Communications in Computer and Information Science   **1604**

More information about this series at https://link.springer.com/bookseries/7899

Nirbhay Chaubey · Sabu M. Thampi ·
Noor Zaman Jhanjhi (Eds.)

Computing Science, Communication and Security

Third International Conference, COMS2 2022
Gujarat, India, February 6–7, 2022
Revised Selected Papers

 Springer

Editors
Nirbhay Chaubey 🄳
Ganpat University
Gujarat, India

Sabu M. Thampi 🄳
IIITM-Kerala
Trivandrum, India

Noor Zaman Jhanjhi 🄳
Taylor's University
Subang Jaya, Malaysia

ISSN 1865-0929   ISSN 1865-0937 (electronic)
Communications in Computer and Information Science
ISBN 978-3-031-10550-0   ISBN 978-3-031-10551-7 (eBook)
https://doi.org/10.1007/978-3-031-10551-7

This Springer imprint is published by the registered company Springer Nature Switzerland AG
The registered company address is: Gewerbestrasse 11, 6330 Cham, Switzerland

Preface

This volume contains the papers presented at the Third International Conference on Computing Science, Communication and Security (COMS2 2022), held at the beautiful campus of Ganpat University, India during February 6–7, 2022. COMS2 2022 was held online, wherein the invited guests, keynote speakers, dignitaries, session chairs, paper presenters, and attendees joined a two-day international conference using Zoom video conferencing. The online conference forum brought together more than 135 delegates including leading academics, scientists, researchers, and research scholars from all over the world to exchange and share their experiences, ideas, and research results on aspects of computing science, network communication, and security.

The conference was virtually inaugurated on the first day by the National Anthem "Jana Gana Mana" with the online presence of academic leaders and luminaries: Shri Ganpatbhai I. Patel (Padma Shri), President and Patron in Chief, Ganpat University, India; Ashutosh Dutta, the Invited Guest of the program and IEEE Fellow, Senior Scientist, and 5G Strategist, Johns Hopkins University, USA; Prabhat Ranjan, Vice-Chancellor, D Y Patil International University, India, and Former Executive Director, TIFAC, Government of India; Sudip Misra, IEEE Fellow, Professor of Computer Science and Engineering, Indian Institute of Technology (IIT), Kharagpur, India; Martin Maier, Professor, National Institute for Scientific Research (INRS), Canada; Balaji Rajendran, Associate Director, Centre for Development of Advanced Computing (C-DAC), Bangalore, India; Mahendra Sharma, Pro. Chancellor and Director General, Ganpat University, India; Rakesh Patel, Pro. Vice Chancellor, Ganpat University, India; Amit Patel, Pro. Vice Chancellor and Executive Registrar, Ganpat University, India; Kiran Amin, Executive Dean of Faculty of Engineering and Technology, Ganpat University, India; and Satyen Parikh, Executive Dean of Computer Science, Ganpat University, India, which declared the conference open for further proceedings.

COMS2 2022 accepted 22 papers as oral presentations (out of 143 full papers received and critically peer reviewed using the Springer OCS System), which were presented during the two days of the conference. All the accepted papers were peer reviewed by three qualified reviewers chosen from our Technical Program Committee based on their qualifications and experience.

In addition to the paper presentations there were five plenary lectures covering the different areas of the conference. Ashutosh Dutta graced the conference and delivered a talk on "5G Security - Opportunities and Challenges". Prabhat Ranjan addressed "Building a Future-focused Research University and Emerging Research Areas". Sudip Misra spoke about "IoT in Healthcare". Martin Maier delivered a talk on "Internet of No Things in the Era of 6th Generation Networks" and Balaji Rajendran addressed "Cyber Resilience: Inspiration from the Internet Addressing Systems".

COMS2 also featured a session track with the following panel members and session chairs: Savita R. Gandhi, Gujarat University, India; Nikhil J. Kothari, Dharmsinh Desai University, India; J.M.Rathod, BVM Engineering College, India; Maulika Patel, CVM

University, India; Anand Nayar, Dua Tan University, Taiwan; Snehal Joshi, Veer Narmad South Gujarat University, India; Vishvjit Thakkar, Gujarat Technological University, India; and Vrushank Shah, Indus University, India.

The proceedings editors wish to thank the dedicated Technical Program Committee members and all the other reviewers for their contributions. We also thank Springer for their trust and for publishing the proceedings of COMS2 2022.

The conference was organized by Ganpat University as a well-reputed private university established through the Government of Gujarat State Legislative Act No.19/2005 on April 12, 2005, and recognized by the UGC under the section 2(f) of the UGC Act, 1956, having a campus which spread over more than 300 acres of land with world class infrastructure and more than 10,000 students on campus. In consideration of its contribution to education in a short period of time, the university has been given Permanent Membership of the Association of Indian Universities (AIU), besides having membership of the Association of Commonwealth Universities (ACU), UK, and the International Association of Universities (IAU), France. Ganpat University offers various unique, quality, industry-linked and sector-focused Diploma, Undergraduate, Postgraduate, and Research-level programs (professional and non-professional) in the fields of engineering, computer science, management, pharmacy, sciences, commerce and social science, architecture, design and planning, maritime studies, law, etc.

In a nutshell, the conference was full of fruitful discussions, igniting the spirit of research. It was indeed a remarkable, memorable, and knowledgeable virtual conference. The success of COMS2 2022 means that planning can now proceed with confidence for the Fourth International Conference on Computing Science, Communication and Security (COMS2 2023) scheduled for February 2023 at Ganpat University, India.

February 2022

Nirbhay Chaubey
Sabu M. Thampi
Noor Zaman Jhanjhi

Organization

Advisory Committee

Ganpatbhai Patel	Ganpat University, India
Mahendra Sharma	Ganpat University, India
Rakesh Patel	Ganpat University, India
Amit Patel	Ganpat University, India

Technical Program Chairs

Nirbhay Chaubey	Ganpat University, India
Sabu M. Thampi	IIITM Kerala, India
Noor Zaman Jhanjhi	Taylor's University, Malaysia

Technical Program Committee

Rajkumar Buyya	University of Melbourne, Australia
K. S. Dasgupta	DAIICT, India
Mohammed Atiquzzaman	University of Oklahoma, USA
A. R. Dasgupta	Space Application Centre, ISRO, India
Akshai Aggarwal	University of Windsor, Canada
Om Prakash Vyas	IIIT Allahabad, India
Savita R. Gandhi	Gujarat University, India
Sabu M. Thampi	IIITM Kerala, India
Dipak Mathur	IEEE Asia Pacific Region 10, India
Sartaj Sahni	University of Florida, USA
Maniklal Das	DA-IICT, India
S. Venkatesan	IIIT Allahabad, India
Deepak Garg	Bennett University, India
Mohit Tahiliani	NIT Karnatka, India
Nilesh Modi	Babasaheb Ambedkar Open University, India
Kevin Dami	University of Detroit, USA
Bala Natarajan	Kansas State University, USA
Virendra C. Bhavsar	University of New Brunswick, Canada
G. Sahoo	Birla Institute of Technology, India
Rajen Purohit	Ganpat University, India
Kiran Amin	Ganpat University, India
Satyen Parikh	Ganpat University, India

Gisa Fuatai Purcel	Commonwelth Telecommunications Organisation, UK
Gyu Myoung Lee	Liverpool John Moores University, UK
Stefano Cirillo	University of Salerno, Italy
Flavio Vella	Free University of Bozen-Bolzano, Italy
Alessandro Barbiero	Università degli Studi di Milano, Italy
Lelio Campanile	Università degli studi della Campania Luigi Vanvitelli, Italy
Asmerilda Hitaj	University of Milano-Bicocca, Italy
Abdallah Handoura	Institut Mines-Télécom, France
Gua Xiangfa	National University of Singapore, Singapore
Raman Singh	University of Dublin, Ireland
Ahmed M. Elmisery	Waterford Institute of Technology, Ireland
Shahzad Ashraf	Hohai University, China
Moharram Challenger	University of Antwerp, Belgium
Dragi Kimovski	Klagenfurt University, Austria
Iwan Adhicandra	University of Sydney, Australia
Payal Mahida	Victorian Institute of Technology, Australia
Tarandeep Kaur Bhatia	Deakin University, Australia
Siddharth Patel	Eaton Corporation, Australia
Marcin Paprzycki	Polish Academy of Sciences, Poland
Sabyasachi Chakraborty	Inje University, South Korea
Sayan K. Ray	Manukau Institute of Technology, New Zealand
Ahmed Al-Sa'di	Auckland University of Technology, New Zealand
Clementine Gritti	University of Canterbury, New Zealand
Samaneh Madanian	Auckland University of Technology, New Zealand
Aravind Nair	KTH Royal Institute of Technology, Sweden
Yehia Abd Alrahman	Chalmers University of Technology, Sweden
Karl Andersson	Luleå University of Technology, Sweden
Jose M. Molina	Universidad Carlos III de Madrid, Spain
Manuel Chica	Universidad de Granada, Spain
Jose Angel Diaz-Garcia	Universidad de Granada, Spain
Carlos Fernandez-Basso	University of Granada, Spain
George Papakostas	Eastern Macedonia and Thrace Institute of Technology, Greece
Dimitris Karampatzakis	International Hellenic University, Greece
Ioannis Tollis	University of Crete, Greece
Christos J. Bouras	University of Patras, Greece
Zitong Yu	University of Oulu, Finland
Paul Aiken	University of the West Indies, West Indies
Rakhee	University of the West Indies, West Indies

Ammar Muthanna	Saint Petersburg State University of Telecommunications, Russia
Noor Zaman Jhanjhi	Taylor's University, Malaysia
Irdayanti Mat Nashir	Universiti Pendidikan Sultan Idris, Malaysia
Jing Rui Tang	University Pendidikan Sultan Idris, Malaysia
Zaliza Hanapi	Universiti Pendidikan Sultan Idris, Malaysia
Encik Ong Jia Hui	Tunku Abdul Rahman University College, Malaysia
Qusay Medhat Salih	University Malaysia Pahang, Malaysia
Dalal A. Hammood	Universiti Malaysia Perlis, Malaysia
Muhammad Asif Khan	Qatar University, Qatar
Ashraf A. M. Khalaf	Minia University, Egypt
Dimiter G. Velev	University of National and World Economy, Bulgaria
Pahlaj Moolio	Pannasastra University of Cambodia, Cambodia
Mudassir Khan	King Khalid University, Saudi Arabia
Lamia Berriche	Prince Sultan University, Saudi Arabia
Lal Bihari Barik	King Abdulaziz University, Saudi Arabia
Shermin Shamsudheen	Jazan University, Saudi Arabia
Tran Cong Hung	Posts and Telecomunication Institute of Technology, Vietnam
Anand Nayyar	Duy Tan University, Vietnam
Pao-Ann Hsiung	National Chung Cheng University, Taiwan
Seyyed Ahmad Edalatpanah	Ayandegan Institute of Higher Education, Iran
Aws Zuheer Yonis	Ninevah University, Iraq
Razan Abdulhammed	Northern Technical University, Iraq
Moharram Challenger	Ege University, Turkey
Sandeep Kautish	LBEF Campus, Nepal
A. A. Gde Satia Utama	Universitas Airlangga, Indonesia
Eva Shayo	University of Dar es Salaam, Tanzania
Anil Audumbar Pise	University of the Witwatersrand, Johannesburg, South Africa
Sarang C. Dhongdi	BITS Pilani, India
Satyabrata Jit	IIT (BHU), India
Pratik Chattopadhyay	IIT (BHU), India
Amrita Chaturvedi	IIT (BHU), India
Amit Kumar Singh	IIT (BHU), India
Amrita Mishra	IIIT Naya Raipur, India
Panchami V.	IIIT Kottayam, India
Bhuvaneswari Amma N.G.	IIIT Una, India
Jitendra Tembhurne	IIIT Nagpur, India
Renjith P.	IIIT Kurnool, India

Sachin Jain	IIIT Jabalpur, India
Priyanka Mishra	IIIT Kota, India
Chetna Sharma	IIIT Kota, India
Eswaramoorthy K.	IIIT Kurnool, India
Pandiyarasan Veluswamy	IIITDM Kancheepuram, India
Sahil	IIIT Una, India
Sanya Anees	IIIT Guwahati, India
Suvrojit Das	NIT Durgapur, India
Aruna Jain	Birla Institute of Technology, India
Amit Kumar Gupta	DRDO, Hyderbad, India
R. Kumar	SRM University, India
B. Ramachandran	SRM University, India
Iyyanki V. Muralikrishna	Independent Consultant, India
Apurv Shah	Maharaja Sayajirao University of Baroda, India
Bhushan Trivedi	GLS University, India
Manoj Kumar	INFLIBNET, India
U. Dinesh Kumar	IIM Bangalore, India
Saurabh Bilgaiyan	KIIT Deemed to be University, India
Raja Sarath Kumar Boddu	Jawaharlal Nehru Technological University, India
Kiran Sree Pokkuluri	SVECM, India
Devesh Kumar Srivastava	Manipal University, India
P. Muthulakshmi	SRM University, India
R. Anandan	VELS University, India
Amol Dhondse	IBM India Software Labs, India
R. Amirtharajan	SASTRA Deemed University, India
Padma Priya V.	SASTRA Deemed University, India
Deepak H. Sharma	K. J. Somaiya College of Engineering, India
Ravi Subban	Pondicherry University, India
Parameshachari B. D.	Visvesvaraya Technological University, India
Nilakshi Jain	University of Mumbai, India
Archana Mire	University of Mumbai, India
Sonali Bhutad	University of Mumbai, India
Anand Kumar	Visvesvaraya Technological University, India
Jyoti Pareek	Gujarat University, India
Sanjay Garg	Nirma University, India
Madhuri Bhavsar	Nirma University, India
Vijay Ukani	Nirma University, India
Mayur Vegad	BVM Engineering College, India
N. M. Patel	BVM Engineering College, India
J. M. Rathod	BVM Engineering College, India
Maulika Patel	CVM University, India
Nikhil Gondalia	CVM University, India

Organizing Committee

Ajay Patel	Ganpat University, India
Ketan Patel	Ganpat University, India
Anand Mankodia	Ganpat University, India
Paresh M. Solanki	Ganpat University, India
Savan Patel	Ganpat University, India
Jigna Prajapati	Ganpat University, India
Pravesh Patel	Ganpat University, India
Ketan Sarvakar	Ganpat University, India
Chirag Gami	Ganpat University, India
Sweta A. Dargad	Ganpat University, India

Contents

Development of Smart Sensor for IoT Based Environmental Data Analysis Through Edge Computing

Abhijit Chatterjee[(✉)]

Space Applications Centre (ISRO), Sensors Development Area, Ahmedabad 380015, India
abhijit@sac.isro.gov.in

Abstract. Internet of Things (IoT) revolutionizes our world with billions of sensors and actuators having ubiquitous sensing abilities which offers shared information to develop a smart environment around us. The proliferation of rich cloud services has introduced an efficient computing technique, edge computing, where processing the IoT data has been carried out at close to the source or edge of the network. Edge computing is advantageous for large volume of data as it addresses the concerns of response time, battery life constraint, band-width, network cost saving, as well as safety and privacy. This paper discusses the implementation of smart IoT indoor environmental sensor using WiFi enabled microcontroller node, streaming the telemetry data to cloud through Raspberry Pi based MQTT broker and analyzing the data through Edge Server and re-duce Publisher-Subscriber (pub-sub) costs by approximately 50% for Google Cloud Platform (GCP) by reducing telemetry data.

Keywords: IoT · Smart sensor · MQTT · Edge · Pub/Sub · Raspberry Pi · ESP32

1 Introduction

IoT comprises of sensor nodes or 'things' which can provide complex services through intelligent interfaces in a large scale by remotely connecting, monitoring, and controlling the existing world entities through the Internet. This network enables connectivity of all IoT things to the Internet for exchanging information sensed by sensing devices/sensors and communicating through designated protocols. Output of a sensor is measurable electrical signal corresponding to any physical quantity namely, temperature, humidity, photon irradiance, pressure, acceleration etc. Smart Sensor is the sensor with onboard computing, decision making and communicating capability for data transfer [1, 2]. Recent introduction of blockchain technology enables address the challenges of IoT [3]. IoT services for industrial or home automation from other techniques due to their ubiquitous and embedded characteristics that affect our daily lives. Smart sensors are the sensing nodes having inbuilt intelligence that interact with the environment of the user to get relevant data that is communicated to the Internet, so that users can control them from anywhere in the world.

© Springer Nature Switzerland AG 2022
N. Chaubey et al. (Eds.): COMS2 2022, CCIS 1604, pp. 1–10, 2022.
https://doi.org/10.1007/978-3-031-10551-7_1

2   Edge Computing

Recently the volume of IoT data has been increased significantly with huge increase in number of 'things' caters to all automation needs of industry, healthcare, smart city, hu-man lifestyles. Volume of data at network edge has been increased in many fold and hence, it would be more efficient to process sensor data at the edge of the network instead of putting all the computing tasks on the respective cloud due to huge unnecessary band-width and computing resource usage. Smart Sensor nodes in IoT are energy constrained things. The wireless communication modules (Wifi, Bluetooth, ZigBee etc.) embedded in nodes are usually energy hungry depends on communication protocol. Hence, offload-ing some computing tasks close to the data source or edge is more cost effective, energy efficient and imposes less burden on cloud [4–6]. Local edge computing extends data processing and storage closer to the large number of smart sensing devices at the edge of the network.

3   System Implementation

This work reports development of environmental smart sensor using Espressif ESP32, a microcontroller unit (MCU) with integrated Wi-Fi and Bluetooth connectivity to con-nect to Raspberry Pi4 based Message Queuing Telemetry Transport (MQTT) broker to measure and send indoor ambient temperature, humidity, air quality data through MQTT protocol. The Edge Server has been implemented within the Raspberry Pi to carry out statistical computation on acquired data of different topics and upload decision in cloud platform. The basic operating scheme has been shown in Fig. 1.

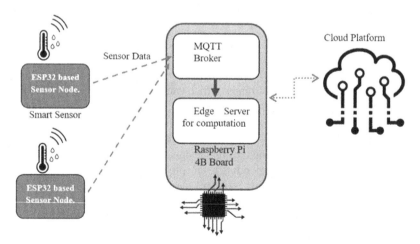

Fig. 1. Block schematic of overall scheme comprising smart sensor nodes, MQTT broker and cloud platform. Multiple smart sensor nodes are connected to broker via Wi-Fi.

4 Experimental Setup

Smart buildings consume significant amount of the energy usage to provide occupants with healthy and comfortable indoor environments. Hence, there has been a noticeable increase in the development of smart sensing systems in recent years, which aim to connect the monitored environment variables (e.g., temperature, humidity, luminosity, and air quality) with building management systems [7]. Indoor air quality monitoring has also become utmost important during cur-rent pandemic situation where poor environmental condition can lead to degradation of human lungs health. The experimental setup consists of two parts: Smart Sensor Node and IoT Edge Server/Broker. Three different types of sensors, viz. PM2.5 Optical Dust Sensor (measures particles with diameter $\leq$ 2.5), MH-Z19 Infrared carbon dioxide (CO_2) Sensor, DHT22 Digital Temperature and Humidity Sensor. The major sensor specifications are given in Table 1 below.

Table 1. Environmental sensors specifications

Optical Dust Particle Sensor (PM2.5)		Non-dispersive infrared (NDIR) CO_2 Sensor (MH-Z19B)		Capacitive humidity sensor and Thermistor (DHT22)	
Parameter	Specification	Parameter	Specification	Parameter	Specification
Detectable particle size	$\geq 1\mu m$	CO_2 measurement capability	$\pm(50ppm+3\%$ reading value)	Temperature measurement capability	-40°C to 80°C (±0.5°C accuracy)
Detectable range	0 to 1.4mg/m³	Output interface	UART, PWM	Humidity measurement capability	0-100% RH readings with 2-5% accuracy
Output signal	PWM (pulse width modulation)	Response Time	< 120 sec	Output Interface	Digital via single bus
Stabilization Time	1 min after Power ON	Preheat time	3 min	Sensing Period	$\approx$ 2 sec

Optical Dust Particle sensor is capable of detecting particles having size larger than one micrometer. Cigarette smoke, house dust, tick, spore, pollen and mildew fall under this category. This sensor has an inbuilt heater to generate heat. Heat creates upward flow of air drawn by the module from surrounding environment. Output PWM low time signifies the particle concentration as per calibration data. It is interfaced with ESP32 PWM pin. CO_2 sensor is based on infrared absorbing gas detection technology with miniature optical circuit. This sensor has been interfaced with ESP32 board through UART pins and DHT22 has been connected with a GPIO. ESP32 has been programmed using Arduino IDE for sensor data collection and transmission of topic wise payload through local wifi. Figure 2(a) and (b) shows formation of integrated smart wire-less sensor where all sensors and battery are connected to ESP32 board.

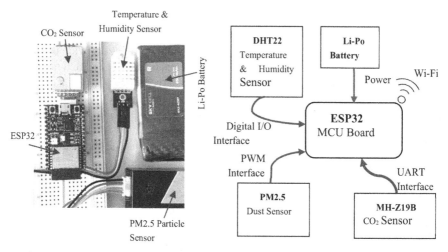

Fig. 2. (a) Photograph of smart sensor with different components. (b) Block schematic of interface between ESP32 and different sensors.

Second part of the setup is Raspberry Pi 4 based standalone unit. It is a commercially available single board computer (SBC) with Quad-core Cortex-A72 (ARMv8) 64-bit processor and integrated Wi-Fi [8] to connect to local Wi-Fi server and smart sensor nodes as shown in Fig. 2. These are the reasons to select Raspberry Pi 4 hardware for this project along with additional advantages of low cost and compact size, ease of configuration. Inbuilt Dual-band 2.4/5.0 GHz wireless LAN, Bluetooth 5.0 makes it more suitable for wireless IoT applications. Mosquitto is a message broker that implements several versions of the MQTT protocol. As it is a relatively lightweight software, Mosquitto suits as the the perfect choice for dealing with the MQTT protocol on Raspberry Pi 4 SBC. Mosquitto MQTT broker is available as part of the Raspbian repository and has been installed in the Raspberry Pi board to connect to MQTT server and Node-RED platform has been used to implement data reception over MQTT and IoT application server.

Basic hardware architecture of Raspberry Pi 4 SBC is given in Fig. 3 below.

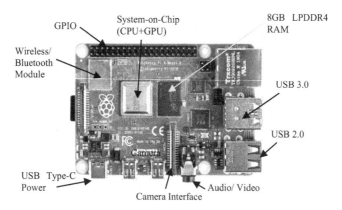

Fig. 3. Raspberry Pi 4 B model SBC board with hardware configuration details

MQTT broker keeps the topic wise information from various sensors and distributes it to subscribed client terminals subscribed for specified topics. Mosquitto is the famous example of an open-source MQTT broker. It is developed by the Eclipse foundation that can be used in various environments. Smart sensor nodes publish acquired data to Mosquitto Broker on specific topics and Raspberry Pi subscribes to the topics through Node-RED. Node-RED is an open-source editor based on JavaScript Object Notation, which facilitates workflow management. Node-Red nodes are very low-code programming tool and required to be interconnected to meet the desired requirements of IoT system. After receiving the wireless sensor data, statistical computations are computed to generate useful information that can be sent to cloud platform. Different research groups reported the popularity of Raspberry Pi platform and its use in implementation of IoT based air quality monitoring and prediction [9–13]. We have used Google Cloud Platform (GCP) and Google IoT Core for as cloud support platform for entire project. Schematic of data flow is shown in Fig. 4. Google Cloud platform, provides a complete solution for collecting, processing, analyzing, and real time visualization of IoT data. It is advantageous due to features like Billing by the second, Security, Big data (Cloud data warehousing, AI Platform, batch and real-time data processing (Dataflow, Pub/Sub, Dataproc), data preparation, analytics (Google Data Studio), Global network and environment friendly.

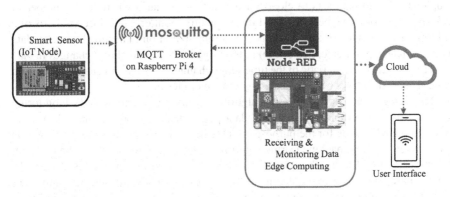

Fig. 4. Schematic representation of data flow from sensor to user. Raspberry Pi is acting as both MQTT broker and subscriber/ Edge processor to smart sensor topic.

5 Results and Discussion

Air quality data has been acquired and transmitted by smart sensor node from morning to evening having duration of around 8 h through MQTT protocol. The aim is to upload sensor data where variation of air quality parameters is beyond threshold limit. So, the decision-making job has been implemented as Edge Computation in Raspberry Pi unit which is subscribed to the topics of sensor node. The received data has been sent to a local file for storage and computation of mean, standard deviation, and peak-to-peak non-uniformity as per Eq. 1 below where Np-p is non-uniformity (in percentage) over acquisition duration T, xi is the time series data from sensors.

$$N_{p\text{-}p} = \frac{\max(x_i) - \min(x_i)}{(\frac{\sum_0^T x_i}{T})} \times 100 \tag{1}$$

This been carried out to identify selected data to be uploaded to cloud storage. Here, the Raspberry Pi also has been acted as Edge to carry out these statistical computations locally instead of uploading entire sensor data to cloud. Figure 5(a, b and c) shows the plot of CO_2 concentration in ppm, ambient temperature in °C and dust particle concentration in pcs/283 ml for entire duration. Three MQTT channels have been used to subscribe to three different sensors. Google IoT Core Connection node provides a connection to a configured instance of the Google IoT Core for device data collection in the Google Cloud. It uses different parameters like Project-ID, Cloud Region, Registry ID, Gateway ID and RSA Private Key file to configure the node to connect the Cloud. The implemented Node-RED flow is shown in Fig. 6 below.

Publisher-Subscriber or Pub/Sub has been used in this project for ingest, streaming and distribute smart sensor data in cloud. This service is available under GCP. It offers the high reliability and automatic capacity management [14]. Cost of the Google Cloud IoT Core depend upon data volume used in a calendar month. Hence, it is economical to upload selected data sets to cloud for a real time scenario where large number of such smart sensors have been involved for air quality monitoring of different parts of a building or plant. This selection is based on computation on real time Telemetry data at edge. Change point detection (CPD) in the Edge Node to find abrupt changes in data when a statistical characteristic of the time series changes [15]. Abrupt changes detect-ed in the sensors data have been indicated by orange circles in Fig. 5.

Research groups reported real-time algorithms run concurrently with the monitoring processes by sensors and process each data point ideally before the next data point arrives at the edge node for the purpose of detecting a change point as soon as possible [16]. However, many machine learning algorithms have been reported for change point detection [17–19]. These techniques include both supervised and unsupervised methods, selected based on the desired outcome of the process. In this work, selected amount of telemetry data after edge computation have been sent to cloud and is shown in Fig. 7 where GCP data flow job graph shows the optimized usage of cloud resources. The pub/Sub requests have only been active during Node-RED sends selected data to cloud after Edge computation locally. Approximately half of messages have been reduced for uploading to GCP cloud instead of uploading entire time series data and hence reduces burden on cloud. Hence, cost of pub/sub service has been reduced up to 50%. This concept is more useful for scenarios where large number of sensor nodes with high volume of data are required to be handled.

Both cloud and device bound Publish/ Subscribe messages are billable in GCP along with MQTT connection and acknowledgement of device configuration. Price is calculated as per Eq. 2 given below.

$$\textbf{Price} = (\text{message size per day}) \times 30 \times \left(\$0.0045 \text{ per MB}\right) \tag{2}$$

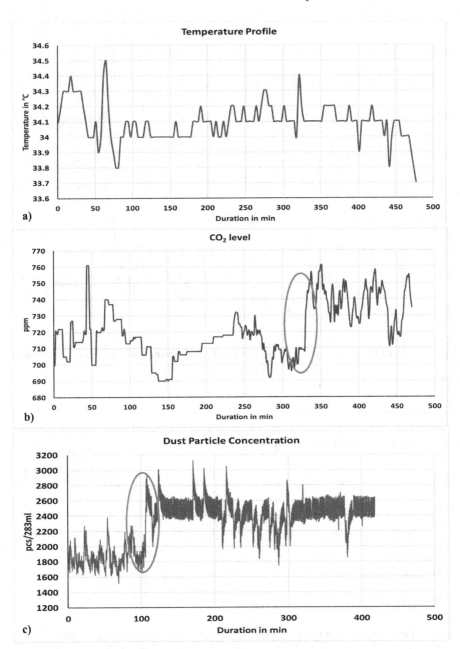

Fig. 5. a) Temperature sensor data. b) CO2 sensor data. c) Dust particle sensor data.

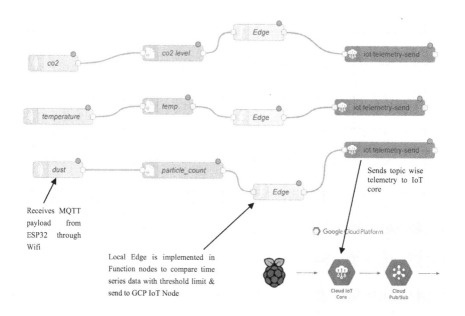

Fig. 6. Node-RED flow to receive data through MQTT, Edge computation and send selected data to Google Cloud.

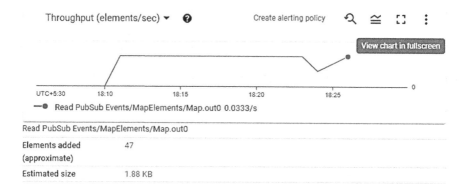

Fig. 7. Snapshot of Google Cloud Throughput monitoring for telemetry data.

The comparison of the cost reduction for uploading IoT sensor data to cloud through local edge computing compared to uploading entire time series data is given in Table 2 below. Where x is the total cost for 480 time-series data points for 8 h of acquisition of each sensor.

Table 2. Cost reduction of IoT data transfer to cloud due to edge computing

Telemetry Data uploading to cloud	Cost of IoT Data transfer to cloud through Pub-Sub
Entire data without Edge	x
Statistical analysis data (mean, SD, NU, min, max)	$\approx \frac{x}{96}$
Critical Values crossing threshold limit	$\approx \frac{x}{2}$

According to research carried out by Cisco, an estimation of 29.3 billion devices will be connected to network worldwide by 2023 [20]. IoT network cost can be increased significantly as the number of IoT devices, an organization deploys, rises. There can be 10% to 30% reduction in costs from using edge computing and an average operational cost savings of 10 to 20% for different industries according to Analysis Mason. Minimization of the energy consumption of users via optimizing the user clustering, computing and communication resources and transmission power has been reported [21].

5.1 Conclusion and Future Direction

IoT based wireless smart sensor has been developed using ESP32 board and local Edge has been implemented in Raspberry Pi 4 board. Environmental sensors data has been acquired for indoor condition and reduced amount of data have been uploaded to cloud after edge computation. Large number of smart sensors will be deployed over distributed area for monitoring different climatic test chambers as part of future work. These climatic and thermos-vacuum test chambers are distributed over geographically different locations. Monitoring of temperature, vibration levels, pressure, particle counts and uploading critical data to cloud to make it available to user as shown in Fig. 8 is an important requirement for IoT based automation.

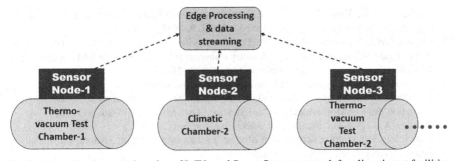

Fig. 8. Future implementation plan of IoT based Smart Sensor network for climatic test facilities.

Hence more number of different sensors will be connected to ESP32 or Raspberry Pi boards for this future need. Other cloud services like AWS also will be explored along with GCP for large volume IoT data streaming and effectiveness of Edge computing on large number of smart sensor data will be analyzed.

Acknowledgement. Authors wish to thank Mr. S.S Sarkar (Deputy Director, SEDA), Mrs. Arti Sarkar (Group Director, EOSDIG/SEDA), Mr. Arup Banerjee (Head, SFSD) and Mr. N.M. Desai (Director, SAC) for providing the necessary opportunity and directions for carrying out these experiments.

References

1. Li, X., Li, D.X.: A review of internet of things—resource allocation. IEEE Internet Things J. **8**, 8657–8666 (2021)
2. Chen, S., Xu, H., Liu, D., Hu, B., Wang, H.: A vision of IoT: applications, challenges, and opportunities with china perspective. IEEE Internet Things J. **1**, 349–359 (2014)
3. Dai, H.-N., Zheng, Z., Zhang, Y.: Blockchain for Internet of Things: a survey. IEEE Internet Things J. **6**, 8076–8094 (2019)
4. Shi, W., Cao, J., Zhang, Q., Li, Y., Lanyu, X.: Edge computing: vision and challenges. IEEE Internet Things J. **3**, 637–646 (2016)
5. Akhtar, M.N., Shaikh, A.J., Khan, A., Awais, H., Bakar, E.A., Othman, A.R.: smart sensing with edge computing in precision agriculture for soil assessment and heavy metal monitoring: a review. Agriculture **11**, 475–512 (2021)
6. Guastella, D.A., Marcillaud, G., Valenti, C.: Edge-based missing data imputation in large-scale environments. Information **12**, 195–205 (2021)
7. Floris, A., Porcu, S., Girau, R., Atzori, L.: An IoT-based smart building solution for indoor environment management and occupants prediction. Energies **14**, 2959–2976 (2021)
8. López, F., Torres F.J., Ramírez, V.A., Núñez, D.A., Corona, R., López, A.R.: Raspberry Pi for implementation of web technology in an automation process. In: 2019 IEEE International Autumn Meeting on Power, Electronics and Computing (ROPEC), pp. 1–6 (2019)
9. Wardana, I.N.K., Gardner, J.W., Fahmy, S.A.: Optimizing deep learning at the edge for accurate hourly air quality prediction. Sensors **21**, 1064–1092 (2021)
10. Lee, Y.-C., Lee, C.-M.: Real-time smart home surveillance system of based on raspberry Pi. In: 2020 IEEE Eurasia Conference on IOT, Communication and Engineering (ECICE), pp. 72–74 (2020)
11. Sajjan, V., Sharma, P.: Analysis of air pollution by using raspberry Pi-IoT. In: 2021 6th International Conference on Inventive Computation Technologies (ICICT), pp. 178–183 (2021)
12. Lai, X., Yang, T., Wang, Z., Chen, P.: IoT implementation of Kalman filter to improve accuracy of air quality monitoring and prediction. Appl. Sci. **9**, 1831–1854 (2019)
13. Medina-Pérez, A., Sánchez-Rodríguez, D., Alonso-González, I.: An Internet of Thing architecture based on message queuing telemetry transport protocol and node-RED: a case study for monitoring radon gas. Smart Cities **4**, 803–818 (2021)
14. https://www.cloud.google.com/pubsub/docs/quickstart-console
15. Kawahara, Y., Sugiyama, M.: Sequential change-point detection based on direct density-ratio estimation. In: SIAM International Conference on Data Mining, pp. 389–400 (2009)
16. Downey, A.B.: A novel changepoint detection algorithm (2008)
17. Camci, F.: Change point detection in time series data using support vectors. Int. J. Pattern Recognit. Artif. Intell. **24**(1), 73–95 (2010)
18. Aminikhanghahi, S., Cook, D.J.: A survey of methods for time series change point detection. Knowl. Inf. Syst. **51**(2), 339–367 (2017)
19. Titsias, M.K., Sygnowski, J., Chen, Y.: Sequential Changepoint Detection in Neural Networks with Checkpoints, pp. 1–17. arXiv:2010.03053v1[cs. LG] (2020)
20. Cisco: Cisco Annual Internet Report (2018–2023), White Paper, Chennai, India (2020)
21. Kiani, A., Ansari, N.: Edge computing aware NOMA for 5G networks. IEEE Internet Things J. **5**(2), 1299–1306 (2018)

Application of Forensic Audio-Video Steganography Technique to Improve Security, Robustness, and Authentication of Secret Data

Sunil K. Moon[⊠]

Department of Electronics and Telecommunication, SCTRs Pune Institute of Computer
Technology, (PICT), Pune, India
skmoon@pict.edu

Abstract. Steganography is the art to conceal any type of secret data into digital media. Its main aim is to maintain data security and authentication. Existing data embedding approaches does not provide information security, authentication and its robustness of secret data. To avoids these limitations this paper uses the Forensic Exploiting Modification Direction (FEMD) algorithm for audio video steganography to increase data security, authentication and its robustness. It uses $3m^2 + 3m + 3$ ary notation to embed three pixels at a time for enhancing embedding capacity and security of secret data. The different types of image processing attacks have been verified on stego video which produces the very good recovery of original and secret data without any distortion. The observed and verified software results confirm that the implemented security model provides better authentication, imperceptibility, robustness, CC (Concealed Capacity), and CR (Concealed Rate) as compared to any existing EMD methods.

Keywords: Data security · Audio-Video steganography · Forensics authentication · FEMD

1 Introduction

In today's internet world, to produce privacy and security to digital media like Facebook, WhatsApp, to make online money transaction is the major issues. Hence to avoids these limitations steganography plays very important role for data security and authentication. To create a security model using steganography, data embedding capacity, security and authentication are the main concerns [1, 2]. The first promising data concealing approach was developed by Zhang and Wang with high embedding secret data in the image by Exploiting Modification Direction [EMD] method. It is used to generate the relationship between the adjacent pixels of the original image where, every secret digit is converted into a $(2n + 1)$-ary notational approach by n pixel which is increased or decreased by 1 pixel at the maximum. The EMD is used to recover the secret data, but it has limitations like embedding capacity, security, and the embedding rate [3]. Xuejing Niu et al. in 2015 proposed a fully EMD-3 technique to modify n pixels groups by 1 to embed secret data in 3n-ary notational system which improves the embedding

© Springer Nature Switzerland AG 2022
N. Chaubey et al. (Eds.): COMS2 2022, CCIS 1604, pp. 11–25, 2022.
https://doi.org/10.1007/978-3-031-10551-7_2

capacity and maintains good image quality at the receiver end, but does not produces authentication [4]. Abbas Cheddad et al. in 2010 have suggested the present status, and disadvantages of image steganography. It elaborates the next level scope of steganography, so that robustness, security, imperceptibility, and proper retrieval of secret data can be further improved [5]. Manasi Subhedar in 2015 et al. produced the currently developed steganography methods with their pros and cons, basic concepts, generation approaches, and information security in the various fields [6]. The recently developed video steganography in spatial and transform domain and which gives the disadvantage and advantages for the previous five years. To generate perfect video steganography, embedding capacity, imperceptibility, and robustness are the key factors, but currently, no one can develop such an algorithm in reality. For implementing a steganographic system in hardware to speeds up the algorithm execution [7]. Mukesh Dalal and Mamta Juneja in 2019 have presented video steganography technology for Standard Definition (SD) and High Definition (HD) to increase the robustness and imperceptibility. To obtain the compromise between imperceptibility and robustness, it should develop the video steganography method which is created for SD and HD videos. The system can reach a high imperceptibility for still image steganography [8].

2 Related Work

In 2018, Saha et al. introduced an EMD technique using a weightage array in which the payload could be varied according to the length of the message at reduced quality distortion. However, once the number of pixels in each pixel group could be known, the weightage array could be easily detected [9]. Leng et al. have proposed a Generalized EMD (GEMD) technique that uses an n-dimensional hypercube around a group of n pixels to achieve a higher payload up to 4.75 bpp [10]. Yanjun Liu et al. in 2017 provides the extended EMD data embedding method to improve the embedding capacity as large as 2.5 bpp [11]. Yanxiao Liu et al. in 2018 implemented a General EMD where n group pixels of cover data are divided into many groups. The embedding capacity can be further increased from general EMD [12]. Zeyad Safaa Younus et al. in 2019 address the weakness of the EMD technique which uses a serial selection of pixels to enhance the robustness of the secret data [13]. Shaswata Saha et al. in 2020 suggested EEMD method by hashed-weightage Array where 2KN-ary numbers are embedded in each K pixels of the original data, where N denotes the number of bits embedded in each pixel. Hence the payload is variable and embedding is done using a dynamic weightage array [14]. In 2019 S.K Moon et al. implemented the audio-video steganography with very good recovery of secret data and produces large embedding capacity and authentication [15]. This paper is organized as follows: The proposed FEMD base conceals an information security model using audio-video crypto steganography is discussed in Sect. 3. The transmitter and receiver section result and their importance is discussed in Sect. 4. The Audio Video system and its performance are discussed in Sect. 5. Section 6 shows the security through different types of attacks on stego video. Section 7 justifies the simulation results and its discussion while the last section indicates the conclusion and references respectively.

3   Proposed Methodology of Information Security

3.1   The Process to Embed Secret Data into Video

The cover input video is split into many still frames and every frame is selected to conceal the secret data like image, text, and audio. Once any type of secret data is embedded into frames of video it is called stego video and this stego video is sent from source to destination. The authentication forensic process checks all the secret data values like PSNE, MSE, CR, and NCF and if it is found to be correct, then sent to destination end otherwise stop in the communication channel as shown in Fig. 1. Before proceeding with the embedding process, the cover video needs to be adjusted as per secret data images. The randomly obtained cover frame pixel components $Z(a, b, c, d)$ are adjusted according to Eq. (1) and Eq. (2), where G (a, b, c, d) denotes the stego pixel component denote the spatial coordinates of the cover frame. The receiver gets the message and retrieves the message using the stego-key which is the same as used by the sender.

$$Z(a, b, cd) = \sum_{i=1}^{n} (G * Z) * \mathrm{mod} * (3m^2 + 3m + 3) \tag{1}$$

$$= for \ G(a, b, c, d) = 255 \tag{2}$$

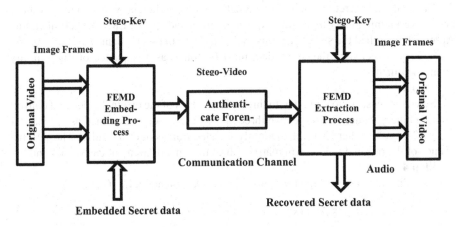

Fig. 1. Security model for video crypto-steganography transmitter

3.2   Video Encoding Process

Each secret data is encoded from the top-left pixel and is coded from top to bottom, left to right. It employed the encoding function along with a secured encryption key. To embed audio into audio, it is converted into several samples and each sample is again converted into the number of bits and every three bits are mapped using the FEMD algorithm. The process of embedding starts after converting the hidden secret data into a sequence of digits with a $(3m^2 + 3m + 3)$ odd base notation system. Suppose the secret information is a binary stream then it is segmented into many binary pieces by m bits and where its decimal value of each piece is represented by G digits in $(3m^2 + 3m + 3)$ ary notation system as shown in Eq. (3) and Eq. (4).

$$YC = \sum_{i=1}^{n} (Z * G) * \mod (3m^2 + 3m + 3) \tag{3}$$

$$K_t = (D - F(x_1, x_2, x_3) * \mod * \left(3m^2 + 3m + 3\right) \tag{4}$$

where D is the secret data size. For m = 1, 9-ary notational and m = 2, 21 ary notational and m = 3, 39 ary notational system.

3.3 The FEMD Process

Step 1.

Select the cover data like Avi, .Flv, Mp4, Mp3, Wav, Tone, Voice and convert it into binary to decimal equivalent to embed the secret data like image, text, Mp3, Wav, Tone Voice,.

Step 2.

Calculate the secret information parameters like size, height, width, sample values, and convert it into binary to decimal equivalent form and apply FEMD Data Embedding Approach to embed the secret data bits m. Let assume the secret database B = $(3m^2 + 3m + 3)$. For recovery, the secret data must be found as a sequence of digits in ary notational method.

Step 3.

Select images, audio, or text with three-pixel values of the original video and convert it into a binary value. The respective three pixels (x_1, x_2, x_3) are defined as X = $x_1 * 1 + x_2 * 2 + x_3 * 3$ where X is the randomly selected frames of cover video. The selected frames of the original video form matrix values in terms of digits of each block index.

Step 4.

Calculate the values of the three-pixel blocks X indicate in Eq. (5)

$$F(x_1, x_2, x_3) = (x_1 * 1 + x_2 * 2 + x_3 * 3) * \mod * B \tag{5}$$

where B = $(3m^2 + 3m + 3)$.

Step 5.

The newly obtained stego-video which contains a large number of selected frames with three stego pixels can be calculated *as shown in Eq. (6)*

$$K_t = (D - F(x_1, x_2, x_3) * \mod * B \tag{6}$$

where D is the secret data digit value. The three-pixel values lie between 0 to 0.49, then it is equal to 0. If it is from 0.5 to 0.99, then it is 1. If it varies from 1 to 1.49, then it is equal to 1 and if this value lies between 1.5 to 1.99, then it is equal to 2 and so on as per the following conditions.

$A = x_1/K_t$, $B = x_2/K_t$, $C = x_3/K_t$. Hence new stego pixel values can be obtain by following conditions $x_1' = x_1 + A$, $x_2' = x_2 + B$, $x_3' = x_3 + C$, $x_1' = x_1 - A$, $x_2' = x_2 - B$ and $x_3' = x_3 - C$. To produce a minimum error and obtain the new possible stego pixel values (x_1', x_2', x_3') the FEMD method generate four various conditions to obtain the three new stego pixel values as.

Case1:
$x_1' = (A + m)$ and $x_2' = B + [(m + 1)$ or $(m + 2)]$, $x_3' = C + [(m - 1)$ or $(m - 2)]$
Case 2:
$x_1' = A - m$ and $x_2' = B - [(m + 1)$ or $(m + 2)]$, $x_3' = C - [(m - 1)$ or $(m - 2)]$
Case 3:
$x_1' = A + [(m + 1)$ or $(m + 2)]$, $x_2' = B - s$, or $B + s$, $x_3' = C + m$
Case 4:
$x_1' = A - [(m + 1)$ or $(m + 2)]$, $x_2' = B + s$, or $B - s$ $x_3' = C - m$
Hence the recover secret data can be obtained using Eq. (7)

$$F(x_1', x_2', x_3') = (x_1' * 1 + x_2' * 2 + x_3' * 3) * \text{mod} * (3m^2 + 3m + 3) \qquad (7)$$

3.4 Process to Embed the Image Into Video with an Example

The secret data as the image has a large number of bits values. Every three bits of the secret image is mapped to bits values of video frames by the FPAM algorithm.

To embed secret data as image into video frames for $m = 1$, $Px = 9$, Let the three pixel values of selected frame of video $(x_1, x_2, x_3) = (5, 7, 9)$, and secret data $D = 3$.
Step 1: $(x_1, x_2, x_3) = (5, 7, 9) = 5*1 + 7*2 + 9 * 3 \bmod 9 = 1$.
Step 2: $K_t = 3 - 1 \bmod * 9 = 7$.
Step 3: $A = 5/7 = 0.71$, $x_1 = 1$, $B = 7/7 = 1$, so $x_2 = 1$, $C = 9/7 = 1.28$, so $x_3 = 1$. The new stego pixel values are $(x_1'', x_2'', x_3'') = (6, 8, 10)$. The recovery of secret data can be obtain using $F(x_1'', x_2'', x_3') = (x_1' * 1 + x_2' * 2 + x_3' * 3)* \text{mod} * (3m^2 + 3m + 3) = 6 * 1 + 8 * 2 + 10 * 3* \bmod 9 = 7$ which is not secret data D. Now to get the secret data $D = 3$, apply four various conditions.
Case 1 $x_1' = (A + m) = 1 + 1 = 2$, $x_2' = B + [(m + 1) = 3$, $x_3' = C + (m - 1) = 1$. Hence new stgo pixel values are $(x_1', x_2', x_3') = (7, 10, 10)$. The recovery of secret data can be obtain using $F(x_1'', x_2', x_3') = (x_1' * 1 + x_2' * 2 + x_3' * 3) * \text{mod} * (3m^2 + 3m + 3) = 7*1 + 10 * 2 + 10 * 3* \bmod 9 = 57 \bmod 9 = 3$ which is equal to secret data D.

3.5 Process to Embed the Audio into Video with an Example

The secret data as audio has a large number of sample values and each sample are converted into bits. Every bit of audio is mapped to bits values of video frames by the FEMD algorithm.

To embed secret data as audio into audio for $m = 2$, $Px = 21$,

Let the three pixel values of selected frame of video $(x_1, x_2, x_3) = (20, 30, 40)$, and secret data $D = 12$, $m = 2$.
Step 1: $(x_1, x_2, x_3) = (20, 30, 40) = 20 * 1 + 30 * 2 + 40 * 3 \bmod 21 = 11$.

Step 2: $K_t = 12 - 11 \bmod * 21 = 20$.

Step 3: $A = 20/20 = 1$, $B = 30/20 = 1.5$, so $x_2 = 2$, $C = 40/20 = 2$, so $x_3 = 2$. The new stego pixel values are becomes $(x_1', x_2', x_3') = (21, 32, 42)$. The recovery of secret data can be $F(x_1', x_2', x_3') = (x_1' * 1 + x_2' * 2 + x_3' * 3)* \bmod * (3m^2 + 3m + 3) = 21*1 + 32 * 2 + 42 * 3* \bmod 21 = 1$ which is not secret data D. Now to get the secret data $D = 12$, apply four various conditions.

Case 1: $x_1' = (A + m) = 3$, $x_2' = B + [(m + 1) = 5$, $x_3' = C_+ (m - 1) = 3$. Hence new stgo pixel values are $(x_1', x_2', x_3') = (23, 35, 43)$. The recovery of secret data can be obtained using $F(x_1', x_2', x_3') = (x_1' * 1 + x_2' * 2 + x_3' * 3)* \bmod * (3m^2 + 3m + 3) = 23 * 1 + 35 * 2 + 43 * 3* \bmod 21 = 222 \bmod 21 = 12$ which is equal to secret data $D = 12$.

4 Transmitter and Receiver Section Result

4.1 At Transmitter Section

The input cover video is converted into the number of frames for concealing the secret data. The secret data is resized into predefined dimensions to make the process simple and easier. Calculation of the typical values of PSNR, MSE, NCF along with a histogram is performed before and after recovery of secret data. The security and authentication of the secret data are done by verifying all the values of security parameters along with the histogram. Figure 2(a) shows the cover video and thumb image as secret data for video steganography and Fig. 2(b) is the randomized secret data with the cover video. Figure 3(a) indicates the randomized secret data and its encrypted form while Fig. 3(b) is the 50th number frame of cover and stego video with the same size, width, and resolution.

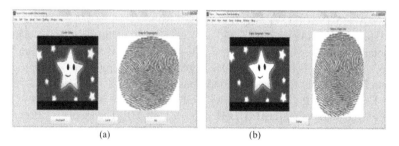

(a)   (b)

Fig. 2. (a, b) carrier video and thumb image for steganography (b) original and randomized data

4.2 At Receiver Section

At the receiver end, the security parameters are calculated once again for stego video. Figure 4(a) shows the received stego video along with secret data and Fig. 4(b) shows the selected frame of stego video and encrypted secret data. Figure 5 indicates the recovered randomized secret data in the encrypted form and decrypted secret data along with the histogram. Figure 6 indicates the spectrograph for various audio samples which are

Fig. 3. (a, b) Randomized secret data and its encrypted form (b) selected frame of original carrier video and steganographic video

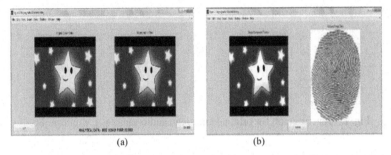

Fig. 4. Received original and stego video and

similar to each other while Fig. 7 gives the spectrograph for original and stego audio samples for tone audio Fig. 8. Shows the indivisible RGB histogram of original and stego video for frame 50.

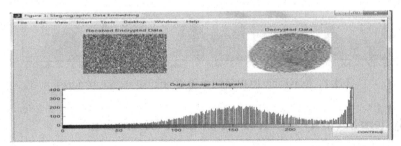

Fig. 5. Recovered randomized secret data encrypted and decrypted secret data along with histogram

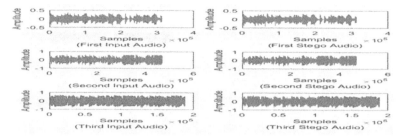

Fig. 6. Spectrograph for original and stego audio samples for mp3 audio.

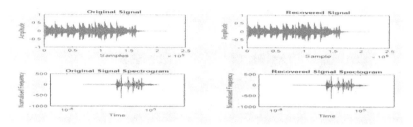

Fig. 7. Spectrograph for original and stego audio samples for tone audio.

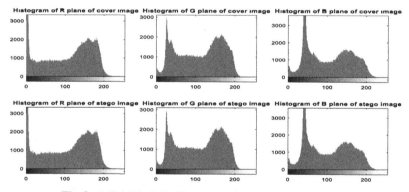

Fig. 8. Indivisible RGB histogram of original and stego video

5 System Security and Its Performance Discussion

The proposed technique is verified for more than twenty-nine images and audio as a secret data by varying the value of m. As the secret data bit m increases, the values of CC and CR also increase and the values of PSNR decreases and it becomes 29.12 dB, with NCF = 0.5 where the proposed security model cannot recover the secret data from the stego video. It is called as significance or critical value of the proposed security model. The simulation results for various secret data of sizes 512 × 512, and samples values as shown in Table 1.

Table 1. Simulations results for various secret data of sizes 512 × 512, and samples values

CR (in bpp)	NCF	m	CC in bits	PSNR (dB) at different ER						
				Thumb	Sign	Home	Baboon	Fruit	Lena	Nature
Simulation results using audio as secret data of samples 667345										
2.19	1	2	4592762	59.31	59.18	59.10	59.16	59.76	59.11	59.14
2.64	1	3	5536481	56.32	56.38	56.41	56.38	56.41	56.38	56.45
2.98	1	4	6249512	54.19	54.11	54.11	54.11	54.11	54.11	54.11
3.5	1	6	7340032	49.66	49.52	49.53	49.52	49.52	49.55	49.39
3.7	1	7	7759462	47.15	47.16	47.16	47.15	47.16	47.18	47.17
3.88	1	8	8136949	44.59	44.52	44.51	44.52	44.52	44.51	44.44
4	1	9	8388608	43.11	43.11	43.11	43.18	43.13	43.16	43.19
4.18	1	10	8766095	41.18	41.12	41.16	41.19	41.17	41.11	41.13
5.85	0.56	33	9876546	29.52	29.47	29.44	29.45	29.48	29.41	29.33
Simulation results using Voice Tone as secret data of samples 996784										
				Mp3	Audio 1	Wav	Mp3	Wav	Audio 2	Audio 3
2.19	1	2	4592762	57.37	57.47	57.37	57.47	57.47	57.37	57.47
2.64	1	3	5536481	55.05	55.15	55.15	55.15	55.15	55.15	55.25
2.98	1	4	6249512	52.62	52.05	52.29	52.52	52.27	52.23	52.23
3.5	1	6	7340032	47.85	47.75	47.72	47.77	47.81	47.77	47.63
3.7	1	7	7759462	45.19	45.15	45.19	45.12	45.17	45.19	45.16
3.88	1	8	8136949	43.18	43.18	43.19	43.18	43.19	43.18	43.14
4	1	9	8388608	40.17	40.17	40.14	40.16	40.18	40.12	40.15
4.18	1	10	8766095	38.52	38.46	38.62	38.51	38.47	38.44	38.31
5.85	0.56	33	9876546	36.51	36.47	36.63	36.48	36.46	36.42	36.35

6   Authentication and Security Analysis

6.1   Blurring and Poisson Noise

The blurring and Poisson noise attacks are tested on selected frames of stego video having 1396 frames with a size of 620 * 620, 540 * 540, 5.3 MB, and audio Mp3 of 8567349 samples. The 0 to 50% Blurring noise reduces and increases the intensity of cover and stego pixels value [16, 17].

6.2 Frame Cropping, Frame Swapping, Frame Replacement, and Frame Exchange

The frame cropping, frame swapping, frame replacement, and frame exchange are applied on selected frames of stego video where a small part of secret data is embedded. The stego frames and audio were crops of 0 to 50% from left to right and top to bottom [16, 17].

6.3 Visual Attack

In this case, the visual attack is applied to the color image with 0 to 50% LSB bit changed. So the proposed algorithm is more secure to visual attacks [16, 17].

6.4 Histogram and Spectrograph

The individual R, G, B histogram of secret data as images and spectrograph of audio as secret data is obtained which is similar to each to other, hence the perceptibility and security increased [16, 17].

6.5 Chi-Squared Attack, Gaussian and Speckle Noise

The observed the effect of Gaussian and Speckle noise attack on original and stego video for the frames number 1 to 10 in terms of the histogram of original and stego frames [15] for m = 3.

6.6 Salt and Pepper Noise and Median Filter

By varying the intensity of stego pixel values 0 to 50%, the modification in pixel values does not deviate from the pixel matrix of stego frame and recovers the secret data with no distortion [16, 17].

6.7 Frame Clockwise and Anti-clockwise, Rotation Attack

All the frames of the stego video and audio (Flv 1700 frames, 680 * 640, 5.6 MB, Mp3 982456 samples) were rotated by 40, 5030, 50, 70, 90, 150, 270, and 360°. The verified results show the stego video and audio are more robust to any frame clockwise and anti-clockwise rotation attack [16].

6.8 Concealed Rate (CR) and Concealed Capacity (CC)

It also gives the information that up to what extend the secret data can be concealed into the cover video so that the concept of any type of steganography remains unchanged [2, 19]. CR rate is calculated by Eq. 8

$$CR = \left[\text{Log}_2 \left(3m^2 + 3m + 3 \right) \right] \tag{8}$$

where m = embedding parameter in bpp

For m = 0, CR = 0.79 bpp, CC = 2656750 bits, m = 1, CR = 1.58 bpp, CC = 3313500 bits, m = 2, CR = 2.19 bpp, CC = 4592762 bits, m = 3, CR = 2.64 bpp, CC = 5536481 bits and so on it is shown in Eq. 9.

$$CC = CR * 512 * 512 * 8 \qquad (9)$$

6.9 Normalized Correlation Factor (NCF)

Normalized Correlation Factor (NCF) is used to verify the similarity between the cover and stego video which is to be correlated [2, 17]. The proposed algorithm FEMD has a very high NCF which is shown in Eq. 10

$$NCF = \frac{\sum_{i=1}^{m} \sum_{j=1}^{n} \left[I(i, j).I'(i, j) \right]}{\sum_{i=1}^{m} \sum_{j=1}^{n} \left[I(i, j) \right]^2} \qquad (10)$$

Where,

m x n = size of the original image
$I(i, j)$ = pixel value of the cover image
$I'(i, j)$ = pixel value of stego image

6.10 MSE, and PSNR

For the perfect steganography, the PSNR value should be in the range of 35 to 70 dB [2]. MSE calculation is shown in Eq. 11 and Eq. 12 (Table 2).

$$MSE = \frac{1}{mxn} \sum_{i=1}^{m} \sum_{j=1}^{n} [I(i, j) - I'(i, j)]^2 \qquad (11)$$

where, m × n = size of the original image
$I(i, j)$ = pixel value of the cover image
$I'(i, j)$ = pixel value of stego image

$$PSNR = 10 \times \log_{10} \left(\frac{255^2}{MSE} \right) \qquad (12)$$

Table 2. Analysis through various attacks

Videos	Frames	Attacks	PSNR	NCF
Video 1	12,24,45	Blurring	58.12	1
Video 2	27,89,25	Poisson noise	58.12	1
Video 3	10,24,110	Chi-squared	58.12	1
Video 4	04,112,270	Frame clockwise	58.12	1
Video 5	54,78,100	Frame anti-clockwise	58.12	1
Video 6	89,115,234	Frame rotation	58.12	1
Video 7	78,95,220	Histogram	58.12	1

7   Simulation Result and Discussion

The simulation results are verified using MTALAB 17.For all the secret data as images and audio, the proposed security model has the value of CR = 1.58 bpp, CC = 3313500 bits. For m = 1 color image and for audio PSNR = 62.12 dB. Forty-three color images like Baboon (512 * 512, Cameraman (512 * 512), Lena 256 * 256), Photograph (256 * 256), Plants (512*512), Signature (512 * 512), Thumb (512 * 512), Vegetable (128 * 128) and audio like MP3 of 874569 samples, Wav 846395 samples, Voice Tone of 764983 samples are used to obtain MSE, PSNR, CR, CE, and NCF. The proposed work has better PSNR, CC, and CR in bpp for color and audio as secret data as shown in Table 3. In the Shaswata Saha et al. 2020, EMD method, as the values of N and K increases the PSNR start to decrease and it becomes 34.01 dB minimum when N and K = 4 while the proposed techniques produce the large values of CC, CR, NCF, and PSNR with color image and audio as secret data as shown in Table 4. Hui-Shih Leng et al. 2019 have applied EMD method on the gray image., As the values of w increase, the payload also increases and the values of PSNR start to decrease and it becomes 30.13 dB minimum when w = 27 and payload = 4.75 bpp. It is the failure value of the Hui-Shih Leng et al. 2019 EMD technique while the proposed techniques produce the large values of CC, CR, NCF, and PSNR with critical values m = 33, CR = 5.85 bpp, and PSNR = 29.12 dB where the FEMD approach fails to recovers the original and secret data with different types of attacks, hence the implemented approach is novel and innovative as given in Table 5.

Table 3. Comparison of existing EMD method and FEMD method

n	Yanjun Liu 2017 [11] ER (bpp) PSNR (dB)		Proposed approach Color images CR PSNR NCF			Audio CR PSNR (dB)	
2	1	52.20	2.19	59.27	1	2.19	59.27
3	1.5	49.23	2.64	56.32	1	2.64	56.32
4	2	45.34	2.98	54.19	1	2.98	54.19
5	2.5	41.84	3.26	52.64	1	3.26	52.64

Table 4. Comparison with Shaswata Saha et al. 2020 and the proposed method

Shaswata Saha et al. 2020 [14]			Proposed approach color images			Audio as secret data		
N	K	PSNR	CR	CC (bits)	PSNR	CR	NCF	PSNR (dB)
1	1	55.34	2.19	4592762	59.27	2.19	1	59.27
2	2	48.53	2.64	5536481	56.32	2.64	1	56.32
3	3	39.50	2.98	6249512	54.19	2.98	1	54.19
4	4	34.01	3.26	6836715	52.64	3.26	1	52.64

Table 5. Comparison of Hui-Shih Leng et al. 2019 and FEMD approach

Hui-Shih Leng et al. 2019 [17]			Proposed approach color images				Audio as secret data		
w	Payload (bpp)	PSNR	m	CR	CC (bits)	PSNR	CR	NCF	PSNR
3	1.5	49.89	3	2.64	5536481	59.27	2.19	1	59.27
4	2	46.74	4	2.98	6249512	55.32	2.64	1	55.32
7	2.81	42.12	7	3.7	7759462	53.19	2.98	1	53.19
9	3.17	39.17	9	4	8388608	49.23	3.26	1	49.23
27	4.75	30.13	33	5.85	9876543	29.12	5.85	1	29.12

8   Conclusion

In this paper, FEMD audio-video-based steganography concept using forensic detection is implemented to improve authentication, imperceptibility, security, and robustness of secret data. Various types of secret data like images and audios are used to embed into the selected frames of video and audio. The FEMD scheme shows better results as compared to all existing EMD techniques to improve the embedding capacity, security and produces a low distortion error at receiver end. Even though this technique is good for images and audio as secret data, it fails to recover secret data when m = 33, CR = 5.85 bpp with PSNR = 29.12 dB which is called the failure value of the system. In the future, it can be enhanced by applying different algorithms or any hardware DSP, FPGA, Arduino processor to increase the security of secret data.

References

1. Mustafa, R.J., Elleithy, K.M., Abdelfattah E.: Video-steganography techniques: taxonomy, challenges, and future directions. In: IEEE Long Island Systems, Applications, and Technology Conference (LISAT), pp. 1–6. https://doi.org/10.1109/LISAT.2017.800196 5,2017

2. Moon, S.K., Raut, R.D.: Innovative data security model using forensic audio-video steganography for improving hidden data security and robustness. Indersci. Int. J. Inf. Comput. Secur. 10(4), pp. 374–395 (2018)

3. Zhang, X., Wang, S.: Efficient steganographic embedding by exploiting modification direction. IEEE Commun. Lett. 10, 781–783 (2006)

4. Niu, X., Ma, M., Tang, R., Yin, Z.: 'Image steganography via fully exploiting modification direction. Int. J. Secur. Appl. 9(5), 243–254 (2015). https://doi.org/10.14257/ijsia.2015.9.5.24

5. Cheddad, A., Condell, J., Curran, K., Kevitt, P.M.: Digital image steganography survey and analysis of current methods. Elsevier J. Sig. Process. 90(3), 727–752 (2010)

6. Subhedar, M., Mankar, V.H.: Current status and key issues in image steganography: a survey. Elsevier Sci. Direct Comput. Sci. Rev. J. 13–14, 95–113 (2015)

7. Sadek, M.M., Khalifa, A.S., Mostafa, M.G.M.: Video-steganography: a comprehensive review. Springer J. Multimedia Tools Appl. Sci. J. 74(17), 7063–7094 (2015)

8. Dalal, M., Juneja, M.: A robust and imperceptible steganography technique for SD and HD videos. Multimedia Tools Appl. 78(5), 5769–5789 (2018). https://doi.org/10.1007/s11042-018-6093-3

9. Saha, S., Ghosal, S.K., Chakraborty, A., Dhargupta, S., Sarkar, R., Mandal, J.K.: Improved exploiting modification direction-based steganography using dynamic weightage array. Electron. Lett. (2018). https://doi.org/10.1049/el.2017.3336

10. Leng, H.-S., Tseng, H.-W.: Generalize the EMD scheme on an n-dimensional hypercube with maximum payload. Multimedia Tools Appl. 78(13), 18363–18377 (2019). https://doi.org/10.1007/s11042-019-7228-x

11. Liu, Y., Chang, C.-C., Huang, P.-C.: Extended exploiting-modification-direction data hiding with high capacity. IEEE ICVIP 2017. http://dx.doi.org/https://doi.org/10.1145/3177404.317 7452

12. Liu, Y., Yang, C., Sun, Q.: Enhance embedding capacity of generalized exploiting modification directions in data hiding. IEEE Access, Digital Object Identifier (2018). https://doi.org/10.1109/ACCESS.2017.2787803

13. Younus, Z.S., Hussain, M.K.: Image steganography using exploiting modification direction for compressed encrypted data. J. King Saud Univ. Comput. Inf. Sci. https://doi.org/10.1016/j.jksuci.2019.04.008,2019

14. Saha, S., Chakraborty, A., Chatterjee, A., Dhargupta, S., Ghosal, S.K., Sarkar, R.: Extended exploiting modification direction based steganography using hashed-weightage Array. Multimedia Tools Appl. 79(29–30), 20973–20993 (2020). https://doi.org/10.1007/s11042-020-08951-1

15. Moon, S.K., Raut, R.D.: Anti-forensic reversible multi frame block to block pixel mapping information concealing approach to increase the robustness and perceptibility. Indersc. Int. J. Spec. Issue Multimedia Inf. Secur. Solu. Soc. Networks 14(3/4), 304–339 (2021)

16. Arab, F., Shahidan, M., Abdullah, S.: A robust video watermarking technique for the tamper detection of surveillance system. Springer J. Multimedia Tools Appl. https://doi.org/10.1007/s11042-015-2800-5.2016

17. Leng, H.-S., Tseng, H.-W.: Generalize the EMD scheme on an n-dimensional hypercube with maximum payload. Springer J. Multimedia Tools Appl. **78**, 18363–18377 (2019)

An Efficient Cluster Based Energy Routing Protocol (E-CBERP) for Wireless Body Area Networks Using Soft Computing Technique

Neha N. Chaubey[1] ⓘ, Lindon Falconer[2](✉), and Rakhee[2] ⓘ

[1] Dharmsinh Desai University, Gujarat, India
[2] The University of West Indies, Mona Campus, Kingston, Jamaica
{lindon.falconer,dr.rakhee}@uwimona.edu.jm

Abstract. The Wireless Body Area Networks (WBAN) is very popular in medical industry and plays a significant role to monitor critical patient information. In the design of WBAN and due to its fundamental nature, routing of patients' critical data to the server in an indoor hospital environment brought challenges. In this paper, an effective cluster-based energy routing protocol (E-CBERP) which uses the ANT colony soft computing technique, is proposed to improve the clustering among WBAN to achieve efficiency, increase network life and throughput. To implement the E-CBERP technique, we have used OMNeT++ discrete-event network simulator. On comparing the performance of our proposed E-CBERP protocol with the traditional existing routing algorithms, the acquired results verify that E-CBERP gives better performance with respect to the Network Lifetime, Energy Consumption, Network Throughput, and Latency.

Keywords: Wireless Body Area Networks (WBANs) · Clustering · ANT Colony · Wireless Sensor Networks (WSNs) · Cluster Head (CH) · E-CBERP

1 Introduction

Wireless Body Area Networks (WBANs) has attained a prominence in the present situation of the covid-19 pandemic across the globe. Various healthcare industries are deploying a variety of devices that can implant inside, outside of the patient body. It has been observed that WBANs have been deployed in various applications scenarios. A recent routing protocol, which has been executed using traditional methods and soft computing approaches is used to increase the network lifetime using the clustering approach. Various routing protocols have been implemented using soft computing techniques for indoor hospital environment scenarios.

In this paper, we extend the scope of WBANs which involves indoor patients whose parameters need to be monitored and sent to the server station wirelessly. Such a scenario is more important where the vitals of a huge population of patients' data is being checked time to time and communicated in real-time. Herein we study different stages namely, neighbor discovery using improved clustering method is executed to find the

© Springer Nature Switzerland AG 2022
N. Chaubey et al. (Eds.): COMS2 2022, CCIS 1604, pp. 26–39, 2022.
https://doi.org/10.1007/978-3-031-10551-7_3

smallest path in order to conserve energy among networks. The main idea is to reduce the processing and communication while choosing the cluster head.

In the proposed algorithm, the clustering process uses the ANT technique [1] for communicating among the other individual nodes based on pheromone trails from one node to another node in the indoor hospital environment. It has been well proven that, in many scenarios, Wireless Sensor Networks (WSN) have been implemented using swarm optimization, Genetic algorithms, and fuzzy computing. The sensor nodes deployed on patients' bodywork with limited resources of communication range. Hence, efficient routing protocols need to design so as to conserve total energy utilisation of the sensor nodes along with the network. These soft computing techniques help to find the shortest path to increase the overall efficiency of the WBAN. Routing protocols [2–4] have been designed to improve these parameters and minimize the load and congestion from source to destination. These techniques are adaptive in nature to find the alternate path whenever there is a node failure or BAN disconnection among the network. Wireless sensor networks (WSNs) is a great enabling technology that can revolutionize information and communication technology. Authors in this paper [5] proposed a new Energy Efficient Clustering algorithm for Wireless Sensor Networks. This algorithm has the ability of selecting a cluster heads of clusters of the network, simulation experiments show that the proposed scheme provides better results than the other existing protocol with respect to energy consumption and consumption delay. Wireless Sensor Networks (WSNs) consist of small nodes with sensing, processing and wireless communications capabilities and routing technique is one of the key concerns in the research area of wireless sensor networks now days [6], authors in this this paper studied important routing protocols and its various challenges such as energy efficiency, quality of service, scalability, storage and computation in WSNs.

Clustering using the ANT technique [7] helps to reduce the traffic and load over the path. Many protocols [8, 9] proposed using clustering technique for its scalability and energy-efficient in WBAN. It organizes its clusters by electing the cluster head formation to receive and transmit its data from all other BAN. Efficient routing protocol LEACH proposed the energy usage of the nodes in network using probability approach [2]. The improved clustering using the ANT technique helps to resolve this adaptive fashion in the network changes by selecting the MDC (Medical Device Coordinator). The route discovery in the network via MDC is based on the minimum cost function. Further, every BAN doesn't have a dedicated MDC in order to process the data using ANT soft computing which is implemented to ensure maximum network lifetime and throughput. This paper is separated into eight sections as given. In Sect. 2, classification of routing protocols for WBAN is presented, Related work of the literature on routing protocols for WBAN is discussed in Sect. 3, and our research motivation is discussed in Sect. 4. Section 5 discusses our proposed technique ECBERP route discovery, route maintenance, and route error, Sect. 6 explains the methodology of evaluation, simulation environment, and simulation parameters. Section 7 discusses results and analyzed them. Lastly, Sect. 8 draws a conclusion and future work.

2   Classification of Routing Protocols for WBAN

Routing protocols is an essential source of energy consumption, choosing an effective route from sensor nodes to the sink node remains a very challenging problem and several researchers are working on it. The routing protocols of WBAN are categorized into (i) Cluster Aware WBAN, (ii) Cross-layered Aware, (iii) Thermal-aware Routing, and (iv) Quality of Service awareness. In Cluster Aware WBAN, the network generates clusters which are a group of sensor nodes and each and every cluster consists of a head which is a medium through which the cluster head communicates with the sink. So, that eventually helps to reduce energy requirement of the node. The basic idea of this category is based on the Low Energy Adaptive Clustering Hierarchy (LEACH) routing protocol for Wireless Sensor Network (WSN).

Many previous studies have proven that this type of protocol is most appropriate for WBAN because it works on balance the energy consumption in the network [10]. Cross-layered Aware: The prime goal of the cross-layered aware protocol is to improve the performance of WBAN through a cross-layered protocol that combines more than one layer. The authors in [11], suggested CLBP, cross-layer protocol work on MAC and network layers, using an interaction graph based on body position, which improves node synchronization and channel access. The Thermal-aware protocol, which depends on the node temperature for path selection. Based on the method presented in [12], the objective of this type of routing protocol is to scale down the heat of this type of network. This is done by ignoring the routes that comprise the hot spots node. To achieve this, a node whose temperature exceeds a certain threshold is considered a hotspot node. In Quality of Service aware, the QoS-aware routing protocols are modular-based protocols wherein different types of QoS metrics have different modules deployed. We need to pay attention to the quality of service, for the reason that this network transmits essential data. This kind of protocol design is a challenging job, due to the complexity of considering different modules for different QoS metrics and coordination between these modules. The QoS in this type of network to be considered are energy efficiency, delay, data critical, reliability, data security, etc. Many protocols in WBAN depend on reliability and delay because it is the most important metric when transmitting critical data [13].

3   Related Work

The Wireless Body Area Network (WBAN) is prominent in health care monitoring of the elderly population which requires remote monitoring continuously in the environment. In literature various other energy-efficient routing protocols are proposed but they lack in achieving network optimal path, conserving maximum energy, and enhancing network efficiency. Nowadays, this field is emerging rapidly with an increase in new ways and procedures for the best path finding to send emergency messages [14]. The dynamic nature of WBAN gives rise to combinatorial optimization problem including making various network metrics more effective like shortest path, minimum energy usage which is hard to solve [15]. Authors proposed a technique, the working of ants on which the ANT colony algorithm is explained [16]. The mechanism explains how ants communicate with each other through pheromone trails. Using this pheromone update, the ant hunts for the shortest path to its destination. The information of the path and obstacles is stored in the memory of ants. All the information regarding the nodes visited and the shortest traveling time from one node to another is stored and using this method of continuous learning the decisions are made [16].

As per standards IEEE 802.15.6, there are different layers of tiers that participate in sensing and communicating from patient devices to the destination. In the architecture, the deployment of the sensors on the patient's hospital environment has a single medical device coordinator (MDC) which participates in sending the information of patients vitals to the end device in a real-time environment without any congestion and link failure as shown in Fig. 1 [2, 17, 18].

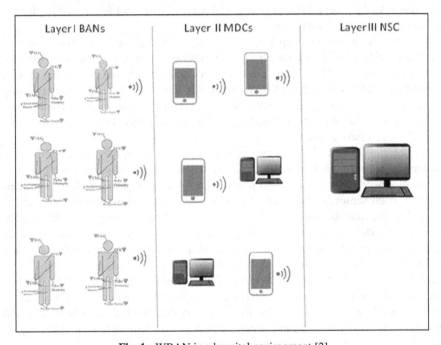

Fig. 1. WBAN in a hospital environment [2]

Many protocols have been proposed to address various issues on QoS, energy-efficient of the data packets in the WBAN to find the best route from source to destination, scheduling, and security issues pertaining to critical data transmission [2, 18, 19]. Authors presented clustering technique with dedicated MDC to each and every BAN device which would be complex in infrastructure and monitoring of many devices in the network [20, 21]. ALARM-NET proposed monitoring of patients residentially without clustering approach. "Anybody" is based on data gathering protocol which is self-organized into clusters that eventually makes the number of direct communications to remote base stations lesser [22, 23]. The authors discussed wearable devices used in WBAN for various medical applications in different scenarios [24].

In [25], an energy-aware routing protocol (EARP) was proposed which was based on a fuzzy control. A fuzzy control model is established by this protocol which comprises of residual energy of node and link quality. Three processes named fuzzification, fuzzy inference, and defuzzification occur and decide best forwarder node. The discussed protocol has three phases i.e. an initialization phase, forwarder node selection phase, and data transmission phase. This EARP protocol divides the data on the basis of importance of data as emergency and periodic, and the fuzzy control model involving residual energy and link quality is used for determining the apt route for these two data transmissions, respectively.

The proposed technique implemented using MATLAB simulation and the simulation results when compared with other prevailing EERDT and M-TSIMPLE protocols, conclude that EARP performs better, in terms of extending network lifetime and improving the reliability of data transmission.

Kushnian Kour and Sandeep Singh Kang in [26] in their research work based on link failure of WBAN for the data transmission efficiency in the network, proposed a model to improve the RPL routing protocol. For implementing and comparing of RPL we use MATLAB with the basic SEAR protocol in terms of various parameters, using this technique, the major issue of link failure is fixed with the parameters of buffer size. They studied that the implemented model performs well in terms of energy consumption, packet loss, and throughput.

Naseer Qureshi et al. [27] projected an innovative way to improve energy utilization. The main concept of this protocol is to choose the fit next jump by calculating the link quality of sensor network nodes and residual energy by computing with the specified equation. Each sensor needs to send data that it exchanges control messages with its neighbors. The neighboring nodes then calculate the residual energy and link quality of neighbor nodes parameters in the network and return to the source nodes the score function value and acknowledgment. This handshaking mechanism which makes the use of control messages increases network overhead and consumes more energy. Sagar et al. [28] proposed a Critical Data Routing (CDR) for WBANs for data routing. The key purpose of this protocol is to lessen energy consumption by sending only critical data to the controller. If any nodes sense critical data directly send that packet to the base station by single hop. Also, each node constructs and updates the routing table periodically.

In [29] authors, presented a review of problems, applications, and performance challenges in WBAN with a focus on security and network reliability related to remote health monitoring. The authors also discussed the performance metrics of WBAN with regard to the network failure using the traditional method. In [30], the energy conservation and detection of alarming status using routing algorithms have been emphasized. The experiment reduces 90% of the energy conservation using Local Processing Unit (LPU). A brief review of the security, challenges, security of WBSNs for patient Health Monitoring in IoT Healthcare Management is discussed in [31]. Ant Colony Optimization which includes discovery of the best route to solve problems using pheromone deposition are given in [32]. Authors in [33] proposed an approach named AntNet for the solution of optimization problems using adaptive routing learning tables in communication networks. The authors in [34] proposed QPRD, the main aim of QPRD is to improve EPR when they classify the patients' information packets into two categories namely Ordinary Packets (OP) and Delay Sensitive Packets (DSP). The QPRD routing architecture can be categorized into seven modules: MAC receiver, delay module, packet classifier, hello protocol module, routing service module, QoS-aware queuing module, and MAC transmitter. The data collection of patient's information is collected in the receiver module of MAC from all neighboring nodes and the packet classifier module bifurcates these as hello packets and data packets. In the end the routing service module accepts the data packets from the higher layers and packet classifier, then they're categorized into ordinary packets or delay-sensitive packets, and chooses the best route for each category.

In [35], the authors focused on various security key algorithms in WBAN. Displaying of real-time BAN data using clustering technique without soft computing has been addressed. It is important to design the clustering with ANT colony optimization to discover the single source shortest path to having better efficiency.

4 Motivation

Finding a single source shortest path in the adaptive environment resolve the issues pertaining to the energy consumption of the nodes using soft computing technique like ANT colony optimization. It reduces the BAN nodes' participation when deploying and transmitting the real-time data in WBAN using the clustering method. In this article, three different data processing operations, like route discovery, route maintenance, and route failure is been addressed using a single Medical Device Coordinator (MDCs) which reduces the infrastructure issues.

5 Proposed Model - Route Discovery

Route discovery is defined as the method of discovering the shortest path route from BAN to the server in the indoor hospital network. It uses forward ants and backward ants starting from lower tier to higher tier and same ants returning back based on the pheromone trails strength. These ants hold the responsibility of finding and maintaining the shortest path from source to destination [17].

$$\text{Modified Probability function} = \frac{D_{ij} * \infty + P_{ij(t)\beta * \tau_i}}{\sum_{i=0}^{N} D_{ij} * \infty + P_{ij(t)} * \beta * \tau_i} \tag{1}$$

Algorithm 1: Route Discovery

Step 1: if the ant reaches node i then
Step 2: if node i ≠ Cluster Head then
Step 3: if (Cluster Head) then
Step 4: choose Cluster Head neighbor using Equation 1 send the ant to it;
          else
Step 5: collect the routing table in ant;
Step 6: inform all other nodes regarding the CH by a message broadcast and
          sent to MDC to forward the data;
          else
Step 7: if (node i==CH) then
     TTL--; /* major amount of jumps of the ants*/

Step 8: if (TTL >0) then
Step 9: choose up next CH neighbor using the probability function;
Step 10: find the function with the highest probability and add present node ID to the
          routing vector to the MDC device;
else
Step 11: destroy the ant

5.1 Route Maintenance

The route maintenance operation is meant to maintain the single source shortest path which is generated by the route discovery process. In this operation, the pheromone is incremented so that the shortest path is sustained and if any node doesn't receive an acknowledgment within a TTL then an error message is transmitted [2]. MDCs keep updated periodically to forward the data received from the BAN within the network and sent to the next tier for further processing in a real-time environment.

5.2 Route Failure

Alternative routes are generated in the network form BAN to MDCs and further next tiers for finding the single-source shortest path. Whenever it receives an error message, the pheromone value is set to zero. An alternate path exists from lower tier to higher tier with the help of the MDCs routing table. Once the packet reaches the MDC, it discovers a new route and starts implementing the ANT technique for the shortest path in the network.

6 Methodology of Evaluation

To check the performance and working of the proposed ECBERP technique, complete experimentation has been conducted and compared the performances of ECBERP with the existing Cluster with ANT colony algorithm, Zk-BAN, and AnyBody with clustering and without clustering using the OMNeT++ Castalia discrete event simulator [36, 37]. Following subsections include all details of the simulation environment and the performance metrics.

6.1 Simulation Environment

In this article, we presented the simulation model of the ECBERP cluster-based ANT technique for data routing in WBAN for 49 to 150 nodes. Simulations were performed in OMNeT++ to show the performance of the routing protocols using the ANT technique to handle the transmission of the critical information without any route failure. The summary of the complete simulation setup is as shown in Table 1.

Table 1. Simulation parameters

Scenario	Parameter	Value
Deployment	Simulator	OMNET++
	Area	50 m * 50 m
	Deployment type	Variable packets
	Total nodes considered	49 to 150 nodes
	Initial node energy	18720 J
	Buffer size	32 packets
	Transmission power	-25 dBm, -15 dBm, -35 dBm
Task	Type of application	Event driven
	Max. size of packet	80K packets
	Traffic type	CBR
MAC	IEEE 802.15.4	Default values
Simulation	Time	1000 ms
Antenna	Antenna type	Omi-directional

6.2 Simulation Parameters

To check the proposed routing protocol's performance, the following four evaluation metrics are considered:

1. Network Lifetime: The total time of network operation until the end node of the network dies is known as network lifetime of the given network.
2. Energy Consumption: To examine the energy requirement of nodes per round, residual energy parameters are taken into consideration to examine the energy usage of the network.
3. Throughput: Transmission rate of the data packets that is successful in a unit time over the network in the simulation process.

4. Latency: In a network, latency is the delay in communication. The time needed for a data packet to be captured, transmitted, processed via various devices, then established at its destination and interpreted.

7 Result and Analysis

This section explains the results which were performed using OMNeT++ using Castalia simulator for the evaluation of the performance metrics of proposed Efficient E-CBERP to compare with Cluster WBAN.

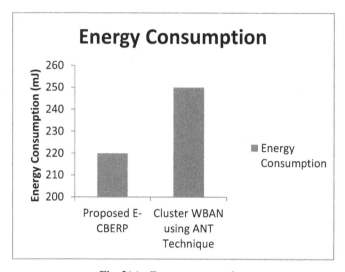

Fig. 2(a). Energy consumption

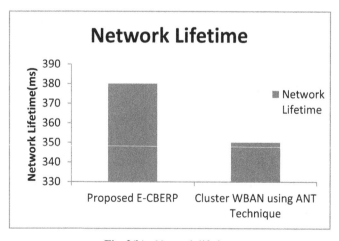

Fig. 2(b). Network lifetime

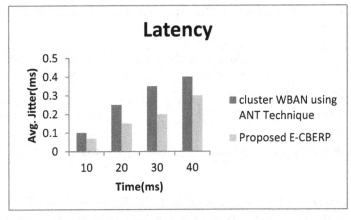

Fig. 2(c). Latency

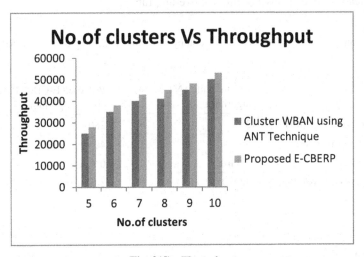

Fig. 2(d). Throughput

Figures 2(a), 2b, 2c, 2(d) represent the analysis of the proposed E-CBERP algorithms by varying networks from 49 nodes to 150 nodes in comparison with a number of clusters, wherein a very stable network behavior is realized for WBAN.

Figure 2(a) depicts the consumption of energy of the proposed E-CBERP is consistently better when compared to the cluster WBAN using the ANT technique. Figure 2(b) represent network lifetime, the E-CBERP shows a better network lifetime than that of the existing routing protocol with a 3% increase with less energy consumption due to more number of clusters formation and a limited number of medical device coordinators (MDCs) in the network environment. Figure 2(c) represent latency, it has been observed that latency of E-BERP is consistently improved while we increase the time from 10 (ms), 20 (ms), 30 (ms) to 40 (ms) while the performance of protocol is significantly affected.

Table 2. Comparison of cluster with ANT colony algorithm with proposed E-CBERP algorithm without clustering

	Cluster with ANT colony algorithm	Proposed E-CBERP ANT colony algorithm
Energy consumption (mJ)	180	150
Network lifetime (msec)	40	50
Latency (msec)	0.7 ms	0.5
Throughput (Packets/msec)	33000	40000

Figure 2(d) shows that throughput of the E-CBERP consistently escalate when a number of clusters were kept varying as per cluster formation during routing of data from source to destination. This significant change with decreased MDCs across the network leads to rise in network lifetime overall (Table 2, 3).

Table 3. Comparison of cluster with ANT colony algorithm with proposed E-CBERP without clustering

	Cluster with ANT colony algorithm	Proposed E-CBERP ANT colony algorithm
Energy consumption (mJ)	295	280
Network lifetime (msec)	35	40
Latency (msec)	0.4 ms	0.3 ms
Throughput (Packets/msec)	32279	33500

Table 4. Comparison of Time complexities of proposed algorithms for WBAN

Algorithm for WBAN	Time complexities
Proposed E-CBERP ANT colony algorithm	$O(1)$
ANT technique	$O(1)$
Cluster using ANT technique	$O(n^2)$

It is clearly visible that the proposed E-CBERP shows very consistent behavior in all performance measure and makes very stable WBAN network (Table 4).

8   Conclusion and Future Work

WBAN schemes demands designs which aims to consume the minimum energy and has the maximum fulfillment of the QoS requirements. Our proposed efficient CBERP using ANT colony algorithm improve network performance stability and prolong the network lifetime. From the results of the simulation we can observe the effectiveness of our proposed E-CBERP algorithm outperforms the existing cluster with ANT colony algorithm, Zk-BAN and AnyBody with clustering and without clustering with respect to the Energy Consumption, Network Lifetime, Latency and Throughput. Our future work will lay emphasis on studying sensor node classification through Adaptive Neuro-based Fuzzy Inference System (ANFIS), its security aspects and also to achieve better energy saving effects we will make the use of green energy technology.

References

1. Omolaye, P.O., Mom,, J.M., Igwue, G.A.: A holistic review of soft computing techniques. J. Appl. Comput. Math. **6**(2), 93–110 (2017)
2. Srinivas, R.M.B.: Cluster based energy efficient routing protocol using ANT colony optimization and Breadth first search. Elsevier Procedia, Comput. Sci. **89**, 124–133 (2016)
3. Panigrahi, B., De, S., Panda, B.S., Luk, J.D.L.S.: Network lifetime maximizing distributed forwarding strategies in ad hoc nwireless sensor networks. IET Commun. **6**(14), 2138–2148 (2012)
4. Qu, Y., Zheng, G., Ma, H., Wang, X., Ji, B., Wu, H.: A survey of routing protocols in WBAN for healthcare applications. Sensors **19**(7) (2019)
5. Chaubey, N.K., Patel, D.H.: Energy efficient clustering algorithm for decreasing energy consumption and delay in wireless sensor networks (WSN). Int. J. Innov. Res. Comput. Commun. Eng. **4**(5), 8652–8656 (2016)
6. Chaubey, N., Patel, D.H.: Routing protocols in wireless sensor network: a critical survey and comparison. Int. J. IT Eng. ISSN: 2321–1776[Online] **04**(02), 8–18 (2016)
7. Moussa, N., El Belrhiti El Alaou, A.: An energy-efficient cluster based routing protocol using unequal clustering and improved ACO techniques for WSNs, Peer-to-peer Networks, Applications, vol. 14, pp. 1334–137 (2021)
8. Panigrahi, B., Sharma, A., De, S.: Interference aware power controlled forwarding for lifetime maximization of wireless ad hoc networks. IET Wireless Sensor Syst. **2**(1), 22–30 (2012)
9. Xiangning, F., Yulin, S.: Improvement on LEACH protocol of wireless sensor network. In: Sensor Technologies and Applications. IEEE Sensor Comm, pp. 260- 264 (2007)
10. Ullah, Z., et al.: Energy-efficient harvested-aware clustering and cooperative routing protocol for wban (e-harp). IEEE Access **7**, 100 036–100 050 (2019)
11. Badreddine, W., Potop-Butucaru, M.: Peak transmission rate resilient crosslayer broadcast for body area networks. aXiv preprint arXiv:1702.05031 (2017)
12. Banuselvasaraswathy, B., Sampathkumar, A., Jayarajan, P., Ashwin, M., Sivasankaran, V., et al.: A review on thermal and QOS aware routing protocols for health care applications in WBASN. In: 2020 International Conference on Communication and Signal Processing (ICCSP), pp. 1472–1477. IEEE (2020)
13. Ibrahim, A.A., Bayat, O., Ucan, O.N., Salisu, S.: Weighted energy and QOS based multi-hop transmission routing algorithm for WBAN. In: 2020 6th International Engineering Conference Sustainable Technology and Development (IEC), pp. 191–195. IEEE (2020)

14. Latha, R., Vetrivelan, P., Jagannath, M.: Balancing emergency message dissemination and network lifetime in wireless body area network using ant colony optimization and Bayesian game formulation. Inf. Med. Unlock. **8** (2017)
15. Xu, G., Wang, M.: An energy-efficient routing mechanism based on genetic ant colony algorithm for wireless body area networks. J. Networks **9** (2014). https://doi.org/10.4304/jnw.9.12.3366-3372
16. Solnon, C.: Ant colony optimization and constraint programming. ISTE and Wiley (2010)
17. Ahmad, A., Javaid, N., Qasim, U., Ishfaz, M., Khan, Z.A., Alghamdi, T.A.: Re-attempt: a new energy-efficient routing protocol for wireless body area sensor networks. Int. J. Distrib. Sensor Networks **2014** (2014)
18. Srinivas, R.M.B.: A soft computing approach for data routing in hospital area networks (HAN). Int. J. Bus. Data Commun. Network. **12**(2), 16–27 (2016)
19. Malan, D., Fulford Jones, T.R.F., Welsh, M., Moulton, S.: CodeBlue: an Ad Hoc sensor network infrastructure for emergency medical care. In: Proceedings of the MobiSys 2004 Workshop on Applications of Mobile Embedded Systems, pp. 12–14 (2004)
20. Dorigo, M., et al.: The ant system: optimization by a colony of cooperating agents. IEEE Trans. Syst. **26**(1), 1–13 (1996)
21. Babu, B.R., et al.: Application of hybrid ANT colony optimization algorithm for solving capacitated vehicle routing problem. Int. J. Comput. Sci. Inf. Technol. **3**(2) (2012)
22. Xiangning, F., et al.: Improvement on LEACH protocol of Wireless Sensor Network. IEEE, Sensor Technologies and Applications (2007)
23. Chen, M., et al.: Energy-efficient differentiated directed diffusion (EDDD) in wireless sensor networks. Comput. Commun. **29**(2), 231–245 (2006)
24. Tavera, C.A., et al.: Wearable Wireless Body Area Networks for Medical Applications. Computational and Mathematical Methods in Medicine, Hindawi (2021)
25. Wang, X., Zheng, G., Ma, H., Bai, W., Wu, H., Ji, B.: Fuzzy control-based energy-aware routing protocol for wireless body area networks. J. Sensors (2021). https://doi.org/10.1155/2021/8830153
26. Kour, K., Kang, S.S.: An energy efficient routing algorithm for WBAN. Turkish J. Comput. Math. Educ. **12**(10), 7174–7180 (2021). https://doi.org/10.17762/turcomat.v12i10.5608
27. Qureshi, K.N., Din, S., Jeon, G., Piccialli, F.: Link quality and energy utilization based preferable next hop selection routing for wireless bodyarea networks. Comput. Commun. **149**, 382–392 (2020)
28. Sagar, A.K., Singh, S., Kumar, A.: Energy-aware WBAN for health monitoring using critical data routing (CDR). Wireless Person. Commun. **112**(1), 273–302 (2020). https://doi.org/10.1007/s11277-020-07026-6
29. Liu, Q., Mkongwa, K.G., Zhang, C.: Performance issues in wireless body area networks for the healthcare application: a survey and future prospects. SN Appl. Sci. **3**(2), 1–19 (2021). https://doi.org/10.1007/s42452-020-04058-2
30. Seemandhar, J., et al.: An Energy Efficient Health Monitoring Approach with Wireless Body Area Networks. arXiv preprint arXiv:2109.14546 (2021)
31. Chander, B.: Wireless Body Sensor Networks for Patient Health Monitoring: Security, Challenges, Applications Security, Challenges, Applications – IoT Healthcare Management, Smart Medical Data Sensing and IoT Systems Design in Healthcare (2020)
32. Blum, C.: Ant colony optimization: introduction and recent trends. Phys. Life Rev. **2**(4) (2005)
33. Di, I.G., Caro, M.: Dorigo AntNet: distributed stigmergetic control for communications networks. J. Artif. Intell. Res. **9**, 317–365 (1998)

34. Khan, Z., Sivakumar, S., Phillips, W., Robertson, B.: QPRD: QoS-aware peering routing protocol for delay sensitive data in hospital body area network communication. In: Proceedings of 7th International IEEE Conference on Broadband, Wireless Computing, Communication and Applications (BWCCA), 12–14 Nov 2012, pp. 178–185. Victoria, BC, Canada (2012)
35. Hussain, S.Z., Kumar, M.: Secured key agreement schemes in wireless body area network, a review. Indian J. Sci. Technol. **14**(24), 2005–2033 (2021). https://doi.org/10.17485/IJST/v14i24.1708
36. Varga, A.: OMNeT++. In: Wehrle, K., Güneş, M., Gross, J. (eds.) Modeling and Tools for Network Simulation. Springer, Berlin, Heidelberg (2010). www.omnetpp.org https://doi.org/10.1007/978-3-642-12331-3_3
37. https://omnetpp.org/download-items/Castalia.html Accessed 25 Jan 2022

Ortho Image Mosaicing and Object Identification of UAV Data

Ruchi Dhall, Rohan Kishore, and Sarang Dhongdi$^{(\boxtimes)}$

Department of EEE, BITS Pilani, K.K Birla Goa Campus, Goa, India
{2019proj032,f20180448,sarang}@goa.bits-pilani.ac.in

Abstract. Real world applications of UAV imagery are growing at a rate faster than ever. Along with this growth comes the need to process the UAV images and extract useful information from them. This paper illustrates a comprehensive python-based algorithm to stitch multiple images gathered from a single UAV and then perform a landscape scan to identify features and other non-homogeneities in the ortho-mosaiced image. The methodology introduced for image stitching involves key point detection using the SIFT algorithm and key point matching using KNN and RANSAC algorithms. The methodology introduced for object identification involves the computation of intensity changes between blocks of pixels in the horizontal direction (H-Scan). These intensity changes are then sorted and filtered before being mapped to feature types such as house roofs, mud trails, forest cover, etc. depending on the image being analyzed. The results indicate that the algorithm can extract meaningful information such as the location and intensity of features from the ortho-mosaiced image. The computational power required to implement this algorithm is extremely minimal, making it a good preliminary algorithm to use for mosaicing and analyzing a set of overlapping UAV images.

Keywords: Unmanned aerial vehicles · Image processing · Object identification · Ortho-Mosaicing

1 Introduction

Aerial surveying and monitoring plays a vital role in a wide range of applications. Civilian applications include resource exploration; monitoring forest fires, oil fields, and pipelines; tracking wildlife; and search and rescue operations in disaster vulnerable areas [33]. Moreover, domestic security applications include border control and perimeter control of nuclear power plants. Military applications are also numerous. The current approach to these applications is to use manned vehicles for surveillance. However, manned vehicles are typically large and expensive. In addition to this, hazardous environments and operator fatigue can potentially threaten the life of the pilot. Therefore, there is a critical need

The work in this paper has sanctioned by Science And Engineering Research Board (SERB-SRG/2019/001204).

for automating aerial monitoring using Unmanned Aerial Vehicles (UAVs) [26]. UAVs provide a platform for intelligent monitoring in application domains ranging from security and military operations to scientific information gathering.

Moreover, with the evolution of UAV remote sensing technologies, research has become widespread in geomatics, disaster monitoring and assessment, national defence, disaster emergency response, and disaster investigation [7]. UAV remote sensing is capable of obtaining the most intuitive high-resolution images of the target area in a short time. This provides an accurate basis for decision making. However, because of limitations in the flying height of the UAV and the focal length of the digital camera, it is difficult to fully capture the entire region of interest in a single image. It is necessary to combine a series of UAV images with overlapping areas into a high-resolution image with a wider field of view [15].

UAVs have gained increasing popularity in remote sensing as they provide a rapid, low-cost and flexible acquisition system for high-resolution data including digital surface models (DSMs), ortho-images, and point clouds. A typical image-based aerial surveying operation with a UAV platform requires flight path planning and Ground Control Point (GCP) measurements for geo-referencing purposes. After image acquisition, images can be stitched or mosaiced, or they can be fed into the photogrammetric process as input. Camera calibration and image triangulation are initially performed in order to generate a DSM or digital terrain model. These products can be finally used for the production of ortho-images, for 3D modelling, or for the extraction of further metric information [17].

In recent years, UAV image stitching or ortho-mosaicing has received increased attention and has become an emerging area in computer vision, photogrammetry, and computer graphics [17]. Due to various uncertain conditions (like the geometric distortion of camera lenses), there are parallax errors and illumination inconsistencies between adjacent UAV images. Consequently, visible seam lines emerge and considerably degrade the quality of the stitched image. Hence, it is of paramount importance to make the color transition natural [14].

After image mosaicing, object detection is one of the most essential means of image processing in computer vision [8]. It is now a critical area of research due to the rapid growth in the applications of computer vision. Object detection can be described as the task of finding the positions and sizes of all objects in an image that belong to a given appearance class. These objects could be cars, buildings, or human faces.

This paper explores and present a comprehensive approach to UAV image processing by describing computationally light-weight algorithms for both image mosaicing and object detection.

2   Literature Survey

The Unmanned aerial vehicle is a low-cost aerial craft that helps in capturing the wide view of any site. These vehicles must be used in different applications to obtain a large number of images without any delay. Because of this, both small and long-lived UAVs adapt well to geo-referencing requirements. The researchers have introduced the use of georeferenced aerial imagery to facilitate UAV navigation [6]. The Multi sensors and hyperspectral platforms, including vision sensors, have been extensively used in drones. Therefore, for effective and efficient mapping of the images which are captured by the UAVs and to make fully autonomous as well as operational UAV network, there is a need to introduce different image extraction and ortho-mosaicing techniques.

The camera attached with a calibrated lens is used to collect digital images automatically, incorporating them with related UAV position and inclination data. The data collected may be used for further digital photogrammetric processing. Normally, the height of the ground or Ground Control Points (GCPs) is employed for differential rectification of collected aerial images in order to achieve proper imaging projection of ground objects before image stitching generates the Digital Ortho-Mosaic Map (DOM). However, this section describes the traditional method which is introduced by the researchers for mosaicing the aerial images as well as extracting the features or objects from the mosaic image.

2.1 Discussion on Image Stitching Methods

In the field of computer vision, photogrammetry, and computer graphics, mosaicing and mapping the aerial images have received much attention and has become an important challenge [17]. The accuracy as well as the challenge of mosaicing the UAV images depends on the three aspects: a) the accuracy of homogenous point matching: b) the curvature of the Earth's surface; and c) the height projection of an object [14]. Therefore, the technology of digital mosaicing or merging all the images which are captured by the single or multi-UAV has been investigated by a number of researchers [12, 21, 23, 30]. The methods which are proposed in [12, 21] by the researchers help in reducing the time of the image stitching process. The structure from motion (SfM) technique was used to construct the methodologies in the papers[12, 21]. When the drones cover the area from a low altitude, the images are get deformed, so before the stitching process, it is very important to remove all the distortion. Therefore, the researchers have proposed an algorithm that helps in reducing distortion or any other deformities from the aerial image [23, 30]. The methods which are introduced in [23, 30] improve the accuracy of the resultant mosaic image map. Another method for mosaicing the drone images which are gathered from an autonomous, small-scale UAV platform was implemented by the researchers in [31]. Also, In [18], researchers have addressed and resolved the inaccuracies that may occur due to the object elevation projection. The method, mosaic the UAV images by considering the position of the drone as well as camera orientation parameters. While stitching the images, the challenge is to verify the feature or common points among all the images because these points can be fallacious. So, in [11] researchers have resolved this challenge and improved the accuracy of the ortho-mosaic map.

2.2   Discussion on Object Detection Methods

Unmanned aerial vehicles (UAVs) are gaining popularity in remote sensing because they provide a rapid, reliable, and flexible collecting approach for high-resolution data including digital surface models (DSMs), orthoimages, and point clouds [4,24]. But scanning and identifying the objects or features from the large area is a formidable task. This motivates researchers to investigate and introduce various machine learning algorithms so that they help in identifying and classifying a certain class of objects from spatial UAV images. This section gives a review of various object detection algorithms which are developed by researchers.

A unique spatial saliency-based hierarchical moving target identification method has been proposed by researchers [27]. They have also used time-space saliency information to enhance the accuracy of the object identification from an image. The experimental results indicate that this method detects objects in aerial video and images with precision and efficiency.. Also, researchers proposed a technique for discovering and identifying object classes from image sequences that are unidentified and unsegmented [9]. The proposed algorithm helps in detecting the number of vehicles on roads or in parking lots from the aerial data. The results signify that the proposed algorithm resolves the urban issues which arise regularly. Moreover, to improve the performance of detecting the object in aerial data, a Scale Invariant Feature Transform (SIFT) and Support Vector Machine (SVM) based methodology has been proposed by the researchers [22]. The algorithm first extracts the features that result in setting the key points by using SIFT function. After that, by using the SVM algorithm, it classifies or detects the objects.

Thus, to identify the objects and extract the characteristics or features of the drone images, various algorithms were proposed by the researchers [5,16,25,29]. These algorithms are based on background extraction and selected feature or key-point extraction approaches. Despite their accuracy, these methods rely heavily on descriptive analysis of characteristics and visual aspects, which takes a long time to evaluate. To overcome this challenge, a Global Density Fused Convolutional Network (GDF-Net) has been proposed by the researchers [34]. Hence, this algorithm is capable of cascading global functions to facilitate learning about object distribution, to detect objects in aerial images.

3   Methodology

3.1   Image Stitching

The increased use of UAVs for aerial photography and mapping has led to the requirement of robust image stitching methods to create seamless image mosaics from multiple individual images [13]. The image stitching algorithm presented below involves identifying common key points among images and matching them with each other. Hence, it is mandatory to have an overlap between the images being stitched. This overlap helps identify how one image is oriented to the other in terms of rotation, translation, scale, and shear. Once this information is obtained, one of the images can be transformed in such a way to seamlessly merge with the other image. Once the merge is complete, image smoothening needs to be performed to blend the overlapping images in such a way that there are no seam lines and duplicated objects [2]. This section describes the steps which are involved in image stitching. And Algorithm 1 illustrates the pseudocode of image stitching methodology.

1. Feature Extraction

   Features/Key Points are detected on each image using the Scale Invariant Feature Transform algorithm [19,20]. Unlike corner detection algorithms, the SIFT algorithm is invariant to scale. The SIFT algorithm first creates multiple scaled images of the original image and classifies them into octaves. Each octave has an image equal to half that of the previous octave. This is done to obtain a series of images of different scales to achieve scale invariance.The Gaussian Blue operator is then used to gradually blur the images inside one octave. The Difference of Gaussian (DoG) method is then used to produce a new series of images from the blurred images. The DoG of images is computed as the difference in the Gaussian blurring of 2 images within an octave with different levels of blurring. The DoG images are then used to create Gaussian Laplacian (LoG) approximations that are invariant to scale. This process is done for all octaves. Each pixel on an LoG image is then compared with neighboring pixels on the same image and corresponding pixels on the next and previous octave LoG images. If the pixel is a local extremum, it is classified as a potentially key point. The feature extraction process can be achieved by using Eqs. 1 to 4.

2. Feature Matching

   Some of the potential key points generated above might not have sufficient contrast with the surrounding pixels and hence are not useful features. Such key points are removed from the set of key points based on a threshold of intensity. If the intensity of a potentially key point is less than a threshold value, it is not considered a key point. After removing the weak key points, the remaining key points are then adjusted for orientation and lighting to make the rotation and illumination invariant. Finally, we end up with key points and their corresponding feature vectors, which tell us about the direction or gradient of the key point [3].

   For this, the K Nearest Neighbor algorithm is used to match these key points of 2 images and the distance between between two feature points is calculated by using Eq. 5. This KNN algorithm returns the k best matches for each feature. Once these matches are identified, a robustness test needs to be performed. Ratio Testing is used to ensure that the key points are matched correctly and the distance between a key point on one image and its match on another image is uniform across all matches.

3. Transformation Estimation

   Once the corresponding matching points are identified on the 2 images, the images need to be merged based on these points. A homography matrix is developed using the RANSAC algorithm [10] which accounts for rotation, translation, scale, and shear. One of the 2 images is transformed using this homography matrix and then merged in a 2-D plane with the other image to get the final stitched image. This can be achieved by using Eq. 6.

4. Output
   This merged image then undergoes all the steps before it gets merged with another individual image and the process goes on till all the images are merged.

3.2   Object Identification

Unmanned aerial vehicles can be used in a variety of applications such as forest fire detection, vegetation monitoring, disaster monitoring and prevention, mapping, traffic monitoring, and optimization, surveillance, etc. Most of these applications require the identification of objects that stand out from the homogeneity of the background. For example, detecting the presence of a drowning human in the sea requires the identification of an individual in the image who will be 'standing out from the homogenous blue background of the sea. Similarly, mapping a forest region requires the identification of pathways and house roofs that stand out from the homogenous green background of the forest. Pixel intensity changes are a good indication of changes in homogeneity and can be used to identify the presence of objects [28,32]. The algorithm presented below is a simple and computationally light method to roughly detect the presence of objects and their locations. This algorithm can be used as a preliminary step in advanced object detection. The steps involved in detecting the object on the stitched image are described in this section. And the Algorithm 2 shows that pseudo-code of the Object Identification Methodology.

1. Image Segmentation:
   Read the image and resize the image to a value (1000 by 1000 pixels)to create an algorithm that is consistent. Then the image is split into multiple small rectangles (50 by 100 pixels) to create smaller blocks of intensity. The average pixel intensity within each smaller block is computed.
2. Image Scanning:
   A horizontal scan is then performed on all rectangles in one row. The average pixel intensity of one rectangle is compared with respect to the mean pixel intensity of the rectangle just to the left of the first rectangle. And the average intensity of pixels is calculated by using Eqs. 7 and 8. It shows that, the absolute value of percentage change in intensity is computed and recorded in a separate list. This process is performed for all rectangles in a row before moving to the next row and performing the same process. By the end of this step, a list containing the percentage changes of intensity of rectangles (w.r.t the rectangles on their immediate left) is obtained.
3. Estimation of Pixel Intensity:
   The change in intensity of the mosaic image is calculated by using Eqs. 9 and 10. The list is then sorted from highest to lowest. Higher the value, more

Algorithm 1. Image Stitching Algorithm for UAV Data

Require: $I = (I_1), (I_2), (I_3), ...(I_n)$ set of aerial images.

Ensure: $Output$ = Stitched Image

1: Read the input images I.

2: Extract the common features from all the images.

- Generation of pairwise homographs by using the Scale Invariant Feature Transformation (SIFT) algorithm. Mathematically, it can be expressed as:

$$H_{(ij)} = K_i R_i R_j^T \tag{1}$$

where, $K_{(i)}$:is the four parameter camera model. It is represented as:

$$K_i = \begin{pmatrix} f_i & 0 & 0 \\ 0 & f_i & 0 \\ 0 & 0 & f_i \end{pmatrix} \tag{2}$$

f_i is the focal length of the camera. R_i is defined as the exponential representation for rotation. It is calculated as:

$$R_i = e^{\theta_i} \tag{3}$$

θ_i is the rotation vector of the camera. There are three rotational vectors $[\theta_1, \theta_2, \theta_3]$. Mathematically, it can be expressed as:

$$[\theta_i] = \begin{pmatrix} 0 & -\theta_{i3} & \theta_{i2} \\ \theta_{i3} & 0 & -\theta_{i1} \\ -\theta_{i2} & \theta_{i1} & 0 \end{pmatrix} \tag{4}$$

Ideally, we would use all the image features that are invariant for this transformation function.

3: After all of the characteristics from all of the images have been retrieved, they must be compared and matched. It can be done by using the KNN. The function can be described as:

- Select a value for K, where K represents the number of training samples in the feature space (k = 4).
- Calculate the distance of unknown extracted points from all the training samples by using the Manhattan distance function. The Manhattan distance function can be expressed as:

$$D = \sum_{i=1}^{n} |x_i - y_i| \tag{5}$$

where, $|x_i - y_i|$: represents the distance between the retrieved data points and the sample points in the images.

- After calculating the distance, a robustness test needs to be performed.
- In this way, common features have been detected from all aerial images.

4: Merge all the images based on the extracted common points. It includes:

- Creating a homography matrix by using the equation:

$$p(H is correct) = 1 - (1 - (p_i))^n \tag{6}$$

where,

p_i =the probability of a feature matching is correct between a corresponding image pair.

- p_H=probability of finding the correct transformation after n trials.
- After generating the homography matrix, one of the images is transformed and merged in a 2-D plane with another image to obtain a stitched image.

5: This stitched image is then further stitched with the other images through steps 1-4.

6: A complete stitched / ortho mosaic image is obtained.

the likelihood of the corresponding rectangle consisting of an object or at least a deviation from homogeneity. So, the higher values in the list and their corresponding rectangles are of primary interest. Based on the landscape and objective of use, a threshold value (for example 0.4 or 40%) is computed and values in the list below this threshold value are discarded and the corresponding rectangles are blackened (intensity 0) in the output image. The remaining values are then segregated and the list is generated as:

- Case 1: If the change in pixel intensity is less than 0.4 (40%), then corresponding rectangles are assigned an intensity of 0.0 (black) in the output image.
- Case 2: If the change in pixel intensity is between 0.4 to 1.0 (40% to 100%), then corresponding rectangles are assigned an intensity of 0.5 (grey) in the output image.
- Case 3: If the change in pixel intensity is greater than 1.0 (100%), then corresponding rectangles are assigned an intensity of 1.0 (white) in the output image.

4. Classified Image: The final output image is obtained with rectangles in black, black gray, dark gray, light gray and white. The lighter the color, the higher the intensity change between that rectangle and the one to its left, and hence, the higher the probability of that rectangle consisting of an object or a deviation from homogeneity. In the example image, the white and light grey rectangles correspond to house roofs and container tops. All the other shades of grey correspond to mud roads, pathways, and other deviations from the green forest homogeneity. The black rectangles broadly correspond to the forest cover.

Table 1. Description of open source UAV-data set

Parameters	Description
Source	Delair Tech DT-18 drones
Location	Congo
Aerage Ground Sampling Distance (GSD)	3.59 cm/1.41 in
Output Coordinate System	WGS84/UTM zone 33S (egm96)
Area Covered	0.0192 km^2
UAV	Delair Tech DT-18
Image acquisition plan	1 flight, grid flight plan
Camera	Delair Tech Big Map
Number of images	15
Image size	2448 × 2048
Image geolocation coordinate system	WGS84 (egm96)

Algorithm 2. Object Identification Algortithm for UAV Data

Require: Ortho-Mosaic Image.

Ensure: Classified Image of Region Detection.

1: Read the stitched or Ortho-Mosaic Image.
2: Segmented the whole mosaic image into small rectangles or blocks as $n * m$, where:
   n indicates the total number of blocks organized in a single line to cover the whole area
   m represents the processing time slots
3: Perform the H-scan on all the segmented rectangles or blocks.
4: Calculate the average intensity of the pixel of each rectangle. Mathematically, it can be expressed as:

$$I_R = \sum_{r=1}^{n_r} (i_r)/N \tag{7}$$

$$I_L = \sum_{l=1}^{n_l} (i_l)/N \tag{8}$$

where,
I_R represents the average intensity of right segmented block.
I_L represents the average intensity of left segmented block.
N Total Number of pixels in the segmented block.
5: Calculate the total change in intensity in the segmented mosaic image. Mathematically, it can expressed as:

$$M = (I_R - I_L)/I_R \tag{9}$$

In terms of percentage, it is calculated as:

$$M = ((I_R - I_L)/I_R) * 100 \tag{10}$$

6: Generate the list (Z) based on the value which is calculated in step 5. The list can be created as:
   – **if** $M \geq 100\%$ **then** $Z = 1$ (represented by white color)
   – **if** $40\% \leq M \leq 100\%$ **then** $Z = 0.5$ (represented by grey color)
   – **if** $M < 40\%$ **then** $Z = 0$ (represented by black color)
   These Z values indicates the homogeneous pixels of an unknown environment in the image and classify by different colors in the output image.
7: The final output image is obtained containing rectangles of black, grey and white colors based on the list which is generated in Step 6.

---

4   Results And Analysis

The algorithms which are discussed in Subsects. 3.1 and 3.2 are tested on the available open-source data set which is provided by ESRI [1]. The detailed description of the dataset is mentioned in Table 1. These methods are implemented using the Python Imaging Library (PIL), Numpy, Pandas, and Open CV (4.5.4) libraries of Python. First, we generate the mosaic image from the set of 15 overlapping aerial images. These images were generated by the Delair

Tech Big Map camera. The set of 15 overlapping images which are taken from the single UAV is shown in Fig. 1. The image stitching algorithm is applied to these images to generate one resultant ortho-mosaiced image. The Fig. 2 signifies that the 15 images are properly stitched without any apparent errors. The above experimental result demonstrates the effectiveness of the image stitching algorithm.

Fig. 1. Set of aerial images

After the image stitching algorithm, the subsequent step is to detect the objects in the mosaic image. For this, the resultant stitched image was divided into 10×20 blocks so as to perform a horizontal line (H-scan), average intensity-based object identification operation. The stitched image which is shown in Fig. 2, consist of forest land, rooftops and mudroads. And the aim is to classify the unknown landscape into these 3 classes. This is achieved by using the average intensity feature and the salient region objection detection algorithm.

The original scene of the area is shown in Fig. 3. The entire image is digitized starting with the first row of the mosaic segmented image. And then, the object detection algorithm is applied. The output image of detected salient regions is obtained and then the appropriate classification of regions into forest land, rooftops, and mudroads is done. The output image is shown in Fig. 4. The Fig. 4 signifies that the image was segmented into 3 colors - white, grey, and black. The white and grey regions also correspond to the salient (deviations from homogeneity) regions in the image. As illustrates in Fig. 4, the white, gray and black regions corresponds to the house roofs, mud roads and forest cover respectively.

Fig. 2. Ortho-Mosaic image

Fig. 3. Segmented configuration of line scan (H-Scan)

Table 2. Statistical results

	White Regions	Grey Regions	Black Regions	All Regions
True Positives (TP)	6	23	119	148
False Positives (FP)	7	13	32	52
False Negatives (FN)	5	29	18	52
Recall Rate (TP/(TP+FN))	54.55%	44.23 %	86.86 %	74.00%
Precision Rate (TP/(TP+FP))	46.15%	63.89 %	79.81 %	74.00%

This classification is then compared with the manual classification of the image to compute the performance of the experimental results obtained. The complete statistical results or the performance metrics of the object identification algorithm are shown in Table 2.

The number of true positives, false positives, and false negatives is illustrate in the Table 2. By using these values the recall rate and the precision rate are calculated. These statistical results indicate that the algorithm is useful in extracting meaningful information such as the location of objects, intensity of objects, etc. about the landscape being scanned by the UAV. The average statistical results, which are illustrated in Table 2, signify that the recall and precision rates are 74% and in this context, these rates are appropriate for tasks involving identifying salient regions. To further improvise and build on the output of this paper, one can train a machine learning model to identify and classify an unknown environment effectively. Moreover, these trained models can then be used for various practical applications like forest fire detection, drowning individual identification, search

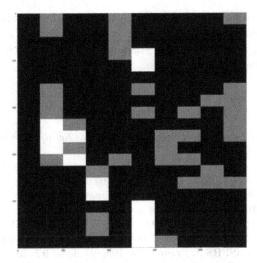

Fig. 4. Classified image of region detection (Here, White Regions, Grey and Black represents: the house roofs or trailer tops, mud roads or rocky patches and forest cover respectively.)

and rescue operations, traffic surveillance, and so on. So, the object identification algorithm can be used as a preliminary image scoping algorithm to broadly get an idea about the contents of the image. Depending on the application, one may use other operations to perform a comprehensive study of the area or region. Furthermore, in this paper, the Algorithms 1 and 2 are implemented by considering the images from a single UAV but usually, more than one UAV would be required to cover a large area. Therefore, these algorithms can potentially be implemented on images obtained from multiple UAVs.

5   Conclusion

This paper introduces an end-to-end algorithm to process and analyze multiple overlapping images taken by a single UAV. The algorithm includes image enhancement, image stitching, image cropping, and object identification. In this paper, feature detection and matching are used for stitching the 15 overlapping aerial images while average pixel intensity comparison across horizontal blocks is used for identifying the different objects such as forest, mud roads, rooftops, and so on. The effectiveness of this algorithm can be gauged based on the experimental results that are obtained. These results are meaningful in terms of providing a preliminary landscape scan of the whole area. However, making use of the various machine learning algorithms helps in extracting more detailed information about the area. This would help in giving a piece of more detailed and accurate information. Moreover, some pre-image processing tasks such as noise removal, dark object subtraction could be performed to make it easier to work with all those aerial data set having noise such as smoke and fog. In the future, the discussed algorithm may be trained in such a way that makes it easier to deal with sudden changes in illumination and shadows of objects which ultimately leads to practical and real-world challenges.

References

1. ESRI Data Set. https://doc.arcgis.com/en/drone2map/get-started/sample-data.htm/. Accessed Dec 2021
2. Brown, M., Lowe, D.G.: Automatic panoramic image stitching using invariant features. Int. J. Comput. Vis. **74**(1), 59–73 (2007)
3. Brown, M., Szeliski, R., Winder, S.: Multi-image matching using multi-scale oriented patches. In: 2005 IEEE Computer Society Conference on Computer Vision and Pattern Recognition (CVPR 2005), vol. 1, pp. 510–517. IEEE (2005)
4. Colomina, I., Molina, P.: Unmanned aerial systems for photogrammetry and remote sensing: a review. ISPRS J. Photogram. Remote Sens. **92**, 79–97 (2014)
5. Cong, M., Han, L., Ding, M., Xu, M., Tao, Y.: Salient man-made object detection based on saliency potential energy for unmanned aerial vehicles remote sensing image. Geocarto Int. **34**(14), 1634–1647 (2019)
6. Conte, G., Doherty, P.: An integrated UAV navigation system based on aerial image matching. In: 2008 IEEE Aerospace Conference, pp. 1–10. IEEE (2008)
7. Deren, L., Ming, L.: Research advance and application prospect of unmanned aerial vehicle remote sensing system. Geomat. Inf. Sci. Wuhan Univ. **39**(5), 505–513 (2014)
8. Fatima, S.A., Kumar, A., Pratap, A., Raoof, S.S.: Object recognition and detection in remote sensing images: a comparative study. In: 2020 International Conference on Artificial Intelligence and Signal Processing (AISP), pp. 1–5. IEEE (2020)
9. Fergus, R., Perona, P., Zisserman, A.: Object class recognition by unsupervised scale-invariant learning. In: Proceedings of 2003 IEEE Computer Society Conference on Computer Vision and Pattern Recognition, vol. 2, p. II. IEEE (2003)
10. Fischler, M.A., Bolles, R.C.: Random sample consensus: a paradigm for model fitting with applications to image analysis and automated cartography. Commun. the ACM **24**(6), 381–395 (1981)
11. Huang, Y., Li, J., Fan, N.: Image mosaicing for UAV application. In: 2008 International Symposium on Knowledge Acquisition and Modeling, pp. 663–667. IEEE (2008)
12. Jia, J., Tang, C.K.: Image stitching using structure deformation. IEEE Trans. Pattern Anal. Mach. Intell. **30**(4), 617–631 (2008)
13. Kern, A., Bobbe, M., Bestmann, U.: Towards a real-time aerial image mosaicing solution. In: International Micro-Air Vehicle Conference and Competition (IMAV) (2016)
14. Li, M., et al.: A stereo dual-channel dynamic programming algorithm for UAV image stitching. Sensors **17**(9), 2060 (2017)
15. Li, M., Li, D., Fan, D.: A study on automatic UAV image mosaic method for paroxysmal disaster. Int. Arch. Photogramm. Remote Sens. Spat. Inf. Sci pp. **39** ,123–128 (2012)
16. Li, Y., Zhang, Y., Yu, J.G., Tan, Y., Tian, J., Ma, J.: A novel spatio-temporal saliency approach for robust dim moving target detection from airborne infrared image sequences. Inf. Sci. **369**, 548–563 (2016)

17. Liu, J., Gong, J., Guo, B., Zhang, W.: A novel adjustment model for mosaicking low-overlap sweeping images. IEEE Trans. Geosci. Remote Sens. **55**(7), 4089–4097 (2017)
18. Liu, Q., Liu, W., Zou, L., Wang, J., Liu, Y.: A new approach to fast mosaic UAV images. Proc. Int. Arch. Photogram. Remote Sen. Spatial Inf. Sci. **38**(1) (2011)
19. Lowe, D.G.: Object recognition from local scale-invariant features. In: Proceedings of the Seventh IEEE International Conference on Computer Vision, vol. 2, pp. 1150–1157. IEEE (1999)
20. Lowe, D.G.: Distinctive image features from scale-invariant keypoints. Int. J. Comput. Vis. **60**(2), 91–110 (2004)
21. McCartney, M.I., Zein-Sabatto, S., Malkani, M.: Image registration for sequence of visual images captured by UAV. In: 2009 IEEE Symposium on Computational Intelligence for Multimedia Signal and Vision Processing, pp. 91–97. IEEE (2009)
22. Moranduzzo, T., Melgani, F.: A sift-SVM method for detecting cars in UAV images. In: 2012 IEEE International Geoscience and Remote Sensing Symposium, pp. 6868–6871. IEEE (2012)
23. Nel, J.F.: Post-processing of UAV-captured images for enhanced mapping by image stitching. In: 2015 IEEE 5th International Conference on Consumer Electronics-Berlin (ICCE-Berlin), pp. 500–504. IEEE (2015)
24. Pajares, G.: Overview and current status of remote sensing applications based on unmanned aerial vehicles (UAVs). Photogram. Eng. Remote Sens. **81**(4), 281–330 (2015)
25. Portmann, J., Lynen, S., Chli, M., Siegwart, R.: People detection and tracking from aerial thermal views. In: 2014 IEEE International Conference on Robotics and Automation (ICRA), pp. 1794–1800. IEEE (2014)
26. Shakhatreh, H., Sawalmeh, A.H., Al-Fuqaha, A., Dou, Z., Almaita, E., Khalil, I., Othman, N.S., Khreishah, A., Guizani, M.: Unmanned aerial vehicles (uavs): a survey on civil applications and key research challenges. IEEE Access **7**, 48572–48634 (2019)
27. Shen, H., Li, S., Zhu, C., Chang, H., Zhang, J.: Moving object detection in aerial video based on spatiotemporal saliency. Chinese J. Aeronaut. **26**(5), 1211–1217 (2013)
28. Sousselier, T., Dreo, J., Sevaux, M.: Line formation algorithm in a swarm of reactive robots constrained by underwater environment. Exp. Syst. Appl. **42**(12), 5117–5127 (2015)
29. Wu, Y., Sui, Y., Wang, G.: Vision-based real-time aerial object localization and tracking for UAV sensing system. IEEE Access **5**, 23969–23978 (2017)
30. Xiong, P., Liu, X., Gao, C., Zhou, Z., Gao, C., Liu, Q.: A real-time stitching algorithm for UAV aerial images. In: Proceedings of the 2nd International Conference on Computer Science and Electronics Engineering, pp. 1613–1616. Atlantis Press (2013)
31. Yahyanejad, S., Wischounig-Strucl, D., Quaritsch, M., Rinner, B.: Incremental mosaicking of images from autonomous, small-scale uavs. In: 2010 7th IEEE International Conference on Advanced Video and Signal Based Surveillance, pp. 329–336. IEEE (2010)
32. Yang, J., Wang, X., Bauer, P.: Line and v-shape formation based distributed processing for robotic swarms. Sensors **18**(8), 2543 (2018)
33. Yao, H., Qin, R., Chen, X.: Unmanned aerial vehicle for remote sensing applications-a review. Remote Sens. **11**(12), 1443 (2019)
34. Zhang, R., Shao, Z., Huang, X., Wang, J., Li, D.: Object detection in UAV images via global density fused convolutional network. Remote Sens. **12**(19), 3140 (2020)

The Novel Approach of Down-Link Spectral Efficiency Enhancement Using Massive MIMO in Correlated Rician Fading Scenario

Niravkumar D. Patel$^{(\boxtimes)}$ (iD) and Vijay K. Patel (iD)

Ganpat University, Mehsana, India
nirav2009ec@gmail.com, vijay.patel@ganpatuniversity.ac.in

Abstract. To shift at higher and wider unused available frequency spectrum for wireless communication application is not an ultimate feasible solution, until and unless the available frequency spectrum is used efficiently. The spectral efficiency is the index of efficient usage of available frequency spectrum. The Massive MIMO technology has been selected as an approach for down-link spectral efficiency enhancement. The spatially correlated Rician fading model is selected for channel fading scenario as it is closer to practical scenario and results are compared with Rayleigh fading scenario throughout. The MMSE, EW-MMSE and LS methods are selected and compared for statistical channel estimation for spectral efficiency enhancement. The MR precoding method is used at BS for DL transmission. The rigorously achievable closed form DL SE expressions are used for analysis. The results show that the MMSE/EW-MMSE estimator is better choice over LS estimator in general. Also the increase in number of antennas at BS can increase the existing performance gap between above mentioned estimators and increase SE in general. The DL SE is higher in Rician fading scenario than Rayleigh fading in both spatially correlated and uncorrelated cases.

Keywords: Massive MIMO system · Spatial correlation · Rician fading · Spectral efficiency · Channel estimation

1 Introduction

The wireless voice and data traffic has followed exponential growth rate since many decades, which is as per the Cooper's law (Cooper 2010, p. 2). The Ericsson mobility report (Ericsson 2021, p. 2) even forecasts growth rate more than 49% annually, which is more faster than Cooper's law. So the Massive MIMO is one of the key enabler technology for this future demands. It is the breakthrough technology in wireless mobile communication, having large number of antennas (i.e. at least ten times of serving UEs) at Base Station (BS) as per (Björnson et al. 2017, p. 6; Ding and Jing 2019, p. 1; Björnson et al. 2016, p. 1; Larsson et al. 2014, p. 186) and this concept of Massive MIMO was firstly introduced by Thomas Marzetta in his seminal paper (Marzetta 2010). The massive number of antennas at BS allows spectral efficiency to be enhanced by beam forming and spatial multiplexing types of key techniques as per (Larsson et al. 2014, p. 187;

© Springer Nature Switzerland AG 2022
N. Chaubey et al. (Eds.): COMS2 2022, CCIS 1604, pp. 54–68, 2022.
https://doi.org/10.1007/978-3-031-10551-7_5

Özdogan et al. 2019, p. 1). The tens of User Equipments (UEs) can be simultaneously served in same coherent time and frequency slot with efficient usage of hundreds of BS antennas. In Time Division Duplex (TTD) mode, Channel State Information (CSI) is estimated in up-link (UL) and assumed same for down-link (DL) as channel is assumed reciprocal in TDD protocol. As result, TDD protocol reduces estimation efforts and time, up to a large extends as per (Björnson et al. 2017, p. 209). The CSI is very important for coherent signal processing and it is obtained by piloting method. The pilot signal is know at both side and it is sent through channel to get channel response. The available channel response of pilot signal is used for CSI acquisition by comparing it with known original pilot available as per (Björnson et al. 2017, pp. 208–209).

2 Literature Review

(Yu et al. 2020, p. 1; Du et al. 2019, p. 1) investigated the SE of system with imperfect CSI for correlated Rayleigh fading models. (Demir and Björnson 2020, p. 2) derived SE for Maasive MIMO in uncorrelated Rician fading scenario. (Chen et al. 2020 p. 1; Cho et al. 2020, p. 1) has analyzed the SE performance for LoS type of channel only, called no fading. Usually in real scenario, channel has direct (LoS) and indirect (NLoS) propagation paths, where the large scale fading results from Line of Sight (LoS) and the small scale fading results from Non-Line of Sight (NLoS) types of propagations as per (Tse and Viswanath 2005, p. 21). As per (Boukhedimi et al. 2020, p. 1; Femenias et al. 2020, p. 1; Jin et al. 2021, p. 1; Liu et al. 2021, p. 1; Peng et al. 2021, p. 1; Boukhedimi et al. 2019, p. 1) the Rician channel fading model can closely represent the real channel fading scenario than Rayleigh one.

This Rician channel model has not much analyzed compared to Rayleigh for Massive MIMO SE as per (Wang et al. 2020, p. 2; Boukhedimi et al. 2019, p. 1). (Boukhedimi et al. 2019, p. 1; Rajmane and Sudha 2019, p. 1) have considered single cell system for SE analysis. Also (Boukhedimi et al. 2019, p. 6) have considered multi-cell scenario but assumed that the LoS can exist only within the cell area and not in between UE and BS belonging from different cells. In large, the Rician channel fading model is limited up to cell boundaries and inter cell channel fading is of Rayleigh fading type only. (Ding and Jing 2019, p. 1; Liu et al. 2020, p. 2) have carried out SE analysis for Massive MIMO system using zero-forcing precoding method. However (Jin et al. 2021, p. 1; Kong et al. 2019, p. 1; Peng et al. 2021, p. 1; Wang et al. 2020, p. 1; Wang et al. 2021, p. 1) has derived SE for Massive MIMO using maximum ration precoding method. As per (HOSANY 2020, pp. 35–36; Rajmane and Sudha 2019, p. 1) maximum ration precoding is simpler than zero forcing precoding in the context of computational complexity. (Liu et al. 2021, p. 1; Özdogan et al. 2019, p. 1; Wang et al. 2021, p. 1; Demir and Björnson 2020, p. 1; Özdogan et al. 2019, p. 1) have derived SE for Massive MIMO using various estimation methods and MMSE estimation found best among all (Arzykulov et al. 2021, p. 2; Boukhedimi et al. 2019, p. 1; Ding and Jing 2019, p. 1; Kong et al. 2019, p. 2; Peng et al. 2021, p. 1; Yu et al. 2020. P. 2; Du et al. 2019, p. 1) all this works assumed imperfect CSI for SE derivation in Massive MIMO, which is the case in real scenario. On the contrary previous works (HOSANY 2020, p. 1; Rajmane and Sudha 2019, p.1; Björnson et al. 2016. P. 119) have assumed perfect CSI for SE analysis in Massive MIMO. Both perfect CSI and imperfect CSI scenarios are considered in (Liu et al. 2020, p. 2) for SE derivation in Massive MIMO.

3   Core Contribution

There are limitations of previous works and it is extended here as follows. (1) Mostly in previous works, fading scenarios are considered uncorrelated, which is not in practice as scattering clusters are finite as per (Björnson et al. 2017, p. 237). and it is broaden by considering correlated scenarios also here to compare it with uncorrelated scenario. (2) Mostly in previous works, fading scenario across the cells are assumed Rayleigh, which is not the reality, because there can be LoS between cell edge UE of cell A to BS of cell B i.e. large areas without obstructions, densification of small cells in given area, and unmanned vehicles serving from air (UAVs). (3) Mostly in previous works, single cell scenario is considered, which is again far away from reality and it is extended by considering multi-cell scenario here. (4) In futuristic mmWave technology, path loss can increase more. As consequence to compensate with that loss, cell area and cell densification in given area can be increased, this increases probability to have LoS more. So LoS existence cannot be avoided absolutely. So the 3GGP model (3GPP Tech. Report 2020, 26) is used in our simulation, where fading is considered as Rician (LoS + NLoS) and compared with Rayleigh (NLoS). To implement above extensive approach, below have been considered:

- In multi-cell system, UE and BS can have Rician or Rayleigh correlated fading channel.
- To acquire CSI, MMSE, EW-MMSE and LS estimation methods are used and MR precoding technique is used for transmit precoding from BS.
  And below has been carried out:
- Average sum DL SE has been analyzed for above mentioned estimation methods and fading scenarios.
- Average sum DL SE has also been analyzed for correlated and uncorrelated fading scenarios.
- Cumulative density function (CDF) of SE per US has also been analyzed for same above estimation methods and fading scenarios.

4   Channel and System Modeling

It is considered that the each BS is equipped with hundreds of antennas in the system. Also the total coverage area is divided in to the L cells and each cell has the dedicated BS equipped with M_j number of antennas. In each cell the K numbers of UEs are served by same BS. The channel between BS and UE is operated in TDD mode, where channel response found constant over coherent slot sized of τ_c samples and channel realization assumed independent over any pair of coherent slots. The coherent slot size τ_c depends on mobility of UE and surrounding environment as per (Björnson et al. 2017, p. 263). The τ_c samples can be divided into τ_P, τ_u, and τ_d samples as per their role, like τ_p samples for UL pilot signaling, τ_u samples for UL data transmission, and τ_d samples for DL data transmission. As per TTD protocol, the channel is assumed reciprocal. As result, the channel is estimated in UL and assumed same in DL, which reduces channel estimation time, resources and efforts compared to FDD protocol. However, before data transmission, channel is estimated by piloting method.

The channel response of propagation is denoted as $h_{lk}^j \in \mathbb{C}^{M_j}$, where l indicates cell number, k indicates UE number and j indicates BS number. These notations are same throughout the paper. The $h_{lk}^j \in \mathbb{C}^{M_j}$ is vector and each element of it represents individual channel response between UE and individual BS antenna. For notational convenience, h_{lk}^j is the UL channel and as per TDD protocol DL channel is $(h_{lk}^j)^H$, in same coherent slot.

The $h_{lk}^j \in \mathbb{C}^{M_j}$ channel considered spatially correlated Rician fading and it is expressed as

$$h_{lk}^j \sim \mathcal{N}_{\mathbb{C}}\left(\overline{h}_{lk}^j, R_{lk}^j\right), \tag{1}$$

where $\forall j, l \in 1, \ldots, L$ and $\forall k \in 1, \ldots K$ and $\mathcal{N}_{\mathbb{C}}$ indicates that the channel realizations are assumed as circularly symmetric complex Gaussian distributed. The $\overline{h}_{lk}^j \in \mathbb{C}^{M_j}$ signify LoS component of channel and $R_{lk}^j \in \mathbb{C}^{M_j \times M_j}$ signify NLoS component of channel in Eq. (1), where $R_{lk}^j \in \mathbb{C}^{M_j \times M_j}$ is positive semi-definite covariance matrix. The Gaussian distribution represents the small-scale fading and large-scale fading can be represented by shadow fading, path loss, radiation patterns of antennas. The large scale fading is represented by R_{lk}^j and $\overline{h}_{lk}^j$. The trace of R_{lk}^j normalized over M_j indicates average channel gain, as shown in Eq. (2). It is also called large-scale channel gain or fading co-efficient.

$$\beta_{lk}^j = \frac{1}{M_j} tr\left(R_{lk}^j\right), \tag{2}$$

5 Estimation Methods

The CSI is very essential for signal processing at receiver and transmitter, which can be acquired by piloting method, where τ_P samples are transmitted as pilot signals in same coherent slot. There is set of pilot sequences, known at UE and BS both and transmitted from UE to BS in UL. In multi-cell scenario, this same set can be reused in more than one cell by UEs and each individual sequence is unique within the cell for each UE. The pilot sequence is denoted as $\varnothing_{jk} \in \mathbb{C}^{\tau_P}$, where $\|\varnothing_{jk}\|^2 = \tau_P$. The pilot sequence set $\mathcal{P}_{jk}$ is expressed as,

$$\mathcal{P}_{jk} = \{(l, i): \emptyset_{li} = \emptyset_{jk}, l = 1, \ldots, L, i = 1, \ldots, K_l\} \tag{3}$$

where k and i are UE numbers and l and j are cell numbers. The $Y_p^j \in \mathbb{C}^{M_j \times \tau_P}$ is the pilot signal received at BS j, expressed as,

$$Y_p^j = \sum_{k=1}^{K_j} \sqrt{P_{jk}} h_{jk}^j \varnothing_{jk}^T + \sum_{\substack{l = 1 \\ l \neq j}}^{L} \sum_{i=1}^{K_l} \sqrt{P_{li}} h_{li}^j \varnothing_{li}^T + N_j^p, \tag{4}$$

where $N_j^P \epsilon \mathbb{C}^{M_j \times \tau_P}$ and $N_j^P \sim \mathcal{N}_\mathbb{C}(0, \sigma_{ul}^2)$. The known UE's pilot sequence $\varnothing_{li}^*$ is multiplied with received Y_p^j signal at BS j to obtain y_{jli}^p as shown in Eq. (5) below,

$$y_{jli}^p = Y_p^j \varnothing_{li}^* = \sqrt{P_{li}}\tau_P h_{li}^j + \sum_{(l',i') \in \mathscr{P}_{li\setminus(l,i)}} \sqrt{P_{l'i'}}\tau_P h_{l'i'}^j + N_j^P \varnothing_{li}^* \qquad (5)$$

where $y_{jli}^p \in \mathbb{C}^{M_j}$ is the enough statistic for estimating h_{li}^j as per (Özdogan et al. 2019, p. 2).

However the statistical channel knowledge required by channel estimator is differ from estimator to estimator and three channel estimators are considered here namely MMSE, EW-MMSE and LS. The statistical distribution of estimated channel can be obtained from the sample mean and sample covariance matrices (Özdogan et al. 2019, p. 2; Kay 1993).

5.1 MMSE Channel Estimator

The channel estimation $\hat{h}_{li}^j$ as shown below in Eq. (6), can be acquired at BS by applying MMSE estimation method to process received pilot signal shown in Eq. (5),

$$\hat{h}_{li}^j = \overline{h}_{li}^j + \sqrt{P_{li}}R_{li}^j \Psi_{li}^j (y_{jli}^p - \overline{y}_{jli}^p) \qquad (6)$$

$$\text{where } \overline{y}_{jli}^p = \sum_{(l',i') \in p_{li}} \sqrt{P_{l'i'}}\tau_P \overline{h}_{l'i'}^j \text{ and } \Psi_{li}^j = \tau_P Cov\{y_{jli}^p\}^{-1} = \\ (\sum_{(l',i') \in p_{li}} P_{l'i'}\tau_P R_{l'i'}^j + \sigma^2 I_{M_j})^{-1} \qquad (7)$$

The perfect channel estimation is ideal case and usually not possible to achieve in practice. There is always some non zero channel estimation error generated, which is defined as $\tilde{h}_{li}^j = h_{li}^j - \hat{h}_{li}^j$ and the covariance matrix of estimation error is expressed as

$$C_{li}^j = R_{li}^j - P_{li}\tau_P R_{li}^j \Psi_{li}^j R_{li}^j \qquad (8)$$

where the trace of C_{li}^j matrix is the mean square error, also defined as $\mathbb{E}\left\{\|h_{li}^j - \hat{h}_{li}^j\|^2\right\}$. The distribution of channel estimation and estimation error can be expressed as below,

$$\hat{h}_{li}^j \sim \mathcal{N}_\mathbb{C}\left(\overline{h}_{li}^j, R_{li}^j - C_{li}^j\right) \qquad (9)$$

$$\tilde{h}_{li}^j \sim \mathcal{N}_\mathbb{C}\left(0_M, C_{li}^j\right) \qquad (10)$$

where $\hat{h}_{li}^j$ and $\tilde{h}_{li}^j$ are independent random variables. It can be noticeable from Eq. (8) and (10) that, the channel estimation error and covariance matrix are not depending on channel mean. Also means of channel vector are deterministic and can be filtered out by receive signal processing and the estimation error does not affected by channel vector means. It is assumed independent channel realization, but it is not necessary that channel estimates are also independent. It can be understood as follows. There are UE_A in cell A and UE_B in cell B using same pilot sequence to estimate the channel. Now, if channel estimation of UE_A is of our interest, then due to having same pilot sequence, channel estimation at BS in cell A between UE_A and BS in cell A is contaminated by unnecessary pilot sequence received by BS in cell A from UE_B in cell B, called pilot contamination. In general it can be said that, it occurs due to the same pilot sequence used by more than one UEs in different cells to reduce pilot over head. The $\hat{h}_{jk}^{j}$ is channel estimation of channel between user equipment k and BS j in cell j, where $(j, k) \in \mathcal{P}_{li}$. However it is expressed as below,

$$\hat{h}_{jk}^{j} = \overline{h}_{jk}^{j} + \sqrt{P_{jk}}R_{li}^{j}\Psi_{li}^{j}(y_{jli}^{p} - \overline{y}_{jli}^{p}) \tag{11}$$

The $\hat{h}_{jk}^{j}$ is correlated with $\hat{h}_{lk}^{j}$ since y_{jli}^{p} common in both expressions and $\Psi_{li}^{j} = \Psi_{jk}^{j}$.

5.2 Element-Wise MMSE Channel Estimator

There can be a case, where full covariance matrices are not available at BS. In such case, MMSE estimation is not as effective as it can be due to lake of statistical information and EW-MMSE estimation is suitable option in such cases (Özdogan et al. 2019, p. 3; Björnson et al. 2017, p. 266). However, EW-MMSE estimates only diagonal elements of matrices and off-diagonal element do not estimated by EW-MMSE, where off-diagonal elements represents correlations between elements. So, EW-MMSE does not required inverse matrix operation, which reduces computational efforts substantially. The EW-MMSE channel estimation is expressed as,

$$\hat{h}_{li}^{j} = \overline{h}_{li}^{j} + \sqrt{P_{li}}D_{li}^{j}\Lambda_{li}^{j}(y_{jli}^{p} - \overline{y}_{jli}^{p}) \tag{12}$$

where $D_{li}^{j} \in \mathbb{C}^{M_j \times M_j}$ and $\Lambda_{li}^{j} \in \mathbb{C}^{M_j \times M_j}$ are diagonal matrices with $D_{li}^{j} = diag\left(\left[R_{li}^{j}\right]_{mm} : m = 1 \ldots M_j\right)$ and $\Lambda_{li}^{j} = diag\left(\left[\sum_{(l',i') \in p_{li}} P_{l'i'}\tau_p R_{l'i'}^{j} + \sigma^2 I_{M_j}\right]_{mm} : m = 1 \ldots M_j\right)^{-1}$. The $\hat{h}_{li}^{j}$ and $\tilde{h}_{li}^{j}$ are distributed as,

$$\hat{h}_{li}^{j} \sim \mathcal{N}_{\mathbb{C}}\left(\overline{h}_{li}^{j}, \Sigma_{li}^{j}\right) \tag{13}$$

$$\tilde{h}_{li}^{j} \sim \mathcal{N}_{\mathbb{C}}\left(0_M, \tilde{\Sigma}_{li}^{j}\right) \tag{14}$$

where $\tilde{h}_{li}^{j}$ is channel estimation error, $\Sigma_{li}^{j} = P_{li}\tau_p D_{li}^{j}\Lambda_{li}^{j}(\Psi_{li}^{j})^{-1}\Lambda_{li}^{j}D_{li}^{j}$ and $\tilde{\Sigma}_{li}^{j} = P_{li}\tau_p R_{li}^{j}\Lambda_{li}^{j}D_{li}^{j} - P_{li}\tau_p D_{li}^{j}\Lambda_{li}^{j}R_{li}^{j} + \Sigma_{li}^{j}$. The $\hat{h}_{li}^{j}$ and $\tilde{h}_{li}^{j}$ are correlated.

In EW-MMSE estimation, estimation of every single element is carried out by processing signal received at each antenna and after that statistics are computed as result. It is noticeable that if off the diagonal elements are zero in covariance matrices then EW-MMSE performs same way as MMSE with lesser computational efforts.

5.3 LS Channel Estimator

There can be a case, when BS does not have any kind of statistical information, in such cases Bayesian estimator are useless and non Bayesian estimator is suitable substitute. The LS estimation is one of these kinds of estimation methods by which h_{li}^j channel can be estimated during propagation (Özdogan et al. 2019, p. 3; Björnson et al. 2017, p. 268). The $\hat{h}_{li}^j$ is LS estimation, which minimize $\|y_{jli}^p - \sqrt{P_{li}}\tau_P \hat{h}_{li}^j\|^2$ and expressed as,

$$\hat{h}_{li}^j = \frac{1}{\sqrt{P_{li}}\tau_P} y_{jli}^p \tag{15}$$

In LS estimation, channel estimation $\hat{h}_{li}^j$ and estimation error $\tilde{h}_{li}^j$ are correlated random variables, distributed as per below,

$$\hat{h}_{li}^j \sim \mathcal{N}_{\mathbb{C}}\left(\frac{1}{\sqrt{P_{li}}\tau_P}\overline{y}_{jli}^p, \frac{1}{P_{li}\tau_P}\Psi_{li}^{j^{-1}}\right) \tag{16}$$

$$\tilde{h}_{li}^j \sim \mathcal{N}_{\mathbb{C}}\left(\overline{h}_{li}^j - \frac{1}{\sqrt{P_{li}}\tau_P}\overline{y}_{jli}^p, \frac{1}{P_{li}\tau_P}\Psi_{li}^{j^{-1}} - R_{li}^j\right) \tag{17}$$

From Eqs. (11), (12) and (15), it is evident that LS channel estimation is simple and less computationally complex than MMSE and EW-MMSE, but it comes at cost of more complex channel estimation statistics a LS estimation have, compared to MMSE and EW-MMSE, which is seen from Eqs. (9), (10), (13), (14), (16) and (17). The non zero mean of $\tilde{h}_{li}^j$ in Eq. (17) confirm the compromise in communication quality, when LS estimation is used.

Also, from Eqs. (6), (12) and (15), it can be confirmed as said previously, that the MMSE estimation required full statistical distribution knowledge ($\overline{h}_{li}^j$ and R_{li}^j), the EW-MMSE estimation required partial statistical distribution knowledge ($\overline{h}_{li}^j$, D_{li}^j, and Λ_{li}^j) and the LS estimation required no statistical distribution knowledge.

6 DL Spectral Effiency Using MR Precoding

The DL data transmissions are τ_d in each coherent slot, where the signal transmitted from BS l is

$$x_l = \sum_{k=1}^{k_l} w_{lk}\varsigma_{lk} \tag{18}$$

where $\varsigma_{lk} \sim \mathcal{N}_{\mathbb{C}}(0, \rho_{lk})$ is the data signal transmitted from BS l for intended UE k in DL and ρ_{lk} is the signal power. The w_{lk} is the transmit precoding vector for spatial diversity determination. The w_{lk} satisfies $\mathbb{E}\{\|w_{lk}\|^2\} = 1$, such that the transmit power allocated to UE k is $\mathbb{E}\{\|\|w_{lk}\varsigma_{lk}\|\|^2\} = \rho_{lk}$. The received signal $y_{jk} \in \mathbb{C}$ at UE k in cell j is,

$$y_{jk} = \left(h_{jk}^j\right)^H w_{jk}\varsigma_{jk} + \sum_{\substack{k=1 \\ i \neq k}}^{K_j} \left(h_{jk}^j\right)^H w_{jk}\varsigma_{jk} + \sum_{\substack{l=1 \\ l \neq j}}^{L} \sum_{i=1}^{K_l} \left(h_{jk}^l\right)^H w_{li}\varsigma_{li} + n_{jk}$$

$$\tag{19}$$

where $n_{jk} \sim (0, \sigma_{dl}^2)$ is independent and identically distributed additive receiver noise. In Eq. (19), first, second and third terms are respectively the desire signal, the intra-cell interference and the inter-cell interference. The ergodic DL capacity of UE k in cell j is lower bounded by (Björnson et al. 2017, p. 276),

$$SE_{jk}^{dl} = \frac{\tau_d}{\tau_c}\log_2\left(1 + \gamma_{jk}^{dl}\right) \text{ bit/s/Hz} \tag{20}$$

where γ_{jk}^{dl} is effective SINR can be expressed as,

$$\gamma_{jk}^{dl} = \frac{\rho_{jk}\left|\mathbb{E}\{w_{jk}^H h_{jk}^j\}\right|^2}{\sum_{l=1}^{L}\sum_{i=1}^{K_l}\rho_{li}\mathbb{E}\left\{\left|w_{li}^H h_{jk}^l\right|^2\right\} - \rho_{jk}\left|\mathbb{E}\{v_{jk}^H h_{jk}^j\}\right|^2 + \sigma_{dl}^2} \tag{21}$$

where the expectations are taken from all sources of randomness.

However, the effective SINR γ_{jk}^{dl} in Eq. (21) can be computed using MR precoding and different estimation methods for DL.

7 Basic Setup and Configuration

The coverage area is assumed of having 16 equal sized cells, where each cell area is 250 m × 250 m having square shape. Also the wrap around topology has been assumed to have equal interference from all directions to the BS. The UEs per cell are considered 10, where distribution of UEs is independent and uniform. Also it is taken care of minimum 35 m distance between UE and BS, while assuming UEs locations. The criterion to assign UE to particular BS among number of BSs options is the channel gain between UE and that selected BS should be largest. The UE location decides large scale fading and nominal angle. The antennas at BS are uniformly and linearly distributed (ULA), where distance between two consecutive antennas are assumed half wave-length.

The average channel response between UE i and BS j in cell l is expressed as (Björnson et al. 2017, p. 181),

$$\overline{h}_{li}^j = \sqrt{\beta_{li}^{j,LoS}}\left[1\, e^{j2\pi d_H \sin(\varphi_{li}^j)} \ldots e^{j2\pi d_H (M-1)\sin(\varphi_{li}^j)}\right]^T \tag{22}$$

where the $\beta_{lk}^{j,LoS}$ is the large scale fading co-efficient, $d_H \leq \frac{\lambda}{2}$ is the two consecutive antenna spacing, and φ_{lk}^j is the angle of arrival (AoA) at UE. In Eq. (22), the co-efficient of large scale fading is defined as $\beta_{lk}^{j,LoS} = \frac{1}{M_j}\|\overline{h}_{li}^j\|^2$, where it is finite for any M_j BS antennas. The $\overline{h}_{li}^j$ in Eq. (22) also represents direct propagation component (LoS). The NLoS propagation is approximately represented by covariance matrix as shown in Eq. (23) below,

$$\left[R_{li}^j\right]_{s,m} = \frac{\beta_{li}^{j,NLoS}}{N}\sum_{n=1}^{N}e^{j\pi(s-m)\sin(\varphi_{li,n}^j)}e^{-\frac{\sigma_\varphi^2}{2}\left(\pi(s-m)\cos(\varphi_{li,n}^j)\right)^2} \tag{23}$$

where N is the number of scattering clusters, $\beta_{lk}^{j,NLoS}$ is the large scale fading co-efficient for NLoS, $\varphi_{li,n}^{j} \sim \mathcal{U}[\varphi_{li}^{j} - 40^{o}, \varphi_{li}^{j} + 40^{o}]$ is the nominal AoA, σ_{φ} is the angular standard deviation (ASD) from the nominal angel, n is the cluster number, s is row number and m is column number of R_{li}^{j} matrix. Here the Gaussian local scattering model (Özdogan et al. 2019, p. 10; Björnson et al. 2017, p. 300) is considered for the covariance matrix $\left[R_{li}^{j} \right]_{s,m}$ of each cluster. The number of scattering clusters $N = 6$, the ASD$\sigma_{\varphi} = 5^{o}$, the channel bandwidth for communication is 20 MHz, the total receive noise power is -94 dBm, the samples per each coherence slot is 200 and the pilot (per UE) in each cell is 10 assumed. The pilots are assigned randomly to the UEs.

As per 3GPP model (3GPP Tech. Report 2020, 26), the LOS probability between UE and BS is modelled, as per below,

$$\text{Probability of LoS} = \begin{cases} \frac{300 - d_{li}^{j}}{300}, 0 < d_{li}^{j} < 300 \, \text{m}, \\ 0, d_{li}^{j} > 300 \, \text{m} \end{cases} \quad (24)$$

It is evident from Eq. (23) that the distance between UE and BS is the only controlling parameter of LoS probability. In existence of LoS, the corresponding large scale fading coefficient is modelled as (3GPP Tech. Report 2020, 17),

$$\beta_{li}^{j} = -30.18 - 26\log_{10}\left(d_{li}^{j}\right) + F_{li}^{j} \, \text{dB} \quad (25)$$

where $F_{li}^{j} \sim \mathcal{N}(0, \sigma_{sf}^{2})$ with $\sigma_{sf} = 4$, is shadow fading co-efficient. In absence of LoS, the corresponding large scale fading coefficient is modelled as (3GPP Tech. Report 2020, 17),

$$\beta_{li}^{j} = -34.53 - 38\log_{10}\left(d_{li}^{j}\right) + F_{li}^{j} \, \text{dB} \quad (26)$$

where $F_{li}^{j} \sim \mathcal{N}(0, \sigma_{sf}^{2})$ with $\sigma_{sf} = 10$, is shadow fading co-efficient. The Rician factor is modeled as (3GPP Tech. Report, 2020, 26), $k_{li}^{j} = 13 - 0.03d_{li}^{j}$ [dB], which is used to calculate $\beta_{li}^{j,LoS}$ and $\beta_{li}^{j,NLoS}$ as shown below in Eq. (25).

$$\beta_{li}^{j,LoS} = \sqrt{\frac{k_{li}^{j}}{k_{li}^{j} + 1}} \beta_{li}^{j} \text{ and } \beta_{li}^{j,NLoS} = \sqrt{\frac{1}{k_{li}^{j} + 1}} \beta_{li}^{j} \quad (27)$$

The calculated $\beta_{li}^{j,LoS}$ and $\beta_{li}^{j,NLoS}$ are used in Eq. (22) and (23) respectively. Also over all large scale fading coefficient can be expressed as,

$$\beta_{li}^{j} = \beta_{li}^{j,LoS} + \beta_{li}^{j,NLoS}, \quad (28)$$

In LTE systems, UEs at the cell edge are allowed to transmit at maximum power and by gradually reducing the power for UEs that are located closer to the BS. The same policy adopted here for UL transmission, because the UL powers affect not only the UL data transmission but also the quality of the channel estimates and indirectly the combining vectors. So to provide fair power allocation to UEs, UL power control policy decided by heuristic approach as below as per (Björnson et al. 2017, p. 464),

$$
p_{jk} = \begin{cases} p_{max}^{ul}, & \Delta > \dfrac{\beta_{jk}^{j}}{\beta_{j,min}^{j}}, \\[2em] p_{max}^{ul} \Delta \dfrac{\beta_{j,min}^{j}}{\beta_{jk}^{j}}, & \Delta \leq \dfrac{\beta_{jk}^{j}}{\beta_{j,min}^{j}}, \end{cases} \tag{29}
$$

where p_{jk} is the transmit power, the p_{max}^{ul} is maximum UL power with value 10 dBm and minimum large scale fading coefficient defined as $\beta_{j,min}^{j} = \min(\beta_{j1}^{j}, \dots \beta_{jk}^{j} \dots, \beta_{jK}^{j})$. The weakest channel UEs can radiate with full power and power radiation decreased proportional to channel strength increment. The policy adopted also for DL as it is for UL for simplicity.

8   Output Results

In this section, simulation is carried out for SE as per above SE equations using MATLAB®.

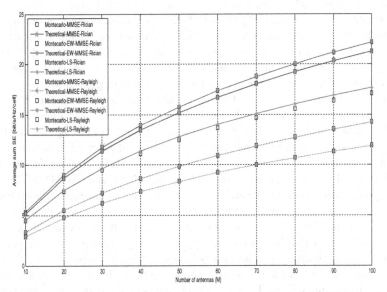

Fig. 1. Averaged Sum DL SE Vs. No. of BS antennas in spatially correlated fading, where k = 10.

The Fig. 1 shows sum SE in DL as function of numbers of BS antennas, averaged over number of realization of various shadow fading and UE locations. The SE carried out for MR precoding, MMSE, EW-MMSE, and LS estimation methods in correlated fading scenario. The SE carried out for Rician and Rayleigh spatially correlated fading. Also SE carried out analytically from equations and practically from Monte Carlo based simulations, where square marker plots indicates Monte-Carlo based simulation and remaining are analytical simulation based plots. The overlapping or closeness of analytical plots (from closed form equations) with practical plots (from Monte-Carlo simulation) validates the carried out results. The DL SE using MMSE estimator is highest in correlated Rician fading case because of acquiring full channel statistics by MMSE estimators, where as DL SE using LS estimation is lowest in same case because of not acquiring channel statistics by LS estimator. The DL SE using EW-MMSE estimator is lower than MMSE but higher than LS estimator in correlated Rician fading case because of acquiring partial channel statistics (diagonals of covariance matrices and average channel gains only). However performance of EW-MMSE is more closer to MMSE because all channel statistics are acquired (as like MMSE) except off diagonal elements of covariance matrices only and in correlated Rician fading case contribution of off diagonal elements of covariance matrices is very less compared to diagonal elements for over all estimation quality. The SE gap between LS and MMSE/EW-MMSE is increasing proportional BS antennas, as LS estimator does not acquiring any type of channel statistics. In Rayleigh fading scenario, DL SE using MMSE estimator is highest compared to EW-MMSE and LS estimators, whereas DL SE of EW-MMSE and LS estimator is identical. The average channel gains and diagonal elements of covariance matrices are significant channel statistics for LoS component of channel propagation. However in Rayleigh fading case, due to lack of strong LoS channel propagation, statistical knowledge of average channel gains and diagonal elements of covariance matrices is not available for over all estimation process. So channel statistics acquirement efforts by EW-MMSE in Rayleigh fading case are worthless and estimation quality of EW-MMSE and LS estimators results identical, which can be seen in Fig. 1. The MMSE estimator gives best performance in correlated Rician or Rayleigh fading scenarios.

The Fig. 2 shows CDF of SE per UE, where random UE locations and shadow fading realisations introduce randomness. It is seen from Fig. 2 that the probability to have SE per UE is higher in Rician fading case compared to Rayleigh fading case. In Rician fading case, for good channel condition the probability of SE per UE is almost equal for MMSE and EW-MMSE, since estimation errors are small. However the difference of probability of SE per UE can be noticed between MMSE and EW-MMSE for weak channel conditions. The good channel condition is defined as having higher probability of SE per UE and weak channel condition is defined as having lower probability of SE per UE. The probability of SE per UE is lowest for LS estimator in Rician fading case for all values of SE per UE. It is noticeable from Fig. 2 that the probability of SE per UE is highest of MMSE compared to other two estimators at very weak channel condition (SE per UE is less than or equal to 0.3 bit/s/Hz) in Rician or Rayleigh fading case. Even for given channel having SE per UE is less than or equal to 1.4 bit/s/Hz, the corresponding probability of SE per UE is higher of MMSE in Rayleigh fading compared to LS in Rician. However, as in Rician, the probability of SE per UE of MMSE is highest in Rayleigh fading case also as shown in Fig. 3, whereas the probability of SE per UE of EW-MMSE and LS estimators is almost equal in Rayleigh fading case.

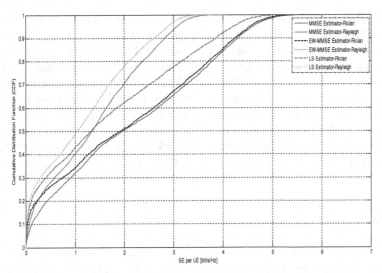

Fig. 2. CDF Vs. DL SE per UE in different fading scenario, where k = 10 & M = 100.

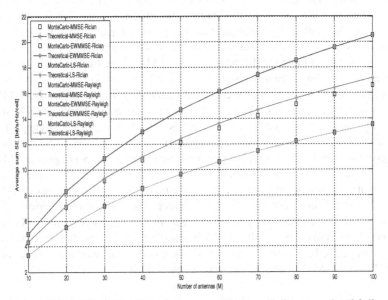

Fig. 3. Averaged Sum DL SE Vs. No. of antennas at BS in spatially uncorrelated fading, where k = 10.

The Fig. 3 shows sum DL SE as function of number of antennas at BS, averaged over number of realization of various shadow fading and user equipment locations. The SE carried out for different estimation methods like MMSE, EW-MMSE, and LS in uncorrelated fading scenario, using same MR precoding transmission method. The DL SE of MMSE and EW-MMSE is identical for uncorrelated Rician fading case as shown in Fig. 3. The only off diagonal elements of covariance matrices are not estimated in EW-MMSE compared to MMSE estimator, reaming estimation part is same for both estimators. However in uncorrelated fading case, off diagonal elements of covariance matrices are zero, so the estimates of MMSE and EW-MMSE are identical. Further, the SE using LS estimator is lower than MMSE/EW-MMSE estimator for uncorrelated Rician fading case, since LS estimator does not utilising and acquiring any type of statistical knowledge of channel. In case of uncorrelated Rayleigh fading, average channel gain (represent the LoS component of channel propagation) and covariance matrices estimation efforts are useless since absence of LoS and covariance matrices are unitary matrices. So all estimates using MMSE, EW-MMSE and LS estimators are same up to deterministic scaling factor and DL SE using same three estimators is same.

9 Conclusion

The average sum DL SE has been discussed throughout for correlated/uncorrelated Rician and Rayleigh fading scenarios in the multi-cell Massive MIMO system. However, MR precoding method is used for DL transmission and DL SE comparison has been carried out for MMSE, EW-MMSE and LS estimation methods. The closed form achievable SE expressions provide insight detailed view of the processing and interference nature. It is observed throughout that the existence of the LoS propagation along with NLoS propagation (like Rician fading) can improve the DL SE compared to the NLoS propagation only (Rayleigh fading). The performance of MMSE and EW-MMSE estimators is identical in all fading scenarios except correlated Rician fading case, where the performance gap is also small. However computational complexity is lower in EW-MMSE compared to MMSE estimator. The performance gap between MMSE/EW-MMSE and LS is comparatively large in all fading scenarios except uncorrelated Rayleigh fading case, where the performance of all three estimators is identical. However LS estimator has lowest computational complexity, but performance is very poor. So in general, MMSE is the best without computational complexity constraint and EW-MMSE is the optimum with computation complexity constraint. In summary, the spatial channel correlation plays important role in choice of optimum estimator. Also the existing performance gap between MMSE/EW-MMSE and LS estimators increases with increase in number of BS antennas as seen from output results. At last in practical scenario, as channel statistics are not fully and perfectly known, the upper and lower performance boundaries are almost set by MMSE/EW-MMSE and LS estimators respectively.

References

Arzykulov, S., Nauryzbayev, G., Celik, A., Eltawil, A.M.: Hardware and interference limited cooperative CR-NOMA networks under imperfect SIC and CS. IEEE Open J. Commun. Soc. **2**, 1473–1485 (2021)

Björnson, E., Hoydis, J., Sanguinetti, L.: Massive MIMO networks:Spectral, energy, and hardware efficiency. Found. Trends® Sig. Process. **11**(3–4), 154–655 (2017)

Boukhedimi, I., Kammoun, A., Alouini, M.S.: Multi-Cell MMSE combining over correlated Rician channels in massive MIMO systems. IEEE Wireless Commun. Lett. **9**(01), 12–16 (2020)

Boukhedimi, I., Kammoun, A., Alouini, M.S.: LMMSE receivers in uplink massive MIMO systems with correlated rician fading. IEEE Trans. Commun. **67**(01), 230–243 (2019)

Chen, R., Zhou, H., Long, W.X., Moretti, M.: Spectral and energy efficiency of line-of-sight OAM-MIMO communication systems. China Commun. **17**(09), 119–127 (2020)

Ding, Q., Jing, Y.: SE analysis for mixed-ADC massive MIMO Uplink With ZF receiver and imperfect CSI. IEEE Wireless Commun. Lett. **9**(04), 438–442 (2019)

Femenias, G., Riera-Palou, F., Álvarez-Polegre, A., García-Armada, A.: Short-term power constrained cell-free massive-MIMO over spatially correlated ricean fading. IEEE Trans. Veh. Technol. **69**(12), 15200–15215 (2020)

Jin, S.N., Yue, D.W., Nguyen, H.H.: Spectral and energy efficiency in cell-free massive MIMO systems over correlated rician fading. IEEE Syst. J. **15**(02), 2822–2833 (2021)

Kong, C., Zhong, C., Matthaiou, M., Björnson, E., Zhang, Z.: Spectral efficiency of multipair massive MIMO two-way relaying with imperfect CSI. IEEE Trans. Veh. Technol. **68**(07), 6593–6607 (2019)

Liu, P., Kong, D., Ding, J., Zhang, Wang, K., Choi, J.: Channel estimation aware performance analysis for massive MIMO with rician fading. IEEE Trans. Commun. **69**(07), 4373–4386 (2021)

Liu, P., Luo, K., Chen, D., Jiang, T.: Spectral efficiency analysis of cell-free massive MIMO systems with zero-forcing detector. IEEE Trans. Wireless Commun. **19**(02), 795–807 (2020)

Marzetta, T.L.: Noncooperative cellular wireless with unlimited numbers of base station antennas. IEEE Trans. Wireless Commun. **09**(11), 3590–3600 (2010)

Özdogan, Ö., Björnson, E., Larsson, E.G.: Massive MIMO with spatially correlated rician fading channels. IEEE Trans. Commun. **67**(05), 3234–3250 (2019)

Özdogan, Ö., Björnson, E., Zhang, J.: Performance of cell-free massive MIMO with rician fading and phase shifts. IEEE Trans. Wireless Commun. **18**(11), 5299–5315 (2019)

Peng, Z., Wang, S., Pan, C., Chen, X., Cheng, J., Hanzo, L.: Multi-pair two-way massive MIMO DF relaying over rician fading channels under imperfect CSI. IEEE Wireless Commun. Lett. (Early Access) 1 (2021)

Wang, M., Yue, D.W., Jin, S.N.: Downlink Transmission of multicell distributed massive MIMO with pilot contamination under rician fading. IEEE Access **8**, 131835–131847 (2020)

Wang, Z., Zhang, J., Björnson, E., Ai, B.: Uplink performance of cell-free massive MIMO over spatially correlated rician fading channels. IEEE Commun. Lett. **25**(04), 1348–1352 (2021)

Yu, X., Hu, Y., Gui, G., Leung, S., Xu, W., Li, Q.: Performance analysis of uplink massive multiuser SM-MIMO system with imperfect channel state information. IEEE Trans. Commun. **68**(10), 6200–6214 (2020)

Boukhedimi, I., Kammoun, A., Alouini, M.S.: 'Line-of-sight and pilot contamination effects on correlated multi-cell massive MIMO systems. In: IEEE Global Communications Conference (GLOBECOM). IEEE, United Arab Emirates (2019)

Cho, H., Park, C., Lee, N.: Capacity-achieving precoding with low-complexity for terahertz LOS massive MIMO using uniform planar arrays. In: International Conference on Information and Communication Technology Convergence (ICTC). IEEE, Korea (South) (2020)

Demir, Ö.T., Björnson, E.: Max-min fair wireless-powered cell-free massive MIMO for uncorrelated rician fading channels. In: IEEE Wireless Communications and Networking Conference (WCNC). IEEE, Korea (South) (2020)

Du, Y., Yu, X., Wang, X., Zhu, Q., Liu, T.: Spectrum efficiency optimization for uplink massive MIMO system with imperfect channel state information. In: 11th International Conference on Wireless Communications and Signal Processing (WCSP). IEEE, China (2019)

Hosany, M.A.: Efficiency analysis of Massive MIMO systems for 5G cellular networks under perfect CSI. In: 3rd International Conference on Emerging Trends in Electrical, Electronic and Communications Engineering (ELECOM). IEEE, Mauritius (2020)

Özdogan, Ö., Björnson, E., Zhang, J.: Downlink performance of cell-free massive MIMO with rician fading and phase shifts. In:IEEE 20th International Workshop on Signal Processing Advances in Wireless Communications (SPAWC). IEEE, France (2019)

Rajmane, R.S., Sudha, V.: Sectral efficiency improvement in massive MIMO systems. In: TEQIP III Sponsored International Conference on Microwave Integrated Circuits, Photonics and Wireless Networks (IMICPW) Conference, IEEE, India (2019)

Kay, S.: Fundamentals of Statistical Signal Processing: Estimation Theory, p. 07458. Prentice Hall, PTR, Upper Saddle River, NJ (1993)

Tse, D., Viswanath, P.: Fundamentals of Wireless Communications. Cambridge University Press (2005)

Björnson, E., Larsson, E.G., Marzetta, T.L.: Massive MIMO: ten myths and one critical question. IEEE Commun. Mag. **54**(02), 114–124 (2016)

Larsson, E., Edfors, O., Tufvesson, F., Marzetta, T.: Massive MIMO for next generation wireless systems. IEEE Commun. Mag. **52**(02), 186–195 (2014)

Cooper, M.: The Myth of Spectrum Scarcity. Technical report DYNA llc (2010). https://ecfsapi.fcc.gov/file/7020396128.pdf

Ericsson: Ericsson mobility report. Technical report (2021). http://www.ericsson.com/mobility-report

Spatial channel model for Multiple Input Multiple Output (MIMO) simulations, 3rd Generation Partnership Project (3GPP), Technical Specification Group Radio Access Network, Technical Report, Release 16, Reference. 25.996, Version. 16.0.0, Upload Date. July 2020, viewed 18 July 2020. https://portal.3gpp.org/desktopmodules/Specifications/SpecificationDetails.aspx?specificationId=1382

Blocking Estimation Using Optimal Guard Channel Policy in GSM 900 System

Promod Kumar Sahu[1]([✉])[iD], Hemanta Kumar Pati[2][iD],
and Sateesh Kumar Pradhan[1]

[1] Department of CSA, Utkal University, Bhubaneswar 751004, Odisha, India
promod_sahu@yahoo.com, sateesh.cs@utkaluniversity.ac.in
[2] Department of CSE, IIIT Bhubaneswar, Bhubaneswar 751003, Odisha, India
hemanta@iiit-bh.ac.in

Abstract. Voice is the king of communication and in 5G world it will be more important than ever, through various types of use cases. A 5G smartphone will not connect to a mobile network unless voice support is available, so enabling this is a must. Voice service requires end-to-end 5G network support to enable the high quality voice service experience for mobile devices. So, we need to consider the whole network chain with IP Multimedia Subsystem (IMS), 5G Core, and 5G Radio access network (RAN)s. To provide seamless voice handover when users move between cells and access technologies, the network must also handle interworking towards 4G, 3G or 2G in case the users move out of 5G coverage. Evolved Packet System (EPS) will be helpful for service providers when they are migrating from 4G to 5G. Circuit Switched FallBack (CSFB) will be helpful for service provider when they are migrating from 2G/3G to 4G. Once the call is set for voice communication, in case user's movement takes place from one cell to another and finds no free channel in that cell then the call will be dropped. To address this issue in this paper we have presented an optimal chan-nel reservation (OCR) policy. This policy reserves channels according to target handoff call dropping probability (HCDP). So, this minimizes the new call blocking probability (NCBP) and keeps the HCDP below the target. We have applied this policy to Global System for Mobile Communication (GSM) 900 system and observed that the HCDP is below the target and NCBP is minimum.

Keywords: New call blocking · Handoff call dropping · Optimal channel · GSM · Mobile cellular networks

1 Introduction

Mobile cellular networks provide services to many users with limited resources. Accommodating more users with desired Quality of Service (QoS) provisioning with limited capacity is a very challenging issue. To this end network resource

© Springer Nature Switzerland AG 2022
N. Chaubey et al. (Eds.): COMS2 2022, CCIS 1604, pp. 69–81, 2022.
https://doi.org/10.1007/978-3-031-10551-7_6

allocation concept plays a vital role. Again, to use network resources efficiently and provide QoS guarantee to various applications resource allocation is important. However, this goal becomes more difficult due to mobility, limited bandwidth, and error-prone wireless channel in wireless mobile cellular networks compared to wired networks. The service area of the wireless mobile cellular network is split into cells. So, that in some distance away the same radio channels may be reused [1,2]. A radio channel, in FDMA can be a frequency band or a code in CDMA in traditional 2G mobile cellular networks or Physical Resource Blocks (PRBs) in LTE like advanced mobile cellular networks. Number of users a cell in wireless mobile cellular network can support is limited to the number of radio channels in FDMA or the number of codes in CDMA based wireless cellular mobile networks. In Long Term Evolution (LTE) the number of users supported is limited to RBs available in the system. The cell/eNB capacity in terms of number of mobile users supported in LTE network providing Voice over Long Term Evolution (VoLTE) service can be found from [3–5]. A Base transceiver station (BTS) in GSM like 2G networks or eNodeB/eNB in LTE like 4G networks connects mobile station (MS)s in the cell it covers. When mobile host wants to communicate with other users it must connect to the BTS/eNB with a new connection request, where a set of desirable QoS requirements are implicitly or explicitly stated.

Considering the huge investment that has gone in to build 4G networks and the huge investment required to build a 5G network, it makes logical sense for the 5G and the 4G networks to interwork with each other. 5G supports both Non-Standalone Architecture (NSA) and Standalone Architecture (SA) implementations [6,7]. Third Generation Partnership Project (3GPP) release 15 standardized the NSA mode of deployment. The 5G networks supported with

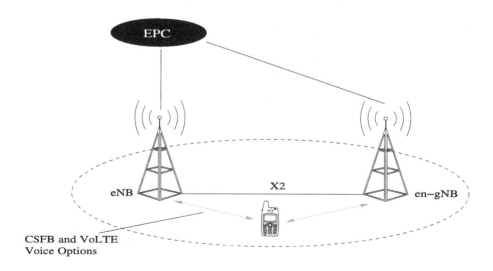

Fig. 1. 5G deployment Option 3.

existing 4G infrastructure in NSA mode. Based on the deployment of 5G network a number of voice delivery options are available. For example Fig. 1 shows Option 3 structure established on E-UTRA New Radio - Dual Connectivity (EN-DC) defined by the 5G NR standard. In this deployment an eNodeB (eNB) of the 4G LTE network acts as the master node and an en-gNB of the 5G network acts as the secondary node. Both of these RAN functions connect to the 4G Evolved Packet Core (EPC). Here based on only 5G an end-to-end voice service is not available and the only voice options are CSFB and VoLTE.

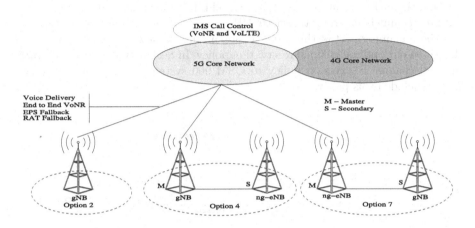

Fig. 2. 5G deployment Option 2, Option 4 and Option 7.

The additional 5G deployment options are Option 2, Option 4 and Option 7 once the 5G core is deployed. When the service provider deploys an IMS network to support the VoLTE service then an end-to-end voice service by using Voice over New Radio (VoNR) is also an option. To meet the QoS flows required for IMS signaling and any resultant voice packets associated with a call the 5G end-to-end network will be used in this approach. In the 5G core this voice option is lost because there is no CSFB capability. This concept is outlined in Fig. 2. Figure 2 also presents RAT Fall-Back and EPS Fall-Back as additional voice options. Both the RAT Fall-Back and EPS Fall-Back consider that the device has registered for IMS services and in on 5G. The EPS Fall-Back or RAT Fallback may be initiated when VoNR is unavailable in the current 5G cell. The EPS Fall-back procedure takes place when the device requests to the IMS that it wants to make a call then the device will be instructed to move from 5G to LTE. At this point the CSFB procedure or even the VoLTE call can be initiated.

When LTE is just used for data transfer, voice calls are handled through the legacy circuit switched mechanisms by falling back to 3G or 2G network as shown in Fig. 3. CSFB works only when the area covered by an LTE network is also covered by the 3G network. EPS will be helpful for service providers when they are migrating from 4G to 5G. CSFB will be helpful for service providers when they are migrating from 2G/3G to a 4G network. In CSFB the 4G MME talks to the 3G Mobile switching center (MSC) through the new SGs interface, to setup the voice call. Once the call setup for voice communication is done, in case user movement takes place from one cell to another and finds no free channel or bandwidth the call will be dropped. To address this issue some channels to be reserved in each cell for this type of handoff calls. Related to this issue some schemes already discussed in [8–20]. Generally, for handome call (HC)s in case more channels are reserved that will decrease HCDP and increase NCBP. To balance these two QoS parameters (i.e., NCBP and HCDP) we present an optimal channel reservation (OCR) policy. This scheme gives optimal number of reserved channels based on target HCDP.

The remaining part of this paper is organized as follows. In Sect. 2, we have described our optimal channel reservation policy. In Sect. 3, we have applied this optimal channel reservation policy to GSM 900 system. Finally, in Sect. 4 we have concluded this paper.

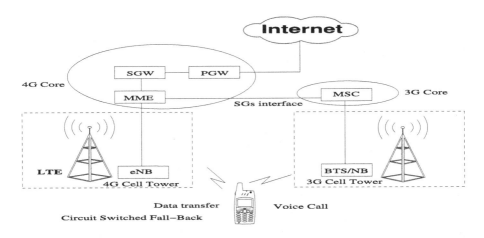

Fig. 3. Circuit switched fall-back.

2   The OCR Policy

In this section, the OCR policy is introduced. First, we present the expression for NCBP and HCDP based on Markovian model and subsequently we present the OCR policy.

2.1   Estimation of NCBP and HCDP

The Markovian model is shown in Fig. 4. Here we considered that total channels available in a cell of a cellular system is C_t and C_T is the threshold. The system accepts both new call (NC) and HC if the used channels in a cell is less than the threshold, and it accepts only HC in case that used channels in the cell is equal

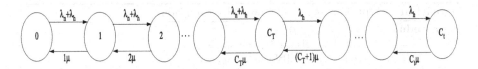

Fig. 4. Markovian model.

to or greater than the threshold and up to C_t. Here λ_n is the NC arrival rate, λ_h is the HC arrival rate, and μ is the service rate. By using these parameters the NCBP denoted by P_{nb} and HCDP denoted by P_{hd} are given below and the detail derivation for this can be found from [10].

$$P_{nb} = \left(\frac{1}{C_T!} \left(\frac{\lambda_n + \lambda_h}{\mu} \right)^{C_T} + \sum_{i=C_T+1}^{C_t} \frac{1}{i!} \left(\frac{\lambda_n + \lambda_h}{\mu} \right)^{C_T} \left(\frac{\lambda_h}{\mu} \right)^{i-C_T} \right) P_0 \quad (1)$$

$$P_{hd} = \frac{1}{C_t!} \left(\frac{\lambda_n + \lambda_h}{\mu} \right)^{C_T} \left(\frac{\lambda_h}{\mu} \right)^{C_t - C_T} P_0 \quad (2)$$

where

$$P_0 = \left[\sum_{i=0}^{C_T} \frac{1}{i!} \left(\frac{\lambda_n + \lambda_h}{\mu} \right)^{i} + \sum_{i=C_T+1}^{C_t} \frac{1}{i!} (\frac{\lambda_n + \lambda_h}{\mu})^{C_T} \left(\frac{\lambda_h}{\mu} \right)^{i-C_T} \right]^{-1} \quad (3)$$

If P_{td} is the targeted HCDP then to obtain the number of channels C_T that satisfy the condition $P_{hd} \leq P_{td}$ is given as follows.

$$P_{hd} = \frac{1}{C_t!} \left(\frac{\lambda_n + \lambda_h}{\mu} \right)^{C_T} \left(\frac{\lambda_h}{\mu} \right)^{C_t - C_T} P_0 \leq P_{td} \quad (4)$$

2.2 Theoretical Estimation of Optimal Number of Reserved Channels

The Algorithm 1 given below is proposed to obtain the maximum number of reserved channels (i.e., optimal number) based on the target HCDP. This algorithm takes NC arrival rate (i.e., λ_n), HC rate (i.e., λ_h), service rate (i.e., μ), the total number of channels in the cell (i.e., C_t) and the target HCDP (i.e., P_{td}) as its input parameters. This scheme returns optimal number of reserved channels (i.e., y) for which $P_{hd}(C_t - y, y) \leq P_{td}$ and $P_{nb}(C_t - y, y)$ is minimum. The process flow of this Algorithm 1 is shown in Fig. 5. In this algorithm the function HandoffcallDrop($\lambda_n, \lambda_h, \mu, C_T, C_t$) estimates the handoff call drop probability using Eq. (2) and function NewcallBlock($\lambda_n, \lambda_h, \mu, C_T, C_t$) estimates the new call blocking probability using Eq. (1). By using this algorithm NCBP (i.e., $P_{nb}(C_t - y, y)$), HCDP (i.e., $P_{hd}(C_t - y, y)$) and optimal number of reserved channels (i.e., y) are calculated under different input traffic conditions.

Algorithm 1. Optimal Reserved Channel Estimation

1: **procedure** $(\lambda_n, \lambda_h, \mu, C_t, P_{td})$
2:    $C_T = C_t$; /* All channels are free channels*/
3:    $P_{nb}(C_T, C_t - C_T)$=NewcallBlock$(\lambda_n, \lambda_h, \mu, C_T, C_t)$;
4:    $P_{hd}(C_T, C_t - C_T)$=HandoffcallDrop$(\lambda_n, \lambda_h, \mu, C_T, C_t)$;
5:    **while** $(P_{hd}(C_T, C_t - C_T) > P_{td})$ **do**
6:       $C_T = C_T - 1$;
7:       $P_{nb}(C_T, C_t - C_T)$=NewcallBlock$(\lambda_n, \lambda_h, \mu, C_T, C_t)$;
8:       $P_{hd}(C_T, C_t - C_T)$=HandoffcallDrop$(\lambda_n, \lambda_h, \mu, C_T, C_t)$;
9:    **end while**
10:    $y = C_t - C_T$;
11:    return(y);

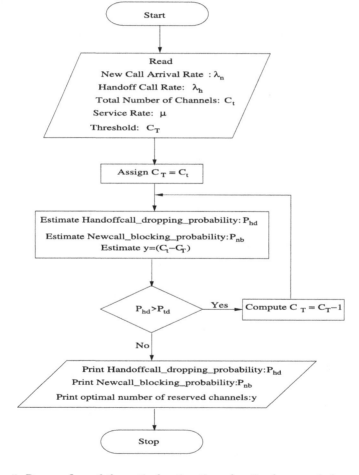

Fig. 5. Process flow of theoretical estimation of optimal reserved channels.

3 Application of OCR Policy to GSM 900 System

In this section first we have discussed the GSM architecture and subsequently introduced the GSM 900 system. Finally, we have applied our OCR scheme to the GSM 900 system and discussed the results obtained.

3.1 GSM Architecture

The GSM architecture is shown in Fig. 6. The GSM network is having three subsystems namely Radio subsystem (RSS), Network switching subsystem (NSS), and Operation support subsystem (OSS). The combination of MS and base station subsystem (BSS) is called RSS comprises all radio-specific entities in the GSM network. The radio subsystem performs the basic functions of connecting the MS to the network. The radio subsystem consists of a number of MSs, BTS and Base station controller (BSC). The interface between MS and BTS is U_m, interface between BTS and BSC is A_{bis} and A is the interface between BSC and MSC. The NSS consists of a number of MSCs. Each MSC of the NSS connects to a number of BSCs. There are also Home location register (HLR)s and Visitor location register (VLR)s. NSS provides the desired interfacing between wireless and fixed networks. The OSS facilitates the operations of MSCs and also control the operation and maintenance of the entire network [21].

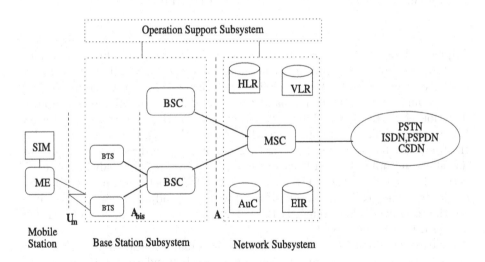

Fig. 6. Architecture of GSM system.

3.2 GSM 900 System

GSM was first introduced as a cellular system explicitly using the 900 MHz band, called the primary band. In GSM system to multiplex air medium among the users a combination of FDMA and TDMA techniques are used. GSM uses a

Table 1. GSM 900 system information.

Features	GSM 900
Spectrum allotted	50 MHz with FDD (i.e., 25 MHz uplink, 25 MHz downlink)
Uplink frequency band	890–915 MHz
Downlink frequency band	935–960 MHz
Access technology	FDMA/TDMA with SDMA
Number of channels	124
Channel bandwidth spacing	200 kHz
Modulation technique	GMSK (BT = 0.3)
Time slot per RF channel	8 slots
Time slot spacing for transmit-receive	3 slots
Transmit-receive frequency spacing or duplex spacing	45 MHz
Frame duration	4.615 ms
Compatibility	ISDN and PSPDN
Transmission power-handset	2 W
Encoding	RPE-LTP, EFR

frequency division duplex (FDD) technique for downlink and uplink separation. So, the downlink and uplink frequencies are different. GSM 900 system uses a frequency band from 935 MHz to 960 MHz in the downlink (BTS transmit, MS receive) and another frequency band from 890 MHz to 915 MHz in the uplink direction (MS transmit, BTS receive) each one 25 MHz. The band separation between downlink and uplink is 45 MHz. Again, the FDMA technique divides the frequency bandwidth of 25 MHz (maximum) in each direction (i.e., both in downlink and uplink) into 125 carrier frequencies, where the bandwidth of each carrier frequency is of 200 kHz. However, the GSM 900 system uses the last carrier frequency channel as a guard band with other adjacent wireless systems. So, the total available channels is 124 [22–24]. Information related to GSM 900 standard is given in Table 1.

In case of GSM 900 standard total channels available in the cell is 124. We can apply our optimal channel reservation policy to this standard. For this standard when a new call arrives if channel is available then it is assigned to that new call. If no channel is available then the new call will be dropped. When a new call is

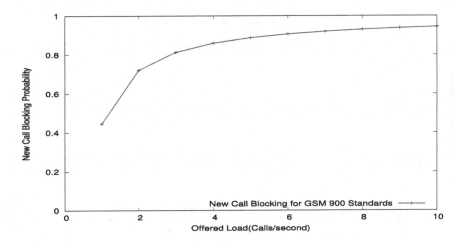

Fig. 7. NCBP vs offered load for GSM 900 system.

dropped then the NCBP will increase. When a handoff call arrives if channel is available then it is assigned to that handoff call. If no free channel is available in the cell then the HC will be dropped and it will increase the HCDP. Generally, handoff call has higher priority than new call, so some channels will be reserved for handoff calls. If more number of channels reserved for handoff call then the HCDP will decrease and it will increase the NCBP. So, based on the target HCDP if the channels are reserved for HC, then the HCDP will be below the target and NCBP will be minimum for that target. Our OCR policy reserves some channels for handoff calls based on the target HCDP. If the target HCDP is changed then the channels reserved for handoff call will also be changed. This policy reserves the maximum number of channels (i.e., optimal number) for HCs based on the target HCDP and it minimizes the NCBP.

3.3   Results and Discussion

We have applied optimal channel reservation policy to GSM 900 system considering the following parameters. In the first case, we have taken the NC arrival rate (i.e., λ_n) from $1\,\mathrm{s}^{-1}$ to $10\,\mathrm{s}^{-1}$ keeping service rate (i.e., μ) as $0.005\,\mathrm{s}^{-1}$ and HC arrival rate (i.e., λ_h) as $0.05\,\mathrm{s}^{-1}$. In the second case, we have taken the HC arrival rate (i.e., λ_h) from $0.01\,\mathrm{s}^{-1}$ to $0.1\,\mathrm{s}^{-1}$ keeping the service rate (i.e., μ) as $0.005\,\mathrm{s}^{-1}$ and NC arrival rate (i.e., λ_n) as $5\,\mathrm{s}^{-1}$. For both of these cases the target HCDP (i.e., P_{td}) is taken as 0.01. Based on the frequency band used in GSM 900 system we have plotted numerical results obtained.

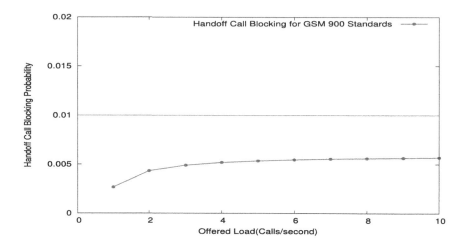

Fig. 8. HCDP vs offered load for GSM 900 system.

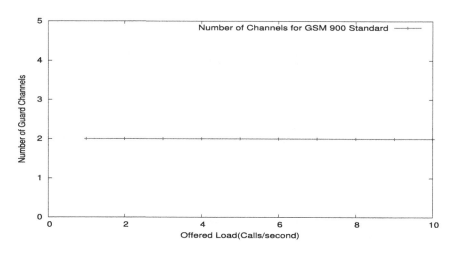

Fig. 9. Optimal number of reserved channels vs offered load for GSM 900 system.

Figure 7 shows NCBP in different offered load conditions for the GSM 900 system. From this Fig. 7 it is observed that NCBP increases with an increase in NC arrival rate for GSM 900 system. Figure 8 shows the HCDP in different offered load conditions for GSM 900 system. From this Fig. 8 it can be observed that HCDP is remaining below the target for GSM 900 system. Figure 9 shows optimal number of reserved channels with different offered load conditions.

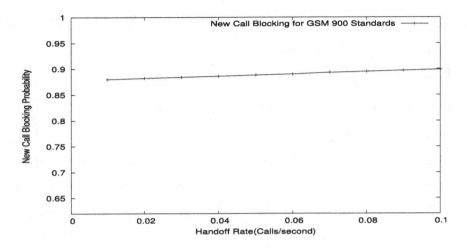

Fig. 10. NCBP vs handoff rate for GSM 900 system.

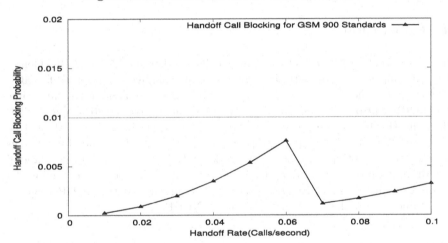

Fig. 11. HCDP vs handoff rate for GSM 900 system.

Figure 10 shows the NCBP in different HC arrival rates for GSM 900 system. From this Fig. 10 it is observed that NCBP is slightly increasing with an increase in HC arrival rate in GSM 900 system. Figure 11 shows the HCDP by varying HC arrival rate for GSM 900 system. From this Fig. 11 it can be observed that HCDP is increasing with an increase in HC arrival rate. Further, it can be found that HCDP is remaining below the target by increasing reserved channels. Figure 12 shows the optimal number of reserved channels with different HC arrival rates for GSM 900 system.

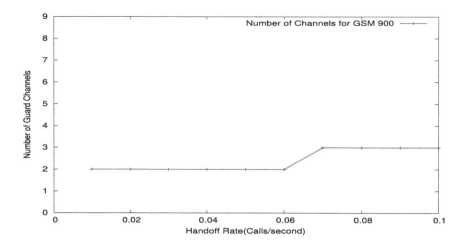

Fig. 12. Optimal number of reserved channels vs handoff rate for GSM 900 system.

4   Conclusion

In wireless cellular networks two types of calls are there i.e., NC and HC. Generally, HCs have higher priority than NCs, so some channels are reserved for HCs. If reserved channels are more then HCDP will be decreased and at the same time the NCBP will be increased. If we reserve channels according to target HCDP then the HCDP will be below the target and at that time the NCBP will be minimum. So, in this paper we proposed an OCR policy for handoff calls. This policy reserved optimal number of channels for HCs based on the target handoff call dropping probability. We applied this policy to GSM 900 system having 124 channels with the target HCDP as 0.01. We observed that the HCDP could be maintained below the target with minimum NCBP.

References

1. Rappaport, T.S.: Wireless Communications: Principles and Practice, 2nd edn. Prentice-Hall Inc., New York (2002)
2. Katzela, I., Naghshineh, M.: Channel assignment schemes for cellular mobile telecommunication systems: a comprehensive survey. IEEE Pers. Commun. **3**, 10–31 (1996)
3. Senapati, R., Pati, H.K.: VoLTE cell capacity estimation using AMR-WB codec. In: International Conference on Advances in Computing, Communications and Informatics (ICACCI), pp. 1885–1889, September 2018
4. Senapati, R., Pati, H.K.: Modelling the region-based VoLTE cell capacity estimation using resource optimisation. IET Commun. **13**, 1225–1235 (2019)
5. Senapati, R., Pati, H.K.: VoLTE cell capacity estimation using AMR-WB codecs and considering VAF, SID, packet bundling, and TTI bundling. Int. J. Commun Syst **32**, 1–16 (2019)

6. Wang, C.-X., et al.: Cellular architecture and key technologies for 5G wireless communication networks. IEEE Commun. Mag. **52**, 122–130 (2014)
7. 3GGP: System Architecture for the 5G System (2018). https://www.3gpp.org/
8. Hong, D., Rappaport, S.S.: Traffic model and performance analysis for cellular mobile radio telephone systems with prioritized and nonprioritized handoff procedures. IEEE Trans. VT **35**, 77–92 (1986)
9. Kulavaratharasah, M.D., Aghvami, A.H.: Teletraffic performance evaluation of microcell personal communication networks (PCN) with prioritized handoff procedures. IEEE Trans. Commun. **36**, 153–163 (1988)
10. Se-Hyun, O., Tcha, D.: Proritized channel assignment in a cellular radio network. IEEE Trans. Commun. **40**, 1259–1269 (1992)
11. Haring, G., Marie, R., Puigjaner, R., Trivedi, K.: Loss formulas and their application to optimization for cellular networks. IEEE Trans. VT **50**, 664–673 (2001)
12. Ni, W., Li, W., Alam, M.: Determination of optimal call admission control policy in wireless networks. IEEE Trans. Wirel. Commun. **8**, 1038–1044 (2009)
13. Ortigoza-Guerrero, L., Aghvami, A.H.: A prioritized handoff dynamic channel assignment strategy for PCS. IEEE Trans. VT **48**, 1203–1215 (2002)
14. Wang, J.L., Chiang, S.Y.: Adaptive channel assignment scheme for wireless networks. Comput. Electr. Eng. **30**, 417–426 (2004)
15. Abdulova, V., Aybay, I.: Performance evaluation of non-prioritized and prioritized call admission control schemes in wireless cellular networks. Wireless Pers. Commun. **78**(1), 69–84 (2014). https://doi.org/10.1007/s11277-014-1736-9
16. Chau, T.C., Wong, K.Y.M., Li, B.: Optimal call admission control with QoS guarantee in a voice/data integrated cellular network. IEEE Trans. Wirel. Commun. **5**, 1133–1141 (2006)
17. Pati, H.K.: A distributed adaptive guard channel reservation scheme for cellular networks. Int. J. Commun Syst **20**, 1037–1058 (2007)
18. Pati, H.K.: A control-period-based distributed adaptive guard channel reservation scheme for cellular networks. Wireless Netw. **19**, 1739–1753 (2013)
19. Sahu, P.K., Pati, H.K., Pradhan, S.K.: A study on static call admission control policies for wireless mobile cellular networks. In: Sekhar, G.T.C., Behera, H.S., Nayak, J., Naik, B., Pelusi, D. (eds.) Intelligent Computing in Control and Communication. LNEE, vol. 702, pp. 229–245. Springer, Singapore (2021). https://doi.org/10.1007/978-981-15-8439-8_20
20. Sahu, P.K., Pati, H.K., Pradhan, S.K.: A study on CAC schemes for homogeneous and heterogeneous wireless cellular networks. In: IEEE International Conference on Computing, Communication and Intelligent Systems, pp. 917–924, February 2021
21. Rahnema, M.: Overview of the GSM system and protocol architecture. IEEE Commun. Mag. **31**, 92–100 (1993)
22. Watson, C.: Radio equipment for GSM. Balston, D.M., Macario, R.C.V. (eds.) Cellular Radio Systems. Artech House, Boston (1993)
23. Winch, R.G.: Telecommunication Transmission Systems. McGraw-Hill, New Yourk (1993)
24. Singal, T.L.: Wireless Communications, 1st edn. Tata McGraw Hill Education Private Limited (2010)

Systematic Review on Various Techniques of Android Malware Detection

Dharmesh D. Dave[(⊠)] [ID] and Digvijaysinh Rathod [ID]

National Forensic Sciences University, Gandhinagar, India
{dharmesh.dave,digvijay.rathod}@nfsu.ac.in

Abstract. Smartphone has become the 4th basic necessity of human being after Food, Cloths and Home. It has become an integral part of the life that most of the business and office work can be operated by mobile phone and the demand for online classes demand for all class of students have become a compulsion without any alternate due to the COVID-19 pandemic. Android is considered as the most prevailing and used operating system for the mobile phone on this planet and for the same reason it is the most targeted mobile operating system by the hackers. Android malware has been increasing every quarter and every year. An android malware is installed and executed on the smartphones quietly without any indication and user's acceptance, that possess threats to the consumer's personal and/or classified information stored. To address these threats, varieties of techniques have been proposed by the researchers like Static, Dynamic and Hybrid. In this paper a systematic review has been carried out on the relevant studies from 2017 to 2020. Assessment of the malware detection capabilities of various techniques used by different researchers has been carried out with comparison of the performance of different machine learning models for the detection of android malwares by assessing the results of empirical evidences such as datasets, features, tools, etc. However the android malware detection still faces several challenges and the possible solution with some novel approach or technique to improve the detection capabilities is discussed in the discussion and conclusion.

Keywords: Android malware detection · Hybrid analysis · Static analysis · Mobile malware

1 Introduction

Due to pervasiveness of the smartphones in the last decade, Android has become the most prevailing mobile operating system on the planet. Among all the digital devices operating system used in the world, Android OS has the highest market share as 41% and in Mobile OS market share the android shares the highest market as 72% among all [1]. Android malware is increasing day by day and according to a report [3] 47% malware infected only android devices out of 27 Million; a total number of malware samples in 2020 which were lower than 5 million till 2016 [2].

Android applications are ubiquitous in daily life. According to statista [4] there are more than 3 million android applications available on google play store as of September

© Springer Nature Switzerland AG 2022
N. Chaubey et al. (Eds.): COMS2 2022, CCIS 1604, pp. 82–99, 2022.
https://doi.org/10.1007/978-3-031-10551-7_7

2020. However there are many malicious applications hidden in various android application market like Google Pslay Store and other third party app store like Appchina, Anzhi, Samsung, etc. The android malwares are uploaded with sophisticated techniques on the google play store or such third party play store(s) to install and execute itself in a silent manner to avoid the any detection by the security protection.

In May 2017 "Judy" android malware has affected over 36.5 million users which is considered one of the largest impact in the history [8]. In August 2019 a popular document scanning application known as "CamScanner" [5] has been found malicious by the researchers of Kaspersky. In October 2019 a new piece of mysterious malware has been found namely "xHelper" that hide itself on the devices on which it is installed and reportedly reinstall itself even after deletion or factory reset of devices [9]. Another one named "Joker" in July 2020 had bypassed Google's Security [6] to spread via Play Store after imposed for the first time, this the malicious application has created fake reviews, versioning techniques and encryption to hide malicious strings to bypass the security. There can be n number of such malwares infected the android devices. After all the verification, assessment and security checks of Google's security the malwares can be spread via google play store or any other third party app market.

To deal with these kind of modus operandi the traditional anti-malware detection mechanism like signature, strings, hashes database, monitoring syscalls are not sufficient. It requires a use of machine learning (ML) with the set of important features to understand the pattern of the malware in order to detect them accurately in timely manner. There are three techniques to detect the android malwares 1. Static 2. Dynamic and 3. Hybrid.

Static Analysis Technique
The static analysis technique relies on the features extracted from the malware sample/file without executing the APK. The malicious APK is unpacked (if required) and decompiled into files (manifest file, class file, etc) which represent the essential information about the application. By using various tools the features like API calls, permissions, Intents, Hashes, Resources, Bytecode, Opcode, Various components, flows, etc Shar, L. K. (2020) [92] can be extracted from the decompiled files. Static analysis is the most popular and used method to detect the android malware, it also consume very less resources and time with minimum risk as mentioned by Koli, J. D. (2018) [43]. But static analysis has the limitation to decompile some unknown obfuscated and packed malwares, also with the malwares that uses anti-reverse engineering techniques.

Dynamic Analysis Technique
In contrast, dynamic analysis seeks to identify the malicious behaviour from the file to overcome the limitation of static analysis techniques. Yan, P. (2017) [22] the malicious application is executed on emulator or on real devices with the tools to extract and collect the dynamic features. Features like API Calls, Runtime Permissions, Network Ops, File Ops, Broadcast receiver, Running Services, System Calls, Network traffic, Taints, Hook, etc as stated in Shar, L. K. (2020) [92]. This technique requires a manual or an automated interaction with the app running in emulator or on real device; to observe the malicious behaviour as it triggers only after certain event or action performed on it. Actual information of applications can be observed through dynamic analysis. But it consumes enormous amount of resources of android OS and time, also it may not detect some malware which prevents themselves from running on the emulator.

Hybrid Analysis Technique

Hybrid analysis is the technique which uses advantage of static and dynamic analysis both. Hybrid analysis is the most comprehensive analysis because it analyse both android app installation files and behaviour of the app runtime. There is a significant growth in utilizing hybrid analysis technique for last 5 years as stated by Sagar, R. (2020) [73].

To understand the various approach and clear vision of android malware detection with all three analysis techniques in the past few years, the systematic literature review has been performed on the relevant studies. The major contributions of this review paper are listed as follows.

I. The review has been performed based on the key aspect of Android malware detection using static, dynamic and hybrid analysis techniques.
II. The analysis of empirical evidences is carried out for all various techniques and compares the efficiency of various approached of android malware detection.
III. The result of empirical evidence shows the performance of all the analysis techniques with the respective best machine learning model.

2   Literature Review Protocol

2.1   Research Questions

In this section the authors have perused certain questions as mentioned below:

RQ1 How does the empirical experiments of android malware detection have been conducted as a part of pilot study?

- Which malware detection method is used (Static, Dynamic or Hybrid)?
- Which dataset is/are used for the detection of android malware?
- What are the support tools used for detection?
- What are the features commonly used in detection?
- Which feature reduction techniques used for android malware detection?
- Which machine learning models are used for android malware detection?

RQ2 What is the overall performance of the techniques in malware detection based on empirical evidence?

2.2   Search Strategy

To obtain the related studies to Android Malware Detection with static, dynamic and hybrid analysis techniques, the author perform a search with Boolean expression like 'AND' or 'OR'. The search term used was (Mobile OR Android) AND (Malware OR Malicious Behaviour) AND (Detect OR Detection) AND (Static Analysis OR Dynamic Analysis OR Hybrid Analysis) AND (Machine Learning).

With this search terms the author has searched across various digital repositories as mentioned below:

- Google Scholar

- MDPI Journals
- IEEE Xplore Digital Library
- ACM Digital Library
- ScienceDirect
- SpringerLink
- ResearchGate

Most of the research papers have been collected from the above mentioned electronic library/repositories apart from any other private resources, in the range of January 2017 to December 2020.

2.3 Study Selection Criteria

To choose the related papers we have used two criteria in all the papers searched from the various repositories mentioned earlier. First, to search the terms that are included in the keywords or title. Second, the empirical experiments that are conducted in the studies.

To filter the irrelevant studies the author have excluded following criteria.

- Papers not in English
- Duplicate Papers
- Windows PE related papers
- Android Security and Android Operating System

After the selection of the studies the authors have checked the quality assessment of the studies as a systematic literature review by the following questions:

- Is the aim of the study is clear?
- Are the Methods of Machine Learning is defined?
- Is Dataset(s) of the study clearly stated?
- Is Feature(s) of the study clearly mentioned?
- Is the Data-Preparation carried out?
- Does the study have clearly stated about ML Algorithms?
- Are performance measures clearly stated?

2.4 Data Extraction of Study

The data extraction is the process to pluck out the information which is necessary for the systematic literature review. The answers of the research questions can be obtained from this data extraction. The extracted information is following the same questions as mentioned in the quality assessment of the study selection criteria.

The author, publication year, publication source (conference/journal) for the primary studies. Static, Dynamic and Hybrid analysis techniques used in the study has been identified by the features of the application used in the study.

Empirical evidences were collected such as dataset(s) used for the experiment, methods used for study, Algorithms used, feature(s) and feature selection techniques, used models and performance measures.

3 Results

In this section the authors have aim to present the results gathered from the preliminary studies. First the author describe the preliminary studies and then according to facts the results of the research questions.

3.1 Description of Study

There were 'n' various studies reviewed by the author and the primary information like publication year and publication source mentioned as below.

Table 1. The result of publication year and publication source

Sr. No.	Publication name	No.	Year
1	ELSEVIER	13	2017–20
2	IEEE	11	2017–20
3	SPRINGER	8	2015–20
4	MDPI	6	2017–20
5	WILEY HINDAWI	3	2019–20
6	ACM	2	2017–20
7	arxiv.org	2	2017–20
8	International Journal of Network Security	2	2017–20
9	IEICE	2	2020
10	PLOS One	2	2016
11	Easychair Preprint	1	2020
12	iJIM	1	2020
13	iJOE	1	2020
14	International Journal of Advanced Computer Science and Applications	1	2020
15	International Journal of Applied Engineering Research	1	2020
16	International Journal of Computer Science and Network Security	1	2019
17	International Journal of Network Security & Its Applications	1	2020
18	International Journal of Engineering & Technology	1	2018
19	IOP Publishing	1	2020
20	JOURNAL OF ADVANCED COMPUTING TECHNOLOGY AND APPLICATION	1	2019
21	JOURNAL OF INFORMATION SCIENCE AND ENGINEERING	1	2016
22	Journal of Intelligent and Fuzzy Systems	1	2018
23	Software Qual J	1	2017
24	TELKOMNIKA	1	2020
25	Research Gate	1	2019

Which includes the table of publications reviewed for this study according to time and source (Table 1).

From the above table it has been observed that the study in this research is evolving by the time and reaching to the new heights every year. Most number of studies are from ELSEVIER, IEEE and SPRINGER.

3.2 RQ1 How Does the Empirical Experiments of Android Malware Detection Have Been Conducted as a Part of Pilot Study?

In reply to RQ1, the empirical evidences are analysed and summarized. There are following steps used in the process of empirical experiments in android malware detection. First step is Data collection, where the details collected related to malicious and benign dataset. Second step is feature extraction and feature reduction, where the details collected related to static and dynamic features and their reduction. Third step is the tools used for the detection of android malware and feature extraction. Forth step is Model selection, where the study of which machine learning models are used to carry out the research, perused. Fifth and final step is Model evaluation, where the study related to method of evaluation and testing of machine learning algorithms were carried out.

i. **Which malware detection method is used (Static, Dynamic or Hybrid)?**
   The aim in this section is to carry out the study related to various android malware detection techniques static, dynamic and hybrid. To study all the techniques, various research and reviews have been studied. Out of which 20 static, 19 Dynamic, 19 Hybrid and 25 Survey papers have been studied.

ii. **Which dataset is/are used for the detection of android malware?**
   To answer this question the details related to various dataset used by various research studies have been collected and it was observed from Table 2 that most of the authors have used Drebin and Malgenome dataset and most of the datasets are old and outdated one. Certain authors have used their private and custom dataset as well.

iii. **What are the support tools used for detection?**
   To answer this question the information related to various tools used in various studies have been collected and it was observed from Table 3 that in dynamic analysis most of the authors have used Monkey tool and for static analysis most of the authors have used androguard. Regarding hybrid analysis, the authors have used mixture of both static and dynamic tools, also some of the authors have not specified any of the tools.

iv. **What are the features commonly used in detection?**
   Features are the key concept as far as machine learning is concerned. To answer this question various static and dynamic features collected from all the studies. Looking at Fig. 1 we can say that permission, intents and API calls are the most used features in the static analysis. It is further observed from Fig. 2 that network traffic, permissions and system calls are the most used dynamic features in our study.

Table 2. The details of Datasets used in various studies

Sr. No.	Dataset	No. of Papers used	YEAR	Paper(s)	No. of sample
1	Drebin	19	2012	[13, 15, 16, 20, 25, 27, 28, 30, 34, 38, 44, 49, 51, 55, 58, 59, 63, 66, 70]	5560
2	Malgenome/Genome	14	2015	[12, 16, 17, 30, 34, 35, 51, 52, 54, 56, 62, 65, 69, 70]	1200
3	Contagio	9	Updated with 4 samples in 2018	[26, 29, 30, 32, 50, 51, 60, 70, 72]	252
4	Not Specified	6	NA	[18, 19, 22–24, 33]	NA
5	AndroZoo	7	Updated and Private	[26, 37, 46, 50, 61, 66, 68]	>1M
6	Virusshare	7	Updated and Private	[37, 47, 50, 56, 59, 66, 68]	3,88,88,256
7	custom/own/self	7	2013 & 2015	[10, 12, 14, 31, 42, 53, 57]	423
8	AMD Dataset	4	2016	[11, 36, 40, 44, 63]	24,553
9	Malshare	2	Updated and Private	[26, 50]	Not specified
10	VT	2	Updated and Private	[26, 50]	>Million
11	ashishb	2	2016	[43, 70]	298
12	Private Github	2	2013	[43, 63, 64]	58
13	AppChina	1	2021	[42]	>1M
14	AndroParse	1	2018	[41]	46683
15	ArgusLab	1	2016	[45]	24,553
16	CIC Android Botnet	1	2014	[48]	1929
17	CIC Android Validaion Dataset	1	2017	[27]	5000
18	Koodous	1	Updated and private	[61]	>3M
19	Androsimilar	1	2013	[55]	24000
20	Droidkin	1	2014	[60]	8000
21	DroidMat	1	2012	[55]	1738
22	PUMA	1	2012	[55]	1811
23	Andromaly	1	2012	[55]	44
24	Info. Sec. Lab of Peking University	1	2018	[39]	46683
25	Intel Security (McAfee Labs)	1	2016	[67]	5000
26	T-Market Live	1	Not Specified	[71]	Not Specified

Table 3. The details of Tools used in various studies

Sr. No.	Tools used	Type	Paper(s)	No. of times
1	Monkey-Tool/Monkey Runner/adb-monkey	Dynamic	[44, 45, 49, 52–54, 60, 64–72]	16
2	Androguard	Static	[26, 28, 33, 40, 43, 48, 50, 56, 58, 61, 62]	11
3	APKTool	Static	[27, 29, 34–36, 50, 58, 65, 66, 72]	10
4	Virustotal	Static	[26, 33, 34, 37, 46, 59, 61]	7
5	Not Specified	–	[25, 30, 31, 38, 39, 41, 63]	7
6	Strace	Dynamic	[45, 51, 52, 54, 58, 69]	6
7	ADB Tool/ADB shell	Static	[44, 46, 54, 57, 66]	5
8	DroidBox	Dynamic	[49, 56, 58, 61, 62]	5
9	Dex2jar	Static	[42, 50, 59, 70, 72]	5
10	tcpdump	Dynamic	[46, 51, 54, 60, 68]	5
11	Android Asset Packaging Tool (AAPT)	Static	[58, 60, 70]	3
12	Baksmali	Static	[36, 58]	2
13	Wireshark	Dynamic	[46, 56]	2
14	T-shark	Dynamic	[47, 68]	2
15	FlowDroid	Static	[37, 61]	2
16	PScout	Static	[27, 71]	2
17	Droidbot	Dynamic	[46, 67]	2
18	APIMonitor	Dynamic	[58]	1
19	APE	Dynamic	[58]	1
20	Cuckoo Droid	Dynamic	[58]	1
21	Robotium	Dynamic	[58]	1
22	JD-cli	Static	[70]	1
23	JD-CORE	Static	[42]	1
24	Frida	Dynamic	[66]	1
25	Dynalog	Dynamic	[67]	1
26	OpenSSL	Dynamic	[68]	1
27	AndroPyTool	Hybrid	[61]	1
28	APICHECKER	Hybrid	[71]	1

(*continued*)

Table 3. (*continued*)

Sr. No.	Tools used	Type	Paper(s)	No. of times
29	Axplorer	Static	[71]	1
30	Dex manager	Static	[72]	1
31	STREAM	Static	[65]	1
32	JADX	Static	[50]	1
33	Android Multitool	Static	[50]	1
34	sublime	Static	[33]	1
35	Euphony	Static	[37]	1
36	dedexer	Static	[37]	1

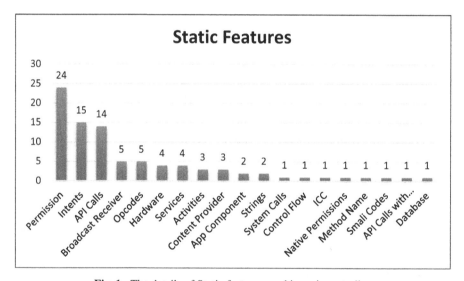

Fig. 1. The details of Static features used in various studies

v. **Which feature reduction techniques used for android malware detection?**
Feature reduction is one of the important task in preparation of the dataset. Surprisingly it is observed in the Fig. 3 that many of the authors are not reducing the features as part of their research and highest no of feature reduction methods used by the authors are custom and vector based. The feature reduction method plays a major role in preparing the dataset for using machine learning algorithms.

vi. **Which machine learning models are used for android malware detection?**
To answer this question the details of classification algorithms have been collected from all the studies and it has been observed from Fig. 4 that most of the authors have

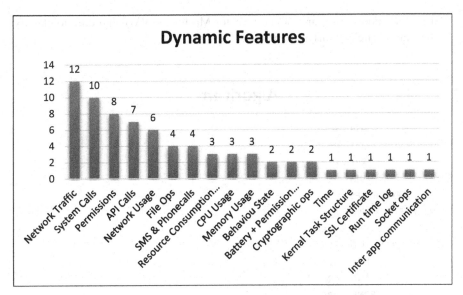

Fig. 2. The details of Dynamic features used in various studies

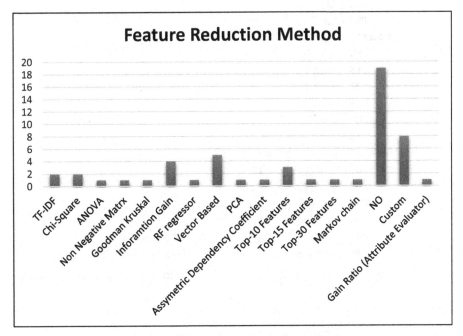

Fig. 3. The details of Feature reduction methods in various studies

used Rain Forest (RF) and Support Vector Machine (SVM) algorithm to classify the android applications as malicious or benign.

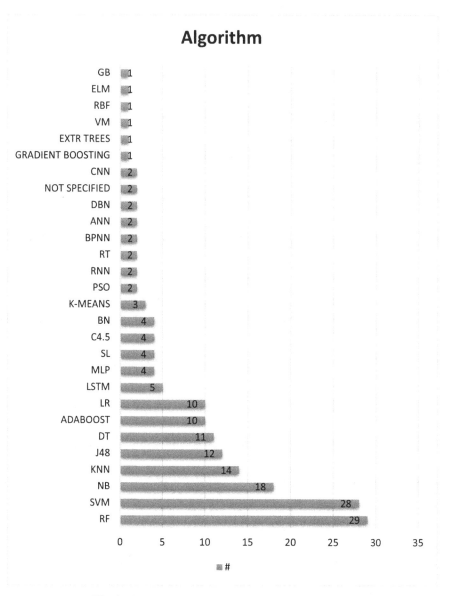

Fig. 4. The details of Algorithms used in all the studies

3.3 RQ2 What is the Overall Performance of the Techniques in Malware Detection Based on Empirical Evidence?

There were three major analysis techniques reviewed in this paper. Static, Dynamic and Hybrid out of which Static analysis has minimum accuracy as 88% and maximum as 99.28%, for dynamic minimum accuracy is 81.50% and maximum is 99.46%, for hybrid minimum accuracy is 89.70% and maximum 99.70%. As per the accuracy percentage of all different methods it is observed that hybrid method can provide better result than only static and only dynamic methods.

4 Discussion

Based of the empirical evidences and analysis of all the studies, hybrid analysis can be considered as the best method for android malware detection as it combines features and techniques of static and dynamic analysis both. It is observed that static analysis by Salah, A. (2020) [25] and by Taheri, R. (2020) [30] that it can give good result but only static analysis technique is not reliable as mentioned by Gong, L. (2020) [71]. Multiple analysis technique can give the more accurate result than single analysis technique as describe by Jannat U. S. (2019) [62] the authors have used multiple static features like permission, intents and API Calls also they have used dynamic features like network flow, file access, socket operations, SMS etc. to get good accuracy over detecting the malware.

Feature reduction is the important part of machine learning process. In our survey it has been observed that most of the authors are not following the standard but there are few papers who have shown the significance of feature reduction methods. Liu, K. (2020) [78] has shown the significance of feature reduction methods with a survey on various feature reduction methods, Alazab, M. (2020) [26] has also used three different feature reduction methods ANOVA, Chi-Square and TF-IDF and compare the result to find the best suite feature reduction method with classification algorithm.

Dataset is a key part of any machine learning related research. In our survey many authors like Xiao, X. (2015) [10], Afifi, F. (2016) [12], Almin, S. B. (2015) [31] have used their private dataset for their research and apart from that most of the users have used Drebin as their dataset. Very few users like Lashkari, A. H. (2018) [94] has created their own dataset with latest android malware samples till 2017.

Almost 98% of the authors have used emulator or simulator in their dynamic and hybrid analysis methods of android malware detection. While it is very good to note that Alzaylaee, M. K. (2020) [67] has shown new dimension and possibility of carrying out android malware detection with hybrid method using real devices to run the malware and extracting the features from those devices.

5 Limitation

Limitation is the universal truth for any system, product or algorithm. During our systematic review on android malware detection we could evident some of the major limitation that are:

i) Either only static or only dynamic analysis techniques used by most of the authors with few features which may result good in accuracy but cannot be considered as reliable in real time usage.

ii) Use of old and outdated datasets, an outdated dataset cannot be reliable as there are many new variant of the malware which uses advanced and sophisticated techniques to evade the detection.

iii) Dataset preparation and feature selection methods not used by most of the authors which lead to an invalid dataset. Liu, K. (2020) [78] has shown the significance of feature reduction methods with a survey on various feature reduction methods, Alazab, M. (2020) [26] has also used three different feature reduction methods ANOVA, Chi-Square and TF-IDF and compare the result to find the best suite.

iv) Testing validation is not done in all the studies. Validation of the testing algorithm is indeed necessary in-order to make it accurate in real time environment.

v) Most of the studies are conducted on the emulator or simulator which may not be the perfect analysis of the malware as there are certain malware which can detect the emulator and hide their characteristics or may get sleep. Sinha, A. (2021) [93] and Alzaylaee, M. K. (2017) [95] have compared the Real Phone vs Emulator on feature extraction and malware detection and proved that Real Phone Accuracy and feature extraction is far better than emulator.

6   Conclusion Future Work

This paper summarizes the various niche techniques used by the researcher for the detection of android malware. This systematic review has studied more than 80 research papers from 2017 to 2020. This paper has followed empirical evidence based approach to identify the related paper for the study and we find that i) most commonly used analysis techniques for malware detection, ii) most widely used dataset for android malware detection, iii) most common static and dynamic features used by the authors, iv) most common feature reduction methods used and v) most used classification algorithms by the authors for the detection of the android malware detection.

Based on the survey there are many future work or opportunities for the researcher to contribute in android malware detection.

i) They may create a latest dataset with latest and various types of the malware samples.

ii) They may use real device to extract the features from malware.

iii) They may create an automated framework where the process of feature extraction from real device and detection algorithm work in a harmonic way.

iv) They may find the best suitable feature reduction method for android malware along with best suitable classification algorithm.

References

1. StatCounter Global Stats - https://gs.statcounter.com/os-market-share
2. Nokia Threat Intelligence Report 2020

3. Nokia Threat Intelligence Report 2019
4. Statista - https://www.statista.com/statistics/266210/number-of-available-applications-in-the-google-play-store/
5. Kaspersky Team: Malicious Android app had more than 100 million downloads in Google Play – Kaspersky (2019)
6. Ravie, L.: Joker Malware Apps Once Again Bypass Google's Security to Spread via Play Store – The Hacker News (2020)
7. Ravie, L.: Watch Out—Microsoft Warns Android Users About A New Ransomware – The Hacker News (2020)
8. Mohit K., Judy Android Malware Infects Over 36.5 Million Google Play Store Users – The Hacker News, May 2017
9. Swati, K.: Mysterious malware that re-installs itself infected over 45,000 Android Phones – The Hacker News (2019)
10. Xiao, X., Xiao, X., Jiang, Y., Li, Q.: Detecting mobile malware with TMSVM. In: Tian, J., Jing, J., Srivatsa, M. (eds.) International Conference on Security and Privacy in Communication Networks, LNICST, vol. 15, pp. 507–516. Springer, Cham (2014). https://doi.org/10.1007/978-3-319-23829-6_35
11. Mercaldo, F., Santone, A.: Deep learning for image-based mobile malware detection. J. Comput. Virol. Hack. Tech. **16**(2), 157–171 (2020). https://doi.org/10.1007/s11416-019-00346-7
12. Afifi, F., Anuar, N. B., Shamshirband, S., Choo, K.K.R.: DyHAP: Dynamic hybrid ANFIS-PSO approach for predicting mobile malware. PloS one **11**(9) (2016)
13. Chen, Z., et al.: Machine learning based mobile malware detection using highly imbalanced network traffic. Inf. Sci. **433**, 346–364 (2018)
14. Jang, J.-W., Yun, J., Mohaisen, A., Woo, J., Kim, H.K.: Detecting and classifying method based on similarity matching of Android malware behavior with profile. Springerplus **5**(1), 1–23 (2016). https://doi.org/10.1186/s40064-016-1861-x
15. Karim, A., Salleh, R., Khan, M.K.: SMARTbot: a behavioral analysis framework augmented with machine learning to identify mobile botnet applications. PloS one, **11**(3) (2016)
16. Khoda, M.E., Kamruzzaman, J., Gondal, I., Imam, T., Rahman, A.: Mobile malware detection: an analysis of deep learning model. In: 2019 IEEE International Conference on Industrial Technology (ICIT), pp. 1161–1166. IEEE (2019)
17. Narudin, F.A., Feizollah, A., Anuar, N.B., Gani, A.: Evaluation of machine learning classifiers for mobile malware detection. Soft. Comput. **20**(1), 343–357 (2014). https://doi.org/10.1007/s00500-014-1511-6
18. Qamar, A., Karim, A., Chang, V.: Mobile malware attacks: Review, taxonomy & future directions. Futur. Gener. Comput. Syst. **97**, 887–909 (2019)
19. Wang, C., Wu, Z., Li, X., Zhou, X., Wang, A., Hung, P.C.: SmartMal: a service-oriented behavioral malware detection framework for mobile devices. Sci. World J. **2014**, 1–11 (2014)
20. Wang, X., Yang, Y., Zeng, Y.: Accurate mobile malware detection and classification in the cloud. Springerplus **4**(1), 1–23 (2015). https://doi.org/10.1186/s40064-015-1356-1
21. Karumudi, B.R., Chandrasekaran, S., Armour, B., Alsmadi, I.: Malware Prediction and Classification Using Advanced Modeling Techniques (2017)
22. Yan, P., Yan, Z.: A survey on dynamic mobile malware detection. Software Qual. J. **26**(3), 891–919 (2017). https://doi.org/10.1007/s11219-017-9368-4
23. Swetha, K., Kiran, K.V.D.: Survey on mobile malware analysis and detection. Int. J. Eng. Technol **7**(2.32), 279–282 (2018)
24. Gyamfi, N.K., Owusu, E.: Survey of mobile malware analysis, detection techniques and tool. In: 2018 IEEE 9th Annual Information Technology, Electronics and Mobile Communication Conference (IEMCON), pp. 1101–1107. IEEE (2018)

25. Salah, A., Shalabi, E., Khedr, W.: A lightweight android malware classifier using novel feature selection methods. Symmetry **12**(5), 858 (2020)
26. Alazab, M.: Automated malware detection in mobile app stores based on robust feature generation. Electronics **9**(3), 435 (2020)
27. Roy, A., Jas, D.S., Jaggi, G., Sharma, K.: Android malware detection based on vulnerable feature aggregation. Procedia Comput. Sci. **173**, 345–353 (2020)
28. Wu, B., et al.: Why an Android App is Classified as Malware? Towards Malware Classification Interpretation. arXiv preprint arXiv:2004.11516 (2020)
29. Deepa, K., Radhamani, G., Vinod, P.: Investigation of feature selection methods for android malware analysis. Procedia Comput. Sci. **46**, 841–848 (2017)
30. Taheri, R., Ghahramani, M., Javidan, R., Shojafar, M., Pooranian, Z., Conti, M.: Similarity-based Android malware detection using Hamming distance of static binary features. Futur. Gener. Comput. Syst. **105**, 230–247 (2020)
31. Almin, S.B., Chatterjee, M.: A novel approach to detect android malware. Procedia Comput. Sci. **45**, 407–417 (2015)
32. Nellaivadivelu, G., Di Troia, F., Stamp, M.: Black box analysis of android malware detectors. Array **6**, 100022 (2020)
33. Christianah, A., Gyunka, B., Oluwatobi, A.: Optimizing Android Malware Detection Via Ensemble Learning (2020)
34. Rathore, H., Sahay, S.K., Chaturvedi, P., Sewak, M.:, December). Android malicious application classification using clustering. In: Abraham, A., Cherukuri, A., Melin, P., Gandhi, N. (eds.) International Conference on Intelligent Systems Design and Applications, AISC, vol. 941, pp. 659–667. Springer, Cham. https://doi.org/10.1007/978-3-030-16660-1_64
35. Ali, W.: Hybrid intelligent Android malware detection using evolving support vector machine based on genetic algorithm and particle swarm optimization. IJCSNS **19**(9), 15 (2019)
36. Egitmen, A., Bulut, I., Aygun, R., Gunduz, A.B., Seyrekbasan, O., Yavuz, A.G.: Combat mobile evasive malware via skip-gram-based malware detection. Security and Communication Networks (2020)
37. Niu, W., Cao, R., Zhang, X., Ding, K., Zhang, K., Li, T.: OpCode-level function call graph based android malware classification using deep learning. Sensors **20**(13), 3645 (2020)
38. Islam, T., Rahman, S.S.M.M., Hasan, M.A., Rahaman, A.S.M.M., Jabiullah, M.I.: Evaluation of N-gram based multi-layer approach to detect malware in Android. Procedia Comput. Sci. **171**, 1074–1082 (2020)
39. Wang, J., Jing, Q., Gao, J., Qiu, X.: SEdroid: a robust Android malware detector using selective ensemble learning. In: 2020 IEEE Wireless Communications and Networking Conference (WCNC), pp. 1–5. IEEE (2020)
40. Ma, Z., Ge, H., Wang, Z., Liu, Y., Liu, X.: Droidetec: Android malware detection and malicious code localization through deep learning. arXiv preprint arXiv:2002.03594 (2020)
41. Dillon, K.: Feature-level Malware Obfuscation in Deep Learning. arXiv preprint arXiv:2002.05517 (2020)
42. Akram, J., Shi, Z., Mumtaz, M., Luo, P.: DroidSD: An efficient indexed based android applications similarity detection tool. J. Inf. Sci. Eng. **36**(1) (2020)
43. Koli, J.D.: RanDroid: Android malware detection using random machine learning classifiers. In: 2018 Technologies for Smart-City Energy Security and Power (ICSESP), pp. 1–6. IEEE (2018)
44. Massarelli, L., Aniello, L., Ciccotelli, C., Querzoni, L., Ucci, D., Baldoni, R.: AndroDFA: Android malware classification based on resource consumption. Information **11**(6), 326 (2020)
45. Abderrahmane, A., Adnane, G., Yacine, C., Khireddine, G.: Android malware detection based on system calls analysis and CNN classification. In: 2019 IEEE Wireless Communications and Networking Conference Workshop (WCNCW), pp. 1–6. IEEE (2019)

46. He, G., Xu, B., Zhang, L., Zhu, H.: On-Device Detection of Repackaged Android Malware via Traffic Clustering. Security and Communication Networks (2020)
47. Wang, S., et al.: Deep and broad URL feature mining for android malware detection. Inf. Sci. **513**, 600–613 (2020)
48. Takawale, H.C., Thakur, A.: Talos app: on-device machine learning using tensorflow to detect android malware. In: 2018 Fifth International Conference on Internet of Things: Systems, Management and Security, pp. 250–255. IEEE (2018)
49. Martín, A., Rodríguez-Fernández, V., Camacho, D.: CANDYMAN: Classifying Android malware families by modelling dynamic traces with Markov chains. Eng. Appl. Artif. Intell. **74**, 121–133 (2018)
50. Alazab, M., Alazab, M., Shalaginov, A., Mesleh, A., Awajan, A.: Intelligent mobile malware detection using permission requests and API calls. Futur. Gener. Comput. Syst. **107**, 509–521 (2020)
51. Su, X., Xiao, L., Li, W., Liu, X., Li, K.C., Liang, W.: DroidPortrait: Android malware portrait construction based on multidimensional behavior analysis. Appl. Sci. **10**(11), 3978 (2020)
52. Bhatia, T., Kaushal, R.: Malware detection in android based on dynamic analysis. In: 2017 International Conference on Cyber Security and Protection of Digital Services (Cyber Security), pp. 1–6. IEEE (2017)
53. Cai, H., Fu, X., Hamou-Lhadj, A.: A study of run-time behavioral evolution of benign versus malicious apps in android. Inf. Softw. Technol. **122**, 106291 (2020)
54. Thangavelooa, R., Jinga, W.W., Lenga, C.K., Abdullaha, J.: DATDroid: dynamic analysis technique in Android malware detection. Int. J. Adv. Sci. Eng. Inf. Technol. **10**(2), 536–541 (2020)
55. Mahindru, A., Singh, P.: Dynamic permissions based android malware detection using machine learning techniques. In: Proceedings of the 10th Innovations in Software Engineering Conference, pp. 202–210 (2017)
56. Kim, D.W., Na, K.G., Han, M.M., Kim, M., Go, W., Park, J.H.: Malware application classification based on feature extraction and machine learning for malicious behavior analysis in Android platform. J. Internet Comput. Serv. **19**(1), 27–35 (2018)
57. Wang, X., Li, C.: KerTSDroid: detecting android malware at scale through kernel task structures. In: 2019 IEEE 25th International Conference on Parallel and Distributed Systems (ICPADS), pp. 870–879. IEEE (2019)
58. Arshad, S., Shah, M.A., Wahid, A., Mehmood, A., Song, H., Yu, H.: Samadroid: a novel 3-level hybrid malware detection model for android operating system. IEEE Access **6**, 4321–4339 (2018)
59. Zhang, Y., et al.: Familial clustering for weakly-labeled android malware using hybrid representation learning. IEEE Trans. Inf. Forensics Secur. **15**, 3401–3414 (2019)
60. Patel, K., Buddadev, B.: Detection and mitigation of android malware through hybrid approach. In: Abawajy, J., Mukherjea, S., Thampi, S., Ruiz-Martínez, A. (eds.) International Symposium on Security in Computing and Communication, CCIS, vol. 536, pp. 455–463. Springer, Cham. https://doi.org/10.1007/978-3-319-22915-7_41
61. Martín, A., Lara-Cabrera, R., Camacho, D.: Android malware detection through hybrid features fusion and ensemble classifiers: the AndroPyTool framework and the OmniDroid dataset. Inf. Fus. **52**, 128–142 (2019)
62. Jannat, U.S., Hasnayeen, S.M., Shuhan, M.K.B., Ferdous, M.S.: Analysis and detection of malware in Android applications using machine learning. In: 2019 International Conference on Electrical, Computer and Communication Engineering (ECCE), pp. 1–7. IEEE (2019)
63. Surendran, R., Thomas, T., Emmanuel, S.: A TAN based hybrid model for android malware detection. J. Inf. Secur. Appl. **54**, 102483 (2020)

64. Demertzis, K., Iliadis, L.: Bio-inspired hybrid intelligent method for detecting android malware. In: Kunifuji, S., Papadopoulos, G., Skulimowski, A., Kacprzyk, J. (eds.) Knowledge, Information and Creativity Support Systems, AISC, Vol. 416, pp. 289–304. Springer, Cham. https://doi.org/10.1007/978-3-319-27478-2_20
65. Vinayakumar, R., Soman, K.P., Poornachandran, P., Sachin Kumar, S.: Detecting Android malware using long short-term memory (LSTM). J. Intell. Fuzzy Syst. **34**(3), 1277–1288 (2018)
66. Kouliaridis, V., Kambourakis, G., Geneiatakis, D., Potha, N.: Two anatomists are better than one—dual-level Android malware detection. Symmetry **12**(7), 1128 (2020)
67. Alzaylaee, M.K., Yerima, S.Y., Sezer, S.: DL-Droid: Deep learning based android malware detection using real devices. Comput. Secur. **89**, 101663 (2020)
68. Kato, H., Haruta, S., Sasase, I.: Android malware detection scheme based on level of SSL server certificate. IEICE Trans. Inf. Syst. **103**(2), 379–389 (2020)
69. Tong, F., Yan, Z.: A hybrid approach of mobile malware detection in Android. J. Parallel Distrib. Comput. **103**, 22–31 (2017)
70. Kabakus, A.T., Dogru, I.A.: An in-depth analysis of Android malware using hybrid techniques. Digit. Investig. **24**, 25–33 (2018)
71. Gong, L., et al.: Experiences of landing machine learning onto market-scale mobile malware detection. In: Proceedings of the Fifteenth European Conference on Computer Systems, pp. 1–14 (2020)
72. Su, M.Y., Chang, J.Y., Fung, K.T.: Android malware detection approaches in combination with static and dynamic features. IJ Network Secur. **21**(6), 1031–1041 (2019)
73. Sagar, R., Jhaveri, R., Borrego, C.: Applications in security and evasions in machine learning: a survey. Electronics **9**(1), 97 (2020)
74. Yusof, R., Adnan, N.S., Jalil, N.A., Abdullah, R.S.: Analysis of data mining tools for android malware detection. JACTA **1**(2), 22–26 (2019)
75. Christiana, A., Gyunka, B., Noah, A.: Android Malware Detection through Machine Learning Techniques: A Review (2020)
76. Kouliaridis, V., Barmpatsalou, K., Kambourakis, G., Chen, S.: A survey on mobile malware detection techniques. IEICE Trans. Inf. Syst. **103**(2), 204–211 (2020)
77. Vasan, D., Alazab, M., Wassan, S., Naeem, H., Safaei, B., Zheng, Q.: IMCFN: image-based malware classification using fine-tuned convolutional neural network architecture. Comput. Netw. **171**, 107138 (2020)
78. Liu, K., Xu, S., Xu, G., Zhang, M., Sun, D., Liu, H.: A review of Android malware detection approaches based on machine learning. IEEE Access **8**, 124579–124607 (2020)
79. Yunus, Y.K.B.M., Ngah, S.B.: Review of hybrid analysis technique for malware detection. In: IOP Conference Series: Materials Science and Engineering, vol. 769, no. 1, p. 012075. IOP Publishing (2020)
80. Talukder, S., Talukder, Z.: A survey on malware detection and analysis tools. Int. J. Network Secur. Appl. **12**(2) (2020)
81. Aslan, Ö.A., Samet, R.: A comprehensive review on malware detection approaches. IEEE Access **8**, 6249–6271 (2020)
82. Pan, Y., Ge, X., Fang, C., Fan, Y.: A systematic literature review of android malware detection using static analysis. IEEE Access **8**, 116363–116379 (2020)
83. Alswaina, F., Elleithy, K.: Android malware family classification and analysis: current status and future directions. Electronics **9**(6), 942 (2020)
84. Alqahtani, E.J., Zagrouba, R., Almuhaideb, A.: A survey on android malware detection techniques using machine learning algorithms. In: 2019 Sixth International Conference on Software Defined Systems (SDS), pp. 110–117. IEEE (2019)
85. Sikder, R., Khan, S., Hossain, S., Khan, W.Z.: A survey on android security: development and deployment hindrance and best practices. Telkomnika **18**(1), 485–499 (2020)

86. Kumar, R., Alazab, M.: Android Malware Detection Techniques (No. 3707). EasyChair (2020)
87. Salem, A.: Towards Accurate Labeling of Android Apps for Reliable Malware Detection. arXiv preprint arXiv:2007.00464 (2020)
88. Selvaraj, P.A., Jagadeesan, M., Sankari, R.G.: Risk score combined malware prediction using machine learning approach. Int. J. Appl. Eng. Res. **15**(4), 422–424 (2020)
89. Huang, J., Huang, W., Miao, F., Xiong, Y.: Detecting improper behaviors of stubbornly requesting permissions in Android applications. IJ Network Security **22**(3), 381–391 (2020)
90. Abdullah, T.A., Ali, W., Abdulghafor, R.: Empirical Study on Intelligent Android Malware Detection based on Supervised Machine Learning (2020)
91. Berger, H., Hajaj, C., Dvir, A.: When the Guard failed the Droid: a case study of Android malware. arXiv preprint arXiv:2003.14123 (2020)
92. Shar, L.K., Demissie, B.F., Ceccato, M., Minn, W.: Experimental comparison of features and classifiers for Android malware detection. In: Proceedings of the IEEE/ACM 7th International Conference on Mobile Software Engineering and Systems, pp. 50–60 (2020)
93. Sinha, A., Di Troia, F., Heller, P., Stamp, M.: Emulation versus instrumentation for Android malware detection. In: Digital Forensic Investigation of Internet of Things (IoT) Devices, pp. 1–20. Springer, Cham (2021). https://doi.org/10.1007/978-3-030-60425-7_1
94. Lashkari, A.H., Kadir, A.F.A., Taheri, L., Ghorbani, A.A.: Toward developing a systematic approach to generate benchmark android malware datasets and classification. In: 2018 International Carnahan Conference on Security Technology (ICCST), pp. 1–7. IEEE (2018)
95. Alzaylaee, M.K., Yerima, S.Y., Sezer, S.: Emulator vs real phone: Android malware detection using machine learning. In: Proceedings of the 3rd ACM on International Workshop on Security and Privacy Analytics, pp. 65–72 (2017)
96. Alzaylaee, M.K., Yerima, S.Y., Sezer, S.: DynaLog: An automated dynamic analysis framework for characterizing android applications. In: 2016 International Conference on Cyber Security and Protection Of Digital Services (Cyber Security), pp. 1–8. IEEE (2016)

Adaptive Rider Grey Wolf Optimization Enabled Pilot-Design for Channel Estimation in Cognitive Radio

D. Raghunatharao[1]([envelope]), T. Jayachandra Prasad[2], and M. N. Giri Prasad[3]

[1] ECE Department, SVR Engineering College, Affiliated to JNTUA, Anantapuramu, Andhra Pradesh, India
raghu.ece@svrec.ac.in
[2] RGM College of Engineering and Technology (Autonomous), Nandyal, Andhra Pradesh, India
[3] Department of ECE, JNTUA College of Engineering, Anantapuramu, Andhra Pradesh, India

Abstract. In recent years, Cognitive Radio (CR) is an advanced and immense technology developed for enhancing the efficiency of spectrum utilization by permitting unauthorized Secondary Users (SUs) functions within service limit of authorized Primary Users (PUs), while creating bearable intervention to the PUs. Typically, secondary network is constructed as Half-Duplex (HD) and are carried out orthogonally in frequency or time domain. CR has been considered as an eminent technology to solve the issue of scarcity of spectrum in wireless communications. The main motive behind constructing CR technology is to increase the efficiency of spectrum utilization. In addition, there is a high need for sensing spectrum and this delay for sensing creates a huge constraint in construction of sensing approaches. This is because of minimum time consumed in spectrum sensing, and later much time is existed for transmission. Hence, this research proposes an effective approach for channel estimation in CR. Here, the optimization of pilot design in CR system is designed depending upon Least-Square channel estimation, where position to insert the pilot symbols are determined using proposed optimization algorithm called Adaptive Rider-Grey Wolf Optimizer (Adaptive RGWO). However, proposed Adaptive RGWO is devised by inheriting adaptive concept with merits of Rider Optimization Algorithm (ROA) and Grey Wolf Optimizer (GWO). Moreover, proposed Adaptive RGWO has achieved minimum BER of 0.0000028 for Rician channel with 768 carriers and minimum MSE of 0.000001 for Rician channel with 512 carriers.

Keywords: Cognitive Radio (CR) · Channel estimation · Orthogonal Frequency Division Multiplexing (OFDM) · Rider Optimization Algorithm (ROA) · Grey Wolf Optimizer (GWO)

1 Introduction

The main principle behind developing CR technology is to increase the spectrum efficiency. Nevertheless, high efficiency needs for spectrum sensing, and its delay creates a

D. Raghunatharao—Research Scholar, JNTUA

© Springer Nature Switzerland AG 2022
N. Chaubey et al. (Eds.): COMS2 2022, CCIS 1604, pp. 100–116, 2022.
https://doi.org/10.1007/978-3-031-10551-7_8

main constraint while designing spectrum sensing methods. This is because of the reason that if minimum period is consumed in spectrum sensing, high amount of duration is required for transmission. So far, number of sensing techniques has been developed in the paper [1–4] to instantly determine one or more free channels. Different types of techniques have been designed to not only integrate effective spectrum sensing approaches but also to enhance the throughput of CR system [5, 6]. CR is the eminent technology to tackle the problem of spectrum shortage. By analyzing the spectrum hole of PUs, CR allows the opportunistic spectrum access for SUs. Hence, CR is an efficient way to enhance the spectrum utilization [7, 8]. Recently, research on CR highly concentrates on resource allocation, spectrum sensing, and CR network cloud. As the fundamental interface technology of 4th Generation (4G), Orthogonal Frequency Division Multiplexing (OFDM) is completely probed and it is considered as the best strategy of physical layer in CR [9–11].

OFDM [12–14] is an eminent approach for broadcasting heavy-bit rate over both internal and external wireless communication systems. Channel parameter detection is a significant approach for enhancing performance of data transmission. Channel parameter estimators can be categorized into two types, such as decision-directed and pilot-symbol-aided [15]. In any demonstration, suitable methodologies for channel-state detection are very crucial for CR models functioning in changing scenarios. Channel-state detection is highly required for determining channel volume to facilitate the transmitter for analyzing its candidate functioning configurations [16, 17]. The channel estimation is generally carried out by embedding pilot tones with a particular time or embedding pilot tones into individual symbol. The former type is the block category pilot channel detection and it has been designed under consideration of slow fading channel. The channel detection for this block-type organization is solely dependent on Least Square (LS) or Minimum Mean-Square (MMSE) [18]. The latter is comb-type pilot channel detection that is developed to meet the requirements for managing if channel variations in one block of OFDM. The comb-type pilot channel detection is comprised with methodologies to evaluate channel at pilot frequencies and it relies on LS, MMSE, and Least Mean-Square (LMS) [19].The embedding pilot tones are based on an algorithm RGWO (Rider Grey Wolf Optimizer) which inherits the optimization techniques of ROA and GWO algorithms [20–22].

The ultimate aim of this research is to establish an effectual approach for channel estimation in CR. Here, the optimization of the pilot design in cognitive radio system is developed based on LS channel estimation where positions to place the pilot symbols is determined using proposed optimization algorithm named Adaptive Rider-Grey Wolf Optimizer (Adaptive RGWO). However, Adaptive RGWO is devised by incorporating the adaptive theory into ROA and GWO.

The key aspect of this paper is explained below:

Proposed Adaptive RGWO: An effectual strategy is proposed for channel estimation in CR, where the optimization of the pilot design in CR system is developed based on LS channel detection. The positions are determined using proposed adaptive RGWO to insert the pilot symbols.

The remaining structure is arranged as follows: Sect. 2 illustrates the literature review of existing techniques of channel estimation in CR that drives the researchers to develop an effectual model. Section 3 explains the system and mathematical model of OFDM system for channel estimation and the proposed Adaptive RGWO for channel estimation in CR is elaborated in Sect. 4. Section 5 introduces discussion of Adaptive RGWO and it comes to a conclusion in Sect. 6.

2 Motivation

This section explains the survey of existing methodologies corresponding to channel estimation in CR along with their pros and cons that drives the researchers to establish an effectual model for pilot channel estimation in CR to improve spectrum efficiency.

2.1 Literature Survey

Various conventional techniques associated with channel estimation in CR are elaborated as follows: Raied Caromi et al. [6] described a sequential channel detection model for multiband CR systems. Here, two scenarios were tested such that the CR users estimated all existing bands and CR users determined one best channel with high gain. This model designed a switch parameter, an estimator, and an ending instruction that considerably reduced both estimation time and estimation error. This method optimally determined the maximum symbols needed for individual channel in a joint optimization issue. More importantly, a sequential mechanism was designed to determine a channel with high gain accurately. However, the method failed to enable a switch using truncation with respect to highly ambiguous samples. Zhenyu Na et al. [11] developed a modified turbo receiver that utilized feedback data for channel detection. Here, the modulator for pilot placing was enhanced to made pilots orthogonal to subcarriers. In order to address the noise enhancement issue, a combination of iterative channel detection approach with threshold control was developed. In order to mitigate the sampling cost, a modified turbo receiver was developed and provided better results over other conventional approaches. P. Demestichas et al. [23] developed a learning method called Bayesian networks for effective channel estimation in CR networks. The major objective of this method was to maximize the certainty level so that the particular configuration can obtain a static bit rate. However, it failed to probe into Bayesian models with even more attributes and its probabilistic connections. Olusegun Peter Awe et al. [24] modeled a network that utilizes a pilot based second order Kalman filter for determining steadily changing channel gain among transmitter of PU and mobile SU. Based on the PU activity, classification decision was provided using adaptive k-means clustering approach. Besides, noise along with interference power was measured using a quadratic polynomial regression method. The developed method offered better results for sensing in CR models of mobile SUs.

2.2 Major Challenges

The issues faced by conventional methods of channel estimation in CR are explained as follows:

The developed approach delivered good Bit Error Rate (BER) and Mean-Squared Error (MSE) performances. However, it failed to maintain the tradeoff between required performance and computing overhead by choosing the iteration number [3].

To integrate the learning method with diverse radio scene analysis is a challenging task. Moreover, optimal selection of connections for a group or all cognitive transmitters in an environment is also a challenging issue [4].

3 System Model of OFDM-Based CR for Channel Estimation

According to the spectrum sensing, pilot design is constructed and it is considered without existing any false alarm rate. After completion of spectrum sensing, PUs that filled subcarriers of OFDM is shut down. On contrast, rest of the active subcarriers is selected that are adopted to choose the symbols for transferring the data to SUs. This generates a sequence that is transformed into time-based signals by exploiting Inverse Fast Fourier Transform (IFFT). To eliminate the intervention among symbols, a cyclic prefix (CP) is utilized whose length is higher while comparing with maximum channel delay distribution. Various channels are developed as a finite-impulse response filter and channel estimation is performed at receiver side after eliminating CP and adoption of FFT. The conversion of multipath fading channel into parallel fading channel is developed utilizing single-tap-zero-forcing channel equalization to minimize low computation. At last, transmitter transmits the result of pilot development to receiver end through control signaling. The pilot designing in CR system is based on Least-Square Channel estimation and locations to place the symbols is estimated using newly proposed adaptive RGWO algorithm that inherits the characteristics of ROA and GWO with adaptive concept. Figure 1 shows the schematic view of proposed model.

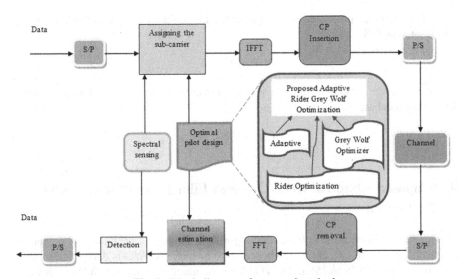

Fig. 1. Block diagram of proposed method

3.1 Mathematical Model of the System

The MIMO-OFDM model is constructed with placing of symbols along with data that is regulated with OFDM modulators and result from such modulators are broadcasted using diverse antennas. The receiver gains transmitted signal by means of demodulators and Channel State Information (CSI) is achieved by means of a training algorithm. It is observed that the training data with optimal scenario gained better results than non-optimality condition. Here, the training samples are designed using proposed optimization algorithm. Let us consider OFDM model with a count of transmitters and b number of end units. At the end side, CE is performed utilizing pilot assisted training, such as LS, and Minimum Mean Square Error (MMSE) and it is computed below,

$$C_{least}^{a,b} = \left(U^{(a)}\right)^{-1} V^b \tag{1}$$

$$C_{MMSE}^{a,b} = P\, L_{IN}\, L_{NN}^{-1}\, V^a \tag{2}$$

The training phase for r orthogonal subcarriers is expressed as,

$$U = \begin{bmatrix} U(0) & 0............ & 0 \\ 0 & U(1)...... & 0 \\ \vdots & \vdots & \vdots \\ 0 & 0..........U(r-1) \end{bmatrix} \tag{3}$$

Here, $U(s)$ denotes pilot tone of sth subcarrier. The training sample is mathematically represented as follows,

$$V = U\, G + N \tag{4}$$

where, G denotes the channel gain, noise vector is indicated as N. The CE depends upon LS is expressed as,

$$C_{least} = U^{-1} V \tag{5}$$

4 Proposed Adaptive RGWO-Based Pilot Design for Channel Estimation

This section elaborates the optimization algorithm enabled for optimal pilot design for channel detection in CR. Here, newly proposed adaptive RGWO is designed by inheriting the features of ROA [5] and GWO [21] with adaptive concept. GWO employs the adaptive switching among the exploitation and exploration phases through the inclusion of adaptive parameters that provides global optimal solution and provides better exploration capabilities. Also, GWO maintains a better tradeoff between exploitation and exploration phases with good optimal avoidance capabilities. The major bottleneck exist in GWO is that the location update is self-contained on fitness since they are dependent upon the position of alpha, beta and gamma wolves. Hence, it is necessary to solve this optimization constrained problem and it is achieved by modifying the update equation of GWO with adaptive concept using RWO, such that the optimal solution becomes very low fit while comparing it with the different wolves and it can be substituted with best solution in the wolf group. Typically, GWO is a metaheuristic algorithm that inspires the hunting mechanism followed by grey wolves in a maximum of 12 wolves. An individual group is guided by a leader known as alpha that provides best solution based on behaviors of whole pack, such as walking, sleeping, and hunting. The alpha is mainly responsible for effectual decision making, whereas the good candidate close to alpha wolf is named as beta. GWO is mainly illustrated in three steps, namely chasing or tracking, encircling and attacking the prey. ROA is depending upon the behavior of riders group approaching the destination in different ways. The group of riders is classified into bypass rider, follower, over taker, and attacker. Finally, winner is selected depending upon the maximum success rate.

4.1 Solution Encoding

Solution encoding illustrates the solution, which is obtained using proposed Adaptive RGWO and to determine the exact position to place the symbols into data, where channel state is estimated by exploiting the training data obtained at end unit. Let us consider length of training data as l, and size of solution vector is denoted as $[1 \times h]$, such that $(h < l)$. Here, h represents the overall count of symbols utilized to construct the training data. The main challenge addressed using proposed adaptive RGWO is optimal positioning of h pilots. Figure 2 illustrates the solution vector.

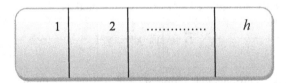

| 1 | 2 | .... | h |

Fig. 2. Solution vector

4.2 Fitness Function

The CE is determined depending upon fitness functions, which is a minimum value. The channel that offers minimum fitness function is considered to invoke the communication and fitness function is expressed as,

$$\mathfrak{I} = \left[\frac{O - O_{least}}{O} \right]^2 \tag{6}$$

Here, O and O_{least} denotes the original channel measure and estimated channel measure utilizing LS, respectively. The minimum function corresponding to training data enables automatic estimation of channel.

4.3 Algorithmic Steps of Proposed Adaptive RGWO for Pilot Design

The algorithmic steps involved in proposed adaptive RGWO is described as below:

Step 1: Initialization

The population of grey wolves is initialized with the optimization functions that enables switching between exploration and exploitation phase and it is mathematically expressed as follows,

$$\vec{X}_i; \ (1 \leq i \leq n) \tag{7}$$

Here, n denotes the number of search agents and position of ith search agent is indicated as $\vec{X}_i$. The optimization parameters consist of coefficient vectors $\vec{v_1}$ and $\vec{v_2}$, random numbers $\vec{y_1}$ and $\vec{y_2}$, and distance $\vec{D}$.

Step 2: Determine the fitness function

The fitness function is employed to estimate the desired solution for inserting symbols for channel detection and it is estimated using Eq. (6).

Step 3: Update position of search agent

In GWO, three phases are explained and the location of alpha, beta, and gamma are improved to evaluate location of food.

Encircling: In this phase, the wolf's position are updated based on the location of prey and it is given as,

$$\overrightarrow{X^{t+1}} = \vec{K^t} - \vec{v_1}.\vec{D} \tag{8}$$

Here, updated position of grey wolf is expressed as $\overrightarrow{X^{t+1}}$ and $\vec{K^t}$ represents previous iteration. The distance among prey and wolf is computed as,

$$\vec{D} = \left| \vec{v_2}.\vec{K^t} - \vec{X^t} \right| \tag{9}$$

where, t implies the iteration and location of wolf in preceding iteration is termed as $\vec{X^t}$. Moreover, $\vec{D}$ denotes the distance among grey wolf and prey. The coefficient vectors are represented as,

$$\vec{v_1} = 2\,\vec{g}.\vec{y_1} - \vec{g} \tag{10}$$

$$\vec{v_2} = 2\,\vec{y_2} \tag{11}$$

Here, $\vec{y_1}$ and $\vec{y_2}$ are made adaptive as,

$$\vec{y_1} = \vec{y_2} = \frac{1}{\left(1 + 1.5e^{-2.6g}\right)}; \quad g \in [0, 1] \tag{12}$$

Here, the values of $\vec{y_1}$ and $\vec{y_2}$ are considered as [0.4, 0.9].

Hunting: The second process in RGWO is hunting mechanism that is guided by alpha wolf. The alpha location is considered to be optimal location of the food. Hence, initial three solutions are estimated depending upon location of alpha, beta, and gamma and such three decisions are represented for enhancing the location of wolves in the group. The initial three solutions is represented as follows,

$$\vec{X_1} = \vec{X_\alpha} - \vec{v_1}.\vec{D_\alpha} \tag{13}$$

$$\vec{X_2} = \vec{X_\beta} - \vec{v_2}.\vec{D_\beta} \tag{14}$$

$$\vec{X_3} = \vec{X_\gamma} - \vec{v_3}.\vec{D_\gamma} \tag{15}$$

The attacker update expression from ROA is adopted to update Eq. (13) and update expression is given by,

$$\vec{X_1} = \vec{X_\alpha} + \left[Cos(Z).\vec{X_\alpha} \right] + D^t \tag{16}$$

Rearranging the above equation and it is given by,

$$\vec{X_1} = \vec{X_\alpha}[1 + Cos(Z)] + D^t \tag{17}$$

$$\vec{X_\alpha} = \frac{\vec{X_1} - D^t}{[1 + Cos(Z)]} \tag{18}$$

where, D^t implies the distance travelled by the rider, Z implies the steering angle and position of first rider is denoted as $\vec{X_\alpha}$. Substituting Eq. (18) in Eq. (13), the modified solution of proposed adaptive RGWO is given by,

$$\vec{X_1} = \frac{[1 + Cos(Z)]}{Cos(Z)} \left\{ \frac{-D^t}{[1 + Cos(Z)]} - \vec{v_1}.\vec{D_\alpha} \right\} \tag{19}$$

Therefore, the position of prey is evaluated as the mean of alpha, beta, and gamma is given by,

$$\overrightarrow{X(t+1)} = \frac{\vec{X_1} + \vec{X_2} + \vec{X_3}}{3} \tag{20}$$

The distance vectors are computed as,

$$\vec{D_\alpha} = \left| \vec{w_1}.\vec{X_\beta} - \vec{X} \right| \tag{21}$$

$$\vec{D_\beta} = \left| \vec{w_2}.\vec{X_\beta} - \vec{X} \right| \tag{22}$$

$$\vec{D_\gamma} = \left| \vec{w_3}.\vec{X_\gamma} - \vec{X} \right| \tag{23}$$

where, $\vec{D_\alpha}$, $\vec{D_\beta}$, and $\vec{D_\delta}$ are the distance vectors, and $\vec{w_1}$, $\vec{w_2}$, and $\vec{w_3}$ specifies the coefficient vectors.

Step 4: Update optimization parameters

The optimization factors $\vec{v_1}$, $\vec{D}$, and $\vec{g}$ are improved at last stage of every iteration for enhancing the position of wolf. The alpha, beta, and gamma wolves are updating its locations depending upon the parameter.

Step 5: Termination

The procedures are repeated until it achieves the desired solution. Algorithm 1 portrays pseudo code of proposed adaptive RGWO.

Algorithm 1: Pseudo code of proposed Adaptive RGWO

S.No	Pseudo code of proposed Adaptive RGWO
1	**Input:** $\overrightarrow{X_1}, \overrightarrow{X_2}, \overrightarrow{X_3}$
2	**Output:** $\overrightarrow{X(t+1)}$
3	Begin
4	Initialize the population $\overrightarrow{X_i}; (1 \le i \le n)$
5	Determine the fitness function using Eq. (6)
6	Update location of search agent using Eq. (19)
7	Update optimization parameters $\vec{v_1}, \vec{D}$, and $\vec{g}$
8	Terminate

5 Results and Discussion

This section explains results and discussion of Adaptive RGWO with respect to evaluation metrics.

5.1 Experimental Setup

The implementation of developed approach is done in MATLAB tool with windows 10 OS, 4 GB RAM, and intel core-i3 processor.

5.2 Evaluation Metrics

The performance of developed Adaptive RGWO is analyzed using performance measures, namely BER and MSE.

5.2.1 BER

BER is defined as the error occurred in the transmission model and it is computed as,

$$BER = \frac{E_{total}}{\lambda} \tag{24}$$

Here, E_{total} denotes the total errors occurred and λ indicates the total number of bits transmitted.

5.2.2 MSE

MSE is computed depending upon difference between actual value and determined value of channel and this MSE value should be minimum for effective solution.

5.3 Comparative Methods

The performance enhancement of Adaptive RGWO is compared and evaluated with conventional methods, such as Optimal Sequential Channel Estimation [6], Iterative + TC [11], GWO [21], ROA [5], and RGWO [22].

5.4 Comparative Analysis

This section elaborates the assessment of developed Adaptive RGWO uisng evaluation metrics by maximizing Signal to Noise Ratio (SNR) from 0 10 20 dB using two channels, namely Rayleigh channel and Rician channel.

5.4.1 Analysis Using Rayleigh Channel with 256 Carriers

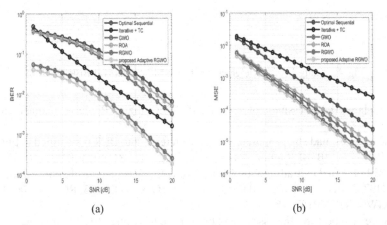

(a)   (b)

Fig. 3. Analysis of Rayleigh channel with 256 carriers (a) BER (b) MSE

Figure 3 portrays the assessment of developed Adaptive RGWO utilizing Rayleigh channel with 256 carriers.

Figure 3(a) illustrates the comparative assessment of proposed approach using BER by changing SNR from 0 to 20 dB. When SNR is 10 dB, BER achieved by proposed Adaptive RGWO is 0.007768213, whereas the existing approaches attained BER of 0.120639624 for optimal sequential channel estimation, 0.025347319 for Iterative + TC, 0.0845525 for GWO, 0.09893875 for ROA, and 0.010348633 for RGWO. By increasing SNR to 20 dB, BER obtained by conventional techniques, such as optimal sequential channel estimation, Iterative + TC, GWO, ROA, and RGWO is 0.006332394, 0.001565402, 0.00314, 0.005015, and 0.00024668. However, BER achieved by proposed Adaptive RGWO is 0.000179077.

Figure 3(b) specifies the comparative assessment of proposed Adaptive RGWO in terms of MSE. If SNR is 10 dB, MSE obtained by proposed approach is 0.000124858, whereas the conventional methods attained the MSE of 0.000734789 for optimal sequential channel estimation, 0.002315099 for Iterative + TC, 0.000206598 for GWO, 0.000263866 for ROA, and 0.000147196 for RGWO.

5.4.2 Analysis Using Rayleigh Channel with 512 Carriers

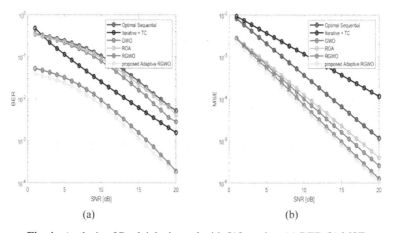

(a)   (b)

Fig. 4. Analysis of Rayleigh channel with 512 carriers (a) BER (b) MSE

Figure 4 shows the assessment of Adaptive RGWO utilizing Rayleigh channel with 512 carriers.

The analysis made by proposed scheme with respect to BER is specified in Fig. 4(a). When SNR is 20 dB, BER attained by proposed Adaptive RGWO is 0.000150403. However, BER obtained by traditional schemes like optimal sequential channel estimation is 0.005249765, Iterative + TC is 0.001565402, GWO is 0.0028425, ROA is 0.00414875, and RGWO is 0.000187988.

Figure 4(b) portrays the assessment of proposed Adaptive RGWO in terms of MSE. If SNR is 20 dB, MSE yielded by conventional methods, such as optimal sequential channel estimation is 0.0000116, Iterative + TC is 0.000116, GWO is 0.00000257, ROA is 0.00000403, and RGWO is 0.00000127. However, the MSE achieved by proposed Adaptive RGWO is 0.00000105.

5.4.3 Analysis Using Rayleigh Channel with 768 Carriers

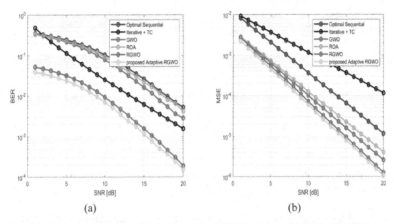

(a)   (b)

Fig. 5. Analysis of Rayleigh channel with 768 carriers (a) BER (b) MSE

Figure 5 portrays the assessment of developed Adaptive RGWO utilizing Rayleigh channel with 768 carriers.

Figure 5(a) illustrates the comparative assessment of proposed approach using BER by changing SNR from 0 to 20 dB. When SNR is 10 dB, BER achieved by proposed Adaptive RGWO is 0.010333, whereas the existing approaches attained BER of 0.145857 for optimal sequential channel estimation, 0.033895 for Iterative + TC, 0.108469 for GWO, 0.123265 for ROA, and 0.013557 for RGWO. By increasing SNR to 20 dB, BER obtained by conventional techniques, such as optimal sequential channel estimation, Iterative + TC, GWO, ROA, and RGWO is 0.008866, 0.002055, 0.004473, 0.006546, and 0.000363. However, BER achieved by proposed Adaptive RGWO is 0.000264.

Figure 5(b) specifies the comparative assessment of proposed Adaptive RGWO in terms of MSE. If SNR is 10 dB, MSE obtained by proposed approach is 0.000125, whereas the conventional methods attained the MSE of 0.000735 for optimal sequential channel estimation, 0.002315 for Iterative + TC, 0.000207 for GWO, 0.000264 for ROA, and 0.000147 for RGWO.

5.4.4 Analysis Using Rician Channel with 256 Carriers

Figure 6 represents the assessment of developed Adaptive RGWO employing Rician channel with 256 carriers.

Figure 6(a) illustrates the assessment of proposed approach using BER. By considering the SNR as 20dB, BER achieved by proposed Adaptive RGWO is 0.00000359, whereas the existing techniques attained BER of 0.0000819 for optimal sequential channel estimation, 0.001565 for Iterative + TC, 0.0000413 for GWO, 0.00004505 for ROA, and 0.00000264 for RGWO.

The analysis of proposed Adaptive RGWO in terms of MSE is illustrated in Fig. 6(b). If SNR is 20 dB, MSE yielded by proposed Adaptive RGWO is 0.00000224. However,

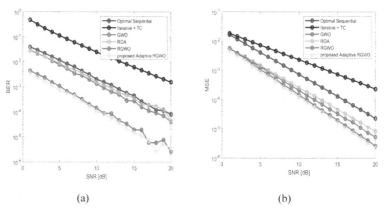

Fig. 6. Analysis of Rician channel with 256 carriers (a) BER (b) MSE

MSE obtained by existing methods, such as optimal sequential channel estimation is 0.0000233, Iterative + TC is 0.000233, GWO is 0.00000532, ROA is 0.00000836, and RGWO is 0.00000261.

5.4.5   Analysis Using Rician Channel with 512 Carriers

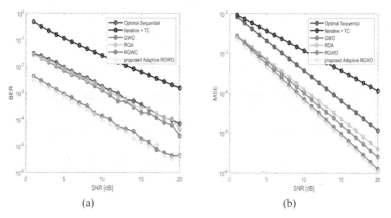

Fig. 7. Analysis of Rician channel with 512 carriers (a) BER (b) MSE

Figure 7 portrays comparative assessment of Adaptive RGWO utilizing Rician channel with 512 carriers.

Figure 7(a) depicts the assessment of Adaptive RGWO with respect to BER. When SNR is 10 dB, BER yielded by Adaptive RGWO is 0.000156042, whereas traditional methods attained BER of 0.002618779 for optimal sequential channel estimation, 0.033894854 for Iterative + TC, 0.001836563 for GWO, 0.002330938 for ROA, and 0.000171387 for RGWO. By increasing SNR to 20d B, the proposed Adaptive RGWO obtained BER of 0.00000410. However, BER achieved by existing techniques, like optimal sequential channel estimation is 0.0000693, Iterative + TC is 0.001565, GWO is 0.0000244, ROA is 0.0000422, and RGWO is 0.0000444.

Figure 7(b) shows the comparative assessment of proposed Adaptive RGWO in terms of MSE. When SNR is 10 dB, MSE yielded by proposed method is 0.0000606 and conventional schemes attained MSE of 0.000368747 for optimal sequential channel estimation, 0.001165882 for Iterative + TC, 0.000102787 for GWO, 0.000125819 for ROA, and 0.0000715 for RGWO. By considering SNR as 20d B, MSE obtained by proposed Adaptive RGWO is 0.00000106, whereas MSE attained by conventional techniques, such as optimal sequential channel estimation is 0.0000116, Iterative + TC is 0.000116, GWO is 0.00000257, ROA is 0.00000403, and RGWO is, 0.00000127.

5.4.6   Analysis Using Rician Channel with 768 Carriers

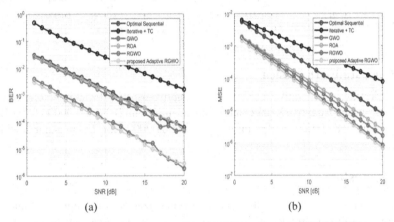

Fig. 8. Analysis of Rician channel with 768 carriers (a) BER (b) MSE

Figure 8 represents the assessment of developed Adaptive RGWO employing Rician channel with 256 carriers.

Figure 8(a) illustrates the assessment of proposed approach using BER. By considering the SNR as 20 dB, BER achieved by proposed Adaptive RGWO is 2.78E-06, whereas 0.001565 for Iterative + TC, 5.06E-05 for GWO, 4.56E-05 for ROA, and 1.82E-06 for RGWO.

The analysis of proposed Adaptive RGWO in terms of MSE is illustrated in Fig. 8(b). If SNR is 20 dB, MSE yielded by proposed Adaptive RGWO is 6.94E-07. However, MSE obtained by existing methods, such as optimal sequential channel estimation is 7.82E-06, Iterative + TC is 7.80E-05, GWO is 1.67E-06, ROA is 2.66E-06, and RGWO is 8.45E-07.

Table 1. Comparative discussion of adaptive RGWO

Channel	Carriers	Metrics/Methods	Optimal sequential channel estimation	Iterative + TC	GWO	ROA	RGWO	Proposed Adaptive RGWO
Rayleigh channel	256	BER	0.0063	0.0015	0.0031	0.0050	0.00024	0.00017
		MSE	0.00002	0.0002	0.000005	0.000009	0.0000026	0.000002
	512	BER	0.0052	0.0015	0.0028	0.004	0.00018	0.00015
		MSE	0.00001	0.0001	0.000002	0.000004	0.000001	0.0000010
	768	BER	0.00525	0.00157	0.00284	0.00415	0.000188	0.00015
		MSE	0.000012	0.000116	0.000003	0.000004	0.0000013	0.000001
Rician channel	256	BER	0.00008	0.0015	0.00004	0.00004	0.000002	0.000003
		MSE	0.00002	0.00023	0.00000532	0.00000836	0.00000261	0.000002
	512	BER	0.00006	0.0015	0.000024	0.0000422	0.0000444	0.000004
		MSE	0.00001	0.0001	0.000002	0.000004	0.000001	0.000001
	768	BER	0.000062	0.00157	0.000051	0.000046	0.0000018	0.0000028
		MSE	0.0000078	0.000078	0.000002	0.000003	0.0000084	0.0000069

5.5 Comparative Discussion

Table 1 portrays comparative discussion of Adaptive RGWO. From the table, it is clear that the proposed Adaptive RGWO has achieved minimum BER of 0.0000028 for Rician channel with 768 carriers, and minimum MSE of 0.000001 for Rician channel with 512 carriers.

6 Conclusion

CR is a promising technology that allows unauthorized SUs to improve efficiency of spectrum utilization. In CR, channel estimation is the necessary parameter and it is more significant to ensure reliable spectrum sensing. The best position to insert the pilot symbols is very substantial for channel estimation in CR and this will considerably improve the spectrum effectiveness and mitigates the spectrum shortage. Therefore, an efficient strategy is developed for channel estimation in CR. The optimization of the pilot design in CR system is developed based on LS channel detection where locations to place the symbols is determined using proposed algorithm named Adaptive RGWO. The developed adaptive RGWO is derived by the integration of adaptive principle with ROA and GWO. Moreover, proposed Adaptive RGWO has achieved minimum BER of 0.0000028 for Rician channel with 768 carriers and minimum MSE of 0.000001 for Rician channel with 512 carriers that shows superior results while comparing it with the conventional methods.

References

1. Lee, W., Akyildiz, I.F.: Optimal spectrum sensing framework for cognitive radio networks. IEEE Trans. Wireless Commun. **7**(10), 3845–3857 (2008). https://doi.org/10.1109/T-WC.2008.070391

2. Liang, Y., Zeng, Y., Peh, E.C.Y., Hoang, A.T.: Sensing-throughput tradeoff for cognitive radio networks. IEEE Trans. Wireless Commun. **7**(4), 1326–1337 (2008). https://doi.org/10.1109/TWC.2008.060869

3. Caromi, R., Xin, Y., Lai, L.: Fast multiband spectrum scanning for cognitive radio systems. IEEE Trans. Commun. **61**(1), 63–75 (2013). https://doi.org/10.1109/TCOMM.2012.101712. 110599

4. Zou, J., Xiong, H., Wang, D., Chen, C.W.: Optimal power allocation for hybrid overlay/underlay spectrum sharing in multiband cognitive radio networks. IEEE Trans. Veh. Technol. **62**(4), 1827–1837 (2013). https://doi.org/10.1109/TVT.2012.2235152

5. Binu, D., Kariyappa, B.S.: RideNN: a new rider optimization algorithm-based neural network for fault diagnosis in analog circuits. IEEE Trans. Instrum. Meas. **68**(1), 2–26 (2018)

6. Caromi, R., Mohan, S., Lai, L.: Optimal sequential channel estimation and probing for multiband cognitive radio systems. IEEE Trans. Commun. **62**(8), 2696–2708 (2014)

7. Hongzhi, M., Zhao, N., Jin, M., Kim, J.M.: Optimal transceiver design for interference alignment based cognitive radio networks. IEEE Commun. Lett. **19**(8), 1442–1445 (2015)

8. Mary, S.A., Nakkeeran, R., Shinu, M.J.: Pilot based mmse channel estimation for spatial modulated OFDM systems. Int. J. Electron. Telecommun. **67.4**, 685–691 (2021)

9. Qi, C., Yue, G., Lenan, W., Nallanathan, A.: Pilot design for sparse channel estimation in OFDM-based cognitive radio systems. IEEE Trans. Veh. Technol. **63**(2), 982–987 (2013)

10. Nicola, M., et al.: Generalized frequency division multiplexing for 5th generation cellular networks. IEEE Trans. Commun. **62**(9), 3045–3061 (2014)

11. Zhenyu, N., et al.: Turbo receiver channel estimation for GFDM-based cognitive radio networks. IEEE Access **6**, 9926–9935 (2018)

12. Ahmad, B.R.S., Saltzberg, B.R., Ergen, M.: Multi-carrier Digital Communications: Theory and Applications Of OFDM. Springer Science & Business Media (2004)

13. Abu, H.M.S., Ahmad, R.B.: Variable pilot channels estimation based on blocktype and combtype pilot arrangement in OFDM system. In: 2016 3rd International Conference on Electronic Design (ICED). IEEE (2016)

14. Inaki, E., et al.: DVB-T2: the second generation of terrestrial digital video broadcasting system. IEEE Trans. Broadcast. **60.2**, 258–271 (2014)

15. Bai, Q., Wang, J., Zhang, Y., Song, J.: Deep learning-based channel estimation algorithm over time selective fading channels. IEEE Trans. Cogn. Commun. Network. **6**(1), 125–134 (2019)

16. Ove, E., et al.: OFDM channel estimation by singular value decomposition. IEEE Trans. Commun. **46.7**, 931–939 (1998)

17. van de Beek, J.-J., Edfors, O., Sandell, M., Wilson, S.K., Borjesson, P.O.: On channel estimation in OFDM systems. In: 1995 IEEE 45th Vehicular Technology Conference. Countdown to the Wireless Twenty-First Century, vol. 2, pp. 815–819 (1995). https://doi.org/10.1109/VETEC.1995.504981

18. Liu, M., Wang, H., Li, Y., Li, P.: Research on pilot-based channel estimation algorithms. In: 2019 IEEE 5th International Conference on Computer and Communications (ICCC), pp. 758–761 (2019). https://doi.org/10.1109/ICCC47050.2019.9064187

19. Kakalou, I., Psannis, K.E., Krawiec, P., Badea, R.: Cognitive radio network and network service chaining toward 5G: challenges and requirements. IEEE Commun. Mag. **55**(11), 145–151 (2017). https://doi.org/10.1109/MCOM.2017.1700086

20. Huda, A.A., Khazal, H.F., Jamel, T.M.: Time Domain Pilot-Based Channel Estimation (TDPCE) using Kalman Filtering for OFDM system. In: IOP Conference Series: Materials Science and Engineering, vol. 1090, no. 1. IOP Publishing (2021)

21. Mirjalili, S., Mirjalili, S.M., Lewis, A.: Grey wolf optimizer. Adv. Eng. Software **69**, 46–61 (2014). https://doi.org/10.1016/j.advengsoft.2013.12.007

22. Raghunatharao, D., Prasad, T.J., Giri Prasad, M.N.: Optimal pilot-based channel estimation in cognitive radio. Wireless Pers. Commun. **114**(4), 2801–2819 (2020). https://doi.org/10.1007/s11277-020-07504-x

23. Demestichas, P., Katidiotis, A., Tsagkaris, K.A., et al.: Enhancing channel estimation in cognitive radio systems by means of bayesian networks. Wireless Pers. Commun. **49**, 87–105 (2009). https://doi.org/10.1007/s11277-008-9559-1

24. Awe, O.P., Babatunde, D.A., Lambotharan, S., AsSadhan, B.: Second order Kalman filtering channel estimation and machine learning methods for spectrum sensing in cognitive radio networks. Wireless Netw. **27**(5), 3273–3286 (2021). https://doi.org/10.1007/s11276-021-02627-w

To Identify Malware Using Machine Learning Algorithms

Shivam Pujari[✉], H. L. Mandoria, R. P. Shrivastava, and Rajesh Singh

Govind Ballabh Pant University of Agriculture and Technology, Pantnagar 263145, Uttarakhand,
India
shivampj@gmail.com

Abstract. Today's world depends on cyberspace since it is very useful for collecting information, data and transporting them in a secured manner. This security
may be broken by various attackers by injecting malware to another device through
various ways such as malicious links generally. Malware is like software that may
harm the system of the user. The most commonly used malware nowadays is ransomware coverts files or any data to unused form by encryption and demands
money for regaining original data. So we need a method to detect it to stop it to
work in any condition like updating its signature etc. We propose a method to
identify different types of malwares including ransomware with the use of API
call data. We achieve the highest accuracy of 0.9636.

Keywords: Malware · Feature extraction · Feature selection · Machine
learning · Weka explorer

1 Introduction

Malware word can be divided into two words 'mal'+'ware' where mal refers to malicious
activity and ware represent software. Hence, we can say the malware is a malicious
activity in software. The common name for a variety of malicious variants of applications,
including viruses, ransomware and spyware, is malware. Malware usually consists of
cyber-attacker-developed code intended to inflict significant data and device harm or to
obtain unauthorized access to a network.

Usually, malware is sent by email in the form of a connection or file which needs
the recipient to select the link or open the file to execute the malware.

The malware which we use in our research is- TeslaCrypt, Vawtrak, Zeus,
DarkComet, CTBLocker, CyberGate, Xtreme, Locky Ransomware and Dridex.

2 Related Work

Shankarapani et al. (2010) present algorithms for identification that can enable the
antivirus community to guarantee a version of a known malware without having to
establish a signature, which can always be detected. By the study of comparisons (based

© Springer Nature Switzerland AG 2022
N. Chaubey et al. (Eds.): COMS2 2022, CCIS 1604, pp. 117–127, 2022.
https://doi.org/10.1007/978-3-031-10551-7_9

on specific quantitative measures), A matrix of similarity scores that can be generated is performed to determine the likelihood that a piece of code under inspection contains a particular malware. The authors present two methods- SAVE and MEDiC.

MEDiC uses analysis assembly calls and SAVE uses API calls for analysis (Static API call series and Static API call set). Authors illustrate where assembly can be superior to API calls. This provides a more rigorous comparison of executables. On the other hand, API calls may be superior to Assembly for their speed and smaller signature. A better detection efficiency can be given by both proposed techniques against obfuscated malware.

Alazeb et al. (2011), employed Zero-day Identification of Malware based on Supervised Learning Algorithms, the API functions were used for feature representation, repeatedly. With the Help Vector Machines algorithm, the best result was obtained with a normalized polykernel. 97.6% accuracy was reached, with a false positive rate of 0.025.

Amin Kharraz et al. (2015) proposed "A Look Under the Hood of Ransomware Attacks" studied ransomware attacks between 2006 and 2014. It tells that we can detect and stop zero-day ransomware attacks by keeping a view of I/O requests and securing the MFT (Master File Table) in the NTFS. The authors suggest mitigating ransomware attacks, system need real-time monitoring.

Sgandurra et al. (2016) have suggested EldeRan tool, which checks characteristic signatures of ransomware by examining a collection of actions in the initial phases of the kill-chain assault flow. EldeRan detects and categorizes Ransomware dynamically by evaluating tasks such as registry operations, Key operations, Windows API calls, directories, and Files operations of a machine. Logical Regression by EldeRanuses to identify each user's classifier algorithm and ML algorithm application, which has additional features for defining and identifying for yet unknown ransomware, build signatures.

Carlin et al. (2017) highlighted the low-level study of both Dynamic and static opcodes to detect malware on the 1,000 samples of labels in the runtime dataset to influence the typical AV labels. They obtained the dataset from VirusShare. The reviewer chose the scale and facility modality. There are 180,000 malware records, and these records are called by MD5 hash with no other metadata. The highest accuracy is 98.4%.

Vinayakumar et al. (2017) proposed "Evaluating Shallow and Deep Networks for Ransomware Detection and Classification" talks about the supervised machine learning method of detection of ransomware. Multi-layer perceptron (MLP) is used for ransomware detection and classification. It proposed a method using API calls for ransomware detection. As a feature for classification, it uses 131 API calls which is the input of MLP architecture.

Takeuchi et al. (2018) introduced Ransomware Detection using Support Vector Machines (SVMs). There are 588 samples in the dataset, which have 312 benign and 276 Ransomware. Virus Total is used to obtain these samples. The authors developed the same vector symbols with different sequences of API calls. The author checked and educated the classifier of the SVM data type. The normal vector symbol accuracy is 93.52%, and 97.48% is the best SVM accuracy.

Greg et al. (2018) recommended the technique of network management for data from traffic so that features can be extracted from it. Those features are used in the classification of ransomware and the used algorithm is Random Forest Binary Classifier. They say the rate of detection is 86%.

3   Proposed Methods

We purposed the method in which we used different machine learning algorithms for the classification of different malware. In this section, we will describe the architecture of our proposed system. Our proposed detection system is attempting to improve the performance of malware detection using API call data.

This system has main modules of raw feature extraction and applying learning algorithms for classification.

3.1   Feature Extraction

We ought to be able to extract the Attributes from the input data such that the algorithm can be fed to it. For instance, In the case of house prices, knowledge may be viewed as a multidimensional Matrix, where an attribute is represented by each column and rows represent the attribute for these properties, numerical values. In the case of the image, it can be data each pixel is interpreted as an RGB color. These features are referred to as traits, and the matrix is known as the Vector of functions. The data extraction method from the files is referred to as Feature Extraction. The purpose of extracting features is to acquire a non-redundant collection of insightful Data. It is crucial to understand that characteristics can reflect the important and valid details regarding our dataset because we do not have them. An exact forecast cannot be made. That is why the extraction of features is always a Non-obvious assignment, which involves a lot of study and checking. Additionally, it is Quite domain-specific, but generic approaches apply badly here.

Non-redundancy is another major prerequisite for a good feature set. Getting redundant characteristics, i.e., characteristics that outline the same data as well as redundant attributes of knowledge, which depend closely on each other's will skew the algorithm and thus have an incorrect Outcome.

Furthermore, if the input data is too large to be fed into the algorithm (has too many characteristics), it can be translated to a reduced vector function (vector, having a smaller number of features). The phase of diminishing the measurements of the vector is referred to as function collection. After this operation, the chosen features are supposed to detail the related data from the Initial set so that, without any precision loss, it can be used instead of initial data.

It is essential to express raw data in some meaningful forms so that we can use it. We use the cuckoo sandbox for feature extraction. Cuckoo sandbox supports a virtual system and monitors the file. We identified the registry key processes IP address and API call as features.

We select API call as a feature because it full fill all requirements. API call outlines everything happening to the operating system. any action we do in the file may be viewed as an API call.

After taking API call sequences of various files including malware we use these data as a training dataset of the machine learning model. We used four machine learning algorithm which is suitable for classification. These classifiers are naïve bayes, Regression, J48 and Random Forest.

4 Experiment

All the experiment is done on Intel (R) Core i54210U CPU machine with 1.70 GHz processor, 32.00 GB of memory. The Microsoft Windows 10 pro is installed on this machine. Ransomware and benign software is analyzed in the Virtual Machine for 20 s. We choose the small running time of 20 s for selecting relevant features before the infection of ransomware in the machine.

4.1 Dataset

We collect 3000 files in which 2000 files are malicious and 1000 files are benign. Malicious files include dridex, ctb-locker cybergate, teslacrypt, zeus, vawtrak, dark comet Xtreme, and locky.

4.2 Cuckoo Sandbox

Cuckoo Sandbox is the platform for investigating open-source malware that makes it easy to get Any file or URL has a comprehensive behavioral analysis in a matter of seconds. We use it in a virtual environment for extracting features.

4.3 Classification

After feature selection of data we trained that data with the help of weka 3.8.5 data mining framework. After that, we took a test dataset of 1156 instances in which 173 samples are benign.

Naïve Bayes Classifier: It classifies data with the assumption of independence among predictors based on Bayes' Theorem. A Naive Bayes classifier believes, in basic terms, that the inclusion of a certain function in a class is unrelated to the existence of any other feature. For example, a fruit may be considered to be a watermelon if it is yellow, round, and about 5 inches in diameter. Even if these characteristics depend on each other or on the presence of the other characteristics, all of these characteristics individually lead to the possibility that this fruit is watermelon and that's why it's known as 'Naive.'

Regression: It is a supervised type of machine learning which predicts resultant value based on given related input features. Forecasting and trend analysis is the main application of it.

J48 Decision Tree: J48 is the improvement of ID3 algorithms (Iterative Dichotomiser 3) developed by WEKA. For constructing a decision tree, it uses both the greedy and top-down approaches.

Random Forest Classifier: Supervised learning ensemble methods which create a forest with n numbers of decision trees. It is developed for both classification and regression analysis. It shows the highest accuracy in comparison to other ensemble methods.

Bagging: Bagging is also called bootstrap aggregation. This is an ensemble learning technique often used to minimize variance in the noisy dataset. This technique selects a random sample of data from a training set in which any data points might be taken many times. These weak models are then trained individually after multiple data samples are collected and depending on the kind of tasks such as regression or classification—the average or majority of those predictions provide a more accurate estimate.

4.4 Weka

Weka is a knowledge analysis environment developed by the University of Waikato. Weka can classify data by machine learning in one click simply. We can apply weka algo on the direct dataset by weka preprocess option in weka explorer or we can call these algorithms by our java program code. Java is used to write weka, so as java is machine-independent it is also open-source and we can use weka on any platform.

5 Result

We obtained desired results from different classifiers as below-

5.1 Naïve Bayes Classifier

Out of 1156 instances 968 instances are classified accurately while 168 instances are classified incorrectly. Hence accuracy is 0. 8373.

=== Summary ===

Correctly Classified Instances	988	85.4671 %
Incorrectly Classified Instances	168	14.5329 %
Kappa statistic	0.838	
Mean absolute error	0.0291	
Root mean squared error	0.1691	
Relative absolute error	16.2603 %	
Root relative squared error	56.5474 %	
Total Number of Instances	1156	

confusion matrix is shown below:

a	b	c	d	e	f	g	h	i	j		<-- classified as
112	12	0	0	18	4	0	3	6	18	|	a = Benign
2	113	1	0	0	2	1	0	0	6	|	b = Dridex
2	0	89	0	0	1	0	0	1	2	|	c = Locky
0	1	0	110	0	1	0	0	0	1	|	d = Teslacrypt
5	11	0	1	46	1	0	2	2	6	|	e = Vawlrak
7	4	0	1	4	82	1	0	2	15	|	f = Zeus
1	0	0	0	0	2	128	0	0	0	|	g = DarkComet
0	1	0	0	0	0	7	120	0	1	|	h = CyberGate
3	0	0	1	0	2	3	0	112	0	|	i = Xtreme
2	0	1	0	0	0	0	0	0	76	|	j = CTB-Locker

5.2 Regression Classifier

Out of 1156 instances 1094 instances are classified accurately while 62 instances are classified incorrectly. Hence accuracy is 0.9463.

=== Summary ===

Correctly Classified Instances	1094	94.6367 %
Incorrectly Classified Instances	62	5.3633 %
Kappa statistic	0.9401	
Mean absolute error	0.0262	
Root mean squared error	0.0984	
Relative absolute error	14.6472 %	
Root relative squared error	32.8856 %	

confusion matrix is shown below:

=== Confusion Matrix ===

a	b	c	d	e	f	g	h	i	j		<-- classified as
171	0	1	0	0	0	1	0	0	0	|	a = Benign
0	113	2	2	6	1	0	0	0	1	|	b = Dridex
0	0	90	0	2	1	0	0	0	2	|	c = Locky
0	1	0	110	1	0	0	0	0	1	|	d = Teslacrypt
0	2	1	1	65	4	0	1	0	0	|	e = Vawlrak
0	3	0	0	6	102	3	1	0	1	|	f = Zeus
0	1	0	0	1	1	128	0	0	0	|	g = DarkComet
0	1	0	0	0	3	6	119	0	0	|	h = CyberGate
0	0	1	0	0	0	0	1	119	0	|	i = Xtreme
0	0	0	0	2	0	0	0	0	77	|	j = CTB-Locker

5.3 J48

Out of 1156 instances 1086 instances are classified accurately while 70 instances are classified incorrectly. Hence accuracy is 0.9394.

=== Summary ===

Correctly Classified Instances	1086	93.9446 %
Incorrectly Classified Instances	70	6.0554 %
Kappa statistic	0.9323	
Mean absolute error	0.014	
Root mean squared error	0.1073	
Relative absolute error	7.8154 %	
Root relative squared error	35.8607 %	
Total Number of Instances	1156	

confusion matrix is shown below:

```
=== Confusion Matrix ===

    a   b   c   d   e   f   g   h   i   j   <-- classified as
  173   0   0   0   0   0   0   0   0   0 |  a = Benign
    0 114   0   0   3   7   0   1   0   0 |  b = Dridex
    0   1  87   1   2   1   0   1   2   0 |  c = Locky
    0   0   0 111   1   0   0   1   0   0 |  d = Teslacrypt
    0   4   1   1  62   4   0   1   0   1 |  e = Vawlrak
    0   6   3   2   4  95   1   2   1   2 |  f = Zeus
    0   0   0   1   0   0 127   3   0   0 |  g = DarkComet
    0   2   0   0   0   1   5 121   0   0 |  h = CyberGate
    0   0   0   0   1   0   0   0 120   0 |  i = Xtreme
    0   0   0   0   2   1   0   0   0  76 |  j = CTB-Locker
```

5.4 Random Forest Classifier

Out of 1156 instances 1114 instances are classified accurately while 42 instances are classified incorrectly. Hence accuracy is 0.9636.

```
=== Summary ===
Correctly Classified Instances        1114          96.3668 %
Incorrectly Classified Instances      42            3.6332 %
Kappa statistic                       0.9594
Mean absolute error                   0.021
Root mean squared error               0.0853
Relative absolute error               11.747 %
Root relative squared error           28.5303 %
Total Number of Instances             1156
```

=== Confusion Matrix ===

```
  a    b   c   d   e    f   g   h   i   j   <-- classified as
171    1   0   0   0    1   0   0   0   0 |   a = Benign
  2  116   0   0   2    4   0   0   0   1 |   b = Dridex
  0    0  92   0   2    0   0   1   0   0 |   c = Locky
  0    0   0 112   1    0   0   0   0   0 |   d = Teslacrypt
  2    0   0   0  72    0   0   0   0   0 |   e = Vawlrak
  3    2   1   0   5  104   1   0   0   0 |   f = Zeus
  1    0   0   0   0    0 130   0   0   0 |   g = DarkComet
  1    0   0   0   0    1   7 120   0   0 |   h = CyberGate
  1    0   0   0   0    0   0   0 120   0 |   i = Xtreme
  1    1   0   0   0    0   0   0   0  77 |   j = CTB-Locker
```

5.5 Bagging

Out of 1156 instances 1102 instances are classified accurately while 54 instances are classified incorrectly. Hence accuracy is 0.9532.

```
=== Summary ===


Correctly Classified Instances       1102          95.3287 %

Incorrectly Classified Instances     54            4.6713 %

Kappa statistic                      0.9478

Mean absolute error                  0.0223

Root mean squared error              0.0921

Relative absolute error              12.4806 %

Root relative squared error          30.7795 %

Total Number of Instances            1156
```

```
    a   b   c   d   e   f   g   h   i   j  <-- classified as
  173   0   0   0   0   0   0   0   0   0 |   a = Benign
    0 116   0   0   5   4   0   0   0   0 |   b = Dridex
    0   0  90   0   1   2   0   0   0   2 |   c = Locky
    0   0   0 111   2   0   0   0   0   0 |   d = Teslacrypt
    0   3   1   0  69   1   0   0   0   0 |   e = Vawlrak
    0   3   2   1   9  97   0   0   2   2 |   f = Zeus
    0   0   0   1   0   1 128   1   0   0 |   g = DarkComet
    0   1   0   0   0   1   6 121   0   0 |   h = CyberGate
    0   0   0   0   0   0   0   0 121   0 |   i = Xtreme
    0   1   0   0   1   1   0   0   0  76 |   j = CTB-Locker
```

We got the Random Forest Classifier has the highest accuracy of 0.9636. The average result of other classification algorithms are given below (Table 1)

Table 1. Comparison of the algorithm in accuracy.

Classifier	Avg TPR	Avg FPR	Fmeasure	Accuracy
Random Forest	0.964	0.004	0.964	0.9636
Regressio n	0.946	0.005	0.947	0.9463
J48	0.939	0.006	0.939	0.9394
Naïve Bayes	0.855	0.015	0.853	0.8373
Bagging	0.953	0.005	0.953	0.9532

6   Conclusion

We have proposed detection of malware and classification with higher accuracy. We have used four classification algorithms to detect malware. We identified malware which success rate is different for different algorithms. Random Forest, Naïve Bayes, Regression and J48 classifier are used for detection which shows accuracy of 0.9636, 0.8373, 0.9463 and 0.9394 respectively. Thus, Random Forest shows the highest accuracy of 0.9636. J48 and Naïve Bayes classifier shows higher accuracy than previous work and Random Forest find almost equal accuracy. We have classified different types of malware which are dridex, locky, teslacrypt, vawtrak, zeus, dark comet, cybergate, Xtreme, and CTB-locker. Thus, we have become successful to detect malware like dridex, vawtrak, dark-comet, and cyber gate using this method. Our method is suitable to classify and detect the polymorphic behavior of malware.

References

Alazab, RVM., Soman, K.P., Poornachandran, P., Nemrat, A., Venkatraman, S.: Deep learning approach for intelligent intrusion detection system. IEEE Access **7**, 41525–41550 (2019)

Alhawi, O.M.K., Baldwin, J., Dehghantanha, A.: Leveraging machine learning techniques for windows ransomware network traffic detection. In: Dehghantanha, A., Conti, M., Dargahi, T. (eds.) Cyber Threat Intelligence. AIS, vol. 70, pp. 93–106. Springer, Cham (2018). https://doi.org/10.1007/978-3-319-73951-9_5

Brewer, R.: LogRhythm, Ransomware attacks: detection, prevention and cure. Netw. Secur. **9**, 5–9 (2016)

Cabaj, K., Gregorczyk, M., Mazurczyk, W.: Software-defined networking-based crypto ransomware detection using HTTP traffic characteristics. Int. J. Comput. Electr. Eng. **66**(8), 353–368 (2018)

Carlin, D., Cowan, A., Kane, P., Sezer, S.: The effects of traditional antivirus labels on malware detection using dynamic runtime opcodes. IEEE Access **5**, 17742–17752 (2017)

Chen, J., Wang, C., Zhao, Z., Chen, K., Du, R., Ahn, G.J.: Uncovering the face of android ransomware: characterization and real-time detection. IEEE Trans. Inf. Forensic Secur. **13**(5), 286–300 (2018)

Cusack, G., Michel, O., Keller, E.: Machine learning-based detection of ransomware using SDN. In: ACM International Workshop on Security in Software Defined Networks and Network Function Virtualization at USA, during 12–15 August, pp. 1–6 (2018)

Haddadi, F., Khanchi, S., Shetabi, M., Derhami, V.: Intrusion detection and attack classification using feedforward neural network. In: 2010 Second International Conference on Computer and Network Technology at USA, during 8–12 July, pp. 262–266 (2010)

Manoun, A., Robert, L., Paul, W.: Malware detection based on structural and behavioral features of API calls. In: International Cyber Resilience Conference' at Perth (Western Australia), during 20–23 August, pp. 13–19 (2011)

Michael, H.L., Andrew, C., Jamie, L.: The art of memory forensics: detecting malware and threats in windows, linux, and mac memory. Int. J. Comput. Secur. **21**, 78–84 (2014)

Pundir, S.L.: Feature selection using random forest in intrusion detection system. Int. J. Adv. Eng. **6**(3), 13–19 (2013)

Rai, M., Mandoria, H.L.: A study on cyber crimes, cyber criminals and major security breaches. Int. Res. J. Eng. Technol. **6**(7), 233–240 (2019)

Rhode, M., Burnap, P., Jones, K.: Early-stage malware prediction using recurrent neural networks. Int. J. Comput. Secur. **77**, 578–594 (2018)

Salman, T., Bhamare, D., Erbad, A., Jain, R., Samaka, M.: Machine learning for anomaly detection and categorization in multi-cloud environments. In: 2017 IEEE 4th International Conference on Cyber Security and Cloud Computing, at New York (USA), during 26–28 June, pp. 97–103 (2017)

Scaife, N., Carter, H., Traynor, P., Butler, K.R.B.: CryptoLock (and Drop It): stopping ransomware attacks on user data. In: 2016 IEEE 36th International Conference on Distributed Computing Systems' at Nara (Japan), during 27–30 June, pp. 303–312 (2016)

Scalas, M., Maiorca, D., Mercaldo, F., Visaggio, C.A., Martinelli, F., Giacinto, G.: On the effectiveness of system API-related information for android ransomware detection. Comput. Secur. **86**, 168182 (2019)

Sgandurra, D., Munoz, L., Mohsen, R., Lupu, E.C.: Automated dynamic analysis of ransomware: Benefits, limitations and use for detection. IEEE Access **9**, 42–45 (2016)

Shankarapani, M.K., Ramamoorthy, S., Movva, R.S., Mukkamala, S.: Malware detection using assembly and API call sequences. J. Comput. Virol. **7**(2), 107–119 (2010)

Shaukat, S.K., Ribeiro, V.J.: RansomWall- a layered defense system against cryptographic ransomware attacks using machine learning. In: 2018 10th International Conference on Communication Systems and Networks at Bengaluru, during 3–7 January, pp. 356–363 (2018)

Shukla, M., Mondal, S., Lodha, S.: Virtualized environment for mitigating ransomware threats. In: Proceedings of the 2016 ACM SIGSAC Conference on Computer and Communications Security' at Vienna (Austria), during 24–28 October, pp. 1784–1786 (2016)

Song, S., Kim, B., Lee, S.: The effective ransomware prevention technique using process monitoring on android platform. Mob. Inf. Syst. **2016**(11), 1–9 (2016)

Takeuchi, Y., Sakai, K., Fukumoto, S.: Detecting ransomware using support vector machines. In: Proceedings of the 47th International Conference on Parallel Processing Companion' at USA, during 13–16 August,. pp. 1–6 (2018)

Vinayakumar, R., Soman, K.P., Velan, K.K.S., Ganorkar, S.: Evaluating shallow and deep networks for ransomware detection and classification. In: 2017 International Conference on Advances in Computing, Communications and Informatics (ICACCI) at Udupi (India), during 13–16 September, pp. 259–265 (2017)

Kharraz, A., Robertson, W., Balzarotti, D., Bilge, L., Kirda, E.: Cutting the gordian knot: a look under the hood of ransomware attacks. In: Almgren, M., Gulisano, V., Maggi, F. (eds.) DIMVA 2015. LNCS, vol. 9148, pp. 3–24. Springer, Cham (2015). https://doi.org/10.1007/978-3-319-20550-2_1

Motor Imagery EEG Signal Classification Using Deep Neural Networks

Abhilasha Nakra$^{(\boxtimes)}$ and Manoj Duhan

Deenbandhu Chhotu Ram University of Science and Technology - [DCRUST], Haryana Murthal, Sonepat, India
nakraabhilasha@gmail.com

Abstract. EEG signals can be considered a secure and safe way to capture human brain activity. EEG signals can play a vital role in motor imagery applications to control hands, feet, etc. Brain computer interface (BCI) is method of connecting human brain to laptop or computer. To control the movement of hands and feet, a BCI system is required. The generated EEG signal is read via computer and, as per EEG signal command, is set for motory movement of the hand and feet. Therefore, in motor imagery EEG applications, proper classification of the EEG signal is desired to distinguish hand and foot movements. In this work, an EEG signal classification is done using Deep Neural Networks (DNN) method and the results are compared with recent notable methods.

Keywords: BCI · EEG · DNN

1 Introduction

In BCI interaction, between the brain and external equipment or appliances, utilizing a series of instructions is established [1–3]. Motor imagery refers to the use of imagined motors to control the hands or other objects. One of the approaches that can be employed for BCI is EEG. EEG is the recommended method because it is non-invasive and inexpensive. It is important to note that an EEG signal contains certain unwanted noise and that these are also non-stationary, so dealing with them is a difficult process. However, several studies have discovered methods to model brain activity. The BCI system is divided into two phases, i.e. offline instruction and online operation. In the online phase, participants' real-time EEG data is translated into commands with the end purpose of allowing external device activation, while in the offline phase, we make the necessary enhancements and alterations to the model [4]. The basic operation of BCI is typically dependent on signal analysis and classification techniques [5]. The examination of EEG data has been discovered to have a considerable impact on classification.

Gunes et al. [6] established a technique that combined the time-domain characteristic with eye movement information. This approach proved effective in identifying and classifying individuals' sleep rates. Nonlinear characteristics of EEG signals, such as multiple entropy signal values, have recently been exploited for categorization [7]. Sharma et al. [8] introduced a technique for empirical model decomposition (EMD).

© Springer Nature Switzerland AG 2022
N. Chaubey et al. (Eds.): COMS2 2022, CCIS 1604, pp. 128–140, 2022.
https://doi.org/10.1007/978-3-031-10551-7_10

Currently, a number of research projects are going on in order to improve and modify categorization algorithms. Linear classifiers and artificial learning based methods are the most popular techniques for categorization in BCI systems [9]. The linear methods are simple but their accuracy is limited due to model limitations like proper modeling of the data [10, 11]. Afterwards, Hsu et al. [12] introduced a novel BCI system model for the classification of EEG signals, with successful performance in adaptive systems. Neural networks [13] and nonlinear Support vector machine (SVM) [14] are two of the most commonly used nonlinear approaches. Recurrent Neural Networks were used by Nihal et al. [15] for the classification of EEG signals. The use of SVM in BCI system was suggested in notable papers [16–19]. The SVM is again a simple method and classification accuracy is good with some limitations. Deep learning has become increasingly popular as a result of the review of graphic processing units (GPUs) [20]. In order to decode and visualise EEG deep learning based method was suggested in [21, 22], the deep learning based methods have excellent accuracy but relatively more complex as compared to linear models.

2   EEG Preliminaries

An EEG signal is a signal that may be used to record human brain electrical activity by properly placing electrodes on the human scalp (Fig. 1). There are numerous positions for placing an electrode on the brain. As different parts of the brain record different activities, proper channel selection is important for a particular class of EEG signal recording [21]. The selected channels for BCI are also shown in Fig. 1.

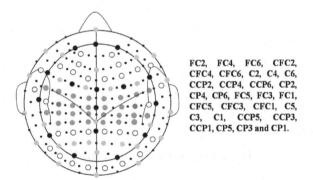

FC2, FC4, FC6, CFC2, CFC4, CFC6, C2, C4, C6, CCP2, CCP4, CCP6, CP2, CP4, CP6, FC5, FC3, FC1, CFC5, CFC3, CFC1, C5, C3, C1, CCP5, CCP3, CCP1, CP5, CP3 and CP1.

Fig. 1. Schematic of electrode placement on the scalp

EEG reveals how distinct neuron networks in the brain communicate with one another. The EEG's frequency fluctuates, and Table 1 shows the classification of the waves. The frequency of the EEG waves is very low therefore both pre-processing and features selections are important in EEG classification.

Table 1. EEG wave frequency and physical state

Wave name	Frequency band	State
Raw EEG	0–4.5 Hz	Awake
Delta	0.5 to 3.5 Hz	Deep sleep
Theta	4 to 7.5 Hz	Drowsy
Alpha	8 to 12 Hz	Relaxed
Beta	13 to 30 Hz	Engaged

The frequency band of importance for BCI motor imagery classification is 8–30 Hz which is further split into two waves: alpha and beta. The division of the EEG wave can be done using wavelet transform as detailed below:

EEG Band Division Using Wavelet Transform

Wavelet transform is a non-stationary time-scale analytic technique; therefore it can be used in EEG signals. It is quite effective in sorting and separating non-stationary signals into their many frequency constituents across distinct time durations.

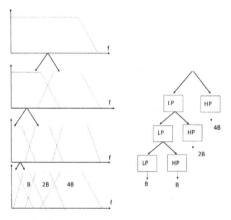

Fig. 2. Frequency division using DWT

Let the maximum frequency of the signal is F_M, then its low pass frequency range is $[0, F_{M/2}]$ and high pass range is $[F_{M/2}, F_M]$, again the low pass signal is further break into low and high frequency components as shown in Fig. 2. This process continues till all the desired bands are recovered.

3 Proposed Work

The proposed method's block diagram is shown in Fig. 3. EEG signal MI task categorization is a three step process: Data preparation, such as decomposition and artifact elimination. The feature extraction procedure is completed in the second stage, and feature classifications are carried out in the last step. The various processes are discussed in subsequent subsections.

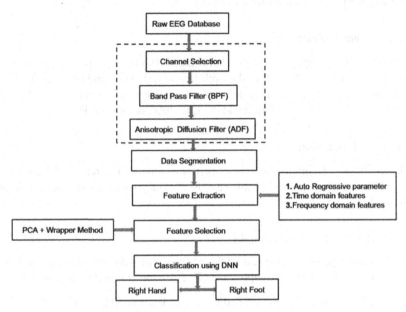

Fig. 3. Block diagram of proposed method

3.1 Channel Selection

An EEG recording is done using 128 channels, making it extremely difficult to analyse such a huge dataset. As a result, we use EEG data for two class MI tasks (right-hand and right-foot). The chosen channels are shown in Fig. 1 [21].

3.2 Band Pass Filtering

EEG signal which is human artifact free in the frequency ranging from of 7–30 Hz, could be obtained by filtering the EEG with the help of a band pass Butterworth filter. The Butterworth filter's mathematical expression is as follows:

$$H(x, y) = 1 - \frac{1}{1 + \left(\frac{d(x,y)B}{d^2(x,y)-d_0^2}\right)^{2n}} \tag{1}$$

The distance between the given window and the centre frequency d_0 is represented by the parameter $d(x, y)$, the bandwidth of the filter is represented by B, and the order of the filter is represented by n.

3.3 Anisotropic Diffusion Filtering

In the process of image processing, the anisotropic diffusion filter (ADF) has been effectively utilized to eliminate high frequency noise along with preserving critical edges [24]. In this work, ADF is used for EEG noise removal.

3.4 Data Segmentation

The next step is data segmentation, on each channel, 168 trials are performed; therefore, the recorded data is of 168×30 trials. Both for the right hand and the right foot, equal data is recorded. The total data is divided into three parts of 50, 30 and 20%, where 50% is for training, 30% is for validation and the rest, 20%, is for testing.

3.5 Feature Extraction

In MI classification technique, feature extraction is crucial. The retrieved features must be as discriminatory as possible between classes. The considered features are detailed below: [23].

3.5.1 Analysis of the Time Domain

The EEG signal is recorded in time domain, where samples are recorded in time domain. Let the EEG signal samples are represented by $E(n)$ and ensemble samples as 's'.

Mean: The EEG signal sub-mean band's value is determined by

$$m = \frac{1}{s} \sum_{i=1}^{s} E_i \tag{2}$$

The aggregate average of the EEG signal's over in s samples in a sub-band is the mean value.

Standard Deviation: The EEG signal deviation from its mean value is evaluated using standard deviation and can be represented as

$$\sigma = \sqrt{\frac{1}{s-1} \sum_{i=1}^{s} (E_i - m)^2} \tag{3}$$

Zero Crossing: The number of times an EEG signal crosses zero is defined as zero crossing, with a small tolerance preserved around zero to counteract noise and artifact and mathematically can be expressed as.

$$\{E_i > 0 \text{ and } E_{i+1} < 0\} \text{ or } \{E_i < 0 \text{ and } E_{i+1} > 0\}$$

$$\text{And } |E_i - E_{i+1}| \geq \varepsilon \tag{4}$$

3.5.2 Frequency Domain Analysis

Signals are characterized in frequency domain in frequency domain analysis, which can be represented as

$$X(k) = \sum_{n=0}^{N-1} x(n)e^{-i\frac{2\pi}{N}kn} \tag{5}$$

Band Power: We define power band as power in a particular band. EEG signal is non-stationary; hence band power cannot be evaluated using the integration of power spectral density (PSD) over considered band. To obtain power signal is divided into blocks and the power of the Mth block is calculated as follows:

$$P_M(k) = \frac{1}{M} \left| \sum_{n=0}^{N-1} x(n)e^{-i\frac{2\pi}{N}kn} \right|^2 \tag{6}$$

3.5.3 Autoregressive Parameter

When it comes to defining time series, the AR model is extremely useful. The PSD can be obtained using Burg method as detailed in [23], which minimizes forward and backward prediction errors.

$$p_x(e^{j\omega}) = \frac{\widehat{E}_k}{\left| \left(1 + \sum_{k=1}^{p} a_k e^{j\omega k}\right) \right|^2} \tag{7}$$

where,

$$\|a\|_p = \left(\sum_{i=1}^{n} |a_i|^p \right)^{1/p} \tag{8}$$

As a result, each training and testing trial yields a total of six features. Out of $128 \times 30 \times 6$, $64 \times 30 \times 6$ features for training, $38 \times 30 \times 6$ features for validation, and $26 \times 30 \times 6$ features for testing.

3.6 Feature Selection

Feature selection in a process of selecting important and relevant features. The selected features can be very large and processing of such large number of features may not be possible or computationally complex. Therefore, feature reduction is necessary. This reduction in features set reduces computationally complexity and improve learning performance. The selected features can be reduced using PCA.

3.6.1 Principal Component Analysis

PCA is a method which is very useful in dimension reduction. The extracted features data is very large in size, and some part of the data is co-related with other part, therefore data redundancy occurs. By carefully, removing redundant data dimension of the original data is reduced without affecting accuracy of the method.

3.6.2 Wrapper Method

This method is an excellent method for important feature selection. The main idea is simple which works similar to Fourier series by representing EEG signal as a summation of 2^n orthogonal signals while minimizing the variance between the estimated and actual signals. This method assumes that the given signal must be bound and integrable, mathematically can be expressed as [24]

$$f(E_1, \ldots E_n) = f_0 + \sum_{v=1}^{2^n-1} f_v(E_v) \tag{9}$$

where,

$$f_v(E_v) = \sum_{j=1}^{k_v} c_{vj} p_{vj}(E_v) \tag{10}$$

In Eq. 14, c_{vj} specifies the parameters that need to be estimated, whereas p_{vf} denotes a set of orthonormalized basis functions. We have a number of options for making the selection of those functions [24]. Here, Legendre polynomials, form tensor products with them are used for this purpose. The c_{vj} parameters are updated while minimizing error using:

$$\text{minimize } J = \sum_{s=1}^{m} \epsilon_s^2 = \sum_{s=1}^{m} (y_s - \hat{y}_s)^2 \tag{11}$$

In above equation, the chosen numbers of samples are denoted by 'm' and the actual and estimated outputs are represented by y_s and $\hat{y}_s$ respectively and represented as

$$\hat{y}_s = \hat{f}(E_{s1}, \ldots E_{sn}) = f_0 + \sum_{v=1}^{2^n-1} \sum_{j=1}^{k_v} c_{vj} p_{vj}(E_{sv}) \tag{12}$$

For feature reduction, samples are removed one by one and new estimate value $\hat{y}_s$ is obtained as in Eq. 13, and this process is continued till the error variance as presented by Eq. 11 is within the limits.

$$\hat{y}_s = f_0 + \sum_{i=1}^{n} \sum_{j=1}^{k_i} c_{ij} p_j(E_{si}) \tag{13}$$

3.7 Classification Using DNN

Figure 4 shows the double layer DNN architecture, here a convolutional and max pooling layers are repeated. The convolutional layer is based on the principle of convolution, in this layer input data is convolved with 3×3 kernel filters. This process captures local features. Next in the max pooling most prominent features are selected by considering a 2×2 filter. Again at the second layer, convolutional and max pooling is performed. Therefore, after second round only the most important features are retained and rest are eliminated. Now with these features feed forward ANN are learned and softmax function is used as classifier. The softmax function is defined as

$$\sigma(z_i) = \frac{e^{z_j}}{\sum\limits_{k=1}^{K} e^{z_k}} \ \forall j\{1, 2, ...K\} \tag{14}$$

The softmax is a kind of probabilistic function, which make sure that the value of $\sigma(z)$ is always positive even when z_j are negative. Further, cross entropy is used for loss minimization. The cross entropy is formulated as

$$L = -\sum_{i=1}^{K} t_i \log(p_i) \tag{15}$$

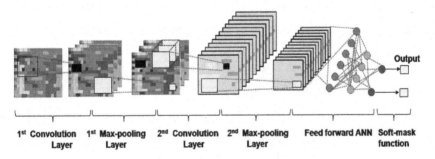

1st Convolution Layer   1st Max-pooling Layer   2nd Convolution Layer   2nd Max-pooling Layer   Feed forward ANN   Soft-mask function

Fig. 4. DNN structure for classification

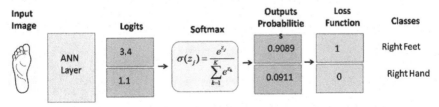

Fig. 5. DNN classification example

The illustrated example is shown in Fig. 5, here the input image is right feet, and after passing through the NN process the logits are 3.4 for right feet and 1.1 for right hand. These values are passed to softmax function, and output probabilities are evaluated. The value of loss function is 0.0955, now as softmax function is differentiable it can be differentiated with respect to weight to bring loss function value as close as possible to zero. Once loss function is minimized corresponding weight values are fixed, and best classification is possible.

4   Results

In this section, results are detailed. In the first part of the results, basic EEG processing results are shown, while in the second part, EEG classification results are shown. Figure 6 shows four subfigures. Figure 6(a) depicts a recorded EEG signal with data plotted for six channels. In Fig. 6(b), the designed BPF is shown with pass-band of 7 to 30 Hz, both amplitude and phase plots are shown with side lobes suppression below 50 dB and in the chosen frequency range phase plot is nearly linear thus filter distortion is within the limits and can be discarded. The band pass filtered signal is plotted in Fig. 6(c), and the noise reduction is clearly visible. The anisotropic diffusion filtered signal is displayed in Fig. 6(d), and baseline noise is greatly reduced.

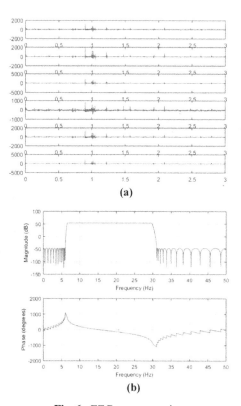

Fig. 6. EEG pre-processing

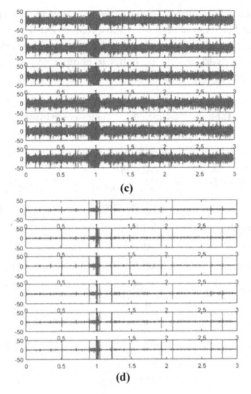

(c)

(d)

Fig. 6. continued

The outcomes of the classification are represented in terms of confusion matrix as presented in Fig. 7, and accuracy of the classification also defined in terms of confusion matrix parameters as detailed in Fig. 7.

True Positives	False Positives
True Negatives	False Negatives

$$Accuracy = \frac{TP + TN}{TP + TN + FP + FN}$$

Fig. 7. Confusion matrix

The proposed method's accuracy is compared to that of recently proposed methods.

It's vital to remember that channel selections, feature extraction, and feature classifications all affect accuracy. The considered work either uses SVM or ANN, DNN as classifier. The proposed work results are better in comparison of recent method and at par with Amin et. al and Kumar et.al works.

Table 2. Classification accuracy comparison

Author	Algorithm	Accuracy %
Lajnef et al. 2015 [25]	ML-DSVM	73
Cai et al. 2018 [26]	ANN + SVM	87.1
Ma et al. 2016 [27]	SVM + PSO	87.14
Chatterjee et al. 2016 [28]	MLP	85.71
Yang et al. 2020 [29]	MLP	76
Sakhavi et al. 2018 [30]	MLP	90.28
Vladimir et al. 2018 [31]	ANN	90.5
Aboalayon et al. 2018 [32]	DL-CNN	92.2
Zhou et al. 2018 [33]	LSTM	91.4
Amin et al. 2019 [34]	DL-CNN	95.4
Kumar et al. 2019 [35]	LSTM	95.5
Fadel et al. 2020 [36]	CNN-LSTM	70.64
Zhang et al. 2019 [37]	DNN	67.76
Proposed	DNN	95.34

The results of our method is superior to other recent methods is due to the use of PCA in feature selection, and we have kept 80% of the total features while rest 20% discarded. The selection of 80-20 is done by considering eigen values. Thereafter wrapper method is further applied for feature refinements. Finally in DNN two stages convolution and max pooling is done to extract most prominent features in classifications (Table 2).

5 Conclusions

Motory image EEG classification has been an important area of research, which is very helpful for physically disabled people. This paper presents a model for Motory image EEG classification using multi domain analysis for feature extraction and use of PCA and wrapper methods for important features selections. These methods are simple still a good numbers of features can be selected while minimizing the size of the datasets. The classification of the dataset is done using the deep neural networks, which is very effective as DNN based system minimizes the loss function and enhances the accuracy. The accuracy of the proposed method is above 95% which is impressive as compared to recent state of arts methods.

References

1. Neuper, C., Scherer, R., Reiner, M., Pfurtscheller, R.: Imagery of motor actions: differential effects of kinesthetic and visual–motor mode of imagery in single-trial EEG. Cogn. Brain Res. **25**(3), 668–677 (2005)
2. Mohammadi, G., Shoushtari, P., Ardekani, B.M., Shamsollahi, M.B.: Person identification by using AR model for EEG signals. In Proceeding of World Academy of Science, Engineering and Technology, vol. 11, no. CONF, pp. 281–285 (2006)
3. Lakshmi, M.R., Prasad, T.V., Chandra Prakash, V.: Survey on EEG signal processing methods. Int. J. Adv. Res. Comput. Sci. Softw. Eng. **4**(1), 84–91 (2014)
4. Lotte, F., Bougrain, L., Cichocki, A., Clerc, M., Congedo, M., Rakotomamonjy, A, et al.: A review of classification algorithms for EEG-based brain–computer interfaces: a 10 year update. J. Neural Eng. **15**, 031005 (2018). 10-031005.28
5. Lotte, F., Congedo, M., Lécuyer, A., Lamarche, F., Arnaldi, B.: A review of classification algorithms for EEG-based brain-computer interfaces. J. Neural Eng. **4**, 1–24 (2017)
6. Gune, S., Polat, K., Dursun, M., Yosunkaya, S.: Examining the relevance with sleep stages of time domain features of EEG, EOG, and chin EMG signals. In: 2009 14th national biomedical engineering meeting, Izmir, Turkey, pp. 1–4 (2009)
7. Acharya, U.R., Hagiwara, Y., Deshpande, S.N., Suren, S., Koh, J.E.W., Oh, S.L., et al.: Characterization of focal EEG signals: a review. Future Gener. Comput. Syst. **9**, 290–299 (2019)
8. Sharma, R., Pachori, R.B., Acharya, U.R.: Application of entropy measures on intrinsic mode functions for the automated identification of focal electroencephalogram signals. Entropy **17**, 669–691 (2015)
9. Xiao, D., Mu, Z., Hu, J.: A linear discrimination method used in motor imagery EEG classification. In: 2009 Fifth International Conference on Natural Computation, vol. 2, pp. 94–98. Tian Jian, IEEE (2009)
10. Hauk, O., Davis, M.H., Ford, M., Pulvermüller, F., Marslen-Wilson, W.D.: The time course of visual word recognition as revealed by linear regression analysis of ERP data. Neuroimage **30**, 1383–1400 (2006)
11. Garrett, D., Peterson, D.A., Anderson, C.W., Thaut, M.H.: Comparison of linear, nonlinear, and feature selection methods for EEG signal classification. IEEE Trans. Neural Syst. Rehabil. Eng. **11**, 141–144 (2003)
12. Hsu, W.Y.: EEG-based motor imagery classification using enhanced active segment selection and adaptive classifier. Comput Biol Med **41**, 633–639 (2011)
13. Titterington, D., MCheng, B.: Neural networks: a review from a statistical perspective. Stat. Sci. **9**, 2–30 (1994)
14. Übeyli, E.D.: Analysis of EEG signals by combining eigenvector methods and multiclass support vector machines. Comput. Biol. Med. **38**, 14–22 (2008)
15. Güler, N.F., Übeyli, E.D., Güler, I.: Recurrent neural networks employing Lyapunov exponents for EEG signals classification. Expert Syst. Appl. **29**, 506–514 (2005)
16. Cortes, C., Vapnik, V.: Support-vector networks. Mach. Learn. **20**, 273–297 (1995)
17. Niu, X.X., Suen, C.Y.: A novel hybrid CNN–SVM classifier for recognizing handwritten digits. Pattern Recogn **45**, 1318–1325 (2012)
18. Manevitz, L.M., Yousef, M.: One-class SVMs for document classification. J. Mach. Learn. Res. **2**, 139–154 (2001)
19. Tarabalka, Y., Fauvel, M., Chanussot, J., Benediktsson, J.A.: SVM-and MRF-based method for accurate classification of hyperspectral images. IEEE Geosci. Remote Sens. Lett. **7**, 736–740 (2010)

20. Craik, A., He, Y., Contreras-Vidal, J.L.: Deep learning for electroencephalogram (EEG) classification tasks: a review. J. Neural Eng. **16**, 031001 (2019)
21. Schirrmeister, R.T., Springenberg, J.T., Fiederer, L.D.J., Glasstetter, M., Eggensperger, K., Tangermann, M., et al.: Deep learning with convolutional neural networks for EEG decoding and visualization. Hum Brain Mapp **38**, 5391–5420 (2017)
22. Nakra, A., Duhan, M.: Motor imagery EEG signal classification using long short-term memory deep network and neighbourhood component analysis. Int. J. Inf. Technol. **14**, 1–9 (2022)
23. Bhateja, V., Singh, G., Srivastava, A., Singh, J.: Speckle reduction in ultrasound images using an improved conductance function based on anisotropic diffusion. In: 2014 International Conference on Computing for Sustainable Global Development (INDIACom), pp. 619–624. IEEE (2014)
24. Sobol, I.M.: Global sensitivity indices for nonlinear mathematical models and their Monte Carlo estimates. Math. Comput. Simul. **55**(1–3), 271–280 (2001)
25. Lajnef, T., Jerbi, K.: Learning machines and sleeping brains: automatic sleep stage classification using decision-tree multi-class support vector machines. J. Neurosci. Methods **250**, 94–105 (2015)
26. Cui, Z., Zheng, X., Shao, X., Cui, L.: Automatic sleep stage classification based on convolutional neural network and fine grained segments. Hindawi Complex **2018**, 9248410 (2018)
27. Ma, Y., Ding, X., She, Q., Luo, Z., Potter, T., Zhang, Y.: Classification of motor imagery EEG signals with support vector machines and particle swarm optimization. In: Computational and Mathematical Methods in Medicine, vol. 2016, p. 8 (2016). Article ID 4941235
28. Chatterjee, R., Bandyopadhyay, T., Sanyal, D.K.: Effects of wavelets on quality of features in motor-imagery EEG signal classification. In: 2016 International Conference on Wireless Communications, Signal Processing and Networking (WiSPNET), pp. 1346–1350. IEEE (2016)
29. Yang, P., Wang, J., Zhao, H., Li, R.: Mlp with Riemannian covariance for motor imagery based EEG analysis. IEEE Access **8**, 139974–139982 (2020)
30. Sakhavi, S., Guan, C., Yan, S.: Learning temporal information for brain-computer interface using convolutional neural networks. IEEE Trans. Neural Netw. Learn. Syst. **29**(11), 5619–5629 (2018)
31. Maksimenko, V.A., et al.: Artificial neural network classification of motor-related EEG: an increase in classification accuracy by reducing signal complexity. Complexity **2018** (2018)
32. Aboalayon, K.A.I., Faezipour, M., Almuhammadi, W.S., Moslehpour, S.: Moslehpour S "Sleep stage classification using EEG signal analysis: a comprehensive survey and new investigation." Entropy **18**, 272 (2016)
33. Zhou, J., Meng, M., Gao, Y., Ma, Y., Zhang, Q.: Classification of motor imagery EEG using wavelet envelope analysis and LSTM networks. In: Proceedings of the Chinese Control and Decision Conference (CCDC), Shenyang, China, 9–11 June 2018
34. Amin, S.U., Alsulaiman, M., Muhammad, G., Mekhtiche, M.A., Shamim, H.M.: Deep learning for EEG motor imagery classification based on multi-layer CNNs feature fusion. Future Gener. Comput. Syst. **101**, 542–554 (2019)
35. Kumar, S., Sharma, A., Tsunoda, T.: Brain wave classification using long short-term memory network based OPTICAL predictor. Sci. Rep. **9**, 9153 (2019)
36. Fadel, W., Kollod, C., Wahdow, M., Ibrahim, Y., Ulbert, I.: Multi-class classification of motor imagery EEG signals using image-based deep recurrent convolutional neural network. In: 8th International Winter Conference on Brain-Computer Interface (BCI) (2020)
37. Zhang, G., Davoodnia, V., Sepas-Moghaddam, A., Zhang, Y., Etemad, A.: Classification of hand movements from EEG using a deep attention-based LSTM network. IEEE Sens. J. **20**(6), 3113–3122 (2019)

Extending WSN Life-Time Using Energy Efficient Based on K-means Clustering Method

Dhulfiqar Talib Abbas AL-Janabi[1], Dalal Abdulmohsin Hammood[1(✉)],
and Seham Aahmed Hashem[2]

[1] The Technical College of Electrical Engineering, Department of Computer Technical
Engineering, MTU (Middle Technical University), Al Doura, 10022 Baghdad, Iraq
{bbc0060,dalal.hammood}@mtu.edu.iq, dalalmmf59@gmail.com
[2] Technical Instructors Training Institute, Technical Electronic Department, Middle Technical
University (MTU), Baghdad, Iraq
dr.seham.ahmed@mtu.edu.iq

Abstract. WSN (Wireless Sensor Networks) can be considered as a wireless network. Sensor nodes are exchanging data between them to transmit data into base station. Sensor contains small battery that is difficult to rechargeable or replacement. So, the challenges are improving the prolong life time of sensor. This paper, presents a k-mean clustering algorithm to enhance energy saving (ES) and prolong life time of sensor node in term of the packet of L-bit towards some destination of distance D. D from sensor nodes to base station is decreased in this work by dividing the region of interest into number of clusters. Each node transmits data into CH (cluster head), then the cluster head transfers the information towards BS (Base station). Energy efficiency is improved as well. Custom Python simulator results show that our work increases energy saving from 14.43% in to 26.61% and the significant improvement of the lifetime of the sensor from 15.03% to 66.78%.

Keywords: WSN · Elbow · Clustering · K-means · Energy saving

1 Introduction

WSN (Wireless Sensor Networks) is a wireless network. Sensor nodes are exchanging data between them to transmit data into base station. Sensor contains small battery that is difficult to rechargeable or replacement. So, the challenges are improving the prolong life time of sensor. Recently, many techniques are proposed to improve life time of networks in wireless communication such as clustering algorithm. K-means is one of algorithm in WSN. The applications of WSN are related to environment, agriculture, building, health care, military as well as industry. It consists of many small devices. These devices are able to compute, cooperate, send the information related to the observed materialistic environment over single-hop WN. The sensor devices sense data and transmits to BS for additional processing in term of processing, sensing, energy, bandwidth, and memory [1–3].

So, it is important to consider D from sensor nods to BS (sending/receiving) in wireless communication. The energy consumption reverse proportion to square distance,

© Springer Nature Switzerland AG 2022
N. Chaubey et al. (Eds.): COMS2 2022, CCIS 1604, pp. 141–154, 2022.
https://doi.org/10.1007/978-3-031-10551-7_11

that is lead to less energy consumption and extend life time of the sensor batteries and the overall networks. The balance process from communication to processing considering how to save energy leads to an advantage of using of periodic wireless sensor networks (PSN). In this papers clustering algorithm are used. K-means algorithm can be considered as a less complicated and lightweight technique, and for choosing the optimal or efficient number of clusters K, we will use Elbow methods. all of this to ensure the efficient energy consumption and prolong of the network. The temperature can be considered as an environment applications of WSN [4]. Sensors batteries is limited in energy saving and it couldn't recharge it, especially critical and hostile environment. Therefore, the power saving is important of the batteries. Thus, the lifetime of WSN is extended. Table 1 clears the techniques of energy efficiency.

Table 1. State of art of energy efficiency techniques

Measurements	Ref	Routing	Genetic	Clustering	K-means	Hybrid	Optimization	Fuzzy logic	Q -Learning
Energy- Accuracy	[5]	–	–	√	√	–	–	–	–
Energy-Lifetime	[6]	–	–	√	√	–	–	–	–
Energy-ccuracy	[7]	–	–	√	√	–	–	–	–
Energy-Lifetime	[8]	–	–	√	√	–	–	–	–
Energy	[9]	–	–	√	√	–	–	–	–
Energy	[10]	√	–	√	√	√	–	–	–
Energy-Lifetime	[11]	–	√	√	√	√	–	–	–
Energy-Lifetime	[12]	√	–	√	√	–	–	–	–
Energy-Lifetime	[13]	√	–	√	√	–	–	–	–
Energy-Lifetime	[14]	√	–	√	√	–	–	–	–
Energy-Lifetime	[15]	–	–	√	√	–	–	–	–
Energy-Lifetime	[16]	–	–	√	√	–	√	–	–
Energy	[17]	–	–	√	√	–	–	–	–
Energy	[18]	√	–	√	√	–	–	–	–
Energy	[19]	√	–	√	√	–	–	–	–
Energy-Lifetime	[20]	√	√	√	√	–	–	–	–
Energy-Lifetime-Packet sent	[21]	√	–	√	√	–	–	–	–
Energy-Data transmission	[22]	–	–	√	√	–	–	–	–
Energy-Lifetime	[23]	–	–	√	√	–	-	√	–
Energy-hroughput-Packet delivery	[24]	–	–	√	√	–	–	–	√
Energy-ifetime- Accuracy	This work	–	–	√	√	–	–	–	–

2 Proposed Method

In this section, K-mean clustering algorithm is used to improve energy efficacy. The goal can be considered as reducing distance between the SNs and the BS and communication process. Then, extending the life time of the SNs as well as the overall network have been enhanced. Figure 1 shows the flowchart of proposed work. The first step is to initialize the energy, thresholding, no. of measuring then the energy test.

2.1 Network Setup and Deployment

A Wireless Sensor Network can be exemplified as a connected graph Gp = (ND, EG). Whereas ND = {ND$_1$, ND$_2$,... , ND$_n$} can be considered as n sensor node set, EG is an edge set. Data is collected by SN during a long time and afterwards transmitted every sensed information towards the hierarchy CH's following level.

At first, energy threshold ε are Initialized. The threshold is 10% of total sensor energy. data sensing measurement number M are 20, 50, and 100. the residual energy for each sensor is tested after finishing the transmitting process of data. if greater than or equal threshold, repeating the process until the residual energy smaller than threshold the sensor is excluded and stop the processing [25].

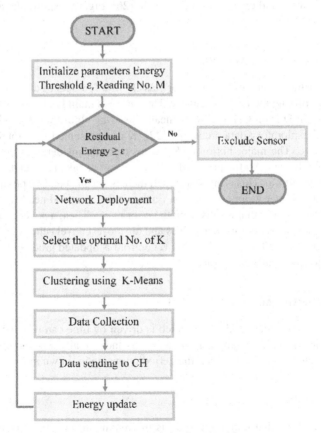

Fig. 1. K-means clustering algorithms

2.2 Choice Optimal Number of Clusters:

Several methods are used by a lot of published papers to decrease D from the sensor nodes to the base station by using a clustering algorithm, the K-means algorithm is a less complicated and lightweight technique, to use the optimal or efficient number of clusters K, we must choice one of the following methods (Elbow, Average Silhouette, Gap statistic). In this part, the elbow method is used as good techniques. This method is shown in Eq. 1. Which it contains distances between all the sample points' of clusters and the centroid of clusters [15]:

$$SSE = \sum_{k=1}^{k} \sum_{xi \in sk} \|xi - ck\|^2 \tag{1}$$

where SSE is sum of squared errors, x is the sensor presented in clusters, Ck is the Kth cluster. The K's optimal value can be located as the value of SSE decreases over the curve very much and creates a smaller angle [26]. Figure 2 shows the algorithm of K-means clustering.

2.3 Network Clustering Algorithms

K-mean clustering is a process to group or classify of a few sets of data into more than one K cluster utilizing the mean of cluster. The l-mean's main goal can be reducing the overall Euclidean D from CH to CM. K-mean clustering algorithm is good researched mechanism of exploratory data analyzing [22]. K is represented by a total of clusters which is positive. The major notion of K-Means can be considered as defining the K centroid for all clusters. All the points of n data sets can be taken and under association with the closest centroid. This is the first step. If there is not any pending points, this move completes and a sooner grouping finishes. Each novel K centroid needs to re-calculate as a cluster's bary-center that results from the prior move. Then, a novel binding should finish among the data set points themselves and the closest novel centroid. There can be a loop. This means that the location of the K centroid is updated gradually to the extent that there is no extra finished updates [5].

2.4 Data Collecting and Sending to CH

Account the model of data collection which is driven by time can be used here that is called Periodic. A novel reading for all time slots individually s is captured by SN i. then, a new vector is shaped by SN i. the periodic sensing is shown in Fig. 3 [27].

2.5 Energy Update

As mentioned above that communication is the maximum energy consumption then must update the energy level of each sensor after sending data if greater than threshold continue, else exclude the sensor.

The model of consuming energy is illustrated in Fig. 4.

K-means Algorithm.

Require: Set of sensors' coordinate M = {M₁, M₂...Mₙ}, K.
Ensure: Set of clusters C = {C₁, C₂...Cₖ}.
1: **for** j ← 1 to K **do**
2:    Cⱼ ← ∅
3: **end for**
4: **for** each set Mᵢ ∈ M **do**
5:    find $\overline{Mi}$; // mean of set Mᵢ
6: **end for**
7: **for** j ← 1 to K **do**
8:    randomly choose centroid xⱼ among $\overline{Mi}$ belongs to Cⱼ
9: **end for**
10: **repeat**
11: **for** each set Mᵢ ∈ M **do**
12:    Assign Mᵢ to the cluster Cⱼ with nearest xi
       (i.e., $|\overline{Mi} - X_{j*}| \le |\overline{Mi} - X_j|$; j ∈ {1, ...K})
13: **end for**
14: **for** each cluster Cⱼ , where j ∈ {1, ...K} **do**
15:    Update the centroid Xᵢ to be the centroid of all sets currently
       in Cⱼ ,so that $xi = \frac{1}{|c_j|} \Sigma_{i \in c_j} \overline{Mi}$
16: **end for**
17: **until** clusters memberships no longer changes
18: **return** C

Fig. 2. The algorithm of K-means clustering

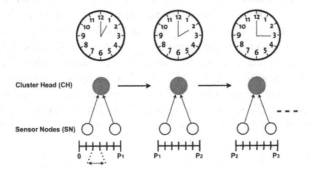

Fig. 3. Periodic sensing of data in sensors node

The energy by which can be under consumption via two parts: the transmission part and the reception part. The transmission's energy needs more power for signaling amplification in accordance with its D where it sets off. Hence, for sending a packet of L-bit towards a point at distance equals D, the exhausted energy can be computed as shown in Eq. 2.

$$E_{tx}(L, D) = (E_{elec} \times L) + E_{amp}D^2 \qquad (2)$$

where E_{elec}: Expended energy for the radio's electronics, E_{amp}: Expended energy via amplifier [28].

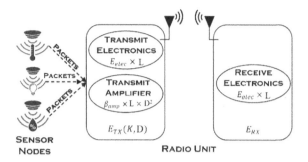

Fig. 4. Radio unit of sensor node

3 Experiment Result

The experiment of our method used python language that is called custom python simulator to validate tis work. In this experiment a collection of temperature monitoring measurement data is collected online from sensors provided by Intel Berkeley's research Laboratory. This type of data is used in many published papers that relate with WSN. The network implemented in this lab consists of x number of sensors arranged in single-hop topology, as illustrated in Fig. 5 .lab consist of 54 Mica2Dot sensors used for many environment monitoring such as light values, voltage, temperature and humidity, fitted in 35×45 m dimension as shown in Fig. 5. In our work temperature is selected for simplicity. Sensors capture the temperature data in lab every 31s.sensed data was compiled into 2.3 million readings as a log file which is utilized in proposed experiment. IEEE 802.15.4 can be utilized via a sensor like MAC protocol. The protocol here can be responsible for getting the interfering of sensors under control. The yellow flag within a few sensor nodes which is shown in Fig. 5 referring that the data of theirs are lost that lead to there are only 47 sensors are chosen and their data is used. The parameters values of our experiments are illustrated in Table 2 [29].

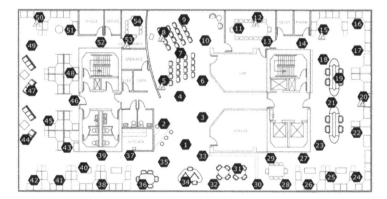

Fig. 5. (Intel Berkeley lab's sensors deployment)

Table 2. Experiment parameters

Parameter name	Value
WSN size	47 sensors
M	20, 50 and 100 sensed data
E_{elec}	50 nJ/bit
β_{amp}	100 pJ/bit/m^2
k	2,3,4
Initial energy	0.2 J

In this work, four scenarios are introduced. First, is the flat network without clustering. An aggregator (BS) location coordinate (X, Y) is (17.5, 22.5) placed in the lab's center. The sensor distributed there sends the data reading towards the aggregator, as shown in Fig. 6. Second, the clustering algorithm is used. The number of clusters K = 2 as shown in Fig. 7 . The SN sends its data to CH, then CH sends data towards BS. The D from SN towards BS can be decreased in this scenario. Third, Fig. 8 shows the number of clusters k is 3. The distance is reduced more than cluster k = 2. Last scenario is When k = 4 the distance is reduced more than k = 2 and 3 as illustrate in Fig. 9.

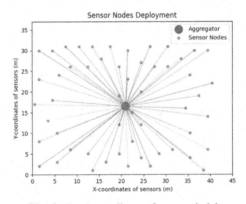

Fig. 6. (x, y) coordinate of sensors in lab

3.1 Data Sets Transmitted

In this section of the experiment, we use clustering technique on network without using any manipulation on the data, for this reason the data sensed by the sensor node are transmitted directly to the BS in the flat network.

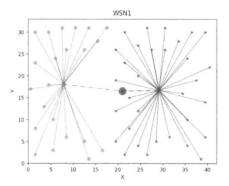

Fig. 7. (x, y) dimension of the lab

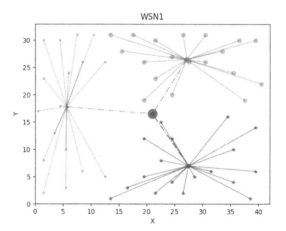

Fig. 8. (x, y) dimension of the lab

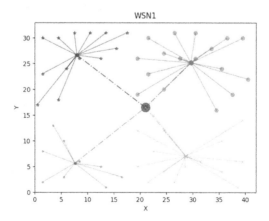

Fig. 9. (x, y) dimension of the lab

3.2 Energy Consumption

The goal for this section can be considered as demonstrating the how our technique can decrease the energy consumption.

The figure below highlights sensor node energy consumption, sensor number and the energy consuming of networks. The consuming of energy is measured by joules when sensor reading measurement (M = 20) in the flat network (black-line) and the network with number of clusters k = 2 is blue - line, k = 3 is red - line, and k = 4 is green-line. It clears that SN energy consumption is 0.00 into 0.25 J while Network energy consumption is 0 into 5 J (Fig. 10).

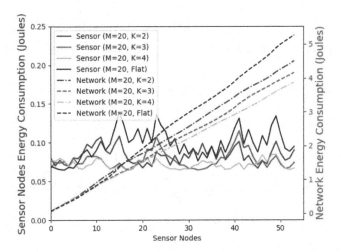

Fig. 10. Network and sensors energy consumption (Color figure online)

Figure 11 illustrates the sensor node energy consumption, number of sensors and network energy consumption. The energy consumption in joules when the sensor reading measurement (M = 25) in the flat network (black-line) and the network with number of clusters k = 2 is blue - line, k = 3 is red - line, and k = 4 is green-line. It clears that SN energy consumption is 0.15 into 0.50 J while Network energy consumption is 0 into 14 J.

Figure 12 illustrates the sensor node energy consumption, number of sensors and network energy consumption. The energy consumption in joules when the sensor reading measurement (M = 100) in the flat network (black-line) and the network with number of clusters k = 2 is blue - line, k = 3 is red - line, and k = 4 is green - line. It clears that SN energy consumption is 0.02 into 1.2 J while Network energy consumption is 0 into 27 J.

We calculate energy saving for all scenario as shown in Eq. 3, and the enhancement of the energy saving in Eq. 4 for all scenario as well.

$$E_{sav}\% = \left(\frac{E_{consum-clus} \times 100}{E_{consum-flat}} \right) \tag{3}$$

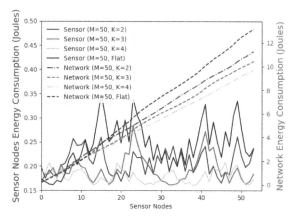

Fig. 11. Network and sensors energy consumption (Color figure online)

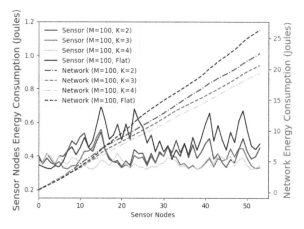

Fig. 12. Network and sensors energy consumption (Color figure online)

where $E_{sav}\%$ is energy saving, $E_{consum-clus}$ is energy consumption using clustering, $E_{consum-flat}$ without clustering.

$$E_{enhans}\% = (100\% - E_{sav}\%) \tag{4}$$

Table 3 illustrates the number of clustering with data sensed measurement for all scenarios.

Accuracy. The accuracy indicates measure loss' ratio, accuracy means the measure loss' ratio after getting it in BS node. we use clustering technique on network without using any manipulation on the data. Data sensed are transmitted directly via sensor node towards BS in flat networks. Accuracy could be enhanced.

Table 3. Energy saving

Data sensed	Number of clusters		
Measurement	K = 2	K = 3	K = 4
M = 20	14.46%	21.04%	26.61%
M = 50	14.43%	20.93%	26.43%
M = 100	14.47%	21.88%	26.51%

3.3 Life Time

Here, we can find an explanation for sensor node's lifetime in flat network that represents in black-line. the clustering technique is used with the cluster number k = 2 as represents in blue - line, k = 3 in red - line, k = 4 with green - line and the sensor reading measurement M = 100. The same initial energy 0.2 J is used for all sensor node in network. The prolong life time of WSN is enhanced. As shown in Fig. 13.

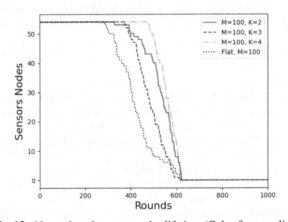

Fig. 13. Network and sensors nodes lifetime (Colur figure online)

We calculate life time for all scenario as shown in Eq. 5, and calculate the enhancement in the life time also in all scenario as shown in Eq. 6

$$LT_{sav}\% = \left(\frac{LT_{clus} \times 100}{LT_{flat}} \right) \tag{5}$$

where LT_{sav} is life time of saving energy, LT_{clus} is life time using clustering, LT_{flat} is life time without clustering.

$$LT_{enhans}\% = (100\% - LT_{sav}\%) \tag{6}$$

Table 4 shows the lifetime enhancement of clustering 2, 3, 4 with M = 100.

Table 4. Lifetime Enhancement

Data sensed measurement	Number of clusters		
	K = 2	K = 3	K = 4
M = 100	15.03%	30.76%	66.78%

4 Conclusion

Energy Saving is main challenging issues in WSN. This paper, presents a k-mean clustering algorithm to enhance energy saving (ES) and prolong life time of sensor node in term of the packet of L-bit towards a point in a distance equals D. D from sensor nodes to BS is decreased here by dividing the region of interest into number of clusters. Each node transmits data into CH, then it transfers the data towards BS. Energy efficiency is improved as well. Custom Python simulator results show that our work increases energy saving from 14.43% in to 26.61% and the significant improvement of the lifetime of the sensor from 15.03% to 66.78%.

In future work, we plan to use one of the data compression algorithms after using the K-means algorithm to provide better energy efficiency and a longer network lifetime.

References

1. Hammood, D.A., Rahim, H.A., Alkhayyat, A., et al.: An energy-efficient optimization based scheme for low power devices in wireless body area networks. J. Comput. Theor. Nanosci. **16**(7), 2934–2940 (2019). https://doi.org/10.1166/JCTN.2019.8197
2. Hammood, D.A., Rahim, H.A., Badlishah Ahmad, R., et al.: Enhancement of the duty cycle cooperative medium access control for wireless body area networks. IEEE Access **7**, 3348–3359 (2019). https://doi.org/10.1109/ACCESS.2018.2886291
3. Hammood, D., Alkhayyat, A.: An overview of the survey/review studies in wireless body area network. In: 2020 3rd International Conference on Engineering Technology and its Applications, IICETA 2020, pp. 18–23 (2020). https://doi.org/10.1109/IICETA50496.2020.9318981
4. Al-Qurabat, A.K.M., Idrees, A.K.: Two level data aggregation protocol for prolonging lifetime of periodic sensor networks. Wireless Netw. **25**(6), 3623–3641 (2019). https://doi.org/10.1007/s11276-019-01957-0
5. Harb, H., et al.: K-means based clustering approach for data aggregation in periodic sensor networks. https://doi.org/10.1109/WiMOB.2014.6962207. ieeexplore.ieee.org
6. Idrees, A.K., et al.: Distributed data aggregation based modified k-means technique for energy conservation in periodic wireless sensor networks. https://doi.org/10.1109/MENACOMM.2018.8371007. ieeexplore.ieee.org
7. Idrees, A.K., Al-Qurabat, A.K., Abou Jaoude, C., Al-Yaseen, W.L.: Integrated divide and conquer with enhanced k-means technique for energy-saving data aggregation in wireless sensor networks. ieeexplore.ieee.org
8. Chawla, H., Verma, P.: Balanced K Means Based Clustering Algorithm for Energy Efficient in Wireless Sensor Networks. Citeseer

9. Jain, B., Brar, G., Malhotra, J.: EKMT-k-means clustering algorithmic solution for low energy consumption for wireless sensor networks based on minimum mean distance from base station. In: Perez, G.M., Mishra, K.K., Tiwari, S., Trivedi, M.C. (eds.) Networking Communication and Data Knowledge Engineering. LNDECT, vol. 3, pp. 113–123. Springer, Singapore (2018). https://doi.org/10.1007/978-981-10-4585-1_10

10. Mahboub, A., Arioua, M.: Energy-efficient hybrid k-means algorithm for clustered wireless sensor networks 7(4), 2054–2060 (2017). https://doi.org/10.11591/ijece.v7i4.pp2054-2060. core.ac.uk

11. Bhushan, S., Pal, R., Antoshchuk, S.G.: Energy efficient clustering protocol for heterogeneous wireless sensor network: a hybrid approach using GA and K-means (2018). ieeexplore.ieee. org

12. Razzaq, M., Devarani Devi Ningombam, S.S.: Energy efficient K-means clustering-based routing protocol for WSN using optimal packet size (2018). https://doi.org/10.1109/ICOIN. 2018.8343195. ieeexplore.ieee.org

13. Devi, R., Energy, T.S.: Energy Efficient Enhanced K-Means Cluster-based Routing Protocol for WSN (2019). academia.edu

14. Lehsaini, M., Benmahdi, M.B.: An improved k-means cluster-based routing scheme for wireless sensor networks (2018). ieeexplore.ieee.org

15. Kumar, B., et al.: Energy Efficient Quad Clustering based on K-means Algorithm for Wireless Sensor Network. ieeexplore.ieee.org

16. Chowdhury, A., De, D.: Energy-Efficient Coverage Optimization in Wireless Sensor Networks Based on Voronoi-Glowworm Swarm Optimization-K-means Algorithm. Elsevier (2021)

17. Park, G., et al.: A novel cluster head selection method based on K-means algorithm for energy efficient wireless sensor network (2013). https://doi.org/10.1109/WAINA.2013.123. ieeexplore.ieee.org

18. Jlassi, W., Haddad, R., Bouallegue, R., Shubair, R.: A Combination of K-means algorithm and optimal path selection method for lifetime extension in wireless sensor networks. In: Barolli, L., Woungang, I., Enokido, T. (eds.) AINA 2021. LNNS, vol. 227, pp. 416–425. Springer, Cham (2021). https://doi.org/10.1007/978-3-030-75078-7_42

19. Wadii, J., et al.: A Combination of Kruskal and K-means Algorithms for Network Lifetime Extension in Wireless Sensor Networks. https://doi.org/10.1109/IWCMC51323.2021. 9498594. ieeexplore.ieee.org

20. Benmahdi, MB., Lehsaini, M.: A GA-Based Multihop Routing Scheme using K-Means Clustering Approach for Wireless Sensor Networks (2020). ieeexplore.ieee.org

21. Benmahdi, M.B., Lehsaini, M.: Greedy forwarding routing schemes using an improved K-means approach for wireless sensor networks. Wirel. Pers. Commun. 119(2), 1619–1642 (2021). https://doi.org/10.1007/s11277-021-08298-2

22. Rida, M., et al.: EK-Means: A New Clustering Approach for Datasets Classification in Sensor Networks. Elsevier

23. Jayaraman, G., Dhulipala, V.R.S.: FEECS: fuzzy-based energy-efficient cluster head selection algorithm for lifetime enhancement of wireless sensor networks. Arab. J. Sci. Eng. 1–11 (2021). https://doi.org/10.1007/s13369-021-06030-7

24. Sathyamoorthy, M., Kuppusamy, S., Dhanaraj, R.K., Ravi, V.: Improved K-means based q learning algorithm for optimal clustering and node balancing in WSN. Wirel. Pers. Commun. 122(3), 2745–2766 (2021). https://doi.org/10.1007/s11277-021-09028-4

25. Harb, H., Jaoude, C.A., Makhoul, A.: An energy-efficient data prediction and processing approach for the internet of things and sensing based applications. Peer-to-Peer Netw. Appl. 13(3), 780–795 (2019). https://doi.org/10.1007/s12083-019-00834-z

26. Et-taleby, A., et al.: Faults detection for photovoltaic field based on K-Means, Elbow, and Average Silhouette Techniques through the Segmentation of a Thermal Image. hindawi.com

27. Abdulzahra, S.A., Al-Qurabat, A.K., Idrees A.K.: Compression-based data reduction technique for IoT sensor networks (2021). bsj.uobaghdad.edu.iq

28. Idrees, A.K., Al-Qurabat, A.K.M.: Energy-efficient data transmission and aggregation protocol in periodic sensor networks based fog computing. J. Netw. Syst. Manage. **29**(1), 1–24 (2020). https://doi.org/10.1007/s10922-020-09567-4

29. Al-Qurabat, A.K.M., Mohammed, Z.A., Hussein, Z.J.: Data traffic management based on compression and MDL techniques for smart agriculture in IoT. Wirel. Pers. Commun. **120**(3), 2227–2258 (2021). https://doi.org/10.1007/s11277-021-08563-4

One-to-One Matching for Cooperative Resource Sharing and Communication in CRNs

Meenakshi Sharma$^{(\boxtimes)}$ and Nityananda Sarma

Tezpur University, Tezpur 784028, Assam, India
amee2187@gmail.com, nitya@tezu.ernet.in

Abstract. Cooperative Spectrum Sharing (CSS) enhances user satisfaction by forming optimal or stable partners for cooperative communication. CSS alleviate spectrum scarcity problem by sharing scare spectrum resources (bandwidth, access time) among cooperative users and thus improves spectrum efficiency. In this paper, a partner-assignment scheme for cooperative communication is proposed for multiple primary users (PUs) and secondary users (SUs) Cognitive Radio Networks (CRNs). In the proposed scheme, PUs and SUs share resource offers where, each PU aims to select most suitable SU as its cooperative partner to relay primary services in exchange of transmission opportunity to the SU in its licensed band. The optimization problem for optimal allocation of access time for cooperative communication as well as for secondary transmission has been formulated. We have used the concept of matching theory to model the partner assignment problem and proposed a polynomial time-based solution. Simulation results reveal that the proposed solution converges to a stable matching for SUs, and optimal matching for PUs. The necessary proofs for the convergence of stability and optimality of the resultant matching are presented in the paper.

Keywords: PUs · SUs · Resource sharing · Optimal allocation · Matching theory

1 Introduction

Internet has become an integral part of human life irrespective of rural and urban society worldwide. Such huge demands of Internet cause heavy utilization of radio spectrum resources. Moreover, the inefficiency involved in traditional spectrum assignment policy consequently results in the spectrum scarcity problem. Cooperative Spectrum Sharing empowered by Cognitive Radio (CR) technology has been proven as a promising solution towards improving spectrum efficiency by allowing unlicensed users (SUs) to cooperatively access the licensed band of licensed users (PUs) in exchange of resource or monetary compensation (Akyildiz et al. 2006; Nicholas Laneman and Wornell 1992; Ahmed et al. 2016). However, resource compensation is found to be more convenient and practical

© Springer Nature Switzerland AG 2022
N. Chaubey et al. (Eds.): COMS2 2022, CCIS 1604, pp. 155–168, 2022.
https://doi.org/10.1007/978-3-031-10551-7_12

than monetary compensation, as the later one needs to deal with some trustworthy billing and trading framework, which is found to be difficult to implement and maintain (Feng et al. 2014). In resource compensation model both PUs and SUs exchange relatively scare spectrum resources during cooperative communication and improve cooperative as well as individual performances assisting each other. In CRN, such resource exchange among the PUs and cooperating SUs is seen in overlay access mode of spectrum sharing, where a PU transmitter (PT) hires a suitable SU as relay to transmit its own signal towards PU receiver (PR) and as compensation provides transmission opportunity to the SU over its licensed band (Liang et al. 2017; Kumar et al. 2012). However, the relay selection and resource allocation for cooperative as well as for secondary communication become challenging problem due to heterogeneous characteristics and conflict of interests associated with PUs and SUs. To analyse and handle such interactions among two disjoint sets of users with cooperative or competitive behaviours, matching theory (Gale and Shapley 1962) is found to be widely used in the scenario like partner (PU-SU pair) assignment and optimal resource allocation.

Many of the recent works in partner assignment and cooperative resource sharing (or allocation) for single PU-multi SUs as well as for multi PUs-multi SUs have been investigated. In (Feng et al. 2014) and (Roumeliotis et al. 2015), utility driven schemes for user pairing and resource sharing problems were formulated and based on the concept of matching theory, suitable users were assigned for cooperation. In (Namvar and Afghah 2015), the access time optimization and utility maximization scheme for both PU and SU was discussed. Using the idea of stable matching, stable PU-SU partners for cooperation were formed that optimized the system utility. In (Gao et al. 2017), partner matching and resource sharing schemes for different matching market scenarios were proposed and established optimal, stable and robust equilibrium suitable for the proposed market scenarios. A TDMA based joint power and time optimization scheme for a multi PUs-multi SUs CRN was proposed in (Bai et al. 2019). Employing β-fair cost function, this scheme succeeded to allocate fair resources among users and improved resource utilization as well as user satisfaction. In (Chang et al. 2020), cooperative relay selection and power allocation schemes among cooperative PU-SU pair was proposed using stable as well as swap matching concept and analysed the utility benefits in both the approaches. A joint optimization problem for relay selection, user pairing and power allocation among the cooperative partners was formulated in (Feiyu et al. 2020); A sub-optimal scheme was proposed which improved energy efficiency of secondary networks. Finally, to evaluate the satisfaction level of cooperative users, a QoS driven secondary communication technique among the SUs was proposed in (Rahim et al. 2020), which significantly improved the overall satisfaction of the SUs while comparing to other contemporary techniques. However, the cooperative resource sharing schemes in multi PUs-multi SUs scenario faces more challenges due to involvement of heterogeneous constraints and competitions among the users, while pairing with the suitable users of opposite set.

In this paper, a matching game based partner assignment framework for multi PUs-multi SUs scenario is proposed, which assigns best suitable PU-SU partners for cooperative communication and allocates optimal resource (access time on PU's band) among them. The proposed one-to-one partner assignment scheme provides maximum possible utility for all selected PU-SU pairs; however, in worst case scenario, a particular SU might have paired with its least preferred PU. Numerical results reveal that the proposed scheme yields optimal matching for the set of PUs and stable matching for the set of SUs.

The rest of the paper is organized as follows. Section 2 presents the description of the system model with considered assumptions and resource optimization framework. In Sect. 3, the proposed one-to-one partner assignment scheme for cooperative communication is described. Simulation results along with performance analysis are discussed in Sect. 4 and finally the paper is concluded with future direction in Sect. 5.

2 System Model and Assumptions

We consider a CRN framework with a set of M PU transceiver pairs denoted as $\mathcal{M} = \{(PT_1, PR_1), .., (PT_i, PR_i), .., (PT_M, PR_M)\}$ and a set of N SU transceiver pairs denoted as $\mathcal{N} = \{(ST_1, SR_1), .., (ST_j, SR_j), .., (ST_N, SR_N)\}$. It is assumed that overlay spectrum access is adopted by PUs and SUs on PU's licensed band, where PUs have the exclusive right over it and SUs access the band in exchange of the relay service to PU transmission. Note that, PU prefers to cooperate with SU if and only if the cooperative capacity is found to be larger than the direct transmission by PU. Meanwhile SU too accepts PU's offer only if SU can maximize its targeted data transmission rate. PU is assumed to be the owner of its licensed band of W MHz bandwidth and channel is used in $TDMA$ mode with time slots of duration T each. We also assume that PUs can adjust their transmission power (POW_{PU}) level, while transmitting their data. For the proposed resource sharing model, we have assumed $TDMA$ channel with each time slot divided into three sub slots based on two decision variables α and β as shown in Fig. 1.

Out of total access time T, the SU assisted cooperative communication takes place over a duration of β time in two phases Phase 1 and Phase 2. In Phase 1, PT_i transmits its data towards the selected relay (or SU) for a fraction of $\alpha\beta$ time duration and in Phase 2, relay node forwards PU data to corresponding PR_i for the next $(1-\alpha)\beta$ time. Finally, in phase 3, the remaining $(T - \beta)$ time is allocated to the assisted relay node as a compensation of relaying PU's service. We have considered that the relay nodes adopted amplify-and-forward (AF) relaying technique for transmitting PU data towards the PU receivers.

2.1 Utility of PUs and SUs

Based on Shannon-Hartley Channel Capacity Theorem, the cooperative capacity (C_{coop}) achieved by the PU due to AF relaying over β time unit and W MHz bandwidth can be written as Eq. (1).

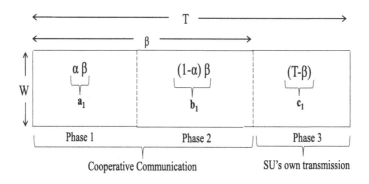

Fig. 1. Time-slot division model of PU band

$$C_{coop} = (a_1 + b_1)W.log(1 + SNR_{s,d} + \frac{x}{y})$$ (1)

where, $\frac{x}{y} = \frac{(SNR_{s,ST}*SNR_{ST,d})}{(SNR_{s,ST}+SNR_{ST,d}+1)}$ and $SNR_{s,d}$, $SNR_{s,ST}$, $SNR_{ST,d}$ are the $SNRs$ received at PR from PT, at ST from PT, and at PR from ST respectively. However, as it is mentioned earlier, PT is able to adjust POW_{PU} in Phase 1. So, the energy consumption of PT in Phase 1 is equal to $POW_{PU} * a_1$ Joules. Therefore, the utility of PU (U_{PU}) can be formulated in terms of maximizing C_{coop} for minimum consumption of energy is as shown in Eq. (2).

$$U_{PU} = \frac{C_{coop} - C_{direct}}{POW_{PU} * a_1}$$ (2)

where, C_{direct} is the capacity achieved by PT via direct transmission and C_{coop} must be $> C_{direct}$. On the other hand, let us assume that each ST has a power budget of POW_{SU} Watt and it uses the same power during both Phase 2 and Phase 3. This makes SU treats PU data as its own while relaying it. Therefore, the total energy consumption of SU (EN_{SU}) is calculated as:

$$EN_{SU} = (POW_{SU} * b_1) + (POW_{SU} * c_1)$$ (3)

where, $(POW_{SU} * b_1)$ is the transmit energy (in Joule) invested by SU during Phase 2 for relaying PU data and $(POW_{SU} * c_1)$ is the transmit energy used by SU during Phase 3 for its own transmission. From Eq. (3), it can be clearly understood that if SU aims to save more energy for Phase 3, it should invest less energy during Phase 2 and this is only possible by allocating minimum possible b_1 for Phase 2.

Finally, SU is awarded with $c_1 = (T - \beta)$ time to access the PU band for secondary transmission. So based on Shannon Theorem, total capacity achieved by an SU (C_{SU}) over W MHz bandwidth and c_1 time unit can be written as shown in Eq. (4).

$$C_{SU} = (c_1 * W).log(1 + SNR_{ST,SR})$$ (4)

Therefore, the utility of SU (U_{SU}) can be formulated in terms of maximizing C_{SU} under reasonable cost values incurred as given in Eq. (5).

$$U_{SU} = \frac{C_{SU}}{EN_{SU} + ER_{SU}} \tag{5}$$

where, ER_{SU} is the expensive rate of SU (discuss in next section) that decides based on the announced resource offers and negotiation among the PUs and SUs. Details of resource allocation process is given as follows.

2.2   Optimal Allocation of α and β

Based on the resource offers announced by PUs and SUs, each PU provides chance to SUs for optimal allocation of α and β. Initially, each interested ST discloses its resource constraints: (i) POW_{SU}, and (ii) c_1^{target} to PUs. Here, c_1^{target} is the minimum required compensation (in terms of access time to access PU's licensed band) asked by the ST to satisfy its targeted transmission rate. Before starting any negotiation with SUs, each PT broadcasts its β_{PU}^{target}, α_{PU} along with a penalty function $P_n(\alpha, \beta, y)$. Here, β_{PU}^{target} is the required β time to obtain transmission objective targeted by PT, α_{PU} ($0 < \alpha_{PU} \leq 0.5$) is the fraction of β time allotted for PT's transmission in Phase 1, and $P_n(\alpha, \beta, y)$ is the penalty function set by PT with the aim to maximize U_{PU}. From SU's utility function (Eq. (5)), it can be observed that SU's utility increases with the increase of c_1 and decreases with the increase of b_1. Hence, SU has a tendency to increase c_1 and decrease b_1 by reducing β up to a possible limit, say, β^{new} (of course $\beta^{new} > \beta_{PU}^{target}$). Therefore, to restrict such self-awareness property of SUs, PT models $P_n(\alpha, \beta, y)$ considering the following two points:

- Based on β^{new} decided by ST, the expensive rate of ST is calculated as, $ER_{SU} = \frac{1}{e^{uv}}$, where $u = \beta^{target}$ and $v = (\beta^{new} - \beta_{PU}^{target})$. Later on, based on the associated ER_{SU} value PT ranks each ST for selection purpose.
- Based on β^{new}, for per unit extra c_1 (c_1^{extra}) achieved by ST, PT reduces α_{PU} by y unit, which is modeled in Eq. (6).

$$\begin{aligned}
\alpha_{PU}^{new} &= \alpha_{PU} - (y.c_1^{extra}) \\
&= \alpha_{PU} - [y.(c_1^{new} - c_1^{target})] \\
&= \alpha_{PU} - [y.((T - \beta^{new}) - c_1^{target})]
\end{aligned} \tag{6}$$

where, α_{PU}^{new} is the newly generated time fraction for PU set by the SU after reducing the β value up to β^{new}, with an intention to maximize c_1^{new}. But, in the race of maximizing c_1^{new}, SU needs to monitor the gradually reduced α_{PU} as well as β^{new} values. As the former increases the size of b_1 and the later increases the size of ER_{SU}. Both the parameters directly affect the cost values of SU and reduce U_{SU}. Therefore, SU needs to decide appropriate value for β^{new} (β^*), so that acceptable ER_{SU} and α_{PU}^{new} can be obtained for cooperation, which satisfies

PU constraints as well as maximizes U_{SU}. So, the optimal allocation of α_{PU}^{new} (α^*) is formulated as given in Eq. (7).

$$\alpha^* = \alpha_{PU} - [y.((T - \beta^*) - c_1^{target})] \tag{7}$$

where, β^* is the optimal time allotted by ST for cooperative communication involving both Phase 1 and Phase 2. The optimization problem for β^* is modelled as given in Eq. (8).

$$
\begin{aligned}
\beta^* &= \max(U_{SU}) \\
&= \max\left(\frac{C_{SU}}{EN_{SU} + ER_{SU}}\right) \\
&= \max \frac{(T - \beta^{new})W.log(1 + SNR_{ST,SR})}{[(((1 - \alpha_{PU}^{new})\beta^{new}) + (T - \beta^{new})) * POW_{SU}] + \frac{1}{e^{uv}}} \\
\text{s.t.} \quad &\beta_{PU}^{target} < \beta^{new} < \beta_{PU}^{max}
\end{aligned}
\tag{8}
$$

where, $\beta_{PU}^{max} = (T - c_1^{target})$. For each β^{new}, the corresponding α_{PU}^{new} is easily found by substituting the value of β^{new} in Eq. (6). However, the optimization problem for β^* (Eq. (8)) is found non-linear nature. Non-linear problems are classified as hard problems and difficult to solve. Heuristic approaches are found widely used to address such problems. Therefore, numerical analysis based heuristic approach can be applied to decide α^* and β^* value. Thus for each PU offer, every SU decides on β^* and corresponding α^* and responds to the PUs with a tuple (α^*, β^*), seeking to be the partner for cooperation.

3   Matching Game Based Proposed Partner Assignment Scheme

The proposed scheme focuses on stable partner assignment for cooperative communication, such that each pair of cooperative partners can be able to maximize their achieved utility. During the assignment, each PU seeks to have most profitable SU as its cooperative partner and similarly each SU aims to match with its most preferred PU. Thus, there arises a win-win situation for both PU and SU. To analyse such mutually beneficial relationships between the users of two disjoint sets in the field of resource sharing among the competitive as well as cooperative users, matching theory is proven to be an effective framework (Yaffe et al. 2010; Cechlrov and Manlove 2005). Some of the relevant definitions (Gao et al. 2017; Chang et al. 2020; Gu et al. 2015) of matching theory which need to be investigated to establish mutually beneficial relationship among the selected PU-SU pairs are given below:

3.1 Basic Definitions of Matching Theory

- **Definition 1** *(One-to-One matching): A One-to-One matching between sets M and N such that $i \in M$ and $j \in N$, can be represented by a One-to-One matching $\mu(.)$, where $\mu(i) = j$ (i is matched with j) if and only if $\mu(j) = i$ (j is also matched with i). Further, $\mu(i) = i$ and $\mu(j) = j$ indicate i and j stay single.*

- **Definition 2** *(Stable matching): In a multi-PU and multi-SU scenario, the stable matching between the PU-SU pair (also termed as unblock PU-SU pair) can be established if both of them satisfy the following two properties :*
  - **Property 1:** *Any i and j of matching μ is willing to maintain the current partnership rather than stay single.*
  - **Property 2:** *Neither i nor j of matching μ can increase their individual utility further, via unilateral deviation (choosing a new partner by betraying current partnership).*

  Otherwise, the PU-SU pair is called as blocking pair that results in an unstable matching.

- **Definition 3** *(Optimal matching): In a multi-PU multi-SU resource sharing scenario, it is possible to construct the optimal matching either from PU's or from SU's perspective. There always exists an optimal matching for each $i \in M$, where every i achieves the maximum possible utility (PU-optimal matching). Similarly, for each $j \in N$, there always exists an optimal matching (SU-optimal matching). But the point to be noted is that a matching or an equilibrium that is optimal for the users of one set will not be optimal for the users of opposite set. That means, users of two different sets cannot achieve optimal equilibrium at the same time.*

Based on the above concepts of matching theory, a matching game based solution strategy has been developed to establish stable assignment of cooperative PU-SU pairs for cooperative communication and resource sharing process in CRNs. The proposed algorithm along with its time complexity analysis and corresponding proofs of the achieved matching types are presented in next section.

3.2 Proposed Algorithm

Time Complexity of Algorithm 1: To analyse the overall time complexity of proposed algorithm, we need to investigate the running time of *while loop* (Step 7) along with its inner *conditional IF statement* (Step 11). Lets analyse the worst case scenario of the algorithm along with its worst case time complexity, where PU_i receives requests from all the N SUs at $Round_1$. Out of these N requests, PU_i selects the SU offer for which maximum U_{PU_i} can be achievable and rejects the others. In $Round_2$, assume the remaining $(N-1)$ SUs send respective request to PU_{i+1} and after selecting the most profitable one, PU_{i+1} rejects the remaining $(N-2)$ requests. This process continues for each entry in PL of SUs i.e. up to M preferences (where M is total number of PUs). Therefore, the worst case running time complexity of the *while loop* along with

---

Algorithm 1: Stable PU-SU pair formation for cooperative communication

---

Input: Provide (α^*, β^*) to each PU.

Output: Formation of stable PU-SU pair.

1 **Initialize:** Matching among the (PU, SU) is null, i.e. $\mu(i) \in M = \mu(j) \in N = \phi$

2 **Preference List (PL) creation by SUs:**

3 Based on (α^*, β^*), each SU computes U_{SU}.

4 Prepares PL for PUs with decreasing order of U_{SU} found so far.

5 According to PL, each SU offers corresponding (α^*, β^*) request, to its most preferred PU.

6 **One-to-One matching:**

7 **while** *(each PU of set M is not mapped with perfect SU)* **do**

8   PU calculates U_{PU} and corresponding ER_{SU} based on received (α^*, β^*) values.

9   PU accepts the request of SU with highest achievable U_{PU} and rejects the rest.

10   For two similar U_{PU} values, PU accepts the request with minimum ER_{SU} value.

11   **if** *SU is rejected by PU* **then**

12   **Repeat (until all entries in PL are processed)**

13   SU updates its PL by substituting the next preferred PU as its current preference and offers corresponding (α^*, β^*) request to it.

14   PU updates its current holding request with the new one if and only if:

15          $(U_{PU_{new}} > U_{PU_{hold}})$ or

16          $(U_{PU_{new}} = U_{PU_{hold}}$ && $ER_{SU_{new}} < ER_{SU_{hold}})$

17   Otherwise, reject the new request.

18   **else**

19   PU_i and SU_j announce as stable partners for cooperation.

20   **end**

21 **end**

---

the ***IF statement*** is $= N + (N-1) + (N-2) + \ldots\ldots\ldots + (N-M) = O(N * M)$, which is a ***polynomial time*** complexity.

Theorem 1. *Proposed algorithm converges to a stable matching, even if the SU pairs with its least preferred PU.*

Proof. According to the PL, each SU aims to attract its most preferred PU. If SU gets rejection by its current preferred PU, it sends request to next preferred PU and this process continues until the SU receives any positive response from the requested PU. Let us analyse the worst case scenario, where SU_j gets the chance to make pair with its least preferred PU_i and obtains utility $U_{SU_j}^{least_i}$. In this state, SU_j has no further PU options to negotiate for maximizing the achieved utility. So SU_j decides to be paired with PU_i instead of being single. Thus, satisfies Property 1 and 2 for SU_j.

However, in the assignment process a PU leaves its current request and accepts a new one only if the later provides higher U_{PU} than the earlier one. This means, if PU_i accepts the request of SU_j, it must provides highest U_{PU_i} among all the previous requests it has received so far. And if it happens, PU_i willingly accepts SU_j as its cooperative partner, which satisfies Property 1 and 2 for PU_i. Therefore, no blocking pairs are emerged in any iterative step of the algorithm, which proves that the final assignment or matching of PU-SU pair is stable.

Theorem 2. *The outcome of the one-to-one matching of the proposed algorithm converges to an optimal matching for the set of PUs.*

Proof. In each round of the proposed algorithm, a single PU may get multiple requests or offers from multiple SUs. Based on such requests, PU calculates corresponding U_{PU} and selects the SU that provides maximum U_{PU}. However, on receiving new offers in imminent rounds, PU accepts the new ones only if U_{PU}^{new} is found $> U_{PU}^{current}$, otherwise it rejects the new request. This indicates if PU_i accepts an offer in $Round_i$ with utility $= U_{PU_i}^{Round_i}$, it must be the highest utility obtained by PU_i so far, which reveals PU always prefers and accepts SU offer with maximum profit irrespective of the round. Hence proves that the proposed algorithm converges optimal matching for each of the PU.

Summary: Analysis of the algorithm revels that in best case when both PU and SU get chance to pair with their first preference, the proposed solution converges to optimal match for PU as well as for SU. However, in worst case, SU might accept the offer of its least preferred PU with certain utility (U_{SU}^{least}), which satisfies SU's target constraint but cannot improve further. So rather than being single, SU accepts the offer and forms a stable match with its least preferred PU. Thus, at the end, the proposed partner selection algorithm turns out to be optimal for the set of PUs and stable for SUs.

4   Simulations Results and Discussion

The simulation study work of the proposed algorithm is carried by MATLAB 7 (R2017a) simulator, in a 64-bit PC with a core i5 processor and 8 GB RAM. We have considered a CR network with randomly distributed M PUs and N SUs. Further, we assume bandwidth $W = 1$ MHz and time period $T = 10$ s. for each PU time slot. The transmission power at each node (PU as well as SU) is set randomly over the range [0.01 to 0.05] W (Su et al. 2012). The PU channels are considered to be AWGN channels and the variance of noise is set as 10^{-10} Watt at all the nodes. Further, the channel gains and path loss exponent are chosen as described in (Sharma et al. 2011).

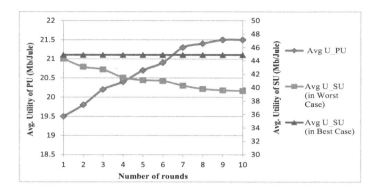

Fig. 2. Graph of utility of PU vs. utility of SU

Figure 2 depicts average U_{PU} (shown in Primary Y axis) and average U_{SU} against number of rounds for both best and worst case (shown in secondary Y axis) for a network with $M = 10$ PUs and $N = 15$ SUs. In each round of the assignment process, PUs get new requests from SUs, and PUs either accept the request with maximum possible utility or reject them. As the rounds proceed, the average utility of PUs either gradually increases or get saturated as shown in the graph. However, the graph for utility of SUs has shown reverse characteristics in this context. Since SUs prepare their PLs by preferring the PUs with maximum U_{SU}. So in best case, both PU_i and SU_j get pair with the most preferred partners and obtain maximum possible utilities. However, in worst case scenario, SU_j gets pair with its least preferred PU due to facing repeated rejection by the previous PUs of its PL. So, in such case utility of SUs is found deteriorate with increase of rounds in the assignment process.

Figure 3 shows the graphs of average U_{SU} for a network with increasing number of SUs (from $N = 5$ to 30) and for some fix number of PUs that is $M = 5$, $M = 10$ and $M = 15$ respectively. As number of SUs increases in the

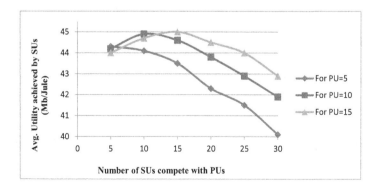

Fig. 3. Avg. utility of SUs for different number of SUs and PUs.

assignment process, the competition among them to get pair with favourable PUs too increases; especially when M is smaller. Therefore, U_{SU} starts to deteriorate as PUs get more SU options to choose for. In the graph of $M = 5$ PUs, U_{SU} is found to be maximum when only 5 SUs involve in the assignment process. Furthermore, with the increase in number of SUs, PUs get chance to negotiate with more SUs and select most profitable SU by rejecting others. So, in worst case, the SUs either to accept the PU offers even it provides low utility (of course > targeted transmission rate) or decide to quite the assignment process. This results the graph of U_{SU} (for $M = 5$) gradually declines as shown in Fig. 3. However, the remaining two graphs for $M = 10$ and $M = 15$ are shown initial increment of U_{SU} when the involved number of SUs is small that is, $N = 11$ and $N = 17$ respectively; after that the U_{SU} starts to deteriorate along with the increase in the number of SUs.

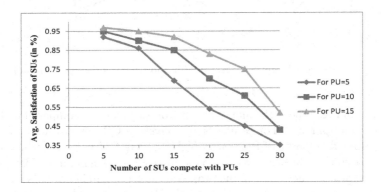

Fig. 4. Avg. satisfaction of SUs for different number of SUs and PUs.

Figure 4 depicts the avg. satisfaction level of SUs with increasing number of SUs participating in the assignment process. Inspire by (Rahim et al. 2020), the satisfaction of SU (SAT_{SU}) for an assigned PU-SU pair can be determined based on the position of assigned PU in the preference list of SU, which is formulated as: $SAT_{SU} = \frac{(M+1)-x}{M}$. Here, M is total number of PUs and x is the position of assigned PU in the preference list of SU. Similarly, the avg. satisfaction of a one-to-one matching having N number of SUs is formulated as: $SAT_{SU}^{avg} = \frac{\sum_{j=1}^{N}(M+1)-x_j}{M*N}$.

In Fig. 4, the graphs of avg. satisfaction of SUs for a CR network as considered in earlier case (Fig. 3) are depicted. When number of PUs in the assignment process is 5 along with 5 number of SUs, the SAT_{SU}^{avg} achieves approximately 95% satisfaction. But as number of SUs increases from 5 to 30 in the assignment process, the option of PUs for choosing most suitable SUs too increases. This restricts the SUs from making preferred pair with PUs, which drastically reduces the satisfaction level of SUs as shown in Fig. 4. Similar graphs of SAT_{SU}^{avg} have been observed for two more cases where number of PUs in the assignment process are increased up to 10 and 15 respectively. However, due to the involvement of more number PUs, the satisfaction level of SUs has improved in both the two cases up to 20% and 48%, while comparing the results with the earlier case (When PUs = 5).

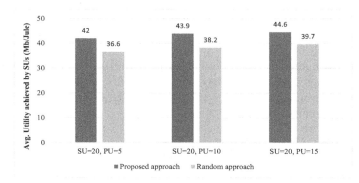

Fig. 5. Proposed approach vs. random approach (Color figure online)

Finally, in Fig. 5 the performance of the proposed model is compared with random selection approach. For comparison analysis, a CR network with $N = 20$ SUs and some fix number of PUs ($M = 5$, $M = 10$ and $M = 15$) is considered. In both approaches, the utility of SUs is found increasing when number of PUs in the assignment process increases. In the proposed model as number of PUs increases, more resource offers are exchanged among the PUs and SUs. This provides opportunity to SUs for negotiate with best PU offer and accordingly fix optimal α and β, which results high utility value for the SUs (blue one). However, in case of random selection approach, the selection of cooperative partner is random. So, there is no guarantee that all the selected PU-SU pairs are suitable cooperative partners for cooperative communication. This results the utility value of SUs decreases than the proposed approach as shown in the graph (red one).

5   Conclusion

In this paper, we have modelled cooperative partner selection and resource allocation problem for multi-PU multi-SU CR networks as a one-to-one matching game. The proposed algorithm provides stable PU-SU pair and allocates appropriate access time among them for cooperative communication. The algorithm converges to (i) optimal matching for the set of PUs, as each PU can be able to obtain the maximum possible utility from its cooperative partner SU, and (ii) stable matching for the set of SUs, as in worst case SUs might have paired with their least preferred PUs. We have provided formal proofs of stability and optimality of the proposed one-to-one matching. Simulation results reveal that the proposed cooperative scheme yields considerable gain in terms of utility achievement for the PU network. While comparing the performance, the proposed model significantly improves SUs utility than random selection approach.

An interesting observation to make is that optimal matching by SUs can be achievable when SUs work cooperatively and apply some combined strategies in requesting PUs for cooperation. But then the matching is no longer a one-to-one; rather it will become a one-to-many matching between the PU and SUs.

Acknowledgement. This work has been supported by IETE Research Fellowship dated 16-08-2021 for the year 2021–2023.

References

Ahmed, E., et al.: Channel assignment algorithms in cognitive radio networks: taxonomy, open issues, and challenges. IEEE Commun. Surv. Tutor. **18**(1), 795–823 (2016)

Akyildiz, I.F., et al.: NeXt generation/dynamic spectrum access/cognitive radio wireless networks: a survey. Comput. Netw. J. **60**(13), 2127–2159 (2006)

Bai, Z., et al.: Energy-efficient resource allocation for secure cognitive radio network with delay QoS guarantee. IEEE Syst. J. **13**(3), 2795–2805 (2019)

Cechlárová, K., Manlove, D.F.: The exchange-stable marriage problem. Discrete Appl. Math. **152**(1), 109–122 (2005)

Chang, M.-K., Mei, Y.-J., Chan, Y.-W., Wu, M.-Y., Chen, W.-R.: Matching game-based hierarchical spectrum sharing in cooperative cognitive radio networks. J. Supercomput. **76**(8), 6195–6218 (2019). https://doi.org/10.1007/s11227-019-02757-1

Yan, F., et al.: Energy-efficient resource allocation in relayaided orthogonal frequency division multiplexing cognitive radio networks with quality of service provisioning. Int. J. Commun. Syst. **33** (2020). https://doi.org/10.1002/dac.4566

Feng, X., et al.: Cooperative spectrum sharing in cognitive radio networks: a distributed matching approach. IEEE Trans. Commun. **62**(8), 2651–2664 (2014)

Gale, D., Shapley, L.S.: College admissions and the stability of marriage. Am. Math. Monthly **69**(1), 9–15 (1962)

Gao, L., Duan, L., Huang, J.: Two-sided matching based cooperative spectrum sharing. IEEE Trans. Mob. Comput. **16**(2), 538–551 (2017)

Gu, Y., et al.: Matching theory for future wireless networks: fundamentals and applications. IEEE Commun. Mag. **53**(5), 52–59 (2015)

Laneman, J.N., Tse, D.N.C., Wornell, G.W.: Cooperative diversity in wireless networks: efficient protocols and outage behavior. IEEE Trans. Inf. Theory **50**(12), 3062–3080 (1992)

Kumar, B., Kumar Dhurandher, S., Woungang, I.: A survey of overlay and underlay paradigms in cognitive radio networks. Int. J. Commun Syst **31**(2), 1–20 (2012)

Liang, W., Ng, S.X., Hanzo, L.: Cooperative overlay spectrum access in cognitive radio networks. IEEE Commun. Surv. Tutor. **19**(3), 1924–1944 (2017)

Rahim, M., et al.: Efficient channel allocation using matching theory for QoS provisioning in cognitive radio networks. Sensors **20**(7), 1–19 (2020)

Sharma, S., et al.: An optimal algorithm for relay node assignment in cooperative ad hoc networks. IEEE/ACM Trans. Netw. **19**(3), 879–892 (2011)

Su, W., Matyjas, J.D., Batalama, S.: Active cooperation between primary users and cognitive radio users in heterogeneous ad-hoc networks. IEEE Trans. Sig. Process. **60**(4), 1796–1805 (2012)

Namvar, N., Afghah, F.: Spectrum sharing in cooperative cognitive radio networks: a matching game framework. In: 49th Annual Conference on Information Sciences and Systems (CISS), Princeton, NJ, USA, pp. 1–5 (2015)

Roumeliotis, A.J., Vassaki, S., Panagopoulos, A.D.: Overlay cognitive radio networks: a distributed matching scheme for user pairing. In: 2015 International Wireless Communications and Mobile Computing Conference (IWCMC), Dubrovnik, Croatia, pp. 172–177 (2015)

Yaffe, Y., Leshem, A., Zehavi, E.: Stable matching for channel access control in cognitive radio systems, Elba, Italy, pp. 470–475 (2010)

Sandbox Environment for Real Time Malware Analysis of IoT Devices

Gaurav Pramod Kachare[1], Gaurav Choudhary[2], Shishir Kumar Shandilya[1], and Vikas Sihag[3(✉)]

[1] School of Computing Science and Engineering,
VIT Bhopal University, Bhopal, India
gaurav.pramod2018@vitbhopal.ac.in
[2] DTU Compute, Technical University of Denmark, Lyngby, Denmark
[3] Sardar Patel University of Police, Security and Criminal Justice, Jodhpur, India
vikas.sihag@policeuniversity.ac.in

Abstract. The explosion in IoT devices' growth becomes the primary target to attackers. It provides a large attack surface to attackers for Distributed Denial of Service (DDoS), Eavesdropping, Privilege Escalation, etc. With a lack of research in IoT security, there are lake solutions to analyze the advanced malware in a secure environment to understand IoT malware behavior. This paper has proposed a sandbox environment concept model that analyses malware, generates automated reports, and solves problems with the existing sandbox. Sandbox uses multiple machine-learning algorithms to analyze malware on three basic levels: static malware analysis, real-time malware analysis, and network analysis. Then by consolidating the report from all this analysis, the sandbox environment generates the report. Static analysis is performed by collecting information from shared libraries, ELF, and other binary files using the Convolutional Neural Networks model generated automated analysis report.

Keywords: Sandbox · Malware · IoT · Security

1 Introduction

Over the years, the Internet of Things (IoT) has become an essential topic of the decade. IoT concepts and implementations completed 20 years in 2021. With the pandemic, the digital revolution enhanced rapidly, and due to the fast internet and enhancements in AI and ML technologies, IoT has become an essential part of our lives. According to International Data Corporation (IDC), there are a forecasted 46 billion connected devices for this year alone, while 31 billion IoT devices will be installed worldwide by the end of 2021. According to statistics smart home sector is also expanding quickly, and estimates are that it will rise by approximately \$54 billion in 2022. According to tech giant Cisco, the ownership of IoT devices will double by the end of 2023. As compared to 2018, On a worldwide scale, 2.1 per capita will increase the ownership of interconnected devices in the next few years.

© Springer Nature Switzerland AG 2022
N. Chaubey et al. (Eds.): COMS2 2022, CCIS 1604, pp. 169–183, 2022.
https://doi.org/10.1007/978-3-031-10551-7_13

Technologies like edge computing are helping in the reduction of cost and improvement computational power of IoT devices, allowing them for temporary data storage before sending over the network, which improves network bandwidth consumption. It also helps to maintain the policies, compliance, and regulation in IoT devices. Also, a rapidly increasing number of IoT increases the collection and transmission of all sorts of data over the internet. All this managing and analyzing data is essential, and so, data analysis, machine learning, and artificial intelligence play a vital role in IoT devices with the help of edge computing data analytics is possible [18,22]. As more and more devices interact sharing data, it becomes easier to train all devices by training one. All this technology developed independently, but we are integrating them all through the use of IoT devices. With the help of all these technological advancements, both organizations and consumers can now experience rapid and effective use of technology, which was not possible before. The Industrial Internet of Things (IIoT) is utilized for productivity maintenance, energy, and resource management, reducing operational costs, and increasing operational safety and productivity. Medical services heavily invest in smart devices, chronic disease monitoring, and smart disease diagnostic devices. According to the forecast of Forst and Sullivan, the internet of medical things (IoMT) is expected to rise to $72.02 billion by the end of the year 2021.

As the IoT industry is growing rapidly and there are numerous hardware, software, and firmware for IoT devices, security becomes the primary concern for IoT devices. These devices were not built with considering security issues. According to the reports, IoT devices are around 33% of all infected devices. The report is aggregated by network traffic monitoring on more than 150 million devices globally. There is a lack of physical hardening, which anyone can exploit with physical access to the device. Cheap IoT devices use unencrypted data transfer and storage mechanisms which then can be attack surfaces for attackers. Some commercial solutions are available for IoT devices like IoT integrators, which help design, architect, and build a proper IoT solution. But the cost and return on investment (ROI) are not appropriate for small organizations. Some vendors provide suitable solutions and regular patches. Endpoint protection (EPP) and IDS can alert users to any malicious activity but are not effective against zero days. Also, there is a sandbox environment to study and contain the IoT malware, which can be global threats later on, but there is no commercial sandbox available for IoT devices [15].

1.1   Problem Statement and Contributions

Over the past few years, IoT has become one of the leading technologies of the 21st-century. Tech analyst company IDC forecasts that there will be 41.6 billion connected IoT devices by 2025. Due to a lack of research and development in IoT security, IoT has become a primary target to attackers as they are highly vulnerable to malware attacks. Malware-infected IoT can be used for attacks like Industrial Espionage and Eavesdropping, Distributed Denial of

Service (DDoS), Cryptomining, etc. Some of the researchers have proposed solutions like v-sandbox where it supports multiple CPU architecture and data from command and control servers (C&C) and auto-generate reports [12]. Also, there are ELF analyzer [6] and IoTPOT [16] honeypot for IoT devices where some of them are more network focused, and others are more optimized for IoT devices. Still, there is no proper solution covering all the components necessary for the sandbox to be efficient and effective. This paper proposes a lightweight sandbox model concept supporting multiple CPU architectures and support data collection from system calls, Command and Control communication, shared libraries, System files, folders along with network data and logs collection without affecting network bandwidth and battery consumption and after utilizing ML algorithms for analysis it generates an automated report.

2   Related Work

A lightweight sandbox for IoT devices is essential as IoT devices have low computational power and a wide variety of hardware [23,24]. Most researchers give importance to Sandbox for IoT devices that support multiple CPU architectures as there is a wide variety of products and embedded systems in IoT devices [6,12]. Along with that, for analysis of malware, there is a need for data from command-and-control systems [2,5,13]. According to recent reports, many IoT attacks are based on changes made on data of shared libraries [12]. For network-based attacks in a sandbox, researchers analyze the network behavior [10,11] and some sandboxes don't affect the network bandwidth. Power optimization is also an important point for comparison while considering the use of sandbox on IoT devices [17]. Some IoT Sandbox can generate a report automatically for further documentation [12].

Many researchers have focused on creating sandboxes on multiple CPU architectures, and some of them are working on most IoT devices. Still, they don't focus on network-based attacks and optimization in-network and battery utilization [1,12]. Whereas some are more focused on optimization, then there is no consideration for the network, Command, and Control, and shared library threats [17,23]. Where some research papers focus on the threat hunting model and don't discuss how threats should be analyzed [9], also, some articles are more focused on how to mitigate the threats using a sandbox environment but support only one CPU architecture. some researchers did an in-depth analysis of signature-based detection but are unable to provide dynamic analysis [2]. No sandbox can satisfy all the points given in the Table 1.

To solve this, sandbox should support multiple CPU architectures, data collected from shared libraries, system calls, file activity, network log, etc. The sandbox should support the command and control server communication, and the sandbox should not affect the network performance and prevent over batter consumption. Network behavior analysis is also important for sandboxing environment. The devices with shallow computation power and network capabilities need to find the integrable solution for IoT devices. Sandbox should provide an automated report after the analysis.

Table 1. The state-of-the-art comparison of solutions for the sandbox environment. {R1-Support Multiple CPU Architectures, R2-Data from Shared libraries, R3-Support Dynamic Analysis, R4-Optimized Battery Consumption And Network Usage, R5-Command and Control server communication, R6-Network Behavior Analysis, R7-Auto-Generated report}

Authors	Key contributions	R1	R2	R3	R4	R5	R6	R7
Le and Ngoe [12]	Develop an adequate IoT sandbox for IoT Botnet detection	Yes	Yes	Yes	No	Yes	No	Yes
Kai-Chi Chang et al. [6]	Created Sandbox supporting multiple CPU architectures using QEMU	Yes	No	Yes	No	Yes	Yes	No
Sahu and Singh [17]	JavaScript-based sandbox to control the execution of IoT programs	No	No	Yes	Yes	No	No	No
Chang et al. [5]	Detection of malware in early stages	Yes	No	Yes	No	No	Yes	No
Alasmary et al. [1]	Created a deep learning model by using control flow graphs	Yes	No	–	No	Yes	No	No
Vaughn et al. [27]	Integrated advanced computational linguistic functions in the sandbox using web interface	No	No	Yes	–	No	No	No
Zhongjin Liu et al. [13]	Designed an Integrated Architecture for Dynamic, Static & behavioral analysis of IoT malware	Yes	No	Yes	No	Yes	Yes	No
Jeon et al. [11]	Performed dynamic analysis of IoT malware in the nested cloud environment	–	Yes*	Yes	No	No	Yes	No
Soliman et al. [23]	Created Taxonomy of different approaches of malware analysis along with pros and cons of each	–	Yes*	Yes	Yes*	No	Yes	No
Sun et al. [24]	Created lightweight scanning & signature-based detection mechanisms for IoT devices	NF	No	No	Yes*	No	Yes	No
Alhanahnah et al. [2]	Generated signature generation and classification scheme using malware dataset	Yes	No	No	No	Yes	Yes*	No
Vasan et al. [26]	Generated threat hunting model based on advanced ensemble learning for IoT malware detection	Yes*	No	Yes	No	No	No	No
Pa Pa and Suzuki [16]	Investigated Iot threat and major compromisations like IoT botnet	Yes	No	–	No	Yes*	Yes	No
Greamo and Ghosh [10]	Discuss about types of virtualization and sandboxes	–	–	Yes	–	–	Yes	–

3   Background

Internet of Things (IoT) refers to a system of interrelated things/devices connected through the internet, which are embedded with sensors, software, and related technologies that autonomously share and collect information. IoT can be any physical device that is connected to the internet to be controlled or transfer information. IoT devices are integrated with CPU, network adapters, and middle-ware. IoT devices use dynamic host configuration protocol for assigning IP to devices for communication. IoT devices use Datagram Transport Layer Security (DTLS), Advanced Message Queuing Protocol (AMQP), etc., for Wired communication. Wireless communication uses Low-power WAN (LPWANs used for machine-to-machine communication), IPv6, Wi-Fi, etc.

3.1 IoT Attacks

IoT devices are more prone to attack by malware. These attacked devices are then used for attacks like Man-in-the-Middle, Eavesdropping, privilege escalation, and Distributed denial of service attacks (DDoS) [3,8]. These attacked IoT devices are bots or zombie, which takes input from a command-and-control (C&C) server. C&C is the machine or servers that attackers use to communicate with infected devices. There are three types of communication between the C&C and bots. Beacon, Command, and Exfiltration. Beacon signals are periodic signals that check the connectivity and sometimes are triggered by system events such as restart or reboot. Command signals, as the name suggests this are the commands from the attacker to bot through C&C. This command is executed immediately or stored for additional processing. The last one is that Exfiltration signals are used to exfiltrate data from the bots or any connected infected device. This kind of command is used in eavesdropping to gather private information such as email, protected documents, etc. malware uses different methods to communicate with the command and control server depending on the environment in which it is deployed. It splits the communication between protocols by using multi-band communication.

3.2 Sandbox Environment

Sandbox is an isolated virtual environment for testing potential malicious code or files without affecting the underlying system and resources by mimicking the production environment's hardware, software, and network configuration. Nowadays, many threats use obfuscation techniques to hide them from detection, and they get activated only when a specific event triggers them. For example, Antivirus is off, exact system time, network and keyboard input, or system calls to understand this behavior. An environment is needed to analyze and report this without affecting the network and system resources. Sandbox executes suspicious files, links, or programs. By utilizing the facility of system snapshots, we can understand the program's behavior or link in the sandbox environment, such as monitoring program network activity, how it's behaving in a particular situation, and the possibility of threat. Sandbox environment also has the facility to save the snapshots of the current state of the instance, which can then be utilized to understand the changes done in the system after malware is executed. Also, we can pause the sandbox environment and get the information about the memory layout API calls and other information, which then can be examined for further analysis, and we can also revert to the saved state in case malware corrupts the environment (Fig. 1).

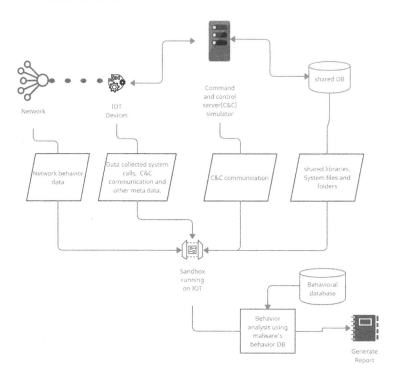

Fig. 1. Functional diagram.

Application of Sandbox Environment. Developers use a sandbox to analyze untested patch code before applying it to the system for quality assurance and robustness check. The testing environment mimics the actual execution environment code can be tested for potential threats and vulnerabilities before deployment. Security researchers also use the sandbox to understand the behavior of malware in a real-time environment and find out ways to detect and protect against them. To protect against any malware, researchers need to understand the functioning of malware, and that can't be performed without a sandbox environment. Sandbox is also utilized as a quarantine for email and attachments as many times email filters detect and quarantine the email and attachments. Still, the user can open these emails and attachments safely so that false positives can be detected without affecting the underlying systems.

3.3 Detection Methods

There are numerous methods available for malware analysis, but malware nowadays uses obfuscation techniques to hide them [4, 21]. Hence, sandbox needs to analyze malware using multiple approaches to classify and identify new obfuscation methodologies and malware behavior before it becomes a global threat. Some of the Detection methodologies are briefed below.

Static Analysis. Static analysis of malware is a method of examining the code without executing the code on the system. It is also known as source code analysis. Using this approach, we can predict the possible malware or vulnerability that can lead to an attack. This can be performed manually on code, but the autonomous approach is more effective and accurate. In IoT devices, malware identification using static analysis in the sandbox environment can be performed using meta-data analysis of the binary files and information available in the Executable and Linkable Format (ELF) files, which can be applied to IoT binaries across multiple CPU platforms [7]. Other traces can be found by opcode instruction which can be acquired by reverse engineering of binary files. There are numerous classification algorithms available to identify malware, such as Logistic Regression (LR). This linearly classifies data into discrete outcomes and by utilizing that detect the malware. Support Vector Machine (SVM) fixes a hyperplane that categorizes samples as malicious or trusted, after which rules are applied to detect false positives. Another approach is the random forest (RF) method. It generates multiple decision trees and merges them to get a more precise and steady prediction. All above are traditional machine learning approaches to detect malware. But there is a more advanced deep learning algorithm that is Convolutional Neural Network (CNN). This algorithm uses image classification to identify malware. There are multiple layers to this approach, such as a convolutional layer, pooling layer, the fully connected layer, which can detect malware more accurately [1]. This method is not the most effective one. It's the first step in malware analysis.

Dynamic Analysis. In contrast to static analysis, dynamic analysis executes the code in a controlled environment and studies code behavior and working. A controlled environment is a sandbox that is entirely isolated and doesn't affect the underlying systems. Static analysis of malware code is fast and straightforward, but it's not effective against advanced malware as they are using obfuscation techniques to hide from detection. To properly understand malware and its working in an actual environment, we need to use dynamic analysis in the sandbox environment. First, all dumps are collected from bash history, API hooks, kernel-loaded modules, and memory dump using tools like volatility.

Considering an example of fileless malware that resides in memory, a memory dump is collected from an isolated sandbox environment, and then data is analyzed using tools and techniques. For dynamic analysis, we can analyze the PE headers and API call analysis. PE headers contain information about imports, exports, timestamps, subsystem sections, and resources, which can help dynamic analysis. API calls play a vital role in dynamic malware analysis as we can understand how malware files execute and perform the action in the sandbox environment. We need to find out malware unpacking methodology, assembly program retrieving, API calls executions using ML algorithm for dynamic analysis [25]. It is an effective and flexible supervised machine learning algorithm. It can solve non-linear problems, and this classifier has high performance and can remove unnecessary inputs autonomously.

Network Analysis. Network analysis is a process to analyze the malware's activity in a network, and it also consists of detecting any possible malware network intrusion at the initial stage. For malware detection in the network, first, the packets are sniffed from the network from tools like Wireshark or by utilizing any centralized proxy server like a Burp. Then the detection can be done using two methods signature-based or anomaly-based. In signature-based malware detection, known malware signatures are used to recognize the malware. The problem with signature-based malware detection is that advanced malware can disguise themselves and avoid detection using garbage code insertion, code permutation, and reaming registers.

In comparison, anomaly or behavior-based malware detection is based on a host's malicious activity or action. Anomaly-based malware detects any suspicious activity by hosts like multiple failed login attempts, local scan by device, remote access from a foreign location, etc. The advantage of this method is that this can be used to identify malware at early stages and can identify zero-day attacks. For malware detection, we can use beacon-based analysis as attackers use command and control servers to make the connection between the attacker and infected systems. As command and control server mimics regular network traffic by utilizing protocols like DNS, HTTPS, etc., [14]. The infected devices periodically check the command and controller servers for any new action or instruction. Most of the time, command and controller servers send no command, which can be detected as the same sort of data is shared between the infected device and server. This can be detected as an anomaly by detection mechanisms. Whatever obfuscation method is used between malware and command and control server, this is noticeable. Every time systems make a request, the random size of data is exchanged for every section. These network behaviors can be detected using an isolation forest machine learning algorithm [25], which is well known for isolating anomalies. It is a type of unsupervised learning algorithm.

4   Proposed Solution

The sandbox has three significant parts-static malware analysis, dynamic malware analysis, and network monitoring. Static malware analysis is an art of reverse engineering where all available information is collected about binary using various methodologies without unpacking or executing the malware. There are many tools for manual static analysis like radare2. But for automated malware analysis, we are using Convolutional Neural Networks (CNNs). CNN is a deep learning approach to solve an image classification problem. It is arranged in a 3D structure where width and height are image length, and image width and depth are RGB channels of the image. First of all, the binaries and Executable and Linkable Format (ELF) files are collected from memory. First, all binaries are converted into an image as shown in the image. The first binary is converted into an 8-bit vector, and then the 8-bit vector is transformed into a grayscale image; and by utilizing this, we can analyze malware portions in detail (Fig. 2).

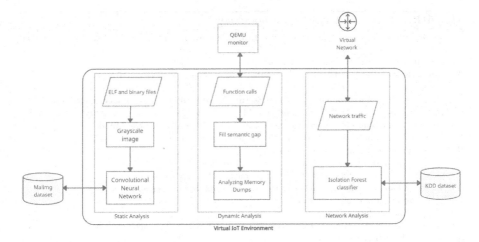

Fig. 2. System model

For feature selection, we can use any image characteristics, texture patterns, frequency of image, etc. by using Global Image Descriptors in python; we can use pyleargist. After finalizing feature selection, we now need to build a CNN model that can be performed using Keras. There are three primary layers in the CNN Convolutional layer, the Pooling layer, Fully-connected layer. Convolutional layer extracts feature we selected in the previous layer from generated grayscale image and then it multiplies values in the filter with the original pixel values. Pooling layer operation is performed for the reduction of the dimension of each feature map. Then the Fully-connected layer is a multi-layer perception and a softmax activation function that predicts a multinomial probability distribution in the output layer (Fig. 3).

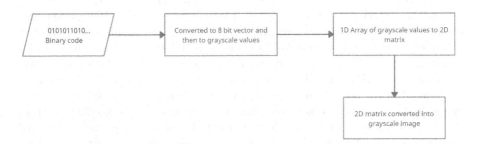

Fig. 3. Binary to grayscale image

Algorithm 1. Static Analysis Methodology

1: **Input**: Malimg dataset, shared libraries, ELF (Executable and Linkable Format) and binary files.
2: **Output**: Detailed Static Analysis Report.
3: Convert binary and Executable and Linkable Format files into grayscale image.
4: Import required packages.
5: Select feature (ex-texture pattern, colour features) using GIST (global image descriptors).
6: Import generated grayscale image and resize it to 64 * 64 pixels.
7: Select first 320 values from grayscale image and store it in array to train model.
8: Build Convolutional Neural Network (CNN) model with 2 layers.
9: Select input size as 32 * 32 for CNN model
10: Reshape train and test image pixels in range 0 to 255.
11: Feed the reshaped values as 32 * 32 * 1 dimension of image as result.
12: Set parameters batch size as 64, epochs as 20 and number classes as 25.
13: According to format build architecture.
14: Compile the model.
15: Fit and train model with appropriate labels and with parameters declared.
16: Test accuracy by using test dataset.
17: **if** Grayscale Image != Malimg dataset **then**
18:    Identify malware family.
19:    Insert image in Malimg dataset.
20:    Generate Report with malware family and accuracy.
21: **else**
22:    Generate Report.
23: **end if**

Dynamic analysis is a process of executing malware in a monitored environment to observe its behavior. When a program is executed, system calls or system calls give us details about files generated, modified, or deleted; websites visited, information transferred, etc. as new malware utilizes obfuscation techniques (fileless malware, dead-code insertion) register reassignment) for hiding themselves from detection. So, the first step in malware analysis is memory acquisition. A controlled environment is needed, which includes the ability to stop the process and examine several aspects of a system for which we need to utilize a tool known as QEMU monitor. It is utilized to give the Virtual Machine complex commands, such as removing or inserting a detachable storage device. Freeze or unfreeze the Virtual Machine and save or restore its state from a disk file. Inspect the VM state without an external debugger. Now live software tools like CaptureGARD or AVML can handle memory acquisition. Once the malware is executed in memory, memory dumps can be acquired at specific intervals in memory and analyzed. Before analyzing, the semantic should be filled, such as the internal structure of file should be extracted from files along with the stack and binary code. Now for the analysis of the dump, we need just to compare dumps of two different time intervals for any changes. We need to take care of time intervals as larger time intervals can affect the detection of system calls as system calls in the stack are there for a shorter duration of time until the function is returned. Then it's get overwritten by the next function call.

Algorithm 2. Dynamic Analysis Methodology

1: **Input**: API calls, malware dataset
2: **Output**: Dynamic Analysis Report.
3: Start malware execution and monitoring.
4: **while** Malware executing **do**
5:     Take periodic snapshot and memory dumps
6:     Hold state if needed using QEMU control
7: **end while**
8: Import required packages.
9: **if** Dataset is not processed **then**
10:     Import dataset and render using csv render.
11:     Generate array with random sample data along with size of sample.
12:     Save and close file.
13: **end if**
14: Identify data and related labels.
15: Select proper features for further analysis.
16: After selecting features divide dataset into group of two as training and test datasets.
17: Fit the taring dataset in the support vector classifier.
18: **if** malware detected using SVM **then**
19:     Generate Report.
20: **else**
21:     Continue
22: **end if**

Network analysis is an integral part of this sandbox as many malware infiltrate data and sometimes require connection to the internet for unpacking, unpacking, and updating malware. This phase continuously monitors a network and generates alerts using the Isolation Forest machine learning algorithm. First, we need to collect data using packet capture tools like Wireshark or tcpdump. Once we have the required data for analysis, we need to read the data set in the KDD dataset into the required dataset. Then we need to transform all non-normal traffic into a single class and anomalous. Then computation of anomalies to normal observations is done, known as contamination parameter, which is used to set the sensitivity of insolation forest. Then we need to split our dataset into abnormal and normal, along with the training and test version of the dataset. Then we need to train the data with train the model with each epoch, and then by using the test dataset, we can verify the accuracy of the model. The detailed approach is discussed in the algorithm given below.

Algorithm 3. Network Analysis Methodology

1: **Input**: Network traffic dump, packet captures (pcap).
2: **Output**: Report of intrusion through network.
3: Periodically capture packets from network.
4: Acquire KDDTrain+.arff file from NSL-KDD dataset.
5: Import required packages and KDDTrain+.arff file.
6: Assign number to field name.
7: Create column with filed name and load dataset with it.
8: **if** Unprocessed Dataset **then**
9:    Encode labels with values from 0 to $n\_classes - 1$.
10:    using transform calibrate values.
11:    return encoded labels.
12:    repeat process for all necessary labels.
13: **end if**
14: Split dataset(data and label) into two parts train dataset and test dataset.
15: Select isolation forest classifier.
16: Train dataset using train dataset.
17: **if** malicious activity detected **then**
18:    Generate alert.
19:    create report.
20: **end if**

To identify if the device is already compromised, we can locate it using the network and time protocols (NTP) as the timestamps play an essential role in finding out the actual time of the incident. If logs are not synchronized, we can conclude that remotely someone tries to access the device multiple times, a command and control server or actual attacker. Often, we need to decode encrypted network communication to utilize tools such a Dshell. This tool decodes the traffic and provides some detection capabilities of command and control server communication. We can use signature-based detection for automated command and control detection using machine learning. Also, we need to verify every result for any possibility of false positives. The above-discussed network anomaly detection approach can also identify the network anomalies like command and control server communication detection but needs to train more to detect all types of command and control communications to infected devices. More research is required for the effective detection of command and control servers and infection network propagation. As the low computation IoT devices send data to cloud or edge computing devices through the IoT gateway or any edge devices for computation or analysis, using the above approach on the computation device is more efficient than running sandbox on the low computation IoT device.

All results generated from the above approaches are sent to the report generation module. This module consolidates all these results in the proper format, and the user inputted required data to generate a correctly formatted report. The user inputted information contains the following fields: case number, the analyst name, organization name, email, mobile no, and automatically input date and time from the current system date and time. All this information is then converted into a PDF file with the file name as the case number. This well-documented report then can be used for further analysis.

5 Discussions

The approach discussed in the paper is having a multilayer approach to identify the malware in a secure, isolated environment as. First, the malware is analyzed statically, then executed, and both network and environment interactions are observed, gathered results are consolidated, and the report is available to the user. This approach is more effective for analysis than any other known approach. Different approaches focus more on specific approaches as V-Sandbox provides dynamic multi-CPU analysis solutions for IoT devices but does not provide proper network communication analysis. IoTBOX, a close source software, only provides network solutions and is not focused on delivering on-device security. IoTPOT explains talent-based attacks answer and supports multiple CPU architectures but focuses on different network attacks and static and real-time analysis. The proposed sandbox analyses shared library, ELF, dynamically linked libraries, API calls, and network communication and supported multiple CPUs.

The proposed sandbox model can be used for multiple purposes. Some of the examples of the use cases are for forensic analysis of IoT devices. To identify any available shreds of evidence and report generation for further analysis. Malware analysis of the zero-day vulnerabilities to identify the obfuscation method used and steps of execution and malware propagation methods is used to find effective ways to detect and contain this malware [19, 20, 28]. To better understand malware's communication methods and detect command and control communications in secure environments. This proposed solution can be less suitable for some lightweight IoT devices. We need to use the high computation device that can be used as an integrated solution for real-time detection. Malware which is using high device power and network resources can affect the sandbox efficiency. To solve this problem, we can use edge computing or similar cloud services.

6 Conclusion and Future Work

IoT devices are becoming primary targets to attackers, and there is not much research done on IoT security. Because of the wide variety of firmware, hardware, and software available for IoT devices, it's hard to provide a unique solution or test each variant. Without a proper testing and analysis environment, we won't be able to analyze new malware. Trying and analyzing malware in a working environment can attack or corrupt the connected and underlying resources. There are existing sandbox environments available in the market. There are some limitations like not all sandbox environments supporting the multiple CPU architectures, being unable to detect command and control server communication from the network and other network attacks, and not providing any optimizations for lightweight IoT devices. All these issues need to be solved to be performed on all the IoT devices and on all categories to understand the malware behavior and obfuscations techniques.

This paper has proposed a concept model for sandbox environment that can run on multiple hardware platforms to perform static analysis. Then, executing it in an isolated sandbox environment performs dynamic and network analysis using different machine learning algorithms. Then it can generates a consolidated report of analysis. Future works include a depth analysis of each machine learning model and optimized results, utilizing PE headers for effective dynamic analysis. Reduce the false positives and implement support for more devices detecting the source of infection in the IoT network with proper command and control server detection.

References

1. Alasmary, H., et al.: Analyzing and detecting emerging Internet of Things malware: a graph-based approach. IEEE Internet Things J. **6**(5), 8977–8988 (2019)
2. Alhanahnah, M., Lin, Q., Yan, Q., Zhang, N., Chen, Z.: Efficient signature generation for classifying cross-architecture IoT malware. In: 2018 IEEE Conference on Communications and Network Security (CNS), pp. 1–9 (2018)
3. Astillo, P.V., Choudhary, G., Duguma, D.G., Kim, J., You, I.: TrMAps: trust management in specification-based misbehavior detection system for IMD-enabled artificial pancreas system. IEEE J. Biomed. Health Inform. **25**(10), 3763–3775 (2021)
4. Borana, P., Sihag, V., Choudhary, G., Vardhan, M., Singh, P.: An assistive tool for fileless malware detection. In: 2021 World Automation Congress (WAC), pp. 21–25. IEEE (2021)
5. Chang, K.-C., Tso, R., Tsai, M.-C.: IoT sandbox: to analysis IoT malware Zollard. In: Proceedings of the Second International Conference on Internet of Things, Data and Cloud Computing, ICC 2017, Association for Computing Machinery, New York (2017)
6. Cheng, S.M., Ban, T., Huang, J.W., Hong, B.K., Inoue, D.: ELF analyzer demo: online identification for IoT malwares with multiple hardware architectures. In: 2020 IEEE Security and Privacy Workshops (SPW), p. 126 (2020)
7. Chiheb, C.: Mastering Machine Learning for Penetration Testing. Packt Publishing, Birmingham (2018)
8. Choudhary, G., Astillo, P.V., You, I., Yim, K., Chen, R., Cho, J.-H.: Lightweight misbehavior detection management of embedded IoT devices in medical cyber physical systems. IEEE Trans. Netw. Serv. Manag. **17**(4), 2496–2510 (2020)
9. Clincy, V., Shahriar, H.: IoT malware analysis. In: 2019 IEEE 43rd Annual Computer Software and Applications Conference (COMPSAC), vol. 1, pp. 920–921 (2019)
10. Ghosh, A., Greamo, C.: Sandboxing and virtualization: modern tools for combating malware. IEEE Secur. Priv. **9**(2), 79–82 (2011)
11. Jeon, J., Park, J.H., Jeong, Y.: Dynamic analysis for IoT malware detection with convolution neural network model. IEEE Access **8**, 96899–96911 (2020)
12. Le, H.V., Ngo, Q.D.: V-sandbox for dynamic analysis IoT botnet. IEEE Access **8**, 145768–145786 (2020)
13. Liu, Z., et al.: An integrated architecture for IoT malware analysis and detection. In: Li, B., Yang, M., Yuan, H., Yan, Z. (eds.) IoTaaS 2018. LNICST, vol. 271, pp. 127–137. Springer, Cham (2019). https://doi.org/10.1007/978-3-030-14657-3_14
14. Livadas, C., Walsh, R., Lapsley, D., Strayer, W.T.: Usilng machine learning technliques to identify botnet traffic. In: Proceedings of the 2006 31st IEEE Conference on Local Computer Networks, pp. 967–974 (2006)

15. Moad, D., Sihag, V., Choudhary, G., Duguma, D.G., You, I.: Fingerprint defender: defense against browser-based user tracking. In: You, I., Kim, H., Youn, T.-Y., Palmieri, F., Kotenko, I. (eds.) MobiSec 2021. CCIS, vol. 1544, pp. 236–247. Springer, Singapore (2022). https://doi.org/10.1007/978-981-16-9576-6_17

16. Pa, Y.M.P., Suzuki, S., Yoshioka, K., Matsumoto, T., Kasama, T., Rossow, C.: IoTPOT: analysing the rise of IoT compromises. In: 9th USENIX Workshop on Offensive Technologies (WOOT 2015) (2015)

17. Sahu, A., Singh, A.: Securing IoT devices using JavaScript based sandbox. In: 2016 IEEE International Conference on Recent Trends in Electronics, Information Communication Technology (RTEICT), pp. 1476–1482 (2016)

18. Sihag, V., Choudhary, G., Vardhan, M., Singh, P., Seo, J.T.: PICAndro: packet inspection-based Android malware detection. Secur. Commun. Netw. (2021)

19. Sihag, V., Vardhan, M., Singh, P.: BLADE: robust malware detection against obfuscation in Android. Forensic Sci. Int. Digit. Invest. **38**, 301176 (2021)

20. Sihag, V., Vardhan, M., Singh, P.: A survey of Android application and malware hardening. Comput. Sci. Rev. **39**, 100365 (2021)

21. Sihag, V., Vardhan, M., Singh, P., Choudhary, G., Son, S.: De-LADY: deep learning based Android malware detection using dynamic features. J. Internet Serv. Inf. Secur. (JISIS) **11**(2), 34–45 (2021)

22. Sinha, R., Sihag, V., Choudhary, G., Vardhan, M., Singh, P.: Forensic analysis of fitness applications on Android. In: You, I., Kim, H., Youn, T.-Y., Palmieri, F., Kotenko, I. (eds.) MobiSec 2021. CCIS, vol. 1544, pp. 222–235. Springer, Singapore (2022). https://doi.org/10.1007/978-981-16-9576-6_16

23. Soliman, S.W., Sobh, M.A., Bahaa-Eldin, A.M.: Taxonomy of malware analysis in the IoT. In: 2017 12th International Conference on Computer Engineering and Systems (ICCES), pp. 519–529 (2017)

24. Sun, H., Wang, X., Buyya, R., Su, J.: CloudEyes: cloud-based malware detection with reversible sketch for resource-constrained Internet of Things (IoT) devices. Softw. Pract. Exp. **47**, 421–441 (2016)

25. Tsukerman, E.: Machine Learning for Cybersecurity Cookbook: Over 80 Recipes on How to Implement Machine Learning Algorithms for Building Security Systems Using Python. Packt Publishing, Birmingham (2019)

26. Vasan, D., Alazab, M., Venkatraman, S., Akram, J., Qin, Z.: MTHAEL: cross-architecture IoT malware detection based on neural network advanced ensemble learning. IEEE Trans. Comput. **69**(11), 1654–1667 (2020)

27. Wright, W., Schroh, D., Proulx, P., Skaburskis, A., Cort, B.: The sandbox for analysis: concepts and methods. In: Proceedings of the SIGCHI Conference on Human Factors in Computing Systems, CHI 2006, pp. 801–810. Association for Computing Machinery, New York (2006)

28. You, I., Yim, K., Sharma, V., Choudhary, G., Chen, I.-R., Cho, J.-H.: Misbehavior detection of embedded IoT devices in medical cyber physical systems. In: Proceedings of the 2018 IEEE/ACM International Conference on Connected Health: Applications, Systems and Engineering Technologies, pp. 88–93 (2018)

Machine Learning for Classification of DOS Attack in Smart Healthcare Networks

Sweta Dargad[1,2,3](✉), Pooja Thakkar[1,2,3](✉), and Sangeeta Giri[1,2,3]

[1] School of CSIT, Symbiosis Skills and Professional University, Pimpri-Chinchwad, India
sweta.dargad@sspu.ac.in
[2] U. V. Patel College of Engineering, Ganpat University, Mehsana, India
pkt01@ganpatuniversity.ac.in
[3] Computer Engineering, Ganpat University, Mehsana, India

Abstract. Healthcare industry has taken 360-degree change when it comes to managing, analyzing and leveraging healthcare data. With 5G technology increased data rates, more reliability and greater capacity, the healthcare system can provide remote services for patients. For remote monitoring of a patient's health, real time data delivery is a must. The crucial requirement of the current time in the healthcare industry is the security of the patient's sensitive and critical data against potential threats. Therefore, it is important that we have security mechanisms ensuring not only authorized parties have access to a patient's sensitive data and medical information but also preserve its privacy and security. By 2022, cyber-crime is predicted to cost \$6 trillion each year. Healthcare industry is continually changing and adopting new aspects in technological transformations. In recent years there has been a broad adoption of Machine learning approaches because of their high level performance in healthcare services starting from the prediction of heart arrest, to medical imaging for detection of tumors and even infections like COVID. AI could help the Healthcare Industry protect their patients' data as well as secure their 5G network of computers across their organization. We have discussed Machine Learning techniques for Data security and privacy and a case study for detecting the intensity of DDOS attack using Decision Tree algorithm on Healthcare application network data. We have also proposed a model which includes 4 interconnecting lifecycle stages- collecting the data, storing the data, processing the data along with the analysis stage and creating knowledge from those data.

Keywords: Machine learning · 5G · IOT · Healthcare · DDOS attack · Security

1 Introduction

To stay up with the newest technological developments, the Indian 5G health-care service business is continuously evolving. It's no surprise that hospitals are embracing the internet to help with their duties in order to improve them-selves and give the finest

---

S. Giri—Contributing author.

© Springer Nature Switzerland AG 2022
N. Chaubey et al. (Eds.): COMS2 2022, CCIS 1604, pp. 184–197, 2022.
https://doi.org/10.1007/978-3-031-10551-7_14

services to their patients. With the development of linked healthcare, which includes improved equipment, monitoring, and tracking capabilities, the aggressive usage of 5G services and AI has made its impact. Improvements in information and communication technology, as well as the need to solve global healthcare and social care issues with data security and privacy, are the major motivations for the implementation of 5G Health care services improved equipment, monitoring, and tracking capabilities, the aggressive usage of 5G services and AI has made its impact. Improvements in information and communication technology, as well as the need to solve global healthcare and social care issues with data security and privacy, are the major motivations for the implementation of 5G Health care services (Fig. 1).

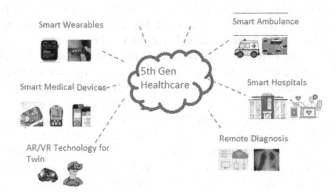

Fig. 1. 5th gen healthcare services

Healthcare information like Home Addresses, Phone Number, Email Ids, Insurance Details, Medical History, Driver License Details, Emergency Contacts, Credit/Debit Card Information, Etc. is in high demand by cyber criminals. [7] 5G, AI [14], and innovative healthcare services have a favorable impact on healthcare delivery. worldwide, including India. While these solutions are beneficial, they will also pose a risk to data security. In India, the digitalization of medical records has resulted in the release of patient data to authorized workers, agents, and contractors of the healthcare industry. Cybercriminals have already targeted the sector in the past, and this trend will only continue. Hospitals can manage this threat in a number of ways.

- **Threats Prevention:** With the minimization of the problems that comprise digital attacks. Firewalls and packet filters can be used to protect the network laid for healthcare services, and access controls lists can be used to minimize user-based risk. IDS/IPS tools can be used in blocking general 5Gsecurity warnings
- **Anomaly detection:** Using packet capture techniques, big data analytics with machine learning approaches, it may be possible to spot threats that pass through basic filters. It is significantly more effective to identify such anomalies when such technologies are embedded into network switches and routers and used as sensor nodes or honey pots
- **Fixing advanced malware:** Attacks aiming to evade basic filters can be detected using signature-based tools like PAYL and POSIDEON. End points are checked

using behavior-based or anomaly-based models integrated with ma-chine learning approaches, maybe leveraging sandboxing. Once a risk has been identified, it must be eliminated from the network in its entirety. Stakeholders can feel certain that their data is safe when such protections are easily integrated with existing technologies. In this paper, we have combined the available resources of Machine Earning Security 5th Gen Healthcare Services and represent the models available for the same.

2 Literature Review

Internet of Things is the network of variable digital machines, computing devices, mechanical devices, or any other thing that will be able to transfer data from a network without any kind of human interaction or Machine intervention. According to the reports of Gartner, in 2020 the world will use 20.4 billion devices for IoT. A lot of technical and security issues come in away when these many devices start connecting. Scalability, Security assurance, Identity, Network management, interoperability, latency, lack of standard are some of the main technical and security issues faced in 5G IoT architecture. The below literature review presents the challenges, crucial factors affecting the 5G healthcare services and how embedding technologies with Machine learning can help resolving such issues in the IoMT which is laid on 5G for healthcare services.

From the last few years Machine Learning (ML) as well as Deep Learning (DL) are superior in the healthcare system. One of the applications is about predicting cardiac arrest from medical images, but there is a performance issue about the robustness and also ML/DL at risk to adversarial attacks.

Here in paper [19] discussed various machine learning techniques in the healthcare system like supervised learning, unsupervised learning, semi-supervised learning, reinforcement learning as well as application of ML such as in prognosis, diagnosis, medical image analysis, treatment and real-time health monitoring. Author has also discussed the methods to ensure private, secure and robust machine learning for the healthcare system. In privacy pre-serving using ML the concepts of cryptographic encryption, differential privacy federated learning are applied. In the literature they have categorized the counter measures against adversarial attacks in three ways as modifying models, modifying data and adding an auxiliary models. Also discussed how graphical causal models are solutions to address distribution shifts, towards responsible ML like general responsibility of AI practices and ML for Healthcare and then tools and libraries for secure and private ML. The important strength of secure ML is based on secure tools and algorithms like Tenser-Flow Federated, CrypTen, PyTorch-DP5, OpenMined6, PySyft7, PyGrid8. Nowadays still many more open research challenges are related to secure, private and robust ML such as Interpretable ML, ML on Edge, Handling Dataset Annotation, Fair and Accountable ML, Model-Driven ML, Distributed Data Management and ML.

Paper [5] discusses about the security issues in IoT devices. They argue that because of different vendors in IoT industry there is very less focus on security of the devices. Their paper focuses on IoT threat detection and mitigation techniques.

Review paper [6] explains the notion of evolution as it has been influenced by the availability of internet technology. The research material produced on numerous papers that focused on published IoT research was examined in depth in this study.

Paper [7] discusses about the 5G architecture and emerging technologies used along. Some use cases and applications are also discussed.

In Paper [16], the authors have discussed methods to visualize and analyze applications of ML & block chain in the zone of medicine. Authors have used VOS viewer software to build and visualize networks that generate the clusters which represent the underlying structure of a document. Based on the technical similarity the clustering results are generated as machine learning, artificial intelligence, blockchain, sensor cluster, IOT cluster. Also dis-cussed the future researches of block chain and machine learning in biomedical monitor, fog computing, activity cognition, security and privacy.

This paper [4] describes how compromised endpoints allow cyber threats to get access to inside networks. Cyber-criminals are increasingly targeting devices like smartphones, tablets, and the Internet of Things (IoT). End-point security is identified utilizing rules or patterns in device-based detection technologies. It also identifies threats when suspicious events according to the attack profile's rules occur on a regular basis. The authors conducted tests in order to identify harmful processes.

In paper [15] authors discuss entropy-based features have been popular for identifying DDoS assaults, although they restrict the types of communication that may be identified. When compared to other techniques, the authors were able to attain greater accuracy and recall values than state-of-the-art approaches.

Nowadays image processing [18] is a huge and worldwide area of research but as well it takes too much memory and computational time. One of the ways is to keep all the data on the cloud. Cloud computing allows users to store and process their data on the internet. Preventing illegal access to medical records and personal health information is the first and most pressing concern. To secure data processing in cloud environments, we present a unique strategy based on machine learning techniques. The hybrid approach of Sup-port Vector Machine and Fuzzy C-means are used to classify the images pixels more accurately. For image enhancement they have used Guassian filtering and pixel intensity. After that they have used the CloudSec module to reduce the risk of medical information. After doing the experiments the evaluation is done by the proposed technique and the result is that the SVM techniques concept is very good for simultaneous image segmentation and data protection. In future they will work on complex images and also will use a homogeneity model rather than pixel color which has components like local image window and filter. It helps to provide the data on cloud with privacy as well encrypted methods will be applied on it.

In the paper [3], Authors have discussed Optimized Deep-CNN towards Attack based on Rider Optimization based Detection in IoT By combining the Development and Operations (DevOps) concepts, this article aims to offer a novel attack detection method. Feature Extraction & Classification are the two steps. The convolution layers in deep convolutional neural network (DCNN) are optimally tuned using Rider Optimization Algorithm (ROA). Authors also discussed possible attacks on IoT Systems.

3   Data Security Privacy Approaches Using Machine Learning Techniques in 5G Healthcare Services

See Fig. 2.

Fig. 2. Machine learning to mitigate attacks on 5th gen healthcare

AI and Machine learning can be used to analyze the big data that we received while using the 5G healthcare services, the data which can be categorized in the form of variability, variety, velocity, volume of data packets in 5G network. IOMT and virtualization of 5G makes it more difficult to handle. Machine learning, expert systems, neural networks, Intelligent agents and pattern recognition can be used to create models which in turn can give us statistics to defect threats in the network using clustering, hypothesis testing, regression analysis (Fig. 3).

Machine learning is the study of obtaining machines to take action in the absence of specific programming. Machine learning has provided us with self-driving vehicles, effective web search, practical speech recognition with a vastly enhanced understanding of the human genome in the past decade. Nowadays machine learning is so common that you actually utilize it hundreds of times in a day without understanding it. Many researchers additionally think it is the most ideal approach to build progress towards human level Artificial Intelligence (AI) [13].

AI is like a man-made brain power application that allows systems the ability to take in and develop as a matter of fact without being unambiguously customized. AI focuses on developing Computer programs which can acquire knowledge and use it to think for themselves. [8] The way to learning starts with, for example, perceptions or information, models, and direct understanding. The key is to allow computers to a just correctly without human intervention or assistance, and to change activities as needed.

3.1   Supervised Learning

Supervised machine learning is of immense help in solving computational problems in the real world. By learning from labelled training data the algorithm predicts results for

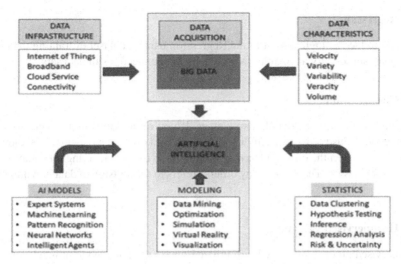

Fig. 3. AI, ML and BigData in Healthcare

unexpected data. Hence designing and deploying these models requires highly qualified data scientists [9]. Data scientists can use their technological knowledge over time to recreate the models in order to preserve the credibility of insights (Fig. 4).

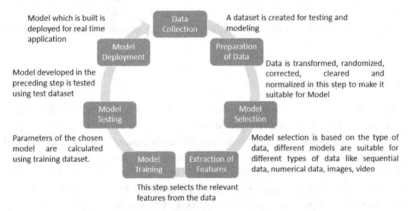

Fig. 4. Machine learning steps for model deployment

Assume you've been given one million coins in 3 kinds of currencies - 1 rupee, 1 lb & 1 Euro. Each and every coin has its own characteristics, such as weight, size, and metal used. Assume you create a model that considers a coin's attribute such as weight, and your model uses weight to determine which denomination it is. As a result, in that model "weight" will be the "Feature," and "currency" will be "Label." As a result, supervised learning models will learn from labelled data.

3.2 Regression

We can produce a single output in the Regression using a dataset of training data [11]. But it isn't sufficiently adaptable to catch complex connections in data sets.

3.3 Classification

It includes collecting the details into classes. If you're thinking about giving someone credit, you may use order to see if they're likely to fail on their payments. It is known as double order when the directed learning computation names incoming information into two distinct classes. The term "many orders" refers to the division of data into numerous categories.

3.4 Unsupervised Learning

Unsupervised algorithms for ML are utilized where the knowledge utilized to train is neither labeled nor named. Unsupervised learning studies how systems can infer the function of describing the hidden structure from unmarked data. The system does not figure out the correct output, but it explores the data and can draw inferences from datasets.

Whenever you put cricket dataset in the model, the machine identifies the pattern of players by plotting wickets on the X axis and runs on the Y axis. By plotting the data, we can see that there are two clusters, one where the player scored a lot of runs but took few wickets, and another where the player scored less runs but took a lot of wickets. There were no labels for batsmen or bowlers in this area. Unsupervised learning is exemplified here.

3.5 Reinforcement Learning

Reinforcement machine learning algorithms are a type of learning algorithm that communicates with its surroundings by producing activity and detecting faults or rewards. This method aids computers and software agents in determining the best actions to do in a particular situation in order to enhance it. Let's imagine you send a system an image of a "CAT" and it incorrectly classifies it as a "Dog," so you offer a negative feedback saying it is a "Cats" image. Next time machine receive a same image, it will be able to correctly identify it dependent upon our feedback. The machine is provide an input &, after executing the algorithm, it produces an output, which the model acquire knowledge from. Some other example: whenever a tagged friend in a photo is recognized in Facebook.

3.6 Support Vector Machines

Development of healthcare services with 5G using machine learning algorithms. Applied in the healthcare services, 5G shows brilliant strength to enable disease like depression, insomnia etc. because 5G healthcare services can be transmitted to remote customers with ultra-low latency as well as ultra-high reliability. But hacking of data is increasing day by day. So AI works brilliantly in healthcare to secure data of patients. Machine learning methods are helping healthcare like hospitals in each and everywhere reduce the hospital staff's burdens which Improve patient health outcomes. Also, AL is used to protect the data and give privacy to help human effort as well as save the data of patients [13].

There are some essential ways in AI which can fight against the 5G healthcare services data security and provide protection against hospitals with medical network devices. First identify emerging malware threats using prediction algorithms of machine learning because if human data is stolen that result of a patient may show a false record then the patient could be at risk. So machine learning can protect these issues by searching for previous data of malware. With the help of a historical dataset, ML trained the model to recognize the malware.

3.7 Decision Tree

Decision trees are ordinarily utilized supervised machine learning algorithms which are utilized by classification as well as regression issues. Decision trees are also one of the predictive modelling approaches which are useful for predicting malware by splitting a dataset related to various conditions link malware (yes) or malware (no) which is useful for increasing the security of data. Formulate a set of decision rules which is made by utilization of training dataset in decision tree algorithm. With the help of decision rules the classes/labels of the test dataset are predicted. Decision tree algorithm which is displayed like a Tree Structure and it is having non leaf nodes. Non leaf nodes behave like a decision maker as well as each and every leaf node representing it as a class/label. So, a decision tree is like a predictor which helps to detect malware for security of patient records.

To predict class/label of a data point regarding data security, some steps need to follow with decision tree like a classifier which is as follow (Fig. 5):

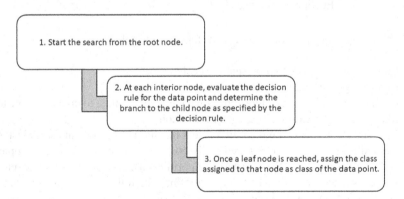

Fig. 5. Steps to be followed for decision tree

In a decision tree the stopping criteria are as follows (Fig. 6):

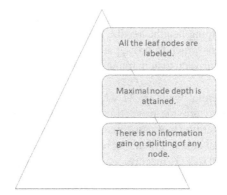

Fig. 6. Stopping criteria for decision tree

Algorithm

The following decision algorithm is constructed as a decision tree which is worked from top-down. By selecting some variables in each and every step that splits the items like malware (False) or malware (True) i.e. present in 5G healthcare service data (Fig. 7):

3.8 Clustering

Clustering is the task of dividing the data points into a number of similar groups. It divides the given collected data into clusters which will be similar. The target of clustering techniques which help to gather similar types of data in the same group and dissimilar types of data in different groups. If the Euclidean distance in between two data is not more than the threshold value, then only the same data are put together in a similar cluster.

$$\text{Euclidean distance} = d(a, b) = \sqrt{\sum_{i=1}^{n} (a_i - b_i)^2} \tag{1}$$

For clustering process some important steps need to follow:

1. Using feature vectors to represent the design.
2. Describing a similarity function.
3. Choosing one clustering algorithm as well as utilizing this, to create the clusters
4. Make decision regarding on clusters formation
5. So many clustering techniques are present like hard clustering and soft clustering. Hard clustering is very computationally costly and nonlinear in time complexity and space complexity. Soft clustering algorithms use ANN, GN, fuzzy set etc.
6. K-means is an important clustering algorithm which is nondeterministic and iterative for a dataset with a predefined number of clusters. It produces centroids for each and every cluster which is produced by a given dataset.
7. Some steps need to follow for k-means algorithm:
8. Choose any of k patterns from given set of pattern for starting cluster which will find the cluster

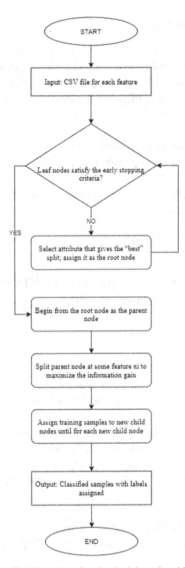

Fig. 7. Flowchart for the decision algorithm

9. Find out the nearest cluster center for the remaining pattern and assign that point in the cluster. If there is no center that stops the process.
10. Recalculate another novel cluster center through the current assigned center.
11. Then go to the second step. In terms of criminal profiles, the K-means clustering technique has a fascinating application. Criminal profiling is a method of grouping information/data on individuals and groups of criminals who have committed crimes. Criminal profiling can be used to identify the kind of criminals involved in a cybercrime that threatens 5G healthcare services and patient records.

3.9 Dimensionality Reduction

Dimensionality Reduction is a method which changes a dataset with huge dimensions into a dataset with little dimension without losing the important data from the dataset. This procedure helps in AI issues to get best quality for classification as well as regression function. Some of the advantages of put in dimensionality reduction in the data are as per the following:

1. Take out redundant features from the dataset.
2. Compressing all the data in this manner reduces the memory needed.
3. Made the calculations quicker.
4. Permits the use of the algorithms appropriate for low dimensional data.
5. Deals with only multi-collinearity issues.
6. Permits to plot as well as visualize the data as much as possible exactly which helps in watching the samples more visible.

4 Case Study: Detecting the Intensity of DDOS Attack Using Decision Tree Algorithm on Healthcare Application Network Data

Description of Data Set
For this example, we used the Kaggle Database that was provided for the application layer-DDOS-dataset. The dataset can be downloaded from https://www.kaggle.com/war dac/applicationlayer-ddos-dataset.

DDoS, that is Distributed Denial of Service attack is a popular, rising attack technique for programmers and hacktivists, in large part because of their simplicity. Exploring the different kinds of DDoS attacks can be testing and tedious. In this model we have distinguished the seriousness of such attacks, say detect the type of DDOS attacks characterized utilizing the Decision tree calculation.

Step1 - The required packages are being loaded.
We import the necessary libraries and packages here. Depending on the platform, your imports must be different.

Step 2 - Loading Preprocessing of data.
We had 156 columns out of which we have identified 78 columns to be used to identify as important metrics. Label 0 is used for "Benign" and 1 is used for identifying "DoS slowloris" and 2 for identifying the attack as "DoS Hulk". We then plotted a scatter-plot which would give us detailed information on how the data is distributed for a few columns with respect to other columns. The metrics "Flow Duration", "Total Fwd Packets" is very

high when the attack is severe and low when it is benign. plotting the correlation matrix of the train data-set.

Step 3 – Create the model creating the model for the decision tree algorithm.
We are also creating a decision tree with different depths for checking the effect on the accuracy level.

Step 4 – Train the model.
We got training data at this point, and a completely configured decision tree to train data.

Step 5 – It is time to Input Test data to check accuracy of the model.
Let check accuracy of our model on test data. We can observe in our output we received 0.99 accuracy with the help of testing dataset. Output Accuracy for Decision tree with depth $= 0.9968172422441902$ (Fig. 8).

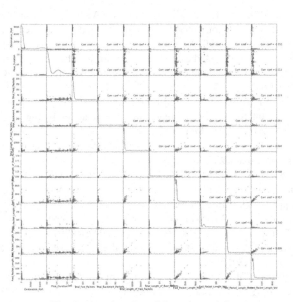

Fig. 8. Density plot of the scattered data

5   Conclusion

Healthcare industry with the 5G technology, which are having lower latency along with greater capacity, the healthcare system can provide remote services for patients. 5G can be used in applications like digital health management, financial records, clinical research and health supply chain management. 5G network deployed in healthcare service to immersive growth in data transfer with the help of data rates as well as speed but in real time some threat and anomaly detected. So this paper represents ML serving some approaches for security of 5G healthcare service data. After discussing the need for security and privacy in 5G healthcare services, we tried to represent the 5G architecture and its functionality in healthcare. Later in this chapter we showed some of the Machine learning approaches involved in providing solutions for privacy and security in 5G healthcare services. The highly network traffic patterns, service based network architecture, and authentication over multiple servers in 5G healthcare service and beyond networks require a relatively robust, agile and fully automated security framework. Such a framework is built-upon smart AI technologies. There is a huge possibility for cyberattacks in the healthcare industry, malware is very harmful for 5G networks which are attacking different systems within a second. So to secure the entire system we will be using various AI algorithms which includes the Decision tree algorithm, SVM, clustering and so on. Prediction algorithm helps to find applications in catch/detect malware attack.

References

1. Khan, R., Kumar, P., Jayakody, D.N.K., Liyanage, M.: A survey on security and privacy of 5G technologies: potential solutions, recent advancements, and future directions. IEEE Commun. Surv. Tutor. **22**(1), 196–248 (2019)
2. Tamilarasi, K., Jawahar, A.: Medical data security for healthcare applications using hybrid lightweight encryption and swarm optimization algorithm. Wireless Pers. Commun. **114**(3), 1865–1886 (2020)
3. Sarma, S.K.: Rider optimization based optimized deep-CNN towards attack detection in IoT. In: 2020 4th International Conference on Intelligent Computing and Control Systems (ICICCS), pp. 163–169. IEEE, May 2020
4. Kim, S., Hwang, C., Lee, T.: Anomaly based unknown intrusion detection in endpoint environments. Electronics **9**(6), 1022 (2020)
5. Karie, N.M., Sahri, N.M., Haskell-Dowland, P.: IoT threat detection advances, challenges and future directions. In: 2020 Workshop on Emerging Technologies for Security in IoT (ETSecIoT), pp. 22–29. IEEE, April 2020
6. Dachyar, M., Zagloel, T.Y.M., Saragih, L.R.: Knowledge growth and development: internet of things (IoT) research, 2006–2018. Heliyon **5**(8), e02264 (2019)
7. Gupta, A., Jha, R.K.: A survey of 5G network: architecture and emerging technologies. IEEE Access **3**, 1206–1232 (2015)
8. Lake, B.M., Ullman, T.D., Tenenbaum, J.B., Gershman, S.J.: Building machines that learn and think like people. Behav. Brain Sci. **40** (2017)
9. Tan, P.N., Steinbach, M., Kumar, V.: Introduction to Data Mining. Pearson Education. Inc., New Delhi (2006)
10. Tobore, I., et al.: Deep learning intervention for health care challenges: some biomedical domain considerations. JMIR Mhealth Uhealth **7**(8), e11966 (2019)
11. Bouktif, S., Fiaz, A., Ouni, A., Serhani, M.A.: Optimal deep learning LSTM model for electric load forecasting using feature selection and genetic algorithm: comparison with machine learning approaches. Energies **11**(7), 1636 (2018)
12. Gupta, G.K.: Introduction to data mining with case studies. PHI Learning Pvt. Ltd. (2014)
13. Thomas, T., Vijayaraghavan, A.P., Emmanuel, S.: Machine Learning Approaches in Cyber Security Analytics. Springer, Singapore (2020). https://doi.org/10.1007/978-981-15-1706-8
14. Benke, K., Benke, G.: Artificial intelligence and big data in public health. Int. J. Environ. Res. Public Health **15**(12), 2796 (2018)

15. Koay, A., Chen, A., Welch, I., Seah, W.K.G.: A new multi classifier system using entropy-based features in DDoS attack detection. In: 2018 International Conference on Information Networking (ICOIN), pp. 162–167 (2018). https://doi.org/10.1109/ICOIN.2018.8343104

16. Anand, A., Rani, S., Anand, D., Aljahdali, H.M., Kerr, D.: An efficient CNN-based deep learning model to detect malware attacks (CNN-DMA) in 5G-IoT healthcare applications. Sensors **21**(19), 6346 (2021)

17. Li, Y., et al.: Literature review on the applications of machine learning and blockchain technology in the smart healthcare industry: a bibliometric analysis. J. Healthc. Eng. **2021** (2021)

18. Marwan, M., Kartit, A., Ouahmane, H.: Security enhancement in the healthcare cloud using machine learning. Procedia Comput. Sci. **127**, 388–397 (2018)

19. Qayyum, A., Qadir, J., Bilal, M., Al-Fuqaha, A.: Secure and robust machine learning for healthcare: a survey. IEEE Rev. Biomed. Eng. **14**, 156–180 (2021)

20. Khamparia, A., et al. (eds.): Computational Intelligence for Managing Pandemics, vol. 5. Walter de GruyterGmbH Co KG (2021)

Traffic Flow Prediction Using Deep Learning Techniques

Shubhashish Goswami[1,2](✉) ⓘ and Abhimanyu Kumar[1]

[1] National Institute of Technology Uttarakhand, Srinagar, India
subh.goswami@gmail.com
[2] Dev Bhoomi Uttarakhand University Dehradun, Dehradun, India

Abstract. In the "Intelligent Transportation System (ITS)", accurate and real-time traffic flow prediction is crucial, particularly for traffic control. To develop a smart city, data related to traffic flow is essential. Many Intelligent Transportation Systems now employ the ongoing technology to predict the traffic flow, reduce road accidents, and anticipate vehicle speed, and so on. However, the prediction that considers some other factors as environmental and weather conditions are considered to be more accurate. Predicting traffic flow is a fascinating research area. To forecast traffic, several different data mining approaches are used. Existing traffic flow forecast approaches are mostly based on shallow traffic prediction methods, which are insufficient for many real-world applications. Since traffic flow shows both spatial and temporal dependency features, as well as being affected by weather, social event data, and other factors, therefore, a new deep-learning-based traffic flow prediction technique such as "Stacked Auto-Encoder (SAE) Convolutional Neural Network (CNN), Long- and Short-Term Memory Neural Network (LSTM)" is proposed in this paper, which considers both "Spatial and Temporal Correlations". The results of the experiments showed the efficiency of suggested approach and compare its performance with several deep learning techniques on a real-world public dataset of Predicting in a complex traffic situation with its accuracy rate.

Keywords: Deep learning (DL) · Traffic flow · Prediction · Intelligent transportation system · CNN · LSTM · SAE

1 Introduction

The "Intelligent Transportation System (ITS) plays a critical role in real-world traffic management and control, benefiting traffic safety, efficiency, and congestion reduction, among other things" [1]. Accurate traffic flow predictions in the highway network offer critical data for ITS to make proactive and effective traffic management choices [2]. Traffic congestion, traffic accidents, and traffic delays, all of which are caused by the exponential rise in the number of motor vehicles, offer significant difficulties and pressure to the transportation process. The most efficient method to address traffic difficulties is to create a dependable traffic management plan based on traffic flow forecasts. The number

© Springer Nature Switzerland AG 2022
N. Chaubey et al. (Eds.): COMS2 2022, CCIS 1604, pp. 198–213, 2022.
https://doi.org/10.1007/978-3-031-10551-7_15

of vehicles moving via the route at every frequency slot is represented by the traffic flow [3].

Furthermore, as people's travel needs grow, so does the number of vehicles on the road, and the city's road network becomes more complicated, making traffic flow more complex and unpredictable. Furthermore, the transportation industry has now reached the big data period. All of this makes it harder for a typical traffic flow prediction system to match the data and produce the best forecast. Furthermore, many Conventional Traffic Flow Prediction (TFP) systems rely on a single time-step prediction, that, however scientifically significant, is inappropriate for the functional development of multi-traffic flow prediction. The "Transportation Management System and the Congestion Analysis early warning sign of the ITS both benefit from accurate long-term TFP" [3, 4].

As a result of the widespread use of traditional traffic sensors and the development of traffic sensing devices, it finally facilitated the emergence of large-scale data transportation [5]. Transportation planning and monitoring are becoming increasingly data-driven [6]. While numerous traffic flow prediction tools and algorithms exist, the majorities of them apply shallow traffic concepts and are still unsatisfactory.

DL, a subtype of the machine learning approach, has recently attracted a great deal of research and business concern. It's been used to solve Classification Problems, NLP, Dimensionality Reduction, Object Recognition, and motion modeling, among other things [7]. Deep learning methods extract intrinsic characteristics in data from the lower to the higher phase using multiple-layer designs or deep frameworks, and they may find massive quantities of structure in the data. Because the architecture of a traffic flow process is complex, DL models could describe traffic characteristics without previous experience, resulting in high TFP performance [5]. The workflow of the TFP using DL Techniques is shown in Fig. 1.

This paper proposes a TFP based on the DL technique. The deep learning method has a high level of accuracy and can efficiently collect spatial information. Deep learning techniques like "Stacked Auto-Encoder (SAE) [5], Convolutional Neural Network (CNN) [8], and Long- and Short-Term Memory Neural (LSTM)", can be used to predict traffic flow data. To extract general traffic flow characteristics, a stacked autoencoder (SAE) method is established, which is trained in a layer-wise rigorous way. It is the first time, to the authors' knowledge, that the SAE method has been utilized to characterize traffic flow characteristics for prediction. "Spatial and Temporal Correlations" are factored in the modeling process. CNN is a type of neural network used to determine spatial correlation from grid-structured data given by images or videos.

CNN has been used to detect spatial correlations in traffic networks from 2D Spatio-temporal traffic data in several studies. Due to the difficulty of describing the traffic network using 2D matrices, numerous studies have attempted to transform the traffic network model at various periods into images and split these images into conventional grids, every grid defining a region. CNNs may be used to establish spatial characteristics between various areas in this method [8].

The RNN approach is generally utilized for tasks that need sequential input. RNNs use a single component input sequence and save performance data on hidden parts which include all prior components' historical data effectively [9]. The "Long Short-Term Memory (LSTM)" exhibits high accuracy in natural language processing [10] and

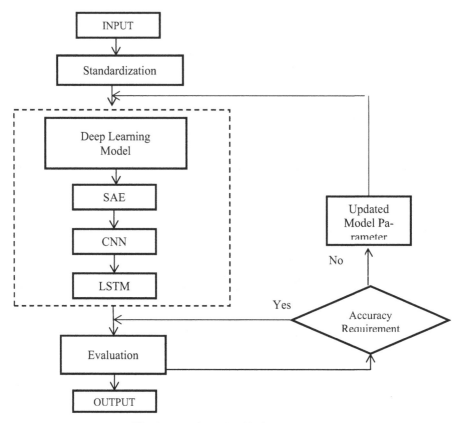

Fig. 1. Workflow of traffic flow prediction

may be used to solve a variety of time series problems. Zhao et al.'s LSTM-based traffic flow forecasting collects temporal information about traffic flow over time. Because this technique solely employs LSTM to analyze the data, it fails to capture spatial information [11]. Various DNN models, on the other hand, specialize in different areas. For example, CNN is better at capturing spatial dependencies in transportation networks; RNN and LSTM are better at capturing temporal dependencies; LSTM may even identify long-term temporal correlation. SAE performs better when it comes to extracting latent characteristics from raw data. Because traffic flow varies depending on both temporal and geographical data, a hybrid composition of several DNN models has become a common technique to enhance traffic forecasting accuracy in recent decades [12].

The following is an overview of the paper's structure: The literature survey is presented in Sect. 2. The key aspects of the deep learning technique are summarized in Sect. 3. The purpose and design of the suggested infrastructure for TFP, as well as how to enhance and combine the fundamental DL techniques to the suggested approach, are also discussed. Section 4 offers empirical studies based on real-world traffic datasets and analyzes the suggested method's performance. Conclusions are presented in the final section.

2   Related Works

With the advancement of intelligent transportation over the last era, TFP has become a major research area in the intelligent transportation field. Many professionals and academics have focused their effort and time on traffic flow prediction work, proposing a wide range of prediction approaches. To explain the numerous aspects of fundamental traffic flow patterns, Reference [13] offers an efficient mixed time series forecasting technique that combines the Auto-regressive Embedded Moving Average Structure with the evolutionary programming methodology.

[14] suggests an integrated TFP method based on traffic flow time series multifractal features. The link between meteorological factors and traffic flow is studied in Reference [15], and a unique overall framework to enhance traffic flow forecast is presented. In addition, [16] presents a traffic prediction technique based on the DBN conceptual framework and multi-task classification to forecast the traffic flow of single and multi-task outputs. [17] proposes a deep code learning technique that is used in the Macao efficient system.

For traffic flow prediction, reference [18] proposes the GRU NN algorithm. In their experiment, they evaluated the predictive accuracy of ARIMA, LSTM, and GRU algorithms and determined that LSTM NNs and GRU NNs outperformed ARIMA. GRU NNs lowered MAE by 10% on average when compared to ARIMA and 5% when compared to LSTM NNs. RNNs with more hidden units will be examined in the next, and the variable length of time sequence inputs may aid RNNs in automatically determining the best time delays.

Integrated DL techniques for TFP have got a huge amount of focus in current decades due to the quick rise of DL theories and applications, as well as the spatial and temporal dependence aspects of traffic flow data. [12] examines combined DL techniques for TFP in depth. It initially presents the different data sources utilized in hybrid traffic flow prediction algorithms, before moving on to the hybrid traffic flow prediction modeling techniques, which range from basic to sophisticated. By examining current methods, one can observe that hybrid methods for traffic flow prediction are getting increasingly sophisticated to capture more information in transportation data. With the growing gathering of finer-grained, multi-type data from transportation networks, the hybrid learning algorithm will likely continue to improve in the future to integrate more data characteristics, allowing for more accurate and scalable traffic flow prediction.

The extensive mobility data and DL regarding traffic forecasts are discussed in [9]. With effective unbiased feature representation, deep learning enhances traffic forecasts. DL theory-based models for traffic data were given in "Large-Scale Transportation Network Congestion Development Forecasting". To avoid traffic delays on a huge transportation network, it is critical to analyze congestion. Traditional congestion forecasting systems rely on static data. With emerging technologies like "Intelligent Transportation Systems (ITS) and the Internet of Things, transportation data is extremely pervasive (IoT)". Introduce a profound limited Boltzmann machine with an RNN design to predict traffic congestion [9]. The system design predicts traffic data more precisely and accurately than current machine learning techniques. Because of the short-term and long-term patterns, predicting traffic statistics is difficult. The prolonged phase of the LSTM model

[10], which is a general technique in deep learning, produces the estimation of short-term traffic data. It outperforms other machine learning techniques currently in use.

In conclusion, a significant number of TFP techniques have been created in response to the rising demand for traffic flow data in ITSs and may employ a variety of approaches from many fields. In any given circumstance, though, it's impossible to claim that one approach is better than another. The accuracy of TFP approaches is governed by the road traffic features inherent in the acquired spatial traffic, and the suggested predictions are based on a small amount of unique traffic information. Furthermore, the literature suggests that employing Neural Networks that had excellent forecasting and resilience, might produce promising outcomes. Even though deep neural networks may train more advanced systems than shallow networks, most contemporary NN-based TFP algorithms only have one hidden layer. With a gradient-based training technique, it is difficult to build a "deep-layered hierarchical NN". This work will evaluate a DL technique for TFP that uses SAEs, CNN, and LSTM.

3 Proposed Work

Deep learning techniques may achieve higher performance by implementing more features and sophisticated frameworks than traditional approaches.

3.1 Stacked Auto-Encoders (SAE)

A Stacked Auto-Encoders (SAE) framework is introduced in this section. The SAE method is a prominent DL model that consists of a stack of auto-encoders. It creates a deep network using autoencoders as building parts [5].

"An Auto-Encoder is a neural network that aims to replicate its input, with the target output being the model's input. An autoencoder with one input layer, one hidden layer, and one output layer" is represented in Fig. 2.

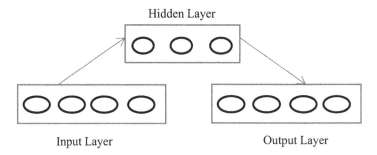

Fig. 2. Auto-encoder

An AE en-codes an input $a^{(m1)}$, to a hidden defines $b(a^{(m)})$, based on (1), and then decodes defines $d(a^{(m)})$ back into a re-construction z(x(i)) termed as in (2), given a series of training samples $\{a^{(1)}, a^{(2)}, a^{(3)}, ...,\}$ where $a^{(m)} \in c^e$, as illustrated in

$$b(a) = p(H_1 a + e) \tag{1}$$

$$d(a) = q(H_2 b + j) \tag{2}$$

In this work, we investigate the "Logistic Sigmoid Function $1/(1 + \exp(-a))$ for $p(a)$ and $q(a)$", where "H_1 is a weight matrix, e is an encoding bias vector, H_2 is a decoding matrix, and j is a decoding bias vector";

We can get the set of parameters that are indicated as ε, by minimizing the reconstructive error $S(A, D)$.

$$\varepsilon = arg_\varepsilon \min S(A, D) = arg_\varepsilon \min \frac{1}{2} \sum_{x=1}^{H} \left| a^{(m)} - D\left(a^{(m)}\right) \right|^2$$

One significant difficulty with an autoencoder is that if the hidden layer is similar in size as or greater than the input layer, the autoencoder might train the identity function. Yet, recent work demonstrates that this is not an issue if nonlinear AE contains more hidden units than the input or if additional limitations like sparsity requirements are enforced [19]. "When sparsity restrictions are applied to the objective function, an AE is transformed into a sparse AE, which takes into account the hidden layer's sparse representation. We will use a sparsity constraint to reduce the reconstruction error in order to obtain the sparse representation".

$$C = S(A, D) + \beta \sum_{n=1}^{A_E} KL(\mu||\hat{\mu}_n) \tag{3}$$

where "β is the sparsity term's weight, A_E is the number of hidden units, μ is a sparsity parameter that is typically a small value near zero, and $\hat{\mu}_n = (1/x) \sum_{m=1}^{M} b_n\left(a^{(m)}\right)$ is the number of hidden units. The average activation of hidden unit n over the training set, and $KL(\mu||\hat{\mu}_n)$ is the Kullback–Leibler (KL) divergence" is defined as,

$$KL(\mu||\hat{\mu}_n) = \mu \log \frac{\mu}{\hat{\mu}_n} + (1 - \mu) \log \frac{1 - \mu}{1 - \hat{\mu}_n} \tag{4}$$

$KL(\mu||\hat{\mu}_n) = 0$ if $\mu = \hat{\mu}_n$, is the property of the KL divergence. It implements the coding sparsity criterion. This optimization issue may be solved using the back-propagation (BP) technique.

An SAE system is constructed by stacking auto-encoders to build a DNN, with the result of the auto-encoder on the layer below functioning as the current layer's input [5]. In SAEs with l layers, the 1st layer is trained like an AE, and the training set is used as inputs. The output of the nth hidden layer is utilized as the input of the $(n + 1)^{th}$ hidden layer after getting the first hidden layer. Numerous AE could be layered hierarchically in this approach. Figure 3 illustrates below.

To use the SAE network for TFP, we must construct a conventional predictor at the upper part. In this study, a logistic classification model is integrated on edge of the system for supervised traffic flow prediction. The SAEs and the predictor are the components of the complete deep architecture system for traffic flow prediction.

3.2 Convolutional Neural Network (CNN)

"CNNs are a form of Feed forward Neural Network with a basic structure and convolution computations". It is one of the most well-known DL techniques. CNNs were first

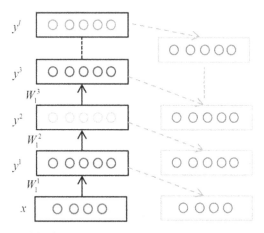

Fig. 3. Training of stacked auto-encoder [5]

studied in the 1980s and 1990s. The first convolutional neural networks were significant delay systems and LeNet-5; after the twenty-first era, with the emergence of the DL approach and the advancement of "Numerical Computing Equipment, Convolutional Neural Networks have evolved significantly and are now used in Image Classification, Speech Recognition, Natural Language Processing, and a variety of other fields" [20].

"The Convolutional Layer, Pooling Layer, and Fully Connected Layer are the 3 aspects of a CNN. The convolutional layer's primary role is feature extraction". The convolutional layer's, convolution kernel shape follows the features of an animal's visual system as it observes objects, focusing on the image's local information first. It could also effectively retrieve the data in the receptive field's local spatial properties. The pooling layer is used for feature extraction and dimension reduction of the feature maps generated by the convolutional layer; the fully connected layer is obtained directly by the convolutional layer and the pooling layer. To achieve the classification model or regression aim, the multi-dimensional abstract feature is given as input and vectorized into vector form. As a result, the features of CNN weight sharing are used in this study to get the spatiotemporal features of traffic flow while decreasing model complexity and computing complexity [20].

Consider the CNN architecture [21], which has two convolution layers and two pooling layers.

"X1: initial convolution, providing it takes a 32*32 matrix, through a convolution of a convolution unit to produce a 28*28 size feature map":

$$x_n^1 = \text{Con2}(W, M_n^1, Valid) + y_n^1; \tag{5}$$

$$r_n^1 = x_n^1; \tag{6}$$

$$z_n^1 = g(r_n^1); \tag{7}$$

where, "Con2 $(W, M_n^1, Valid) + y_n^1$ indicates a narrow convolution, and g denotes the activation function".

"P2: initial pooling, pooled frame for 2*2, size of feature map 28*28 pooled into 14*14 pool mapping, total pool maps derived":

$$p_n^2 = \alpha_n^2 \ \text{low} \ (z_n^1) + y_n^2; \tag{8}$$

$$r_n^2 = p_n^2; \tag{9}$$

$$z_n^2 = g; \tag{10}$$

where "p = low (x) denotes subsampling in the following sequence: p = $\alpha low(x) + y$; α and y are the scalar factors".

"X3: Using a convolution core $M_{nh}^3(h = 1, 2, \ldots, G_1$, each 14*14 of the feature map in this layer is developed of all pool maps in the layer x_n and all G_1 pool maps in the pool map, resulting in a total of 10*10 size sprofs of the feature maps":

$$x_n^3 = \sum_{h=1}^{G_1} Conv2\left(z_h^2, \ M_{nh}^3, \ valid\right) + y_{nh}^3; \tag{11}$$

$$r_n^3 = p_n^3; \tag{12}$$

$$z_n^3 = g(r_n^3); \tag{13}$$

"P4: Pooled once more, frame for 2*2, pooling a 10*10 feature map into a 5*5 pool map, resulting in a pool map of F3":

$$p_n^4 = \alpha_n^4 \ \text{low}(z_n^3) + y_n^4; \tag{14}$$

$$r_n^4 = p_n^4; \tag{15}$$

$$z_n^4 = g(r_n^4); \tag{16}$$

The input gate determines if the current feature is effective, the output gate determines if the recent data is valuable, and the forget gate remembers the earlier inaccurate data decision. Finally, the sequence z_n^4 (n = 1, 2,..., G_3) is expanded into a vector, which is then connected in an appropriate way to form a long vector as input to the full-connection layer network.

3.3 Long- and Short-Term Memory (LSTM) Neural Network

The LSTM neural network is an updated version of Hochreiter et passim.'s neural network. Gradient explosion or gradient disappearance is an issue that can develop during the training system of the new RNN as time and the number of network layers expands, making it very hard to obtain data about preceding long-distance data. In opposed to RNN, the fundamental element of the LSTM hidden layer is a memory unit, which incorporates a self-connected memory cell and three gate units that regulate information flow: input gate, output gate, and forget the door. The input and output gateways control the flow of information into and out of neurons, respectively. The forget gate has the authority to manage memory cells and control whether they should be forgetting or remembering beforehand. This can answer the difficulty of gradient vanishing, as well as its ability to remember history for an extended time. The current condition of the data is the key to choosing the optimum time interval automatically. The "LSTM is suitable for processing and identifying interval and delay events in time series because this can learn long-term and short-term submitted of time series and the neural network comprises memory units". As a result, the time-series patterns of traffic flow are generated using LSTM in this paper [20].

The weights of the hidden and output layer are defined by and V, respectively, whereas the transition weights of the hidden level are symbolized by W. The element-wise multiple of the input and the earlier network hidden phase ht−1 produces the network's hidden phase at time t. Equation 17 shows the hidden state at time t. Figure 4 shows the flowchart of the LSTM model.

$$Kt = \partial(Gh_x x_t + W_{hh}h_{t-1} + B) \tag{17}$$

"Ghx is the weight between the input and recurrent hidden nodes, Whh is the weight between the recurrent node and the previous time step of the hidden node itself, and b and sigmoid activation are the bias and non-linear (sigmoid) activation, respectively". Although RNNs outperforms other algorithms in time series prediction, they still have problems that need to be addressed. Figure 4 shows the construction of the LSTM-NN with one memory block. Input, output, and forget gates are present in the memory block, and they provide the write, read, and reset functions on each cell, respectively. The working mechanism of LSTM is shown in Eqs. 18–22.

$$b_t = \lambda(w_x i_t + Wh_i l_{t-1} + WC_i a_{t-1} + k_i) \tag{18}$$

$$s_t = \lambda(w_x \alpha i_t + Wh_f l_{t-1} + WC_f a_{t-1} + k_f) \tag{19}$$

$$a_t = s_t c_t + b_t \alpha(W_x i_t + W_\beta \widehat{\mu_t} + k_s) \tag{20}$$

$$k_t = \delta\big(W_x i_t + W_{x0}l_{t-1} + \alpha_0 a^t + k_0\big) \tag{21}$$

$$l_t = k_t(ya_0) \tag{22}$$

The LSTM model has been shown to be superior in order to achieve accuracy. The LSTM is an extensively used RNN that can reap the benefits of the pattern of timing changes in time series. Due to RNN's gradient disintegration limits, LSTM implemented the notion of a cell, (i.e.) exactly the same except inserting a block instead of a hidden layer inside the RNN. The input gate analyzes whether the current feature is beneficial, the output gate assesses whether the current information is valuable, and the forget gate takes account of the previously entered invalid information [21].

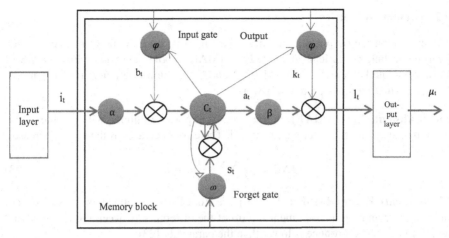

Fig. 4. Flow-chart of LSTM model

4 Experimental Results and Analysis

4.1 Traffic Flow Data Description

The "Caltrans Performance Measurement System", which is open to the public and available to transportation academics, maintains the extensively utilized traffic flow data. The PeMS database captures raw traffic flow data from 40,000 loop detectors deployed along various highway routes in California, including major urban regions [22]. "Three deductive detectors put in the Interstate 5 (I5) highway stretch in San Diego, California, were used to capture raw traffic flow data. The three detectors are placed in the I5 segment's arterial, on-ramp, and off-ramp areas". Table 1 contains further information on the three detectors, including the "Freeway Identity, Detector Number, Detector Position, Traffic Flow Direction, and Lane Count". The experimental traffic flow data was gathered between "September 1, 2019, and September 30, 2019", with a 5-min sample frequency. Before performing the data de-noising and prediction function, we pooled traffic flow data from nearby lanes [1].

Table 1. Comprehensive data description for 3 detectors [1]

Location	Freeway	Detector Number	Lane Number
X	I5	1125067	4
Y	I5	1118237	3
Z	I5	1123795	2

4.2 Evaluation Metrics

The evaluation metric plays a significant part in evaluating the performance of Deep Learning techniques. "Mean Absolute Error (MAE), Root Mean Square Error (RMSE), Mean Absolute Percentage Error (MAPE), and Correlation Coefficient (R)" [1] are the four evaluation methods used in this work.

Mean Absolute Error (MAE): Varies from 0 to positive infinity, with a value of 0 if the anticipated and true values are identical. The error decreases as the value decreases.

$$MAE = \frac{1}{Z} \sum\nolimits_{x=1}^{Z} \left| b_x - \widehat{b_x} \right| \tag{23}$$

Mean Square Error (RMSE): The "Square Root Error is defined as the square root of the square and the measurement n ratio of the difference between the expected and actual values". The variance is lower than the parameter [23].

$$RMSE = \sqrt{\frac{1}{Z} \sum\nolimits_{x=1}^{Z} \left(b_x - \widehat{b_x} \right)^2} \tag{24}$$

Mean Absolute Percentage Error (MAPE): The "average of the absolute value of the departure of all individual observations from the arithmetic mean [23], also defined as the absolute deviation of the average". Because the average absolute error avoids the problem of errors leveling out, it can properly represent the amount of the real forecast mistake.

$$MAPE = \sum\nolimits_{x=1}^{Z} \left| \frac{\hat{b}_x - \overline{\hat{b}}_x}{b_x} \right| \tag{25}$$

Correlation Coefficient (R): It calculates the linear relationship between the anticipated and actual values. The closer to 1, the more important [23].

$$R = \frac{\sum_{x=1}^{Z} \left(b_x - \overline{b} \right) \left(\hat{b}_x - \overline{\hat{b}} \right)}{\sqrt{\sum_{x=1}^{Z} (b_x - \overline{b})^2 (\hat{b}_x - \overline{\hat{b}})^2}} \tag{26}$$

4.3 Results

This study examines the performance of the suggested Deep learning approaches to those of SAE, CNN, and LSTM. SAE, CNN, and LSTM parameter values are comparable to those seen in state-of-the-art. Figure 5 illustrate the predicted outcomes. Convolutional neural networks are better at extracting spatial data than they are at retrieving temporal features. A well-known time series ML approach, the LSTM was primarily utilized to remove temporal characteristics. To reduce noise and detect missing data, a stacked denoise autoencoder is utilized [24]. Missing values in the provided data have an impact on the results of additional estimation and forecasting. For road traffic, each precision of forecast results is critical since it saves accidents, collisions, and further congestion.

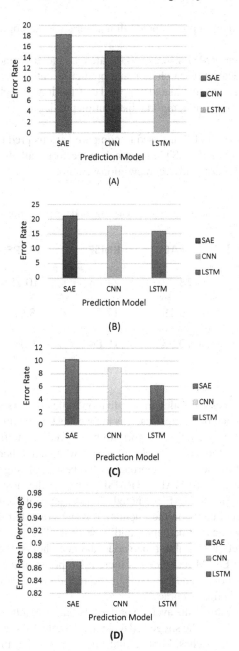

Fig. 5. Comparison of prediction algorithm based on error rate. (A): Mean absolute error rate (MAE). (B): Mean square error (MSE). (C): Mean absolute percentage error (MAPE). (D): Correlation coefficient (R).

Considering missing data improves prediction accuracy in all approaches, according to the results.

"MAEs, MREs, and RMSEs" are used to calculate the differences between forecast and actual values. Because researchers make predictions at many locations and times, the forecasting accuracy of spatial and temporal distributions is highly vital. To evaluate the performance of spatial and temporal distribution predicting, a coefficient correlation (R) is defined.

RMSE, MAE, MRE, and R are used to compare various prediction methods. Table 2 and Fig. 5 illustrates that the LSTM approach outperforms all other approaches on the basis of error rate reduction and accuracy improvement.

Table 2. Evaluation of deep learning model's prediction results

Prediction Model	MAE	RMSE	MAPE	R
SAE	18.27	21.03	10.25	0.87
CNN	15.19	17.67	8.92	0.91
LSTM	10.53	15.84	6.15	0.96

Table 2 also describes the following evaluation indicators. As seen in the table, the individual SAE approach prediction result is the weakest of the three, with higher error slots and a poor fit effect. The CNN algorithm has a prediction effect that is similar to that of a simple neural network approach and is somewhat better than the SAE technique. The prediction result of the LSTM approach is the best of all suggested deep learning techniques since it has the least MAE and RMSE, as well as the most well-fitting R-value.

It can be shown that the SAE predicted value is generally constant, and that the prediction is most accurate when the fluctuation is not great, but that the performance is low during the significant fluctuation and peak time. The "CNN technique is more accurate in the prediction of stable time series and peak hours, but not in the terms of low fluctuations. The LSTM technique is more appropriate in the prediction of stable time series and peak hours, and can well fit the real-time series of traffic flow while maintaining high prediction accuracy".

The experimental value is the average of the calculation results in order to accurately evaluate the performance of the suggested technique. Table 2 shows the prediction error results for the three approaches. Table 3 and Fig. 6 shows that the LSTMs algorithm has enhanced prediction accuracy in traffic flow prediction when compared to the other three approaches.

Table 3. Comparison of various prediction algorithm based on accuracy

Prediction Algorithm	Accuracy (%)
SAE	79.25
CNN	83.27
LSTM	87.95

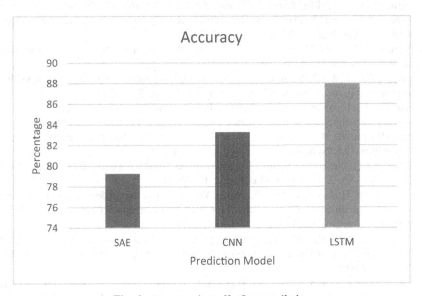

Fig. 6. Accuracy in traffic flow prediction

5 Conclusion

This paper proposed a Traffic Flow Prediction approach by Deep Learning techniques. Data is gathered from several sources, and criteria are chosen. The suggested algorithm's performance is measured using metrics such as RMSE, MAPE, MAE, and R. For data collecting, the proposed approaches employ a multimodal framework. A deep learning model is used to make a prediction for each data source. To extract the spatial information of neighboring crossroads, the method incorporates CNN. The LSTM collects the traffic flow's time-series information, which it then integrates with the extracted spatial and time-series information in the SAE technique for prediction. The results show that the LSTMs approach has greater prediction accuracy than a system that simply examines time or space characteristics, and thus can accurately represent changing traffic flow conditions.

References

1. Chen, X., et al.: Traffic flow prediction by an ensemble framework with data denoising and deep learning model. Physica A **565**, 125574 (2021)
2. Do, L.N., Vu, H.L., Vo, B.Q., Liu, Z., Phung, D.: An effective spatial-temporal attention based neural network for traffic flow prediction. Transp. Res. Part C: Emerg. Technol. **108**, 12–28 (2019)
3. Li, Y., Chai, S., Ma, Z., Wang, G.: A hybrid deep learning framework for long-term traffic flow prediction. IEEE Access **9**, 11264–11271 (2021)
4. Yu, B., Song, X., Guan, F., Yang, Z., Yao, B.: k-Nearest neighbor model for multiple-time-step prediction of short-term traffic condition. J. Transp. Eng. **142**(6), 04016018 (2016)
5. Lv, Y., Duan, Y., Kang, W., Li, Z., Wang, F.Y.: Traffic flow prediction with big data: a deep learning approach. IEEE Trans. Intell. Transp. Syst. **16**(2), 865–873 (2014)
6. Chen, C.P., Zhang, C.Y.: Data-intensive applications, challenges, techniques and technologies: a survey on big data. Inf. Sci. **275**, 314–347 (2014)
7. Hinton, G.E., Salakhutdinov, R.R.: Reducing the dimensionality of data with neural networks. Science **313**(5786), 504–507 (2006)
8. Yin, X., Wu, G., Wei, J., Shen, Y., Qi, H., Yin, B.: Deep learning on traffic prediction: Methods, analysis and future directions. IEEE Trans. Intell. Transp. Syst. (2021)
9. Karthika, B., UmaMaheswari, N., Venkatesh, R.: A research of traffic prediction using deep learning techniques. Int. J. Innov. Technol. Explor. Eng. (IJITEE) **8**, 725–728 (2019)
10. Zhao, R., Yan, R., Wang, J., Mao, K.: Learning to monitor machine health with convolutional bi-directional LSTM networks. Sensors **17**(2), 273 (2017)
11. Saravanan, S., Venkatachalapathy, K.: A deep hybrid model for traffic flow prediction using CNN-rGRU. Int. J. Anal. Exp. Modal Anal. **11** (2019)
12. Shi, Y., Feng, H., Geng, X., Tang, X., Wang, Y.: A survey of hybrid deep learning methods for traffic flow prediction. In: Proceedings of the 2019 3rd International Conference on Advances in Image Processing, pp. 133–138, November 2019
13. Xu, C., Li, Z., Wang, W.: Short-term traffic flow prediction using a methodology based on autoregressive integrated moving average and genetic programming. Transport **31**(3), 343–358 (2016)
14. Zhang, H., Wang, X., Cao, J., Tang, M., Guo, Y.: A hybrid short-term traffic flow forecasting model based on time series multifractal characteristics. Appl. Intell. **48**(8), 2429–2440 (2017). https://doi.org/10.1007/s10489-017-1095-9
15. Koesdwiady, A., Soua, R., Karray, F.: Improving traffic flow prediction with weather information in connected cars: a deep learning approach. IEEE Trans. Veh. Technol. **65**(12), 9508–9517 (2016)
16. Huang, W., Song, G., Hong, H., Xie, K.: Deep architecture for traffic flow prediction: deep belief networks with multitask learning. IEEE Trans. Intell. Transp. Syst. **15**(5), 2191–2201 (2014)
17. Li, D., Deng, L., Cai, Z., Yao, X.: Notice of retraction: intelligent transportation system in Macao based on deep self-coding learning. IEEE Trans. Industr. Inf. **14**(7), 3253–3260 (2018)
18. Fu, R., Zhang, Z., Li, L.: Using LSTM and GRU neural network methods for traffic flow prediction. In: 2016 31st Youth Academic Annual Conference of Chinese Association of Automation (YAC), pp. 324–328. IEEE, November 2016
19. Palm, R.B.: Prediction as a candidate for learning deep hierarchical models of data. Technical University of Denmark, p. 5 (2012)
20. Jiang, L.: Traffic flow prediction method based on deep learning. J. Phys. Conf. Ser. **1646**(1), 012050 (2020)

21. Chen, X., Xie, X., Teng, D.: Short-term traffic flow prediction based on ConvLSTM model. In: 2020 IEEE 5th Information Technology and Mechatronics Engineering Conference (ITOEC), pp. 846–850. IEEE, June 2020

22. Wang, Z., Pyle, T.: Implementing a pavement management system: the Caltrans experience. Int. J. Transp. Sci. Technol. **8**(3), 251–262 (2019)

23. Hassan, A., Mahmood, A.: Deep learning approach for sentiment analysis of short texts. In: 2017 3rd International Conference on Control, Automation and Robotics (ICCAR), pp. 705–710. IEEE, April 2017

24. Yang, B., Sun, S., Li, J., Lin, X., Tian, Y.: Traffic flow prediction using LSTM with feature enhancement. Neurocomputing **332**, 320–327 (2019)

Meta Heuristic Backtracking Algorithm for Virtual Machine Placement in Cloud Computing Migration

T. Lavanya Suja$^{(\boxtimes)}$ ⓘ and B. Booba ⓘ

Department of CSE VISTAS, Chennai, India
lavanyasujat@gmail.com

Abstract. Cloud serves as a repository for voluminous data generated in internet. Situations prevailing before and after pandemic reveal the fact that cloud computing served as a backbone for almost all industries across the globe by its humongous computing facility. This necessitates numerous algorithms for the best usage of cloud resources namely virtual machines (VM). One such technique is our proposed meta heuristic Backtracking algorithm for finding an alternative place for VMs to be placed after migration from overloaded places. The performance metrics such as number of hosts shutdown, mean execution time and standard deviation of the execution time of the proposed meta heuristic Backtracking algorithm are compared against existing VM placement algorithms like Inter Quartile Range, Minimum Migration Time, Maximum Correlation and Random Selection, show a commendable improvement. The results show introducing meta heuristic techniques in a successful algorithm like Backtracking optimize the influential factors of Service Level Agreements (SLA) by increasing an 8% of total number of hosts shutdown, decreasing a 10.4% of time in mean execution time and decreasing a 33.5% of time in standard deviation of execution time.

Keywords: Cloud computing · VM placement algorithm · Meta-heuristic · Backtracking · Over utilization

1 Introduction

According to National Institute of Science & Technology (NIST) [11], the definition of cloud computing is "cloud computing is a model for enabling ubiquitous, convenient, on-demand network access to a shared pool of configurable computing resources (e.g., networks, servers, storage, applications and services) that can be rapidly provisioned and released with minimal management effort or service provider interaction". In cloud computing the Service Level Agreement (SLA) is laid down enlisting the factors that should be satisfied throughout the service. This may include 100% server availability, provision for scaling up and down etc. If the SLA factors are not followed the Cloud Provider pay a penalty to the cloud consumer and for giving the services in SLA seamlessly the cloud consumer pays the provider so, SLA factors gain importance in cloud business. Thus,

© Springer Nature Switzerland AG 2022
N. Chaubey et al. (Eds.): COMS2 2022, CCIS 1604, pp. 214–225, 2022.
https://doi.org/10.1007/978-3-031-10551-7_16

resource allocation is always an evergreen situation where optimal solutions are poured into the cloud infrastructure utilization.

The proposed algorithm is an attempt to provide an optimal solution in a meta-heuristic way. Heuristics and algorithms are inseparable and several techniques like hill climbing, backtracking and many probabilistic approaches have given optimal solution for historic problems like N-Queens, Travelling Salesman, sum of subsets etc. The research motivation came from the history of backtracking and its efficiency in providing solutions in an easy and straight forward way which is easy to understand and simple enough to adopt. The proposed meta heuristic backtracking algorithm replaces the statistical method, Inter Quartile Range (IQR) for deciding on the overloaded hosts (PM) with the components like requested RAM, bandwidth requested and requested million instructions per second. The main contribution of backtracking technique is reducing the number of comparisons done in each VM residing in PM thus saving energy in terms of time and cost. The introduction of cloud computing and the importance of VM migration is explained below.

1.1 Cloud Computing and VM Migration

Cloud computing is a "Pay per use" service provided through internet. The cloud consumers rent their resources needed from the cloud providers. The example for cloud consumers can be individuals, small and big commercial and non-commercial organizations etc. The cloud providers are Amazon, Google Cloud, Microsoft, IBM etc. The cloud services have started from 3 major ones namely "Software as a service (SaaS, Platform as a Service (Paas) and Infrastructure as a service (IaaS)" to nowadays "Anything (X)" can be got as a service from cloud. To name a few they are Database, Storage, Identity, Desktop, Security etc.

The Datacenters (DC) in cloud is comprising of one or more servers which can be viewed as collection of Physical Machines (PM). Inside the PM there can more than one logically separated cores or Virtual Machines (VM). Each VM is responsible for the job execution. As the cloud services has become all pervasive and ubiquous, the infrastructure of the cloud and its maintenance has become more and more essential, as a result, have taken a center stage in the cloud market. The provisioning and effective usage of the resources like DC, PM, VM are very mandatory nowadays. This will also contribute to reducing the carbon emissions due to cloud usage and pave way for Green Computing. The energy efficiency is the fundamental need of any algorithm, henceforth it is decided to adopt a meta heuristic Backtracking algorithm for VM allocation to jobs by checking its load in it. Below is the brief introduction about Backtracking and how it is made meta heuristic for the research problem.

1.2 Backtracking

Backtracking [14] is an age-old technique which had successfully solved historic problems like Travelling Salesman, N-Queens, Sum of Subsets, Knapsack and even Sudoku puzzles. Usually there will be 2 constraints namely Implicit and Explicit given in the technique. An optimum solution is the one which satisfies both the constraints.

Problems can be solved by Trial-and-Error method which is a quite simple approach. Several mathematical techniques started from this point. The Trial-and-Error approach is called as Heuristic in mathematical techniques which is nothing but trying out all sort of chances. This can also be termed as Greedy technique in algorithms. Unfortunately, the search space of this technique is exceptionally large and when the problem's choices are more, then finding the solution becomes extremely hard termed as Non-Deterministic Probability hard (NP-hard) problems as the probability of finding a solution is exceedingly small because of the volume of the search space. For e.g., Travelling Salesman problem, N-Queen's problem etc.

To reduce the search space or options to be explored for finding a solution to a problem, some higher order problem solving skills are employed by the human community. Those techniques are termed as Meta-heuristic which help in filtering out the non-fruitful search options. These meta-heuristic techniques are nothing but introducing a next level criterion (criteria) to proceed further in the solution space. By employing these meta-heuristic techniques, the search space is trimmed down and eliminated from unfruitful options to be explored. There by the time and energy are saved in the journey of finding solution.

In Cloud business there are so many problems which involves reduction of energy usage. One such thrust area is VM Allocation for job submission and VM Selection for migration. These two are the main tasks that are considered here. For VM allocation we have proposed a new meta heuristic Backtracking algorithm and for VM Selection an already existing Minimum Migration Time criterion is taken. With these combinations the performance parameters are studied and compared with the already existing statistical approaches.

The rest of the paper is organized as introduction to the concepts such as cloud computing and VM migration, Backtracking, then with the related work followed by proposed method, experimental setup, results and finally with the conclusion and future scope.

2 Related Work

The authors [1] present a detailed review on VM consolidation which is a main element in VM placement in PM. There are 2 types of consolidation namely Static and Dynamic. In Static type the previous history of utilization is the driving factor of consolidation whereas in Dynamic type the short time recent history of utilization alone is enough, and it includes migrations of VM from one PM to other. Dynamic type further can be Centralized and Decentralized consolidation. Several works related to VM consolidation emphasize the fact that consolidation should be Dynamic and factors like Minimum Migration Time, SLA aware factors and Energy consumption. Various mathematical techniques and Genetic Algorithms serve this purpose, but they prove that this is a multi-objective problem and meta-heuristic techniques are the most needed along with a parent technique.

Having proposed 4 statistical techniques for VM Selection and 3 techniques [2] for VM Placement the combinations of them are tested for their performance. Out of them 3 combinations namely THR-MMT, IQR-MMT, MAD-MMT and LR-MMT are the top performance algorithms. Each of them gives optimal solution for SLA violations, energy usage, power usage and number of VM migrations. The authors conclude that online algorithms with adaptive heuristic outperform their counterparts, and this confirms the fact that there are various factors in which optimum value can be dependent upon. Our proposed algorithm therefore uses meta-heuristic technique like Backtracking along with the existing Minimum Migration Time for VM placement and VM selection, respectively.

The authors [3] propose Emperor Penguin Optimization algorithm for VM consolidation in the energy aware context. The results are compared with other nature inspired algorithms like Binary Gravity Search Algorithm (BGSA), Ant Colony Optimization (ACO), and Particle Swarm Optimization (PSO). The results they show that their proposed algorithm is efficient in minimizing energy consumption, SLA violations and widening the requirements of QoS for providing the cloud service in a capable way. In their simulation and comparison EPO algorithm work on multi objectives and consumes an average of 55.96% of energy and reduces an average of 47.12% SLA violations claimed to be a better performance than the above existing algorithms.

The parameter minimum migration time is the criteria for the new algorithm proposed for VM migration in [4]. The authors claim that their proposed algorithm achieves better efficiency and response on customer requirements and restrict number of SLA violations. The minimum migration time algorithm also uses Backtracking technique for trying out VMs suitable for migration from a host which speed up the process of the proposed algorithm.

Forecasting the utilization is the technique proposed in [5]. The Simple exponential smoothening technique is employed to predict the CPU utilization of the VM, Hosts and thereby the Data center. The method employed avoids unnecessary VM consolidation on Over utilization and underutilization, hence saves energy and reduces the number of migrations as they show in simulation results.

In [5] the proposed Energy aware Proactive Host load detection algorithm is compared to two of the best statistical techniques-based algorithms namely IQR-MMT and IQR-MC. The results show better performance for the proposed method. In a similar way in this paper our proposed method is compared with 4 Optimal online deterministic algorithms on the performance metrics related to energy and SLA.

A simple forecast is applied on the VM by calculating the Expected Failure Rate by using a Non-Homogeneous Poisson process distribution. The hosts are categorized as Under, Over and Normal Loaded, then each job from the job list is assigned to a minimum Expected Failure Rate and Underloaded host. The authors of [6] explains that their simulation results prove that their proposed AFTRA algorithm reduces the Makespan, energy consumed, maximize the Success rate and VM utilization. One important factor they have not considered is the cost which plays the tradeoff between service and price.

The Predicting Cloud Computing System (PCCS) [7] uses a workload analyzer to predict the workload of the host based on the history and checks whether it is over or underutilized. In contrary to the above algorithm AFTRA, cost is included as a main factor, but the Hard disk capacity and network Bandwidth are not introduced as parameters for weightage. The simulation results show that PCCS decreases the Turnaround time considerably and overall improvement rate in all the parameters are considerable. Mainly

SLA related parameters like SLA compliance, fault detection are improved because of prediction and self-healing nature of the algorithm.

Specifically, task execution time, load, and cost of it are taken into consideration by authors of [8] in their improved Whale optimization algorithm (WAO) for Cloud task scheduling (IWC). The experimental setup was run in 3 different modes, one during small scale (jobs < 101), medium scale (jobs < 1001) and large scale (jobs < 10001). Their results show the IWC performs well by decreasing the overall cost that its counterparts such as ACO and PCO. Though the time cost remains almost same for all the 3 algorithms in medium & large-scale run, there is a substantial difference in load cost and price cost brought by IWC. The authors says that because of the meta heuristic functions used in WOA this optimization is possible.

The proposed P2C algorithm [9] considers burst time and resource utilization factors which the authors of [9] advocates very essential for the better performance of theirs. A comparison of results is done with FCFS, MCT and MaxChild and the graphs show that the P2C algorithm decreases the execution time than the existing methods especially when the load is heavier and number of jobs greater than VMs. The resource provisioning is done in a Parent to Child relationship by looking into the dependencies between them. This time-based algorithm is another way of approaching a task scheduling problem.

Like the above problem discussed in [9], the authors of [10] also take up the same datasets for comparing their algorithm's performance. The problem is Task Scheduling in VMs and the technique they have chosen is an improved Teaching-learning based optimization (TBLO) namely Generalized TBLO. Their results claim that their GTBLO technique reduces the cost of execution than its counterparts.

The above literature review can be summarized by the below table, Table 1. In the comprehensive review it is observed that there are 3 mostly adapted techniques namely Mathematical, Statistical and Nature inspired algorithms, Our proposed algorithm uses an age old technique called Backtracking and employs meta heuristic techniques for finding out whether a host is overutilized or not.

3   The Proposed Method

In cloudsim3.0.3 the system architecture is built like the below diagram Fig. 1. The simulation starts by creating the Data Center (DC), the DC Broker, PMs, VMs and their corresponding lists. As the jobs are submitted to the VMs, two main jobs take place, namely VM Placement for jobs and VM Selection for migration.

In our proposed method the Meta Heuristic Backtracking (MH_BK) technique is used for finding whether a host, PM is overutilized or not. It is checked for finding a place to the job allocated in VMs inside this PM. A similar work in [4] is done by using backtracking and a new algorithm for finding out VM placement but the only criteria is the VMs having minimal migration time whereas in our proposed meta heuristic approach a combination of 3 parameters such as totalmips, totalRam, totalBw requested by the

Table 1. Summary of literature review

Name of the algorithm	Approach used	Parameters considered
Optimal online deterministic [2]	Statistical techniques	Energy consumption, Mean & Standard deviation of execution time
Emperor Penguin optimization [3]	Nature inspired	Energy consumption and SLA violations
Efficient virtual machine Migration [4]	Mathematical	Migration time, SLA violations
Energy aware Proactive Host load detection [5]	Statistical forecast	Performance degradation, SLA & Number of Hosts shutdown
Adaptive fault tolerant resource allocation [6]	Statistical forecast	PM overload categorization, Expected failure rate of job
Predicting cloud computing [7]	Statistical Prediction	Cost, SLA & fault rate
Whale optimization [8]	Nature inspired	Cost & Price
Multi-dependency and time-based resource scheduling [9]	Mathematical	Burst time, resource utilization

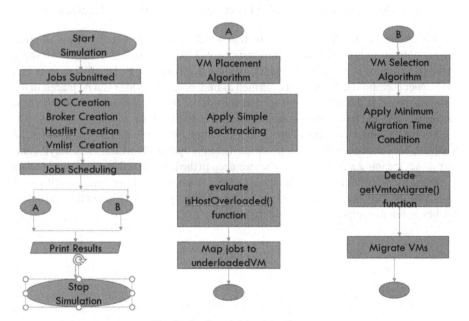

Fig. 1. System architecture diagram

VM inside a host is checked against available counterpart's (PM) resources. If the total requested quantities are more than what is present in the Host, then the host is termed as "overutilized" and the VMs residing in it will be added to VMs to be migrated list, otherwise this host (PM) serve as place for VMs to be allotted for jobs. The explanation of proposed meta heuristic Backtracking algorithm is given below.

3.1 Meta Heuristic Backtracking Algorithm

Backtracking [14] as per theory will have 2 constraints namely Implicit and Explicit. In our method the implicit constraints are the mandatory conditions which are checked for each VM in the Host, such as requested totalmips, requested totalRam and requested totalBw, are checked whether they are below the mips, Ram and Bw the Host have. If these implicit constraints are violated in between any iteration then backtracking is done, meaning, the loop is made to break. Thus, the time wasted for other VMs to be checked are eliminated. This checking saves time and energy as there are thousands of VM in some hundreds of PM according to our system configuration.

The explicit constraint is to check whether utilization is above the permissible limit. The limit is calculated by comparing the utilization and upper threshold. If utilization is greater than upper threshold then the Host is termed as Overutilized, otherwise Host is Underutilized and hence this is the place where VMs to be migrated will be brought in. Thus Hosts (PM) are checked for Overutilization or not. Here the above mentioned upper threshold is calculated by the below formula.

$$\text{upperThreshold} = 1 - \text{getSafetyParameter}() * \text{getUtilizationThreshold}() \quad (1)$$

The above Eq. 1 is the heuristic function which will decide whether the host comprising of thousands of VMs is overutilized or not. After calculating the upperThreshold value from Eq. 1, it is checked against its current utilization. If the utilization is less than upperThreshold then the host is termed as underutilized so jobs can be placed in the host, otherwise. if the utilization is greater than upperThreshold then the host is termed as overutilized and hence no jobs will be placed inside the host.

For the calculation of upperThreshold, two factors must be carefully chosen to strike a balance between over and underutilization. In our proposed algorithm the SafetyParameter = 0.2, meaning a 20% more can be stretched in the load of the Host to accommodate the migrated VMs, UtilizationThreshold = 0.8, which is the higher limit of utilization for a VM. In this way the proposed algorithm with the given experimental setup below fetches optimal results in terms of energy and SLA.

Pseudocode of Metaheuristic Backtracking

```
boolean isHostOverUtilized(PowerHost Host)
        initialize utilization=0.
        calculate upperThreshold;
        addHistoryEntry(host, upperThreshold);
        For Each VM in VMList of Host do
                Update totalRequestedMips;
                Update totalRequestedBw;
                Update totalRequestedRam;
if ((totalRequestedBw > host.getBw()) ||   (totalRequestedRam > host.getRam()))
                break;   //backtrack
        End For
        double utilization = totalRequestedMips / host.getTotalMips();
        if ((utilization > upperThreshold) ) return true;
        else    return false;
```

Algorithm 1. Metaheuristic Backtracking

The above meta heuristic backtracking is an idea to refine the checking of discovering the overutilized hosts which consists of hundreds of VMs. This algorithm basically checks for each VM inside the host, whether requested parameters are greater than the host's parameter. If so, no need to check for utilization so it backtracks and go for next host. Hence it removes the unnecessary iterations and saves time and energy as a result.

4   Experimental Setup

The experimental set up in Cloudsim3.0.3 has the following configuration. The configuration of the PM is, Operating System is Linux with Architecture of ×86 and virtual machine monitor as Xen. The DC models are HP ProLiant ML110 G4 servers and HP ProLiant ML110 G5 servers as per the system configuration given in [15]. The dataset is taken from Planet lab on the date "20110303" [12] is fed for both the proposed and existing algorithms to measure the performance characteristics. First the Backtracking algorithm with metaheuristic approach is executed and the output is compared against existing statistical approaches is given below.

All the graphs below are drawn with output parameters from 4 existing statistical and 1 proposed algorithm. The naming conventions used for each algorithm is abbreviation _safetyParameter of the respective algorithms. The safety parameters of first 4 statistical approaches are 1.5 and the proposed metaheuristic backtracking 0.2. The reason for the wide difference in the value of safety parameter is because the existing algorithm uses the inter quartile range of the data in the dataset [12] and multiply with the safety parameter, whereas the proposed algorithm multiplies the safety parameter with the utilization threshold of the host directly in Eq. 1. The below Table 2 gives an expansion for the existing and proposed algorithms.

Table 2. Expansion of algorithms.

Abbreviation	Expansion	Safety parameter
IQR_MMT_1.5	Inter Quartile Range- Minimum Migration Time	1.5
IQR-MC_1.5	Inter Quartile Range- Maximum Correlation	1.5
IQR_MU_1.5	Inter Quartile Range- Minimum Utilization	1.5
IQR_RS_1.5	Inter Quartile Range- Random Selection	1.5
MH-BK_0.2	Metaheuristic Backtracking	0.2

In the below Fig. 2, the parameter taken for consideration is number of hosts shutdown during the simulation time of one day using the above dataset [12]. It is found that there is an increase of 6974 from a maximum value so far in the existing approaches 6420.

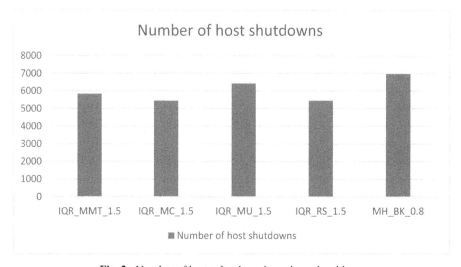

Fig. 2. Number of hosts shutdown in various algorithms

In Fig. 3, the next parameter to be considered is mean execution time for VM selection, Host selection and VM reallocation. In all the 3 parameters mentioned above our proposed algorithm has taken less values compared to all existing approaches.

In the last Fig. 4, Standard deviation of time taken for VM selection, Host selection and VM reallocation is measured for existing and proposed approaches. The bars drawn, clearly indicate the execution time's standard deviation is much lesser than the existing approaches' values.

algorithms.

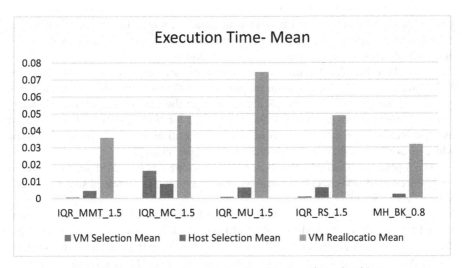

Fig. 3. Comparison of mean execution time in various algorithms

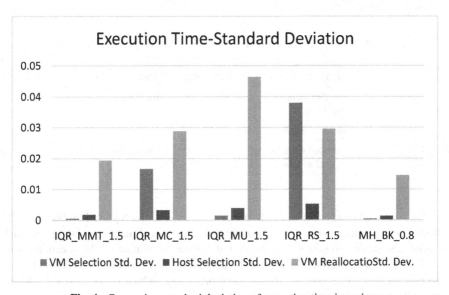

Fig. 4. Comparing standard deviation of execution time in various

5   Results

To evaluate the performance of the proposed algorithm, the output parameters related to SLA and energy are taken into consideration. To compare the performance, we have taken some best performing algorithms using statistical methods like Inter Quartile Range (IQR), Local Regression (LR) and Local Regression Robust (LRR).

The dataset used is from [12] and the load taken on "20110303" is used for this test run. The results in Fig. 1 show that our proposed MH-BK algorithm firstly increase the number of Hosts shutdown which saves considerable energy. It clearly states that VM consolidation happens from underutilized hosts so that VMs in it are migrated and the underutilized Host is put to a sleep mode or shutdown.

Secondly in Fig. 2, the Mean execution time of parameters namely VM Selection, Host Selection and VM Reallocation are plotted, and the bars show that the all the mean execution time are lesser in MH-BK algorithm than the existing algorithms. Similarly in Fig. 3, the Standard deviation of Execution time for VM Selection, Host Selection and VM Reallocation are also lesser in MH-BK algorithm than the existing algorithms which clearly shows that the data is clustered near the mean [13].

The 3 parameters namely Number of hosts shutdown is increased, mean execution time is decreased, and execution time's standard deviation is decreased so it becomes a muti-objective problem to solve.

As a result, the proposed meta heuristic Backtracking algorithm increases the number of hosts shutdown from 6420 to 6974 which is 8% of improvement. A commendable 10.4% decrease in mean execution time is achieved by adopting meta heuristics in decision making of finding overloaded hosts from 0.03581 to 0.318. A substantial decrease of 33.5% in standard deviation is experienced from 0.0198 to 0.01451. The data are tabulated below in Table 3.

Table 3. Parameters and their influenced percentage by MH_BK Algorithm

Parameter name	Percentage	Effect
Number of hosts shutdown	8%	Increased
Mean of execution time	10.4%	Decreased
Standard deviation of execution time	33.5%	Decreased

The above table says it is a multiobjective solution to the research problem of VM allocation as parameter, number of hosts has been increased than the existing approach whereas the other two parameters mean and standard deviation of the execution time are decreased. The percentage of increase may be 8% but it is a good number though. The percentage of decrease are considerable percentage which really adds value to the approach and thereby time and energy are saved.

6   Conclusion and Future Scope

It is evident from the results by choosing a cautious value as Utilization Threshold (0.8) and Safety parameter (0.2), the algorithm consumes less energy, more hosts are shutdown thus saves energy & cost, execution time taken for VM selection, Host Selection and VM reallocation is less and therefore the mean and standard deviation of them gets reduced. This is a positive improvement brought by this algorithm. The number of hosts shutdown is increased by metaheuristic backtracking algorithm in simulation now seem to be a favourable situation to save more energy but must be explored that this is the same reflection in the real scenario. Further study related to the cost and energy parameters must be brought in to support the inference observed. To make the fact clear, in future a robust method will be chosen for VM selection algorithm which is used to select VMs for migration depending upon overutilization, underutilization factors and datasets from other 9 days from Planetlab to look for optimal solution. A combination of these 2 algorithms will provide more optimal results for better infrastructure and SLA management.

References

1. Donyagard Vahed, N., Ghobaei-Arani, M., Souri, A.: Multiobjective virtual machine placement mechanisms using nature-inspired metaheuristic algorithms in cloud environments: a comprehensive review. Int. J. Commun. Syst. **32**(14), e4068 (2019)
2. Beloglazov, A., Buyya, R.: Optimal online deterministic algorithms and adaptive heuristics for energy and performance efficient dynamic consolidation of virtual machines in cloud data centers. Concurr. Comput. Pract. Exp. **24**(13), 1397–1420 (2012)
3. Samriya, J.K., Chandra Patel, S., Khurana, M., Tiwari, P.K., Cheikhrouhou, O.: Intelligent SLA-aware VM allocation and energy minimization approach with EPO algorithm for cloud computing Environment. Math. Probl. Eng. **2021**, 1–13 (2021)
4. Chien, N.K., Dong, V.S.G., Son, N.H., Loc, H.D.: An efficient virtual machine migration algorithm based on minimization of migration in cloud computing. In: Vinh, P.C., Barolli, L. (eds.) ICTCC 2016. LNICSSITE, vol. 168, pp. 62–71. Springer, Cham (2016). https://doi.org/10.1007/978-3-319-46909-6_7
5. Fard, S.Y.Z., Sohrabi, M.K., Ghods, V.: Energy-aware and proactive host load detection in virtual machine consolidation. Inf. Technol. Control **50**(2), 332–341 (2021)
6. Sathiyamoorthi, V., Keerthika, P., Suresh, P., Zhang, Z.J., Rao, A.P., Logeswaran, K.: Adaptive fault tolerant resource allocation scheme for cloud computing environments. J. Organ. End User Comput. **33**(5), 135–152 (2021)
7. Sohani, M., Jain, S.C. Fault tolerance using self-healing SLA and load balanced dynamic resource provisioning in cloud computing. Jordon J. Comput. Inf. Technol. **7**(2), 206–222 (2021)
8. Chen, X., et al.: A woa-based optimization approach for task scheduling in cloud computing systems. IEEE Syst. J. **14**(3), 3117–3128 (2020)
9. Prakash, V., Bawa, S., Garg, L.: Multi-dependency and time based resource scheduling algorithm for scientific applications in cloud computing. Electronics **10**(11), 1320 (2021)
10. Ram, S.D.K., Srivastava, S., Kumar Mishra, K.: A variant of teaching-learning-based optimization and its application for minimizing the cost of workflow execution in the cloud computing. Concurr. Comput. Pract. Exp. **33**, e6425 (2021)
11. Final Version of NIST Cloud Computing Definition Published: NIST (8 January 2018). https://www.nist.gov/news-events/news/2011/10/final-version-nist-cloud-computing-definition-published
12. beloglazov/planetlab-workload-traces: GitHub (n.d.). https://github.com/beloglazov/planetlab-workload-traces. Accessed 28 June 2021
13. What Does Standard Deviation Show us About Our Data? (n.d.). http://science.halleyhosting.com/sci/soph/inquiry/standdev2.htm. Accessed 28 June 2021
14. Horowitz, E.: Fundamentals of Computer Algorithms (Computer Software Engineering Series) (New edition). Computer Science Press (1978)
15. SPECpower_ssj2008. (n.d.). http://Www.Spec.Org., http://www.spec.org/power_ssj2008/results/res2011q1/power_ssj2008-20110127-00342.html. Accessed 29 June 2021

Achieving Energy Efficiency in Life-Logging Applications of Internet of Things Using Data Compression Through Incorporation of Machine Learning and Edge-Cloud Architecture

Vishal Barot[1](✉) and Ritesh Patel[2]

[1] LDRP Institute of Technology and Research, Gandhinagar, Gujarat, India
vishal_ce@ldrp.ac.in
[2] U & P. U. Patel Department of Computer Engineering, CSPIT, Gujarat, India
riteshpatel.ce@charusat.ac.in

Abstract. Life logging applications for physiological and behavioral analysis of humans make use of smart wearable devices for capturing the various biosignals of a human. These devices have a combination of sensors that capture the respective biosignals and report the recorded data to the edge device (usually a mobile phone) which in turn acts as a primary communicator delivering the data over cloud for storage and future analysis. As this huge amount of data is transmitted from edge device to the cloud, IoT devices are forced early exhaustion, due to higher energy consumption. We propose a SZ based lossy compression technique on edge devices. To evaluate our proposal we implemented the algorithm over automobile drivers' stress recognition dataset from PhysioNet that resulted in a reduction of the dataset size by 103 times after compression. As information loss is a primary constraint while compressing data, we performed stress prediction over the decompressed data using a fully connected neural network with an accuracy of 98.01% which is more than the accuracy achieved for predictions made on the original - uncompressed dataset.

Keywords: Internet of Things · Machine learning · Stress level prediction · Data compression · Energy consumption optimization

1 Introduction

Sensors, actuators, wearable IoT devices and other "Things" in Internet of Things (IoT) are extensively being used in the current times and are predicted to become an inseparable part of human lives in the near future. Processing of the recorded data over the device itself imposes a large computation overhead over these battery backed devices that are prone to early extinction due to energy drain. This leads to a need of transmitting the recorded data over cloud, for processing. Although, cloud with its ubiquitous computation and storage capacity

© Springer Nature Switzerland AG 2022
N. Chaubey et al. (Eds.): COMS2 2022, CCIS 1604, pp. 226–243, 2022.
https://doi.org/10.1007/978-3-031-10551-7_17

can overcome the computation bottleneck of IoT devices, transmission of the massive recorded data over cloud imposes a huge communication overhead over the network which also can lead to extinction of the battery backed IoT devices.

An estimate suggests that with advancements in IoT applications and their growing deployments, the IoT devices globally would consume around 46TWh energy by the year 2025 [1]. This makes working on conservation of energy of IoT devices, an interesting domain of research. The easiest way is replenishing of batteries of these battery backed IoT devices but the process of replenishing them is time consuming, inconvenient, high costing and even hazardous in a certain cases [2]. An IoT application consists of three parts: collection of data, processing of data and transmission of data [3]. Of all the three parts, transmission of data is believed to consume the most energy [4]. Node to edge device transmission using technologies such as Bluetooth, RFID or other local range communication technologies [5] is not as energy consuming as edge device to cloud transmission [6]. In order to protect edge devices from draining away due to higher energy consumption during transmission, a concrete approach needs to be designed [7]. For the same, techniques such as edge - cloud - IoT integration, for example a an architecture composed of three layers (tiers) is implemented in sensor based systems connecting the wearable device to edge device such as mobile phone which in turn is connected to cloud. In this architecture, sensor data or some part of it is processed within the network or near the network, on most cases that is on edge device itself to avoid a massive transmission of data to cloud [8]. Apart from performing a part of processing over edge device, another technique that is gaining momentum is compression of data. Compression leads to reduction of the overall volume of data transmitted thereby reducing the energy consumption [9].

We propose an energy efficient SZ lossy compression technique over edge device to compress the data to be transmitted to cloud thereby reducing the size of data transmitted leading to lesser energy consumption. To validate our proposal, we have applied the SZ lossy compression technique over stress recognition in automobile drivers' dataset from PhysioNet [10]. For determining the effectiveness of the proposed technique, two parameters namely energy consumption and information loss were considered. Energy consumption was measured in terms of size of the compressed data obtained after applying SZ lossy compression technique as compared to that of original data. Smaller size of compressed data that would now be transmitted as compared to original data infers a reduction in energy consumption. Information loss was measured in terms of stress prediction accuracy as calculated for decompressed dataset over cloud and compared with that on original dataset. An equal or higher accuracy of over decompressed dataset suggests no information loss despite compression-decompression.

Rest of the paper has been organized as follows: Sect. 2 presents a review of the literature related to IoT based life logging applications and data compression approaches; Sect. 3 describes the proposed technique for life logging applications along with our case study, Sect. 4 detail the dataset, experiment conducted and the results; Sect. 5 is the conclusion.

2   Related Work

As the usage of wearable sensors, actuators and other similar other smart embedded devices has increased, tracking human physiological, psychological and behavioral states in routine as well as their interaction with the environment has become easier [11]. IoT has facilitated collection of biosignals such as heart-rate, respiration rate, blood oxygen as well as electrocardiogram (ECG) monitoring at a very low cost proves a recent study [12]. Making use of maps and timelines recorded using cell phones along with the wearable sensor readings enables regular spatial and temporal routine analysis of humans [13]. This collection of data and analytics enhance real time monitoring of the current psychological state or health condition of humans and act as a decision support tool in providing personalized advice being given to individuals, encouraging a healthy lifestyle and a facilitated routine based on a detailed analysis from statistical perspective [14].

Several studies have discussed such applications of IoT data analytics that are particularly called "Life logging Applications" as they deal with human health, routine and behavioral analysis. For example, life logging can be used for gaining significant insights into a common phenomenon affecting both personal and work lives of people, stress [15]. Thomas Fischer [15] who discussed about organizational stress and its balance first concluded on basis of a literature review over 155 articles that devices such as smart mobile phones and smart watches that can be used to track the routine as well as a few biosignals of individuals as also concluded by Weiss [16] in his research wherein he used machine learning for recognition of activities based on patterns tracked by smart watches. Kunc [14] investigated 130 research papers and explained summarizing them the significance of human behavioral aspects at work places contributing to life logging applications in healthcare domain. They concluded that collection of behavioral data and evaluating it will infer adoption of new mechanisms at organizational level for managing the employee stress level.

Kulev [12] presented how biosignals like blood oxygen, ECG, respiratory rate, pulse rate and photoplethysmography can be gathered by wearable devices and used for recognizing and monitoring individual human activities. He also proved how interventions in the routine lead to an increase or decrease in the physical activities of an individual. Vilarinho [13] presented an IoT and machine learning based model for activity recognition as well as fall recognition. The collected data samples making your of android phones collecting 11,771 samples of both human activities and falls performed by a group of 30 participants who belonged to age group 18 to 60. These measurements were classified as activities performed by a person in daily routine (ADL) and falls. Using this data, they prepared a classifier that could classify activities under nine different categories of ADL and eight different types of falls categories. They made use of k-NN, SVM, ANN and random forest for modeling and presented their accuracies as results. However, they suggested that CNN and RNN would result in better accuracies for activity recognition.

Rashidi [17], Patel [18], Avci [19], Mazilu [20], Kranz [21] and Stiefmeier [22] proved in their studies that data from sensors is the foundation of the smart assistive devices that help in identifying human activities like different hand gestures, cooking activities, fall detection, running, sitting, sleeping, walking, typing, painting, reading, writing etc. This human activity recognition can be used in smart homes, rehabilitation centers, in healthcare domain to facilitate medical and behavioral assessment of humans. The industries too can benefit from this type of setup as this can help them assess the productivity of their employees in terms of working hours, postures, time spent in breaks etc. Francisco [23] presented an IoT data analytics model using CNN and RNN. They identified human activities like standing, sitting, bicycling, walking, drinking from cup etc. from published datasets such as mHealth [24] and opportunity [25]. They trained an eight layer deep network named DeepConvLSTM gave high accuracy despite trading off system performance. They used baseline CNN for comparison and showed how DeepConvLSTM helped distinguish between gesture that were similar in nature such as opening and closing of door while the baseline CNN showed errors in recognizing these activities.

Ji Ni [26] presented a healthcare analytics model that works in 2 stages. In stage one, a multiple objective genetic programming algorithm is used for reducing the dimensions of life logging data. Stage two has a hidden markov model (HMM) implemented for prediction of status of human activity over time. For validating the model proposed, they collected real data including number of steps, duration etc. for 118 to 401 days from 10 participants in UK. For comparing the accuracy of their model, they showed their model MOGP-HMM could give better predictions of human activity status than SVMs using different kernels. They concluded that their model could be easily adopted not only in the healthcare domain but also in business analytics.

Jun Qi [27] shows a comparative analysis of measure and recognition of physical (PARM) in constrained or controlled environment and unconstrained or uncontrolled environment. The paper gives a review of techniques used for data fusion in PARM application enabled by IoT paradigm. They have critically examined the activity recognition and measure from 3D perspective viz. devices, persons and timeline. From their study, they have concluded that if the data fusion techniques are designed and deployed successfully, they will enable monitoring the human activities using low cost devices leading to safer preventive care.

Muaddi Alharbi [28] studied usage of wearable trackers in older adults. It was noticed that the step count measure, MVPA, ECG and HR readings were accurately measured and that the older adults showed adherence over longer usage. P. Yang [29] focused on pre-processing the diverse human life patterns gathered by heterogeneous wearable devices since the huge uncertainty persisting due to heterogeneity of the data makes its lesser useful in healthcare.

Majdi Rawashdeh [30] presented an experiment over activity recognition in smart home environment. This experiment was conducted using available datasets that recorded human activities like in bed, bed to toilet, breakfast, work, dinner, sleep, watch TV, meditate, bath, read and other routine activities. Algorithms like Naïve Bayes, SVM and J48 were used to train a classifier for further predictions. Results in terms of accuracy reflected an improvement when training dataset was varied by changing number of attributes, activities and sensor deployment at home.

Liao [31] has applied Global Positioning System (GPS) so as to track the location of individuals and recognize or predict the on-going activity on the basis of their in-home location. Although we now have sensors that can do the same in a much easier way with least cost, what is more interesting is the methodology adopted is that they used hidden markov models for association of activities with locations. In [32], Liao has integrated an IoT sensor network for life logging instead of GPS and made use of a Bayesian Network for pattern recognition and human activity prediction.

Samarah [33] worked upon health related data sensing taking privacy into consideration. They proved that while most of the human activities are atomic - occur rapidly in succession, the algorithms that were applied for prediction worked well for pre segmented data and that they gave lesser accuracies when atomic actions were considered. Hossain in 2018 [34] and 2019 [35] presented voice pathology detection approach and cloud-assisted video transmission for recording the life logs of individuals.

Hesham El-Sayed [36] has presented a bigger picture on collaboration of technologies like edge, cloud and IoT for the purpose of data analytics. They have suggested that since the data collected by the IoT sensor networks is sent over cloud for processing and actuations, it increases the overhead, response time traffic. If smart phones, wearable devices and other board units were made to work on the edge of network for analysis of the gathered data and extraction of knowledge, network resources could be saved and response time could be improved. Yet another technique that can help reduce overhead is data compression [8].

There are several data compression techniques such as content aware (sensitive) compression approach on the basis of similarity of frames [37]. Such applications are quite common in applications like IoT streaming services. Deepu [38] presents a data compression scheme that is hybrid in nature for power reduction in WSNs. The hybrid scheme provides both lossy and lossless compression. The scheme includes automated context aware selection of data rate leading to power conservation in wireless devices. As proved by Joseph Azar [7], compression of data on sensor nodes using lossy compression technique would reduce the overall energy consumption due to a reduced size of data being transmitted after compression. The compressed file is decompressed over edge device and then used for further processing and analysis.

3   Proposed Architecture

As per the proposed architecture, initially the driver's physiological data gets recorded by various physiological sensors giving us data about driver's heart rate, respiration rate, electrocardiogram and galvanic skin responses of hands and legs.

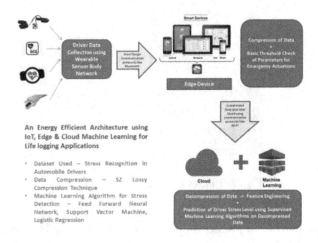

Fig. 1. Proposed architecture

In our case study, for validating our proposed technique, we have worked upon this data that is stress recognition in automobile drivers database published on PhysioNet [10]. Having collected this data over sensor node in a real time scenario as described in the architecture, this data is transmitted to the edge node. Here, the sensors are considered to have been fixed in a wearable device which acts as the sensor node in our case and the edge device here is the mobile phone. Hence the data recorded by wearable sensor device is sent to the mobile phone using local communication technology such as bluetooth. On the edge node, SZ lossy compression technique is used for data compression and the compressed data is then transmitted to cloud using Internet. Over cloud, the data is decompressed, stored and later used for analysis like prediction of stress level of drivers using various supervised learning algorithms, a comparison of whose accuracies has been shown (Fig. 1).

As the transmission using bluetooth, between the wearable sensor device and the mobile phone doesn't impose much of a transmission overhead as compared to transmission between mobile device and cloud using internet, the data compression on edge device before data transmission over cloud reduces the amount of data transmitted thereby leading to a reduction in the energy consumed in transmitting the data. One major consideration here was the information loss. Although data compression reduces energy consumption, if there is loss of information due to compression, the technique fails. Hence, having decompressed the compressed data, we then run a supervised classification algorithm over the data to predict the stress level of drivers. This was done using various supervised machine learning algorithms such as SVM, logistic regression, feed forward neural network [7] and fully connected neural network proposed by us. The accuracy achieved from predictions made over decompressed data turned was higher

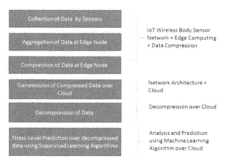

Fig. 2. Phases of proposed architecture

than that achieved from prediction made on original data. This happened as SZ lossy compression technique used has an inbuilt data cleaning and noise removal mechanism [7].

The subsections below explain each of the steps mentioned in Fig. 2 in detail. Section 3.2 explains the dataset, Sect. 3.2 details the SZ lossy compression technique used, Sect. 3.3 explains the preprocessing done over the decompressed dataset over cloud before prediction and Sect. 3.4 describes the stress prediction algorithm.

3.1 Dataset

The dataset used is stress recognition in automobile drivers database published on PhysioNet [10]. With various sensors to record respiratory rate, heart rate, galvanic skin response (GSR) of hands and legs and electrocardiogram (ECG) of 17 different drivers while they drove on a path that was pre-reserved, a wearable sensor body network was created. This drive was done in and around Boston, Massachusetts for a span of 50 to 90 min. The dataset has 9 attributes in all. They are as follows: driver id, heart rate (HR), galvanic skin response for foot, galvanic skin response for hand, elapsed time (ET), electrocardiogram (ECG), electromyography reading (EMG), marker and respiration rate (RESP). Table 1 depicts the dataset of Driver 6 showing a few tuple with all the attributes. The dataset suggests the following: 1. In rest - "low stress" 2. In average traffic - "moderate stress" 3. On busy streets - "high stress"

3.2 Lossy Compression

Error controlled lossy compression techniques not only give a good compression ratio, but they also keep the data integrity maintained such that the data after decompression remains valid to the users [39]. Different datasets work well with

Table 1. Sample records from the dataset

Elapsed time	Driver	ECG	EMG	Foot GSR	Hand GSR	HR	Marker	RESP
'0:04.960'	6	−0.082	0.186	8.939	18.928	93	12.34	36.83
'0:04.962'	6	−0.082	0.186	8.939	18.928	93	12.34	36.83
'0:04.964'	6	−0.079	0.186	8.939	18.928	93	12.34	36.83

different techniques. The techniques those are very popular for data reductions are SZ [40] and ZFP [41]. Out of various compression techniques like ZFP, Gzip, NUMARCK, FPC, ISABELA, SZ and FPZIP. SZ has got the best decompression time [42]. Out of ZFP and SZ, the compression ratio of SZ is 80% more than that of ZFP [40].

As Tao [39] stated in 2019, the SZ algorithm compresses multidimensional data in time series. There is a great constraint it puts upon the loss of data due to its error bound feature that allows us to specify the amount of error while restoring data on decompressing it. SZ lossy compression technique compresses input data files that are in binary format [39]. But for our case, since the data is in floating point values, we need to modify the SZ algorithm to adapt to floating point values [7] (Fig. 3).

Data Collection by Wearable Device:
      while energy_level_of_node > 0 and sensor_active_status == ON
      for each time period T
           collect data in M*N format (readings*features)
           for each time period P of T
                transmit data to edge device

SZ Lossy Compression over Edge device:
      Input: M*N (readings * features)
      while energy_level_of_edge_device> 0 and mobile_edge_device_status == ON
      for each time period T
           flatten data (convert 2D array to 1D array)
           compress 1D array using adaptive curve fitting models
           #linear curve fitting or quadratic curve fitting or preceding neighbors fitting
           Select the model yielding closest approximation
           Transform fitted data into integer quantization factors
           Encode using Huffman tree
           transmit data over cloud

Fig. 3. SZ lossy compression algorithm [7]

3.3   Dataset Preprocessing

Once the compressed data is transmitted over cloud, it is decompressed so as the perform analysis over it. So as to make stress predictions on the basis of the decompressed data, the data is first preprocessed. The steps involved in preprocessing of the dataset are shown in Fig. 4. The marker is first converted to binary labels so as to address this as a stress prediction problem. Later, noise removal and data cleaning techniques are applied over the dataset especially for electrocardiogram (ECG) and galvanic skin response (GSR) features followed by feature engineering over these two specifically for extraction of information by attribute expansion.

Fig. 4. Dataset preprocessing steps

Frank in his study [43] suggests that the stress level classes can range from two to five or more different levels of stress. The technique wherein there is prediction made upon two classes is called detection and in our case it becomes "Stress Detection". While in a certain cases unsupervised learning algorithms can be used for defining labels- levels of stress on basis of similar characteristics but it can also be done with the help of self reporting questionnaires. We converted the marker values from "low stress", "moderate stress" and "high stress" to stress detection classes "stressed" and "not stressed" depicted by binary classification classes +1 and −1 signifying driving and resting respectively. For each driver's records, we initially plotted the "marker" attribute. On enhancing the visibility of peaks, they helped convert "marker" into binary "stressed" and "not stressed" labels. Figure 5 represent the graph plotted to identify stress and no stress states using peak.

The under mentioned observations were made by inspecting the peak in the plotted graph for each driver.

1. +1 stress start - int: From the reading of the graphs (of markers) of these drivers, the initial period is resting (not stress or 1) and the later is stress (−1). The key represents the drive id and the value represents the index

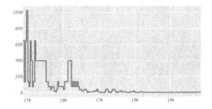

Fig. 5. Inspection of peak of marker

where the peak was observed. The peak represents the change in the state. '11': 33248, '16': 39149, '09': 23232, '17a': 46541, '12': 36445 Here, for driver 11, the entry 33248 is the demarcation of the change in state from no stress to stress.

2. +1 stress int-end: From the reading of the graphs (of markers) of these drivers, the initial period is stressful (stress or −1) and the later is not stress (+1). The key represents the drive id and the value represents the index where the peak was observed. The peak represents the change in the state. '06': 7424, '07': 13023, '17b': 48077, '10': 26272, '08': 16224 Here, for driver 06, the entry 7424 is the demarcation of the change in state from stress to no stress (Table 2).

Table 2. Snapshot from driver 6's dataset

ET	Driver	ECG	EMG	Foot GSR	Hand GSR	HR	Marker	RESP	Stress
'04.96'	6	−0.08	0.18	8.93	18.92	93	12.34	36.83	1
'04.96'	6	−0.07	0.186	8.93	18.92	93	12.34	36.83	1
'09.99'	6	−0.10	0.18	8.85	18.72	75	12.29	35.15	−1
'09.99'	6	−0.11	0.18	8.85	18.72	75	12.29	35.15	−1

After converting the markers to binary, data cleaning, noise removal and smoothing techniques were applied upon the dataset, specifically on attributes ECG and GSR. Data cleaning was performed by removing noise from ECG signal using Bypass filter. Figure 5 shows the difference between the filtered and original ECG signal. The GSR value is cleaned by multiplying the negative values with −1 and for entries with value 0, considering the preceding entry instead (Fig. 6).

Next, feature engineering was performed on each driver's dataset individually. The attributes ECG and GSR have been expanded using feature engineering as suggested in [44]. Attributes of ECG has been expanded to 10 new attributes

Fig. 6. Noisy ECG signal

using the highest value of ECG in each iteration (r_peak). Table 3 shows the attributes obtained by feature engineering ECG while Table 4 shows attributes obtained by feature engineering GSR that has been expanded to 5 different attributes.

Table 3. Feature engineered attributes from ECG signals

The interval between 2 consecutive R_R peaks is called RR interval	
RMSSD	inter-beat (RR) interval's root mean quare
sdNN	Standard deviation RR interval
meanNN	Mean RR interval
cvNN	RMSSD/meanNN
medNN	Median absolute deviation of RR interval
medianNN	absolute value's median of the consecutive difference in between 2 intervals
mcvNN	medNN/medianNN
pNN50	Number of interval difference of consecutive RR intervals > 50 ms by total RR intervals
pNN20	Number of interval difference of consecutive RR intervals > 20 ms by total RR intervals

3.4 Stress Prediction

Stress level prediction of drivers has been done making use of supervised learning classifiers like support vector machine, logistic regression and fully connected neural network. The decompressed data that includes attributes heart rate, respiration rate and all the engineered features of ECG and GSR is made use of for predicting stress. SVM is a classifier that helps in fining the optimal most separating hyperplane differentiating classes. It is widely used with linearly non

Table 4. Feature engineered attributes from GSR signals

meanGSR	GSR signal mean
meanSCR	SCR signal mean
meanSCL	SCL mean
maxSCR	Maximum value of SCR signal
slopeSCL	maximum SCL value – minimum SCL value

separable and high dimensional data [45]. Logistic regression is a classifier that defines a relationship between a nominal variable and a certain dependent factors that could be discrete, continuous or binary in nature [45].

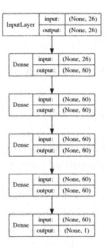

Fig. 7. FCNN architecture [7]

We made predicted stress using two different fully connected neural networks (FCNN) that yield different accuracies. The first architecture is as suggested in [7] has got 17 input neurons corresponding to 17 features and 60 neurons in the hidden layers. Stochastic gradient descent (SGD) with 'Adam' optimizer and binary cross-entropy are used for optimization. For validation of the hyper parameters, 10-Fold cross validation is used with 300 epochs and 0.01 learning rate as suggested in [7]. Figure 7 shows the architecture of this FCNN.

We then tried predicting stress using our proposed fully connected neural network design with 250 epochs, 0.01 learning rate, 'Adam' optimizer, 20% validation split and 20% training split. Figure 8 shows the architecture of this FCNN designed by us for this dataset. Accuracy achieved using our proposed FCNN is more than that achieved using SVM, logistic regression or FCNN [7]. This accuracy is consistently higher over both decompressed as well as original dataset.

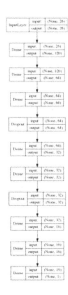

Fig. 8. Proposed FCNN architecture

4   Results and Discussion

The result of the proposed technique has been evaluated in two contexts. Energy consumption was measured in terms of size of the compressed data obtained after applying SZ lossy compression technique as compared to that of original data. Smaller size of compressed data that would now be transmitted as compared to original data infers a reduction in energy consumption. Information loss was measured in terms of stress prediction accuracy as calculated for decompressed dataset over cloud and compared with that on original dataset. An equal or higher accuracy of over decompressed dataset suggests no information loss despite compression-decompression.

4.1   Energy Consumption

Using SZ Lossy Compression technique, the data is compressed on the edge device before being transmitted to Cloud. A reduction in the amount of data transmitted leads to reduction in the amount of energy consumed while transmitting data. Table 5 shows comparison of file sizes of the original dataset and the compressed dataset. There is a reduction of around 103 times has been achieved using SZ Lossy Compression Technique over the Dataset.

4.2   Prediction Accuracy

Initially, the original dataset was used to train a bare FCNN model with 16 neurons in the input layer, 32 neurons in the hidden layer and 1 neuron in the

Table 5. Data compression in terms of file sizes

	Dataset	Size
1	Original Dataset	3,968,221 bytes
2	Compressed Dataset	38,527 bytes
	Reduction in size	103 times

output layer. There was no data cleaning performed and the dataset was original and not compressed. As shown in Table 6, the accuracy obtained over this model was 50.1%. The same model when tested with dataset after removing noise from ECG gave an accuracy of 65.59%. On using extracted features of ECG, the accuracy increased to 88.12%.

On using support vector machine & logistic regression for predicting stress over feature engineered dataset, the accuracy obtained is 79.67% and 71.88% respectively. On using the architecture as suggested in [7] that has 17 input neurons corresponding to 17 features and the hidden layers with 60 neurons, the prediction over the feature engineered dataset rose to 96.87%. On training our proposed Fully Connected Neural Network that we designed with 250 epochs, 0.01 learning rate, 'Adam' optimizer, 20% validation split and 20% training split, the accuracy obtained is 97.56%. Table 7 shows a summary of these classifiers tested over the Original Dataset.

Table 6. Stress prediction accuracies of various models over original dataset

No.	Original dataset	Atr.	Model architecture	Accuracy
1.	Original dataset as collected (no feature engineering)	6	16->32->1 [7]	50.1%
2.	Noise removal from ECG attribute (no feature engineering)	6	16->32->1 [7]	65.59%
3.	ECG Noise Removal + ECG Feature Engineering	16	16->32->1 [7]	88.12%
4.	ECG Noise Removal + ECG Feature Engineering + GSR Feature Engineering	27	17->60->60->60->60->1 [7]	96.87%
5.	ECG Noise Removal + ECG Feature Engineering + GSR Feature Engineering	27	Support Vector Machine (SVM)	79.67%
6.	ECG Noise Removal + ECG Feature Engineering + GSR Feature Engineering	27	Logistic Regression	71.88%
7.	ECG Noise Removal + ECG Feature Engineering + GSR Feature Engineering 27	-	Proposed (extended) FCNN Architecture (Fig. 7)	97.56%

When the data is decompressed over cloud, the above mentioned algorithms are applied over the decompressed data for stress detection and Table 7 summarizes the accuracies obtained by applying these classifiers over decompressed dataset.

Table 7. Stress prediction accuracies of various models over decompressed dataset

No.	Decompressed dataset	Atr.	Model architecture	Accuracy
1.	ECG Noise Removal + ECG Feature Engineering + GSR Feature Engineering	27	17->60->60->60->1 [7]	97.11%
2	ECG Noise Removal + ECG Feature Engineering + GSR Feature Engineering	27	Support Vector Machine (SVM)	80.10%
3	ECG Noise Removal + ECG Feature Engineering + GSR Feature Engineering	27	Logistic Regression	72.21%
4	ECG Noise Removal + ECG Feature Engineering + GSR Feature Engineering	27	Proposed (extended) FCNN Architecture (Fig. 7)	98.01%

Table 8 shows a comparison of the accuracies of various supervised learning algorithms on original and decompressed dataset.

Table 8. Stress prediction accuracy comparison over original and decompressed datasets

No.	Classifier	Original dataset	Decompressed dataset
1	FCNN [7]	96.87%	97.11%
2	Support Vector Machine (SVM)	79.67%	80.10%
3	Logistic Regression	71.88%	72.21%
4	Proposed (extended) FCNN Architecture	97.56%	98.01%

The results prove that the accuracy of Stress Detection over decompressed dataset is more than that obtained over original dataset. The reason for this is that the SZ Lossy Compression technique filters out noise as an inclusive step [46]. Out of all the classifiers tried, our proposed FCNN gets the highest accuracy.

5   Conclusion

SZ lossy compression technique works well helping reduce the energy consumed in transmitting data from edge device to cloud making sure there is no information loss. As data is compressed on edge device, the volume of data to be transferred from the edge device to cloud significantly reduces; thereby reducing the energy consumed in transmission. For real time applications, there can be a minor issue faced due to network latency but if the necessary actuation conditions are placed upon the IoT device or edge device, necessary actions can be initiated on conditioning the data collected at the edge device itself. This technique could work well for applications related to studying, predicting or analyzing physiological and behavioral pattern of individuals. The stress detection results obtained using various supervised classifiers suggest that the accuracy of prediction is better over decompressed dataset as compared to original due to noise removal feature of SZ lossy compression technique. In future, we would like to implement a machine learning based compression algorithm so as to achieve a higher compression ratio.

References

1. Liu, X., Ansari, N.: Toward green IoT: energy solutions and key challenges. IEEE Commun. Mag. **57**(3), 104–110 (2019)
2. Chang, K.-D., Chen, C.-Y., Chen, J.-L., Chao, H.-C.: Internet of things and cloud computing for future internet. In: Chang, R.-S., Kim, T., Peng, S.-L. (eds.) SUComS 2011. CCIS, vol. 223, pp. 1–10. Springer, Heidelberg (2011). https://doi.org/10.1007/978-3-642-23948-9_1
3. Anastasi, G., Conti, M., Di Francesco, M., Passarella, A.: Energy conservation in wireless sensor networks: a survey. Ad Hoc Netw. **7**(3), 537–568 (2009)
4. Razzaque, M.A., Bleakley, C., Dobson, S.: Compression in wireless sensor networks: a survey and comparative evaluation. ACM Trans. Sens. Netw. (TOSN) **10**(1), 1–44 (2013)
5. Zeng, M., Yadav, A., Dobre, O.A., Poor, H.V.: Energy-efficient joint user-RB association and power allocation for uplink hybrid NOMA-OMA. IEEE Internet Things J. **6**(3), 5119–5131 (2019)
6. Miettinen, A.P., Nurminen, J.K.: Energy efficiency of mobile clients in cloud computing. HotCloud **10**(4–4), 19 (2010)
7. Azar, J., Makhoul, A., Barhamgi, M., Couturier, R.: An energy efficient IoT data compression approach for edge machine learning. Futur. Gener. Comput. Syst. **96**, 168–175 (2019)
8. Lee, K., Murray, D., Hughes, D., Joosen, W.: Extending sensor networks into the cloud using amazon web services. In: 2010 IEEE International Conference on Networked Embedded Systems for Enterprise Applications, pp. 1–7. IEEE, November 2010
9. Sen, J.: Security in wireless sensor networks. In: Wireless Sensor Networks: Current Status and Future Trends, pp. 407–408 (2012)
10. Dataset Source. Name of Dataset: Stress Recognition in Automobile Drivers: Drivedb. https://archive.physionet.org/cgi-bin/atm/ATM
11. Micucci, D., Mobilio, M., Napoletano, P.: UniMiB SHAR: a dataset for human activity recognition using acceleration data from smartphones. Appl. Sci. **7**(10), 1101 (2017)
12. Kulev, I., Pu, P., Faltings, B.: Discovering persuasion profiles using time series data. In: Proceedings of the Neural Information Processing Systems Time Series Workshop (2016)

13. Vilarinho, T., et al.: A combined smartphone and smartwatch fall detection system. Presented at the (2015)
14. Kunc, M., Harper, P., Katsikopoulos, K.: A review of implementation of behavioural aspects in the application of OR in healthcare. J. Oper. Res. Soc. (2018). https://doi.org/10.1080/01605682.2018.1489355
15. Fischer, T., Riedl, R.: Lifelogging for organizational stress measurement: theory and applications. In: Fischer, T., Riedl, R. (eds.) Lifelogging for Organizational Stress Measurement. SIS, pp. 1–37. Springer, Cham (2019). https://doi.org/10.1007/978-3-319-98711-8_1
16. Weiss, G.M., Timko, J.L., Gallagher, C.M., Yoneda, K., Schreiber, A.J.: Smartwatch-based activity recognition: A machine learning approach. In: 2016 IEEE-EMBS International Conference on Biomedical and Health Informatics (BHI), pp. 426–429. IEEE, February 2016
17. Rashidi, P., Cook, D.J.: Keeping the resident in the loop: adapting the smart home to the user. IEEE Trans. Syst. Man Cybern.-Part A Syst. Hum. 39(5), 949–959 (2009)
18. Patel, S., Park, H., Bonato, P., Chan, L., Rodgers, M.: A review of wearable sensors and systems with application in rehabilitation. J. Neuroeng. Rehabil. 9(1), 1–17 (2012)
19. Avci, A., Bosch, S., Marin-Perianu, M., Marin-Perianu, R., Havinga, P.: Activity recognition using inertial sensing for healthcare, wellbeing and sports applications: a survey. In: 23th International Conference on Architecture of Computing Systems 2010, pp. 1–10. VDE, February 2010
20. Mazilu, S., Blanke, U., Hardegger, M., Tröster, G., Gazit, E., Hausdorff, J.M.: GaitAssist: a daily-life support and training system for Parkinson's disease patients with freezing of gait. In: Proceedings of the SIGCHI Conference on Human Factors in Computing Systems, pp. 2531–2540, April 2014
21. Kranz, M., et al.: The mobile fitness coach: towards individualized skill assessment using personalized mobile devices. Pervasive Mob. Comput. 9(2), 203–215 (2013)
22. Stiefmeier, T., Roggen, D., Ogris, G., Lukowicz, P., Tröster, G.: Wearable activity tracking in car manufacturing. IEEE Pervasive Comput. 7(2), 42–50 (2008)
23. Ordóñez, F.J., Roggen, D.: Deep convolutional and LSTM recurrent neural networks for multimodal wearable activity recognition. Sensors 16(1), 115 (2016)
24. Banos, O., et al.: mHealthDroid: a novel framework for agile development of mobile health applications. In: Pecchia, L., Chen, L.L., Nugent, C., Bravo, J. (eds.) IWAAL 2014. LNCS, vol. 8868, pp. 91–98. Springer, Cham (2014). https://doi.org/10.1007/978-3-319-13105-4_14
25. Roggen, D., et al.: Collecting complex activity datasets in highly rich networked sensor environments. In: 2010 Seventh International Conference on Networked Sensing Systems (INSS), pp. 233–240. IEEE, June 2010
26. Ni, J., Chen, B., Allinson, N.M., Ye, X.: A hybrid model for predicting human physical activity status from lifelogging data. Eur. J. Oper. Res. 281(3), 532–542 (2020)
27. Qi, J., Yang, P., Newcombe, L., Peng, X., Yang, Y., Zhao, Z.: An overview of data fusion techniques for internet of things enabled physical activity recognition and measure. Inf. Fusion 55, 269–280 (2020)
28. Alharbi, M., Straiton, N., Smith, S., Neubeck, L., Gallagher, R.: The use of wearable trackers by older adults and data management: a systematic review. Maturitas (2019)
29. Yang, P., et al.: Lifelogging data validation model for internet of things enabled personalized healthcare. IEEE Trans. Syst. Man Cybern. Syst. 48(1), 50–64 (2016)

30. Rawashdeh, M., Al Zamil, M.G., Samarah, S., Hossain, M.S., Muhammad, G.: A knowledge-driven approach for activity recognition in smart homes based on activity profiling. Futur. Gener. Comput. Syst. **107**, 924–941 (2020)

31. Huanga, W., Lib, S.: An Approach for Understanding Urban Human Activity Patterns with the Motivations Behind (2019)

32. Liu, L., Wang, S., Su, G., Huang, Z.G., Liu, M.: Towards complex activity recognition using a Bayesian network-based probabilistic generative framework. Pattern Recogn. **68**, 295–309 (2017)

33. Samarah, S., Al Zamil, M.G., Aleroud, A.F., Rawashdeh, M., Alhamid, M.F., Alamri, A.: An efficient activity recognition framework: toward privacy-sensitive health data sensing. IEEE Access **5**, 3848–3859 (2017)

34. Hossain, M.S., Muhammad, G., Abdul, W., Song, B., Gupta, B.B.: Cloud-assisted secure video transmission and sharing framework for smart cities. Futur. Gener. Comput. Syst. **83**, 596–606 (2018)

35. Hossain, M.S., Muhammad, G., Alamri, A.: Smart healthcare monitoring: a voice pathology detection paradigm for smart cities. Multimedia Syst. **25**(5), 565–575 (2019)

36. El-Sayed, H., Sankar, S., Prasad, M., Puthal, D., Gupta, A., Mohanty, M., Lin, C.T.: Edge of things: the big picture on the integration of edge, IoT and the cloud in a distributed computing environment. IEEE Access **6**, 1706–1717 (2017)

37. Hsu, C.C., Fang, Y.T., Yu, F.: Content-sensitive data compression for IoT streaming services. In: 2017 IEEE International Congress on Internet of Things (ICIOT), pp. 147–150. IEEE, June 2017

38. Deepu, C.J., Heng, C.H., Lian, Y.: A hybrid data compression scheme for power reduction in wireless sensors for IoT. IEEE Trans. Biomed. Circuits Syst. **11**(2), 245–254 (2016)

39. Tao, D., Di, S., Liang, X., Chen, Z., Cappello, F.: Optimizing lossy compression rate-distortion from automatic online selection between SZ and ZFP. IEEE Trans. Parallel Distrib. Syst. **30**(8), 1857–1871 (2019)

40. Di, S., Cappello, F.: Fast error-bounded lossy HPC data compression with SZ. In: 2016 IEEE International Parallel and Distributed Processing Symposium (IPDPS), pp. 730–739. IEEE, May 2016

41. Lindstrom, P.: Fixed-rate compressed floating-point arrays. IEEE Trans. Visual Comput. Graphics **20**(12), 2674–2683 (2014)

42. Lu, T., et al.: Understanding and modeling lossy compression schemes on HPC scientific data. In: 2018 IEEE International Parallel and Distributed Processing Symposium (IPDPS), pp. 348–357. IEEE, May 2018

43. Frank, K., Robertson, P., Gross, M., Wiesner, K.: Sensor-based identification of human stress levels. In: 2013 IEEE International Conference on Pervasive Computing and Communications Workshops (PERCOM Workshops), pp. 127–132. IEEE, March 2013

44. Ollander, S.: Wearable sensor data fusion for human stress estimation (2015)

45. Salazar, D.A., Vélez, J.I., Salazar, J.C.: Comparison between SVM and logistic regression: Which one is better to discriminate? Revista Colombiana de Estadística **35**(2), 223–237 (2012)

46. Liang, X., et al.: Error-controlled lossy compression optimized for high compression ratios of scientific datasets. In: 2018 IEEE International Conference on Big Data (Big Data), pp. 438–447. IEEE, December 2018

Cab Fare Prediction Using Machine Learning

Kevan Mehta$^{(\boxtimes)}$, Aashil Shah, and Samir Patel

Pandit Deendayal Energy University, Gujarat, India
{kevan.mce18,aashil.sce18,Samir.patel}@sot.pdpu.ac.in

Abstract. In recent years, the taxi service industry has been booming and is expected to experience significant growth in the short term. Due to this growing demand, many companies have sprung up to offer cab rides to users. However, few companies charge higher fares for the same route. Therefore, customers have to pay an unwanted high amount even though the prices should be lower. The main objective is to estimate travel costs before booking a cab to have transparency and avoid unfair practices. Our system is designed to allow individuals to estimate taxi trip fares by using various dynamic conditions such as weather, cab availability, cab size, and the distance between two locations. The data that is already present helps in creating a mathematical model that records essential trends. This model is used to predict the future or suggest optimal outcomes. Different techniques and methods have been used to implement this system, e.g., Machine Learning, Supervised Learning, Regression Techniques, Random Forest, and parameter tuning (increasing model accuracy).

Keywords: Machine learning · Supervised learning · Random forest tuning · Random forest · Decision tree

1 Introduction

People prefer to use a cab to travel from one place to another in today's world rather than using public transport. Public transport is inconvenient for people as it is crowded and takes longer to get to your destination. Therefore, the quickest solution is to use private cabs and achieve their goal at their comfort level. Due to the higher reliance on cabs in metropolitan cities, some companies like Uber Ola sometimes charge higher fares than are required. As a result, people are forced to pay more than the required amount. This action is not fair and causes financial loss for no reason. For this reason, we have decided to develop a model that predicts the exact fare between two locations. People can check their fares before booking a cab. So that people can see that they are paying the right amount for the distance.

In supervised learning, the algorithm creates a mathematical model from data consisting of inputs and outputs. As examples of supervised learning, the classification and regression algorithms can be cited. In the unsupervised learning case, the algorithm develops a mathematical model from data consisting only of inputs and no output labels. The goal of unsupervised learning algorithms is to find patterns in data, such as by collecting or compiling data points. Machine Learning focuses on predictive data-based predictions, while data analysis focuses on finding unknown features [7].

© Springer Nature Switzerland AG 2022
N. Chaubey et al. (Eds.): COMS2 2022, CCIS 1604, pp. 244–254, 2022.
https://doi.org/10.1007/978-3-031-10551-7_18

Supervised learning algorithms are divided into two broad categories classification and regression. Classification algorithms are used when we want to classify the data into different groups or categories that have been learned from the training data. Regression algorithms are used to predict the unknown or future variables based on the data of the input variables from the data set. The first step in modeling is to identify the problem and select the appropriate category. Because the problem "cab fare" goes hand in hand with prediction.

2 Literature Review

The authors of [1] have created a mobile application for taxi routes as well as a safe tracking fare rate. The app provides the exact location of the taxi, the cost of the trip, and the same route. While predicting a huge fare limit on travel time delays. They used a tracking system that uses GPS to track the coordinates as they travel to overcome it. It also offers other services such as ride-sharing and one-time payments to ensure customer satisfaction. The app provides the current location of the user via SMS. Additionally, it includes customer feedback on the go, evaluating service provider performance.

In [2], the research paper focuses on taxi fare prediction using Deep Learning and Stacking Classifier. However, the authors first used the Deep Learning approach with fewer features in their dataset than previously used. The paper uses factors such as time and day to predict the cab fare. The results were not optimal, but they were faster than the stacking classifier method and aimed to implement more additional features and test parameters to make their model more accurate and convenient.

The authors in [3] showed an approach in predicting future taxi demand using machine learning. They used the Recurrent Neural Network (RNN), which can be trained with historical data and predict demand for taxis. They considered certain features to forecast fares, such as drop-off and pickup points. The authors have collected data for the previous three years for all the routes departing from the airport and predict taxi demand hourly and for a given period. This model will determine a pattern of past markets and forecast future demand for taxis. In the future, they aim to expand it to other inputs such as predicting cab demand during holidays and festivals.

Another approach is [4]. It displays several techniques by which cab fare can be predicted. All the approaches use distance, time, and passenger count to indicate the cab fare. However, the model accurately predicts the fare but does not consider every factor required to predict fare. The above factors lead to the limitation of the model. The model will not perform as expected when several other parameters include weather conditions and cab availability. After completing the modelling, they found that Random Forest is the best fit technique. The authors state that when there are more factors to predict the fare, overfitting of data will occur, which will reduce the model's accuracy, and to overcome it, one needs to use complex ridge regression techniques.

A novel approach is presented in [5], which aims to predict fare using algorithms based on regression and classification techniques using machine learning. The authors used the latitude and longitude of the pickup and drop locations and passenger count. The paper showed a comparative analysis by implementing various algorithms and found that Random Forest provided pinpoint accuracy with the data sample. The accuracy can be improved by using Xgboost regression or ridge regression techniques.

An Approach is displayed in [6]. The paper reveals effective and accurate cab-sharing solutions using key feature extraction. It mainly solves the problem of excessive traffic on the road and reduces the fares for rides. Hence, it aims to reduce the number of routes by sharing the taxi. The authors first illustrate the faults in the current system and then propose a method to help users reach their destination at the optimum time with less cost and without any difficulty.

3 Advantages of Proposed System

Our system predicts fare based on weather conditions such as wind, pressure, rain, humidity and clouds, location-based, availability, and cab type. Most of the prior research did not consider weather conditions as a factor to predict the fare. Moreover, we have used the name of places instead of mentioning latitude and longitude to make it more convenient for the creators and users to work on it. Previously built systems provided less fare accuracy, which is not feasible to implement the model in real life. Additionally, we have also increased the accuracy of the fare which takes less time for determining the fare. However, we tried our best to gain the utmost precision by using the finetuning technique.

4 Methodology

The random forest algorithm creates various trees (decision trees) and integrates their outputs to improve the ability to perform normally. An ensemble method is a method for merging trees. Random Forests solve regression and classification problems since they combine weak learners (individual trees). In regression problems, dependent variables are constant; in classification problems, the dependent variable is categorical.

The random forest algorithm predicts the outcome based on the predictions of the decision trees. It averages the outcome of the decision trees, and the more trees it has, the more accurate it is.

There are several reasons for using a Random Forest algorithm: More accurate than decision tree algorithm, solving the issue of overfitting, increases precision, generates forecast without requiring many configurations in packages (like scikit learn) and providing an effective way of handling missing data; after identifying the approach.

The next step is to process the data. Data monitoring refers to data analysis, data processing, and visualization of data through graphs and plots. This is commonly referred to as Exploratory Data Analysis (EDA) [8].

4.1 Data

The goal is to create a model that will predict the cost of a continuous cab ride for each cab based on a number of factors such as weather, time, location, and cab availability. This problem statement falls below the estimation, which is related to predicting future continuous prices (values that don't change the cost of a cab ride). Fig. 1, 2 shows a sample of the data set used to predict the cab fare.

	distance	cab_type	time_stamp	destination	source	price	surge_multiplier	id	product_id	name	datetime
0	0.44	Lyft	1.544950e+12	North Station	Haymarket Square	5.0	1.0	424653bb-7174-41ea-aeb4-fe06d4f4b9d7	lyft_line	Shared	1970-01-01 00:25:44.949989376
1	0.44	Lyft	1.543280e+12	North Station	Haymarket Square	11.0	1.0	4bd23055-6827-41c6-b23b-3c491f24e74d	lyft_premier	Lux	1970-01-01 00:25:43.280001024
2	0.44	Lyft	1.543370e+12	North Station	Haymarket Square	7.0	1.0	981a3613-77af-4620-a42a-0c0866077d1e	lyft	Lyft	1970-01-01 00:25:43.370047488
3	0.44	Lyft	1.543550e+12	North Station	Haymarket Square	26.0	1.0	c2d88af2-d278-4bfd-a8d0-29ca77cc5512	lyft_luxsuv	Lux Black XL	1970-01-01 00:25:43.550009344
4	0.44	Lyft	1.543460e+12	North Station	Haymarket Square	9.0	1.0	e0126e1f-8ca9-4f2e-82b3-50505a09db9a	lyft_plus	Lyft XL	1970-01-01 00:25:43.459962880
...	...	...	...	...	...	...	...	...	...	...	...
693066	1.00	Uber	1.543710e+12	North End	West End	13.0	1.0	616d3611-1820-450a-9845-a9ff304a4842	6f72dfc5-27f1-42e8-84db-ccc7a75f6969	UberXL	1970-01-01 00:25:43.710048256

Fig. 1. Sample cab data set

	temp	location	clouds	pressure	rain	time_stamp	humidity	wind	date_time
0	42.419998	Back Bay	1.00	1012.140015	0.1228	1545003901	0.77	11.25	1970-01-01 00:00:01.545003901
1	42.430000	Beacon Hill	1.00	1012.150024	0.1846	1545003901	0.76	11.32	1970-01-01 00:00:01.545003901
2	42.500000	Boston University	1.00	1012.150024	0.1089	1545003901	0.76	11.07	1970-01-01 00:00:01.545003901
3	42.110001	Fenway	1.00	1012.130005	0.0969	1545003901	0.77	11.09	1970-01-01 00:00:01.545003901
4	43.130001	Financial District	1.00	1012.140015	0.1786	1545003901	0.75	11.49	1970-01-01 00:00:01.545003901
...	...	...	...	...	...	...	...	...	...
6271	44.720001	North Station	0.89	1000.690002	NaN	1543819974	0.96	1.52	1970-01-01 00:00:01.543819974
6272	44.849998	Northeastern University	0.88	1000.710022	NaN	1543819974	0.96	1.54	1970-01-01 00:00:01.543819974
6273	44.820000	South Station	0.89	1000.700012	NaN	1543819974	0.96	1.54	1970-01-01 00:00:01.543819974
6274	44.779999	Theatre District	0.89	1000.700012	NaN	1543819974	0.96	1.54	1970-01-01 00:00:01.543819974
6275	44.689999	West End	0.89	1000.700012	NaN	1543819974	0.96	1.52	1970-01-01 00:00:01.543819974

Fig. 2. Sample weather data set

The predictor and target variables are as follows:
Predictors:

- distance: indicates the distance between two places.
- cab_type: which type of cab it is.
- Destination: the place where the cab ride started.
- source: the place where the cab ride ended.
- surge_multiplier: indicates how much demand the cabs are in.
- product_id: indicates the cab id.
- Name: shows the names of different cab types
- Datetime: date at which the customer took the ride.

Target: price (Fig. 3)

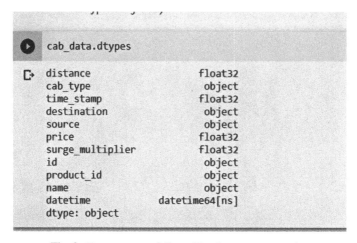

Fig. 3. Data structure followed by data type conversion

4.2   Pre-processing (Missing Value and Outlier Analysis)

As portrayed in Fig.1,2. there is a lot of noisy data. The very first step that every machine learning project needs to undertake is Data Cleaning which includes the following points as per our project:

1. Separating combined variables
2. There are some negative and NaN values in the dataset, so we have to remove those values.
3. Passenger count in a vehicle cannot be more than six or less than 1. So, we need to incorporate it into the data set.
4. There are some outlier figures in the data set, so we need to remove those (Fig. 4).

	distance	time_stamp	price	surge_multiplier
count	693071.000000	6.930710e+05	637976.000000	693071.000000
mean	2.190057	1.530152e+12	16.543797	1.013870
std	1.138935	1.390676e+10	9.319172	0.091467
min	0.020000	1.543200e+12	2.500000	1.000000
25%	1.280000	1.543440e+12	9.000000	1.000000
50%	2.160000	1.543740e+12	13.500000	1.000000
75%	2.920000	1.544830e+12	22.500000	1.000000
max	7.860000	1.545160e+12	97.500000	3.000000

Fig. 4. Refined data

4.3   Feature Selection

Because all variables are numerical, the correlation matrix extracts the critical features. We observed that every variable was necessary for determining the fare as each variable has its significance in different situations. Thus, we retained all the parameters for determining the final cab fare. Figure 5, shows only a few variables out of the entire list of variables.

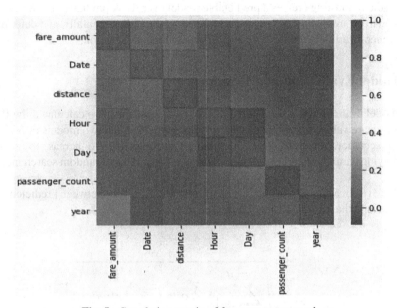

Fig. 5. Correlation matrix of few parameters used

4.4   Model Development

After determining all predictive variables, we used the regression models in our processed data to predict the target variable. The following are the models we have built: Linear Regression, Decision Tree, Random Forest, and Gradient Boosting.

Linear Regression can be defined as finding the relationship between two things i.e., dependent variable (y) and independent variables (x) using a straight line. The straight line signifies how close is the dependent variable to the straight line. The closer to the straight line the more accurate is the value of the dependent variable.

A decision tree is just a bunch of nested if-else statements in a tree structure. At each step along the way, there will be a condition, and we continue down either on the true or false branch. We keep doing it till we reach the last branch. That last node will be the result of decision tree. It helps in accurately predicting the output variable but can sometimes lead to inaccurate results if one doesn't carry it out carefully.

Decision trees are divided into three main parts:

• Root Node: performs initial partition

- Terminal Nodes: that predict the outcome are also called leaf nodes.
- Branches: arrows that connect nodes, indicating the flow from the root to the other leaves.

A random forest is a process in which a machine follows an ensemble method that works by building several decision trees during training and providing the output as a class that is the mode for all trees for each decision.

Gradient boosting creates a predictable model over weak predictive models, usually decision trees, into predictable models by building them incrementally, and determining their generalization by optimizing any differentiable loss function.

5 Model Evaluation and Results

The model evaluation has been performed in two steps: First, we calculated the RMSE and R-Square values for all the models and determined which two models provided the highest accuracy. Secondly, after determining that we went on to increase the accuracy by applying parameter tuning techniques using grid search and random search methods.

- RMSE (Root Mean Square Error): measures the differences between predicted model values and the observed values (Fig. 6).

$$RMSE = \sqrt{\frac{\sum_{i=1}^{n} (X_{obs,i} - X_{mo\,del,i})^2}{n}}$$

Fig. 6. RMSE Formula

- R Squared (R^2): This statistical metric indicates how close the data is to the fitted regression line. It explains how much of the volatility in the target variable is explained.

The smaller the result, the better is the model's performance: The R-Squared formula is used to understand how the independent variables best describe the model's variance. For the R-Squared, the value closer to 1, the better is the model's performance: Table 1 describes its error metrics according to the underlying model.

Table 1. Comparison between algorithms before applying hyper tuning

Model name	RMSE	R Squared
Linear regression	0.25	0.77
Decision tree	0.28	0.7
Random forest	0.23	0.79
Gradient	0.22	0.81

Compared to the proposed algorithm with others, Random Forest has an R Square value close to 1. It shows that the performance of the given model is excellent and accurate. In addition to the accuracy, we have found by determining the R Square value of the random forest algorithm, we have tried to improve the results using the parameter tuning technique. Results are shown in Table 2.

Table 2. Results post applying hyperparameter tuning

Model name	Parameter	RMSE	R Squared
Random search CV	Random forest	0.24	0.79
	Gradient boosting	0.25	0.77
Grid search	Random forest	0.23	0.8
	Gradient boosting	0.24	0.79

Here we have used two parameters to tune the model:-

- Random Search CV: It uses a random combination of the hyperparameters is used to find the model solution. The number of iterations depends on time and resources.
- Grid Search CV: It is a model that tests all combinations of values passed in a dictionary and examines the model for each combination using the cross-validation method. After testing the function, we find the accuracy/loss of all hyperparameter combinations. So, we can choose the one that works best.

Finally, I used to predict the target variable for the data set. Results that I found out are the following:
Some more visualization facts:

Number of Passengers and Fare
We can see in the below figure that single passengers are the most frequent travelers, and the highest fare also seems to come from cabs that carry one passenger (Fig. 7).

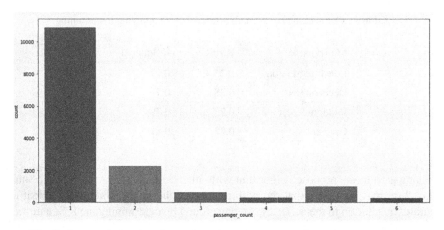

Fig. 7. Bar graph showing the total number of passengers for each passenger count

Hours and Fares

- During hours between 6 pm and 11 pm the frequency of cab boarding is very high due to peak hours.
- Fare prices from 2 pm to 8 pm are slightly higher than all other times (Fig. 8).

Fig. 8. Cab demand analysis during the entire day

Week Day and Fare

Cab fare is high on Friday, Saturday, and Monday, maybe during the weekend and first day of the working day they charge because of high fare demand of cabs (Fig. 9).

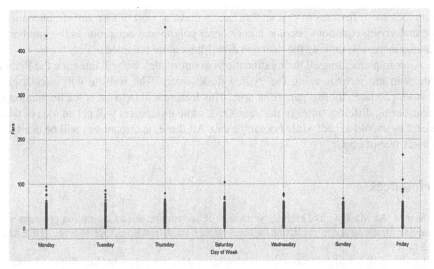

Fig. 9. Cab Fare prices during different days of the week

6 Limitations

Our system is limited to displaying fare for a single route (from source to destination), but several ways might be available to reach the goal in real life. It is possible that the manner with which we expected fare might have a longer distance. It is possible that the path with which we predicted fare might have a longer distance. So, we need to find the shortest route with the least cost and reach the passenger fastest to the destination. Moreover, the cab fare might not be 100% accurate as it does not consider every parameter.

7 Conclusion

Until now, our model has completed testing of the sample dataset, and the results that we found out were quite promising. We found that Random Forest proved to be the best-fit algorithm for this type of analysis. We further increased the model's accuracy using parameter tuning with the help of Grid Search CV and Random Search CV. As the accuracy of this model is around 85–90%, we wish to expand it to use it for real-time analysis and optimize it for the shortest path possible between any two places. After accomplishing that, our model will be a good fit for public use. Finally, a web application will also be developed to quickly access the tool without any problem.

8 Future Work

The authors aim to extend the project to predict fare for the shortest route. This will help users reach their destination in the shortest time, and the least cost will be charged. To further improve the accuracy of the model, complex ridge regression and Xgboost technique can be used to maximize the accuracy of the model. Moreover, we would like to include more features to predict the fare to make it work under any circumstances. The underlying equations become higher-order polynomial equations as the number of features increases, making the data and algorithms more complex.

After implementing all the modifications to our model, we will integrate the Python code with the website using the Python flask library. The website will also display previous cab fares for that particular area. This feature will help users see fluctuation in prices during different times of the year. Over some time, users will get an idea of what price they should expect while booking a cab. All these functionalities will be available to users free of cost.

References

1. Saxena, A., Madhavi, R., Mohite, S.: Design of taxi routing & fare estimation program with security tracking and re-prediction for smart phones. Int. J. Res. Eng. Appl. Manage. (IJREAM). 5 (2017)
2. Upadhyay, R.: Taxi fare rate classification using deep networks. In: Lui, S. (ed.) Encontro Português de Inteligência ArtificialAt, Portugal (2017)
3. Wang, W., Lu, Y.: Analysis of the mean absolute error (MAE) and the root mean square error (RMSE) in assessing rounding model. IOP Conf. Ser. Mater. Sci. Eng. **324**, 012049 (2018)
4. Panda, G.: Machine learning using exploratory analysis to predict taxi fare. Int. J. Res. Appl. Sci. Eng. Technol. (2019)
5. Banerjee, P., Kumar, B., Singh, A., Ranjan, P., Soni, K.: Predictive analysis of taxi fare using machine learning. Int. J. Sci. Res. Comput. Sci. Eng. Inf. Technol. 373–378 (2020)
6. Chelliah, B., Singh, J., Chaturvedi, D., Singh, A.: Taxi fare prediction system using key feature extraction in artificial intelligence. Turkish J. Comput. Math. Educ. (2021)
7. Tomar, D., Agarwal, S.: A survey on data mining approaches for Healthcare. Int. J. Bio Sci. Bio Technol. **5**(5), 241–266 (2013)
8. Abdul Rahuman Aslam, M.A., Gobinathan, V., Krishnan, K., Rajasekaran, G.: Prediction of cab demand using machine learning. Int. Res. J. Eng. Technol. (IRJET). **6**, 1–8 (2019)

Device to Device Communication over 5G

Md.Tabrej Khan[1(✉)] [iD] and Ashish Adholiya[2]

[1] Faculty of Computer Science, Pacific Academy of Higher Education and Research University,
Udaipur, Rajasthan, India
tabrejmlkhan@gmail.com
[2] Faculty of Management, Pacific Academy of Higher Education and Research University,
Udaipur, Rajasthan, India

Abstract. The dependency on small cells, the cost of establishing a 5G infrastructure, and traffic at the Base Transceiver Station (BTS) can be reduced by distributing ideal data over an active WiFi connection in nearby mobile devices. Besides, unloading and distributing the unused data over WiFi to nearby devices will not affect the speed of 5G. Therefore, without compromising on the promised speed by the 5G cellular network, a massive sum of ideal 5G data can be distributed via a WiFi connection to other nearby handsets connected to the given 5G cellular network. Recent studies have suggested a "delayed offloading" methodology to offload ideal 5G data to a nearby environment with an active WiFi connection. In the present study, we propose a device-to-device (D2D) method for rerouting ideal 5G cellular data from an inactive WiFi using the "delayed offloading" principle to a neighboring headset with an active WiFi connection provided by the given 5G cellular network. However, if there is not a single handset found in an active WiFi environment, the offloaded 5G data will be sent to BTS in a conventional manner.

Keywords: 5G · Device-to-device communication · Cellular network

1 Introduction

1.1 5th Generation

In the new world of the Internet of things (IoT) and fifth-generation (5G), data is increasing explorational such as videos in this reference, data traffic increase 50% every year. [1, 2]. This new generation proposes the use of millimeter-wave (mmWave) frequencies to offer a completely new spectrum and multi-Gigabit-per-second (Gbps) data rates to a mobile device [3]. The 5G is based on the millimeter wave, whereas the 2G, 3G, and 4G networks are based on microwave frequency. The 5G provide a higher bandwidth (about ten times greater than today's 4G LTE) to support a large number of uses in term of data speed up to 10 Gbps and lower data traffic outstanding. Figure 1 shows the different wired and wireless technologies and their corresponding data speeds [4].

With all the advantages of the millimeter-wave, there remain some challenges. The millimeter waves have lower penetrating powers than microwaves, and thus it will not be easy to transmit such signals over a great distance or even through building walls.

© Springer Nature Switzerland AG 2022
N. Chaubey et al. (Eds.): COMS2 2022, CCIS 1604, pp. 255–273, 2022.
https://doi.org/10.1007/978-3-031-10551-7_19

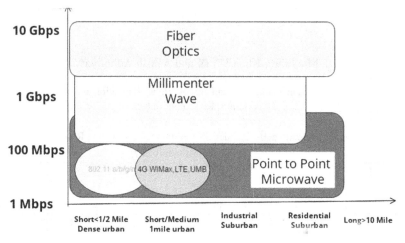

Fig. 1. Distance/Topology/Segments versus data speeds

Therefore, addressing this problem and many other, many new techniques such as the use of femtocells, beamforming, network slicing, etc. have been introduced and proposed in recent papers.

The 5G wireless technology will also make use of cloud computing. This will allow intelligent and efficient handling of all the data, further reducing traffic and delays.

1.2 5th Generation Advantages

The 5th generation of telecommunication networks proposes to bring much good into the world. 5G will achieve up to 10 times the speed of the existing 4G networks. The immensely high data speeds themselves bring forward lots of advantages. For example, it will help improve the population's lifestyle and make work more efficient.

1.3 5th Generation Disadvantages

The 5th generation of telecommunication networks proposes to bring much good into the world. 5G will achieve up to 10 times the speed of the existing 4G networks. The immensely high data speeds themselves bring forward lots of advantages. For example, it will help improve the population's lifestyle and make work more efficient.

2 Literature Review

This paper [5], show that d2d communication in 5G is a significant area for research. In addition, it analyses the past research paper in terms of resource allocation. Finally, machine learning (ML) and deep learning (DL) will help offload the data traffic from the base station (BTS). The previous user also uses this trace to predict the location using the Hidden Markov Model (HMM) algorithm. HMM is helpful to find the shortest route [6].

The paper [7] gives WCETT, the Weighted Cumulative Expected Transmission Time to offload to BTS through multi-hop D2D communication. According to [7], the 1st term of WCETT expression, that reproduced $(1 - \beta)$, computes the assets expended in a given path, whichever the channels utilized, and secondly, the channel diversity represented by the 2nd term, subjective by β [8]. In [9], the authors mention first on-the-spot WiFi offloading and second delayed WiFi offloading. In this paper, we are using the latter; delayed offloading. In delayed offloading, all the user's traffic will be sent over WiFi when there is an active WiFi connection in the user's handset; else, all traffic is forwarded to the cellular interface after the traffic has waited for a deadline in the queue for the WiFi to come back.

Cisco [10] predicts that by 2025, more than 11.6 billion mobile-connected devices and traffic will reach an annual rate of 30.6 Exabytes (8×10^6 Terabytes) per month. This considerable amount of mobile device traffic will be challenging for the cellular network to handle all on its own.

[6] measured the average round-trip delay of 6.71 ms for one-hop D2D where 20 ping packets were sent from a transmitting device to a 70 m far apart receiving device. The maximum discovery distance and transmission rate for D2D communication are 354 m and 50 Mbps, respectively, greater than WiFi, 35 m and 11 Mbps (IEEE 802.11b), respectively.

In this paper, they review the recent article related to d2d communication found that traffic congestion is the main issue for delay packets. Path selection is one of the best challenges in B5G [11].

This paper prosed the DAIS algorithm, artificial intelligence-based transmission in the d2d network. Finally, it achieved a low computational load and high spectral efficiency [12].

In [13], the author experimented with SImuTE for network-assisted routing for d2d. The result shows around 35% saving in energy of base station and 15% packet transfer.

3 Methodology

The design and simulation of telecommunication studies are all based on probabilistic equations. For 5G, stochastic geometry has been used to build its model. Queuing theory is also an essential part of any communication.

3.1 Stochastic Geometry

Probability theory has a branch of Stochastic geometry (SG), which discusses random elements. Random mosaics, random networks, random unions of convex sets, random graphs, and the cluster are part of Stochastic geometry. This area includes many applications due to its strong relation with communication theory and spatial statistics. Nodes geometric pattern, response times, or congestion are handled through queuing theory, part of Stochastic geometry (SG).

It analyzes the extensive wireless communication network in a probabilistic way. Dealing with the Euclidean plane or space makes it more vital to explore the network. By the characteristics (connectivity, stability, capacity, etc.) as functions of a relatively small number of parameters.

3.2 Deterministic vs. Stochastic Geometry

Deterministic and stochastic geometry are the two known available approaches for cellular network designing and analysis. GSM, UMTS, and LTE networks have used deterministic based on a hexagonal cell to design the cellular network's coverage [14]. The deterministic method is only effective for networks with a fixed number of cell radii. When 5G is implemented will have many access nodes, co-tier interference, cross-tier interference, new backhauling solution, cloud system, and many more. The cell site area will not be hexagonal, and each cell site area will differ from the other. On top of all these, the cell sites will have a high-powered base station under which there will be many small cells. The small cells will be inside the larger cell covered by the high-powered base station, creating cross-tier interferences. The existing hexagonal methods will be a total failure for designing a heterogeneous network as they are only suitable for topologies with fixed cells. There is HetNet stochastic approach better result, so it is used for prediction.

Stochastic geometry is the study of random spatial patterns. Stochastic geometry can be used to model K-tier heterogeneous network, where the small base stations are positioned by a stochastic process in an unexpected random way. In stochastic geometry, the properties of the heterogeneous networks like small cells positions and macrocells positions, location of user's and user's mobility, co-tier and cross-tier interferences between access nodes are considered an arbitrary stochastic process of specific probability distribution (pdf) [15].

3.3 Different Stochastic Probability Distribution

The most effective probability distribution to model small cells in a heterogeneous network is still a debate. In addition, there are different node positioning models, and work is going on to include as many parameters as possible to generate a more realistic topology related to the 5G network.

Poisson Point Process (PPP): PPP can easily model a heterogeneous network with an infinite number of nodes in the endless coverage area. PPP define the base station position of different tier cellular networks [16].

Binomial Point Process (BPP): BPP is also used to model the position of base stations of single or K-tier cellular networks, except that the network node number is finite and the coverage area is also limited. The wireless sensor network behaviour in LAN used the BPP model [17].

Matern's Hard-Core Point Process (Matern's HCPP): HCPP is a developed model of PPP. There are many problems with PPP, such that PPP returns random network topology without any limitations of a minimum distance between neighbour transmitters.

Thus, with PPP planning, some BSs may appear in the same place or very close to each other. This results in unrealistic network topology and inaccuracy in modeling and calculating distance-dependent network parameters such as transmission power and signal to interference to noise ratio (SINR). HCPP is used to model a more realis-tic network topology by exploiting the strict minimum distance between any base station pair. HCPP is obtained from PPP eliminating all points which are not satisfying. However, HCPP is more complex and provides inaccuracy in simulation because of violation of the probabilistic distribution of network parameters [18, 19].

Voronoi Tessellation: It is used to model the arbitrary coverage area of small cells in a dense urban location. It uses the PPP or HCPP or other probability distribution to know the position of the small cells, and then it defines the coverage area for all the small cells. Voronoi tessellation is formed by taking pairs of neighbour points and drawing an equidistant line between them and perpendicular to the line joining both ends [20].

Poisson Cluster Process (PCP): In real life, user equipment (UEs) is concentrated around social places, bus stations buildings, and shopping centres with a hotspot or WiFi. So PCP considers that users are found clustered together most of the time, and hence there will be more small cells required in a building or shopping malls. PCP method creates network topology with K-clustered access nodes [21].

New parameters are being added to such stochastic models to make the model more realistic. Some parameters are crucial and must be included in the stochastic modelling for the position of small cells, while others provide minor improvement in the stochastic model.

3.4 Queuing Theory

Queuing theory is explicitly used to analyse and design any system that involves waiting in lines for a service, such as restaurants, banks, mobile data, etc. The queues can be formed at the receiving end, transmission end, or both ends. They act as data buffers and protect data packets from crashing into one another. However, queues can be a wasteful downtime.

The notation usually identifies queuing models: I/S/s/C, where I denotes the inter-arrival time distribution, S denotes the service time distribution, s denotes the number of servers, and C represents the number capacity of the queue [22]. If C is omitted, it is assumed that $C = \infty$. The inter-arrival time is the time between the arrival of one customer and the arrival of the next customer. It is calculated for each customer after the first and is often averaged to get the mean inter-arrival time, represented by lambda. Service time is well-defined as the time needed to serve a customer. There are lots of different queuing models, and a few single server models have been discussed below:

Markov(M)/Markov(M)/1: In exponential or Poisson distribution Markov (M) is commonly used. Hence an **Markov(M)/Markov(M)/1** queue included one server, inter-arrival time and service time which is exponentially distributed [23, 24]. The integral equations for M/M/1 models are:

$$L = \sum_{n=0}^{\infty} n(1-\rho)\rho^n = \frac{\lambda}{\mu - \lambda} \tag{1}$$

$$L_q = \sum_{n=1}^{\infty} (n-1)P_n = \frac{\lambda^2}{\mu(\mu - \lambda)} \tag{2}$$

$$W = \frac{1}{(\mu - \lambda)} \tag{3}$$

$$W_q = \frac{\lambda}{\mu(\mu - \lambda)} \tag{4}$$

where L denotes expected no. of customers in the system, Lq indicates desired queue length, waiting time of system represent W, and waiting time in queue represent Wq.

M/G/1: Here, the inter-arrival time is given by exponential distribution, and the general distribution provides the service time. This model involves non-exponential distributions and offers the following equations:

$$L_q = \frac{\lambda^2 \sigma^2 + \rho^2}{2(1-\rho)} \tag{5}$$

$$L = \rho + L_q \tag{6}$$

$$W_q = \frac{L_q}{\lambda} \tag{7}$$

$$W = W_q + \frac{q}{\mu} \tag{8}$$

where L denotes the expected no. of customers in the system, Lq denotes desired queue length, system waiting time represents W and waiting time in queue represents Wq.

A modified M/G/1 queue has been used for the HetNet [21]. The queuing model introduced in [21] is an M/G/1 model with limited feedback. This feedback mimics the possibility of an outage. High interference, fading, lower availability of power resources, no coverage by any base station (BS) within the HetNet, etc., are some of the main reasons for the outage. Therefore, the probability associated with this transition would be the outage probability seen from the UE's perspective. This queue model is illustrated in Fig. 2(a–b) shows the time diagram notation.

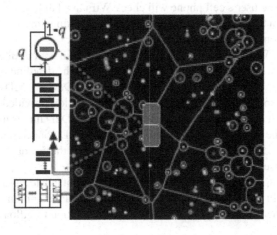

(a) Queue Model

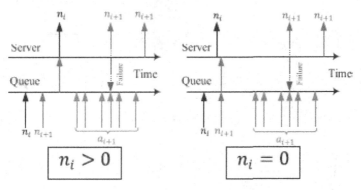

(b) Time Diagram Notation

Fig. 2. UE queue model in a 3-tier HetNet

4 Result

4.1 New Routing Scheme

Currently, a considerable amount of research has been done on WiFi offloading and D2D communication to offload and reroute the data to neighboring devices in an active WiFi environment. The "WiFi offloading" and D2D communication mechanism of offloading 5G data direct a minimum amount of traffic to BTS, thereby reducing the dependency on small-cells and reducing the cost of establishing a 5G infrastructure. [9] The present study can be regarded as a comprehensive work where the data packets are unloaded over an active WiFi environment. Otherwise, if active WiFi is inaccessible, the data packets are offloaded via cellular network until a deadline is gotten. The current proposed routing scheme is presented below:

Scenario 1: The user's cell phone will check WiFi availability. If WiFi is available, it will send its data to WLAN with the help of WiFi offloading, managing base stations' power consumption, traffic overload, and higher data rate.

Scenario 2: If WiFi is unavailable, data traffic flow will wait until a given deadline. In the meantime, when the data is in a queue waiting for the deadline period to end, the data in an inactive WiFi environment will run a Device 2 Device (D2D) communication with the neighboring handsets for an active WiFi connection provided by the same 5G cellular network. If a handset with active WiFi is found, a D2D link is made between the two handsets in the two WiFi environments. Once the D2D connection has been made, the handset in an ideal WiFi connection offloads most of the 5G data over WiFi to the neighboring handset in the same 5G cellular environment.

Scenario 3: Suppose the user's cellular handset does not locate any adjoining handset with an active WiFi connection. Then using the usual cellular communication data in the inactive environment will communicate with the base station to offload the 5G cellular data.

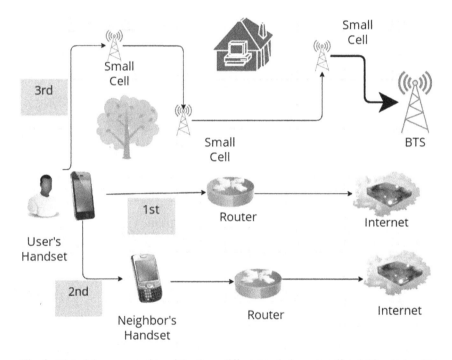

Fig. 3. Pictorial representation of the three different techniques to offload 5G cellular data

Markov's Chain. 2D Markov chain was used to model their WiFi queue. In the pre-sent study, their model was extended by considering D2D in the Markov chain, as shown in Fig. 2. States with {i, Wi-Fi} represent WiFi connectivity, {i, Cellular} represent states with only cellular connectivity and states with D2D connectivity {i, D2D}. Here, the number of customers represents i in the system (service+queue). While in the WiFi states, the system empties at the rate of μ and in both D2D state and cellular at a rate of $i\xi$. The frequency of offloading the abandoned data packets in the WiFi queue is represented as $i\xi$. Upon termination of the deadline, the neglected data packets are offloaded by the D2D state/cellular state.

Table 3. Shorthand Notation and Variables.

Variable	Definition/Description
λ	Average packet arrival rate at the mobile user
η	The rate of leaving the WiFi state
μ	The servicing rate while in WiFi state
γ	The rate of leaving the cellular state
τ	The rate of leaving D2D state
ξ	The reneging rate or the rate of abandoning WiFi state
i	Number of customers in the system (service + queue)
{i, Wi-Fi}	WiFi connectivity state
{i, Cellular}	Cellular connectivity state
{i, D2D}	D2D connectivity state

WiFi Queue. Cisco predicts that by 2025, more than 11.6 billion mobile-connected devices and traffic will reach an annual rate of 30.6 Exabytes (8×10^6 Terabytes) per month. This considerable amount of mobile device traffic will be challenging for the cellular network to handle all on its own. One solution to this problem is to deploy a substantial number of small cells in our environment. But telecommunication companies are feeling reluctant to bear the enormous cost of buying, installing, and maintaining these small cells. To date, WiFi offloading seems to be an easy and inexpensive solution to the problem. WiFi-AP are already found at the customer's end: WiFi routers installed at homes and work. The company needs to install fewer small cells when sending the user's traffic over WIFI. We proposed an excellent environment for telecommunication companies so they can reduce the traffic at BTS.

In [9], the author mentions two types of WiFi offloading 1) on-the-spot offloading and 2) delayed offloading. In this study, we are using the latter; delayed offloading. In delayed offloading, all the user's traffic will be sent over WiFi when there is an active WiFi connection in the user's handset; otherwise, all traffic is sent over the cellular interface once the deadline is reached. We extended this routing scheme and made it better and less dependent on small cells by including D2D in the routing scheme.

It has been presumed that the 5G cellular network will be available at all times, and the data of the inactive user handset gets offloaded as per the First Come First Served (FCFS) queuing principle. Each time the WiFi link gets gone, the packets available in the WiFi queue will be provided with a deadline. The deadline time of the packets increases from the first to the last queued data packets, i.e., the first data packet in the queue will

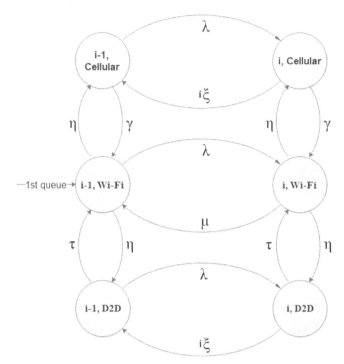

Fig. 4. The 2D Markov Chain for the Wi-Fi queue in delayed offloading with consideration to D2D.

have a lower deadline time than the second packet in the WiFi queue. Consequently, provided the WiFi link does not appear in the given deadline period, the First Come First Served (FCFS) queuing discipline was used to offload packets data to the neighboring handset via D2D or cellular network.

One-hop device-to-device (D2D) Communication. D2D communication is another promising solution in minimizing the cost of implementing 5G cellular infrastructure and reducing traffic at the BTS. D2D communication in the cellular network refers to the direct communication between the mobile users without Base Station (BS) or the core network elements. Many papers have shown procedures for neighbor discovery and data offloading using D2D communication. Our routing scheme restricts one-hop D2D communication, which involves transmitting data by a single hop. The reason for limiting to only one-hop D2D is that current technology is only just enough to do one-hop D2D and proves unreliable for multi-hop D2D.

D2D is of two types: Network-centric and Device centric. Network-centric means communication between mobile users depends on the network infrastructure. This means that the user of a particular network, Airtel, will only do D2D. Whereas the proximate device manages device-centric means network setup. This means that the user of a specific mobile handset, for example, Samsung, will only be able to do D2D will each other. So, users of the same mobile network operator or same banded handsets can allow each other to offload their data.

In [6] and [10], the author measured the average round-trip delay of 6.71 ms for one-hop D2D, where 20 ping packets were sent from a transmitting device to a 70 m far apart receiving device. The maximum discovery distance and transmission rate for D2D communication are 354 m and 50 Mbps, respectively, greater than WiFi, 35 m and 11 Mbps (IEEE 802.11b), respectively [8].

In the present routing schema, the user's set will explore any other set with an active WiFi link to a WLAN in its nearby environment. Once such a handset has been identified, the user's handset will try to link with the neighbor's handset via allocating an IP address as suggested by the authors in the article [25]. Abstract Protocol Notation (APN) based algorithm required by the user's set to determine adjoining set with an operational WiFi link has been described below:

Step 1 : Consider the boolen variable *WiFiAck* = *true* and *WiFi Reply* = *true*
Step 2 : Initialize the variable *find WiFi* = *true*
Step 3 : Start to *find WiFi send request (WiFiAck)* to broadcast.
Step 4 : Timer start for reply during this time *find WiFi* = *false*
Step 5 : When *Recive reply (WiFi Reply)* from server stop reply timer
Step 6 : If WiFi reply is true then send *acknowledgement to find IP addressother − wise it will be end*.

Provided below is Abstract Protocol Notation (APN) based the algorithm showing how the adjoining set with an active WiFi link would reply to the request of the customer's set:

Step 1 : Consider the Variable *Available_WiFi* = *True* and *WiFi Reply*
Step 2 : Start to check *receive request (WiFi Reply)* from client.
Step 3: if *Available_WiFi* = *True* and *WiFi Reply* = *True* then reply to client otherwise *WiFi Reply* = *False*

The user's handset transmits an invitation to locate an operational WiFi handset in a given environment. A timer is turned on as the message is sent from the user's handset. If a confirmatory response of the active WiFi handset approaches, the user's handset sends one more invitation to create a D2D link with the operational WiFi handset of a neighboring environment. Or else, if there is no neighboring active WiFi handset, the packets of the user's handset will offload the data packets to the cellular network (Fig. 5).

Total Expected Delay. A data packet experiences a delay at every stage along its transmission as it moves from a source to a given destination. The types of total delay experienced by a data packet are queuing, transmission, nodal processing, and propagation delay. Our model assumes that the data traffic reaches with rate λ through a Poisson process, the available and unavailable WiFi phase and the deadline as an exponential distribution with rate "η," "γ," and "ξ," respectively. Moreover, the file sizes are also exponentially distributed. The WiFi queue is constructed using the Markov chains principle as represented in Fig. 4. The Eq. 9 states the total expected delay of the proposed model:

$$E[D] = p_1 D_{WiFi} + p_2 D_{D2D-WiFi} + p_3 D_{CELLULAR} \qquad (9)$$

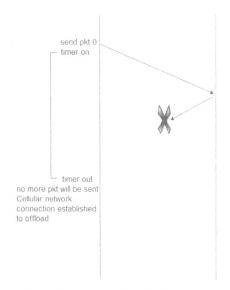

send pkt 0
timer on

timer out
no more pkt will be sent
Cellular network
connection established
to offload

Fig. 5. Pictorial representation of the mechanism involved in timing out of timer upon deadline.

Here p_1 is the possibility of WiFi availability in the customer's set, D_{WiFi} signifies a total end-to-end delay related to unburdening data via WiFi, p_2 represents the probability of active WiFi availability in the neighbor's handset provided that the user's handset does not have an active WiFi. Likewise, $D_{(D2D-WiFi)}$ in Eq. 9 signifies a sum of end-to-end delay linked to offloading data packets to the neighboring handset using WiFivia one-hop D2D communication. The probability that the D2D communication and WiFi are unavailable provided that the cellular network is continuously offered is denoted by p_3, and likewise, a complete end-to-end delay linked to offloading via the cellular network is represented by $D_{CELLULAR}$.

To calculate the end-to-end delay for scenario-2 where the D2D transmission is possible with the neighbor's handset, and the user' WiFi is unavailable, the delays namely, the delay happened to owe to delaying until the deadline in the WiFi queue is terminated, the delay sustained is to accomplish D2D transmission and lastly the delay accrued while transmitting data packets over the neighbor's active WiFi network need to be accounted separately. Therefore, the study offers WCETT (Weighted Cumulative Expected Transmission Time) through multi-hop D2D communication to offload data packets to BTS. Thus, the WCETT [21] is represented as:

$$WCETT = (1 - \beta) \times \sum_{i=1}^{n} ETT_i + \beta \times \max X_j \tag{10}$$

where $Xj = \sum_i ETTi$ and $ETT = ETX \times \frac{S}{B}$.

ETX stands for the number of anticipated retransmission before a packet is effectively transferred, the packet's size is denoted by S, and B signifies the bandwidth of the link. the first term of WCETT expression that multiplied $(1 - \beta)$ computes the resources expended in a given path, whichever the channels utilized, and secondly, the channel diversity represented by the second term, weighted by β. From Eq. 10, we can calculate the delay equation for one–hop D2D as follows:

Meant for Unit-hop

$$X_J = \sum_i ETT_i \tag{11}$$

$$X_1 = \sum_1 ETT_1 \tag{12}$$

$$X = ETX \times \frac{S}{B} \tag{13}$$

Therefore,

$$WCETT = (1 - \beta) \times \sum_{i=1}^{n} ETT_i + \beta \times \max X_j \tag{14}$$

$$WCETT = (1 - \beta) \times ETX \times \frac{S}{B} + \beta \times ETX \times \frac{S}{B} \tag{15}$$

$$D_{One-hopD2D} = WCETT = (1 - \beta) \times ETX \times \frac{S}{B} + \beta \times ETX \times \frac{S}{B} \tag{16}$$

From the research paper, we get the model's delay related to calculating the delay faced by a packet while the data is offloaded over WiFi. The equation required to calculate the delay in the model for offloading data over WiFi is shown below:

$$E[T] = \frac{1}{\lambda}\left[\left(1 + \frac{\gamma}{\eta}\right)\frac{\lambda - \mu(\pi_w - \pi_{0,w})}{\xi} + \frac{(\lambda - \mu)\pi_w + \mu\pi_{0,w}}{\eta}\right] \tag{17}$$

$$D_{WiFi} = E[T] = \frac{1}{\lambda}\left[\left(1 + \frac{\gamma}{\eta}\right)\frac{\lambda - \mu(\pi_w - \pi_{0,w})}{\xi} + \frac{(\lambda - \mu)\pi_w + \mu\pi_{0,w}}{\eta}\right] \tag{18}$$

The end-to-end delay in data to offload via D2D over WiFi is estimated as:

$$E[D] = p_1 D_{WiFi} + p_2 D_{D2D-WiFi} + p_3 D_{CELLULAR} \tag{1}$$

$$E[D] = 0 + p_2 D_{D2D-WiFi} + 0 \tag{20}$$

$$E[D] = p_2 D_{D2D-WiFi} \tag{21}$$

here,

$$D_{D2D-WiFi} = D_{Deadline} + D_{D2D} + D_{WiFi} \tag{22}$$

Simulation. We have employed the MATLAB to model the packet arrival rate versus transmission delay for scenario-2, as shown in Fig. 6. The target rate is $\xi = 0.9s^{(-1)}$, and

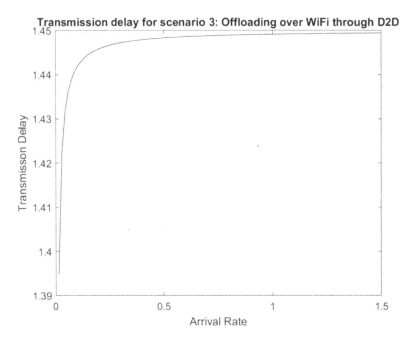

Fig. 6. Pictorial representation of the average delay in offloading over WiFi via D2D.

the deadline time is selected to be 1.11 s. The data rate for transmission over WiFi is 1Mbps, the bandwidth for D2D is 6 GHZ, and the packet size is 7.5 Mbyte.

This showed three scenarios that could occur while offloading data from the user's handset. The scenarios depend on the availability of WiFi and the feasibility of D2D communication. The Equ models the total expected delay. 1. Furthermore, the MATLAB simulation is shown too.

The MATLAB/Simulink simulation software was used to model and test the newly proposed routing scheme. In addition, to replicate the data offloading scheme, the SimEvents library of Simulink was utilized smartly, and the description and results of the simulation are provided in the below subtopics:

SimEvents Model. The SimEvents library has been profoundly used for the designing of the proposed system. Firstly, a FIFO was applied, and subsequently, an data packages generator was employed to duplicate the files. Subsequently, M (Markov)/M (Markov)/1 model was employed. There's only one server, and both the service time and the inter-arrival time were fixed to exponential distribution such that the model ensues the M/M/1 model. The timeout time was selected based on a small survey, and based on the survey for the simulation two minutes was selected. The Simulink model and the survey results are pictorially represented in Figs. 7 and 8, respectively.

The proposed routing model simulation results using a 500 units simulation time are represented in Figs. 9, 10, 11, and 12. The Figs. 9, 10 and 11, respectively illustrates the utilization factors of WiFi, D2D, and Cellular network. The Fig. 12 pictorially represents the average queue length of D2D route and WiFi route. The average queue length signifies

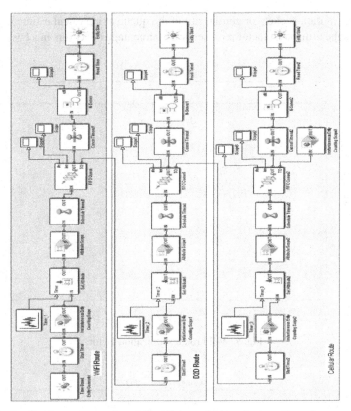

Fig. 7. SimEvents library based Simulink model based on novel routing system

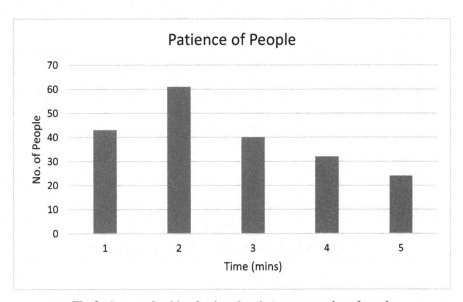

Fig. 8. Survey of waiting for time (in mins) versus number of people

the number of data packets or entities are in the queue at a particular time in a specific server, and the utilization factor represents the percentage of servers in a busy state, and.

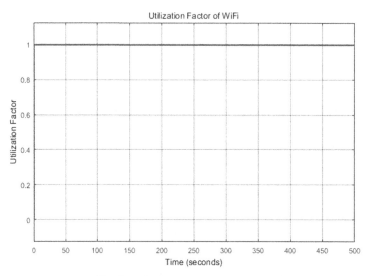

Fig. 9. WiFi route's utilization factor.

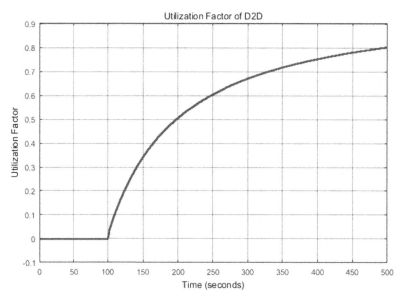

Fig. 10. Of Device to Device route's utilization factor.

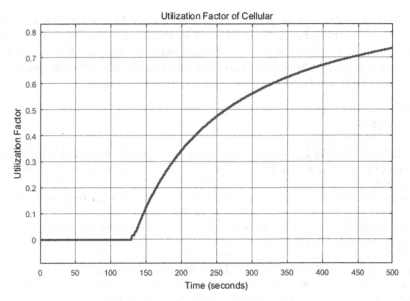

Fig. 11. Cellular network's utilization factor.

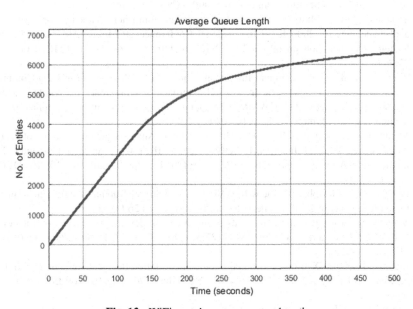

Fig. 12. WiFi route's average queue length.

5 Conclusion

We propose a scenario that could occur while offloading data from the user's handset. The designs depend on the availability of WiFi and the feasibility of D2D communication.

The total expected delay was modeled and simulated via MATLAB simulations. Results of MATLAB simulations are better in terms of total expected delay time. In Future studies, work will be based on machine learning and network layer. Moreover, machine learning techniques will be employed to enhance the beamforming selection, and thereby, the network layer will help reduce the latency, improving the results.

References

1. Gubbi, J., et al.: Internet of Things (IoT): a vision, architectural elements, and future directions. Futur. Gener. Comput. Syst. **29**(7), 1645–1660 (2013). https://doi.org/10.1016/j.future.2013.01.010
2. Rappaport, T.T.: Spectrum Frontiers : The New World of Millimeter-Wave Mobile Communication. New York University Tandon School of Engineering (2016)
3. Rappaport, T.S., et al.: Millimeter wave mobile communications for 5G cellular: It will work! IEEE Access **1**, 335–349 (2013). https://doi.org/10.1109/ACCESS.2013.2260813
4. Churchill, S.: Millimeter Frequencies Proposed for 5G, 19 July 2012
5. Yao, L., et al.: V2X routing in a VANET based on the hidden Markov model. IEEE Trans. Intell. Transp. Syst. **19**(3), 889–899 (2018). https://doi.org/10.1109/TITS.2017.2706756
6. Qin, H., et al.: An experimental study on multi-hop D2D communications based on smartphones. In: 2016 IEEE 83rd Vehicular Technology Conference (VTC Spring), May 2016, pp. 1–5. IEEE (2016). https://doi.org/10.1109/VTCSpring.2016.7504128
7. Toham, C., Jan, F.: Multi-interfaces and multi-channel multi-hop ad hoc networks: overview and challenges. In: 2006 IEEE International Conference on Mobile Ad Hoc and Sensor Systems, October 2006, pp. 696–701. IEEE (2006). https://doi.org/10.1109/MOBHOC.2006.278636
8. Zhou, X., et al.: The Design and Implementation of FPGA Subsystem in D2D Communication Based on LTE Network. In: 5th IET International Conference on Wireless, Mobile and Multimedia Networks (ICWMMN 2013), pp. 5.07–5.07. Institution of Engineering and Technology (2013). https://doi.org/10.1049/cp.2013.2424
9. Mehmeti, F., Spyropoulos, T.: Is it worth to be patient? Analysis and optimization of delayed mobile data offloading. In: IEEE INFOCOM 2014 - IEEE Conference on Computer Communications, April 2014, pp. 2364–2372. IEEE (2014). https://doi.org/10.1109/INFOCOM.2014.6848181
10. By 2020, 75% of Mobile Traffic will be Video [Cisco Study]. Tubular Insights, 2018. https://tubularinsights.com/2020-mobile-video-traffic/. Accessed 26 Dec 2018
11. Malathy, S., et al.: Routing constraints in the device-to-device communication for beyond IoT 5G networks: a review. Wirel. Netw. **27**(5), 3207–3231 (2021). https://doi.org/10.1007/s11276-021-02641-y
12. Ioannou, I., et al.: Distributed artificial intelligence solution for D2D communication in 5G networks. IEEE Syst. J. **14**(3), 4232–4241 (2020). https://doi.org/10.1109/JSYST.2020.2979044
13. Bastos, A.V., Silva, C.M., da Silva, D.C.: Assisted routing algorithm for D2D communication in 5G wireless networks. In: 2018 Wireless Days (WD), April 2018, pp. 28–30. IEEE (2018). https://doi.org/10.1109/WD.2018.8361688
14. Leese, R.A.: A unified approach to the assignment of radio channels on a regular hexagonal grid. IEEE Trans. Veh. Technol. **46**(4), 968–980 (1997). https://doi.org/10.1109/25.653071
15. Dhillon, H.S., et al.: Modeling and analysis of K-tier downlink heterogeneous cellular networks. IEEE J. Sel. Areas Commun. **30**(3), 550–560 (2012). https://doi.org/10.1109/JSAC.2012.120405

16. Blaszczyszyn, B., Karray, M.K., Keeler, H.P.: Using Poisson processes to model lattice cellular networks. In: 2013 Proceedings IEEE INFOCOM, April 2013, pp. 773–781. IEEE (2013). https://doi.org/10.1109/INFCOM.2013.6566864

17. Zhu, C., et al.: A survey on coverage and connectivity issues in wireless sensor networks. J. Netw. Comput. Appl. **35**(2), 619–632 (2012). https://doi.org/10.1016/j.jnca.2011.11.016

18. Teichmann, J., Ballani, F., van den Boogaart, K.G.: Generalizations of Matérn's hard-core point processes. Spat. Statist. **3**, 33–53 (2013). https://doi.org/10.1016/j.spasta.2013.02.001

19. Haenggi, M., et al.: Stochastic geometry and random graphs for the analysis and design of wireless networks. IEEE J. Sel. Areas Commun. **27**(7), 1029–1046 (2009). https://doi.org/10.1109/JSAC.2009.090902

20. Xu, X., Li, Y., Gao, R., Tao, X.: Joint Voronoi diagram and game theory-based power control scheme for the HetNet small cell networks. EURASIP J. Wirel. Commun. Netw. **2014**(1), 1–12 (2014). https://doi.org/10.1186/1687-1499-2014-213

21. Mirahsan, M., Schoenen, R., Yanikomeroglu, H.: HetHetNets: heterogeneous traffic distribution in heterogeneous wireless cellular networks. IEEE J. Sel. Areas Commun. **33**(10), 2252–2265 (2015). https://doi.org/10.1109/JSAC.2015.2435391

22. Approximations TM, Formulas BQ, Notation Q, et al. (n.d.) Tutorial for the use of Basic Queueing Formulas, pp. 1–9

23. Foruhandeh, M., Tadayon, N., Assa, S.: Uplink Modeling of K -tier heterogeneous networks: a queuing theory approach. IEEE Commun. Lett. **21**(1), 164–167 (2017). https://doi.org/10.1109/LCOMM.2016.2619338

24. Wang, J.Y.: Queueing Theory, 1–24 (2009). https://doi.org/10.1016/S0723-2020(11)80062-7

25. Mohsin, M., Prakash, R.: IP address assignment in a mobile ad hoc network. In: MILCOM 2002, Proceedings, pp. 856–861. IEEE (2002). https://doi.org/10.1109/MILCOM.2002.1179586

Energy Efficient Allocation of Resources in NOMA Based (MU-HCRN) with Perfect Spectrum Sensing

S. Prabhavathi$^{(\boxtimes)}$ ⓘ and V. Saminadan

Department of Electronics and Communication Engineering, Puducherry Technological University, Puducherry, India
{smprabhavathi,saminadan}@pec.edu

Abstract. Allocating Resources in NOMA Based MU-Heterogeneous Cognitive Radio Networks (MU-HCRN) with Perfect Spectrum Sensing in an energy-efficient manner considering assured Quality-of-Services (QoS) is addressed. The major goal is optimally allocating spectrum bands more efficiently while consuming less power, less interference and increased throughput for each subordinate users. Dynamic Search Power Allocation (DSPA) algorithm is proposed with power constraints. Using dynamic programming optimal solutions, with each users throughput makes optimal power allocation. Performance metrics used in this proposed algorithm are spectrum efficiency, energy efficiency, and sum rate, to optimize the use of limited spectrum resources ensuring higher transmission rates for multi-user (MU). Depending on channel conditions power levels are adjust and allocated to the subordinate users. From the Simulations our Dynamic Search Power Allocation can achieve higher energy efficiency, a greater sum rate, and efficiency of spectrum is good than the conventional methods.

Keyword: Cognitive radio networks · NOMA · Resource allocation · Energy efficiency · QoS

1 Introduction

Cognitive radio (CR) was evolved to resolve the spectrum shortages, because of increasing demand in wireless applications and the under-utilization of frequency spectrum.

Using a perfect spectrum sensing technique, it is feasible to determine the spectrum's state by sensing the unused spectrum of Primary Users (PUs). Sensing should have a high detection probability for secondary users to communicate efficiently in underutilized bands in order to safeguard all users from interference. MU-HCRN must be capable of supporting large numbers of users while maximizing spectrum efficiency.

(CRN) requires energy-efficient power allocation. In [1–3] under poor spectrum sensing, (RA) in multiuser OFDM-based CRN with heterogeneous services is investigated. In a CR network, resource allocation tries to maximize energy efficiency, spectrum usage,

© Springer Nature Switzerland AG 2022
N. Chaubey et al. (Eds.): COMS2 2022, CCIS 1604, pp. 274–285, 2022.
https://doi.org/10.1007/978-3-031-10551-7_20

and fairness. Energy efficiency checks how effectively power is used for data transmission, [4] Addressed the EE power distribution in CRS for heterogeneous users without taking sensing failures into account. In [5–7] resource allocation in downlink NOMA Networks and HCRN are addressed. In [8–12] energy efficiency of NOMA network with FTPA are discussed.

[13] uses RF energy harvesting in underlay mode to describe and solve the energy effectiveness problem of a cognitive wireless network. The throughput threshold is utilized to meet various application QoS requirements.[14] offered an innovative cooperative game theory-based strategy to resource allocation and sharing, ensuring maximum return through cooperative node selection. This strategy saves energy while maximizing resource utilization. [15] Showed that the Markov Random Field (MRF)-based resource allocation technique is feasible and presents detailed findings and performance analyses. In [16], under channel uncertainties, a downlink robust RA algorithm is suggested in CRN.

We present "energy-efficient resource allocation for (MU-HCRN)" based on Non-Orthogonal Multiple Access NOMA with spectrum sensing to secure multiple users' communication. In addition, by allocating optimal transmission powers among various users, network throughput is improved.

This work maximizes energy efficiency for (MU-HCRN) with numerous QoS constraints and transmitter power limitations.

1. A system outline has been established to increase the EE for NOMA-based HCRN with spectrum sensing.
2. Dynamic power allocation algorithm based on dynamic programming optimal solution is proposed.
3. A perfect spectrum sensing for HCRN in the presence of transmit power, interference, and QoS constraints allows the EE to be maximized and the normal communication to be protected.
4. We conclude with simulation results to verify how the proposal is improving performance.

The study is organized as follows: Sect. 2 provides the system outline. Power and SINR constraints are proposed in Sect. 3. Sect. 4 contains the simulation scenario as well as discussions. Finally, Sect. 5 brings the conclusion.

2 System Outline

2.1 System Outline for Spectrum Sensing (SS) and NOMA-Enhanced HetNets System

The system model for NOMA enhanced HCRN is shown in Fig. 1 Each Macro cell contains number of small cells with unlicensed Secondary users (SU_1, SU_2, SU_3....SU_K) who do not have any authority to access the spectrum or resources and m primary licensed users (PU_1, PU_2, PU_3....PU_m) who have the authority to access the spectrum. Macro Base Station (MBS) is located in the center of each MC with radius Rm as its coverage, and a Small cell Base Station (SBS) is located in the center of each SC with radius Rs as its coverage. All K SBSs are cognitive and NOMA functioned. The fusion center is located at the centre which collects the sensed information from all the secondary users (SU_1, SU_2, SU_3....SU_K) which is located at macro cell in the network.

NOMA is employed in the (HCRN), which allocates the transmit power of the secondary users and primary users based on their location with the base station non-orthogonally instead of allocating the resources orthogonally as in "(OMA)" technique. And depending on their channel conditions, the broadcast power is allocated that is channel state with fine condition is allocated with minor power because there is no any interference or fading occurred in it and the channel state with poor state due to multi channel interference and fading due to large transmission distance is allocated with more broadcast power to ensure the maximum broadcast rate.

The cognitive phase consists of four main task, in that phase spectrum sensing performs the main role of detecting the spectrum gap in the radio spectrum environment, to better understand the unlicensed secondary users performs spectrum sensing to detect the existence of spectrum gap. Spectrum gap means if primary licensed user is not using the spectrum in the radio frequency environment, spectrum hole is created. If primary user is accessing the spectrum means gap is not there, it is occupied. Spectrum mobility makes transition to the better spectrum that is available. Spectrum administration makes decision on allocating the best accessible spectrum bands to the unlicensed users. Spectrum distribution is the output of the cognitive phase; it enables the licensed primary users to share their resources with the unlicensed secondary users.

The spectrum management function uses the spectrum sensing information to analyze spectrum opportunities and take spectrum access decisions.

Perfect Spectrum Sensing with no sensing errors that is false alarm (When the subcarrier is available but the sensing result is busy) and missed detection (When the subcarrier is occupied by PU but the sensing end result shows that it is vacant) can be assumed with high Signal-to-Noise Ratio (SNR). For our work we consider only the high (SNR) signal without considering the low (SNR) signals from the energy statistics. It evaluates the signal intensity to be above a threshold to define the primary user presence, ensuring maximum detection probability and minimal sensing mistake.

Each CRN's bandwidth is split into Y subcarriers, and each subcarrier's bandwidth is Bn Hz and thus the nth CRN has Yn subcarriers. For SU's, the subcarriers in the nth CRN are separated into available and unavailable subcarriers Y_n^a, Y_n^u.

Miss Detection (MD) and False Alarm (FA) are the Sensing errors in CRN. When the subcarrier is occupied by PU but the sensing end result shows that it is vacant, in that case MD occurs. When the subcarrier is available but the sensing result is busy, FA occurs.

The factors $Q_{n,y}^{misd}$ and $Q_{n,y}^{fa}$ describes probabilities of MD and FA. $H_{n,y}^1$ and $H_{n,y}^2$ are used in the nth CRN to indicate if the PU is available or not in the Yth subcarrier. $O_{n,y}^1$ and $O_{n,y}^2$ are used in the nth CRN to indicate if the Yth subcarrier is unavailable or available.

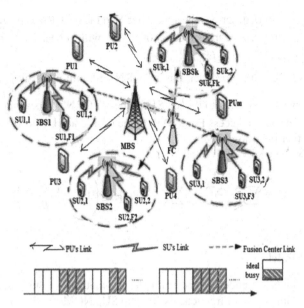

Fig. 1. System model

The four spectrum sensing scenarios are as follows:

$$
\begin{aligned}
P\{O^1_{(n,Y)}|H^1_{(n,Y)}\} &= 1 - Q^{misd}_{(n,Y)} \\
P\{O^2_{(n,Y)}|H^1_{(n,Y)}\} &= Q^{misd}_{(n,Y)} \\
P\{O^2_{(n,Y)}|H^2_{(n,Y)}\} &= 1 - Q^{fa}_{(n,Y)} \\
P\{O^1_{(n,Y)}|H^2_{(n,Y)}\} &= Q^{fa}_{(n,Y)}
\end{aligned}
\tag{1}
$$

The chance that the Yth subcarrier is really utilized by PUs and it's unavailability in the nth CRN can be stated as

$$
\begin{aligned}
\theta^1_{(n,Y)} &= P\{H^1_{(n,Y)}|O^1_{(n,Y)}\} \\
&= \frac{P\{O^1_{(n,Y)}|H^1_{(n,Y)}\}P\{H^1_{(n,Y)}\}}{P\{O^1_{(n,Y)}|H^1_{(n,Y)}\}P\{H^1_{(n,Y)}\}+P\{O^1_{(n,Y)}|H^2_{(n,Y)}\}P\{H^2_{(n,Y)}\}}
\end{aligned}
\tag{2}
$$

where $Q^L_{n,y}$ denotes the chance that PU will occupy the Yth subcarrier in the nth CRN. The chance that the Yth subcarrier in the nth CRN is not utilized by PUs and is thus available to the SUs is given by $\theta^2_{n,y}$.

In CRN, a secondary user's total attainable rate is calculated as

$$
R_x = B_n \cdot \sum_{x=1}^{X} \sum_{y \in Y^a_n} \rho^Y_{x,n} r^Y_{x,n}
\tag{3}
$$

$$
\rho^Y_{(x,n)} = \begin{cases} 1, \text{ in } n^{th} \text{ CRN,} & \text{the } Y^{th} \text{ subcarrier was assigned to SUx} \\ 0, \text{ Others} \end{cases}
\tag{4}
$$

where $\rho_{x,n}^Y$ can be 1 or 0, describes the subcarrier Y in the nth CRN is occupied with SUs or not. And $r_{x,n}^Y$ is the rate of transmission of xth SU with subcarrier Y in the nth CRN, which is written as $r_{x,n}^Y = log_2(P_{x,n}^y \gamma_{x,n}^y)$.

(SNR) of xth SU with subcarrier Y in n^{th} CRN with unit power is $\gamma_{x,n}^y = \frac{H_{x,n}^y}{\sigma B_n}$.

$P_{x,n}^Y$ is the power assigned to the xth SU in the nth CRN's subcarrier Y, and $H_{x,n}^y$ is channel gain of nth CRN Access Point (AP) to the xth SU across the Yth subcarrier. σ is the density of thermal noise power.

The HCRN's capacity is given as

$$C = \sum_{x=1}^{X} \sum_{n=1}^{N} \sum_{y \in Y_n^a} B_m \, log_2 \left(1 + \frac{P_{x,n}^Y H_{x,n}^Y}{\sigma B_n}\right) \qquad (5)$$

2.2 NOMA Model

CR- NOMA adopts the underlay spectrum sharing method, in this paradigm all users interfere in the same range of frequencies. To help SU_i, NOMA's SIC technology is used to filter out signal interference from users until the desired signal is decoded. The weak user (the one who is longer from the base station) receives more power; whereas the strong user receives a lower transmit power (user near to the base station). Superposition coding combines all of the user's data.

Super imposed signal is

$$Y(n) = \sqrt{P\alpha_1} \cdot S_1(n) + \sqrt{P\alpha_2} \cdot S_2(n) + \sqrt{P\alpha_3} \cdot S_3(n) + \ldots\ldots \qquad (6)$$

Let α be the percentage of total power P allotted to user i with $\alpha_1 < \alpha_2 < \alpha_3 < \alpha_4$ being the order of power allocation.

The SIC at the receiver decodes high-powered signals first; the signal at user U_i can be represented mathematically as $y_i = h_i x + w_i$.

The received output signal is y_i, channel gain is h_i, the transmitted overlaid signal is x, and the user U_i is subjected to w_i noise. The signal obtained for a MU- NOMA is defined as $Y = h_1 \sqrt{P\alpha_1} \, S_1(n) + h_2 \sqrt{P\alpha_2} \, S_2(n) + h_3 \sqrt{P\alpha_3} \, S_3(n) + w\ldots\ldots$

$R_i = log_2 \left(1 + \frac{\beta_i P |h_i|^2}{P|h_i|^2 \sum_{K=i+1}^{N} \beta_k + \sigma_n^2}\right)$ is the data rate which depends upon the power distribution, that is how much power is assigned to the secondary users based on the transmitting distance from the base station, channel's gain, and the multiple users located in the (HCRN).

3 Power and SINR Constraints

For NOMA based HCRN, transmission power limits, interference, and guaranteed QoS constraints are used to provide primary and secondary users' regular communication with increased secondary user network throughput, maximum number of multiple user access and improved energy efficiency.

Equation (8) describes that the power of both PU and SU are less than or equal to the base station's maximum power, Pmax (i.e., PBS and SBS). The total transmit power of 40 (dBm)10 w is used at the base station. Hence the power constraint expression is:

$$P_{PU} \leq Pmax$$
$$P_{SUi} \leq Pmax \tag{7}$$

Each SU's QoS should be ensured by meeting the following criteria.

$$\gamma_{PU} \geq \gamma_{PU}^{th}$$
$$\gamma_{SU} \geq \gamma_{SU}^{th} \tag{8}$$
$$R_n \geq R_{min}$$

In Eq. (9) γ $^{th}_{PU}$ is the (SINR) threshold that the PU must meet for normal communication between primary and secondary users in the network.

The threshold that the ith SU must meet to communicate normally is represented by γ $^{th}_{SU}$.. And R_{min} is the SU's minimum capacity requirement that is how much data rate it can handle in the network. To provide QoS, SU's capacity must be larger than Rmin. The secondary users receive subcarriers with good channel condition.

The interference constraint is as follows:

$$\sum_{i=1}^{N} P_{SUi} h_{SUi,PU} \leq I_{PU}^{th} \tag{9}$$

The interference threshold of Primary user is I_{PU}^{th}, P_{SUi} is the ith SU's power, and $h_{SUi,PU}$ is the SU$_i$ to PU channel gains.

4 Optimization Problem Formulations

This work addresses the maximization of energy efficiency, system throughput maximization problem, maximizing the number of multiple user access, and the power control problems between multiple users with specific QoS constraints (i.e., minimum (SINR), power constraints and interference temperature constraints).

To determine the best solutions, constrained Dynamic Programming Optimization Problem is applied. It is feasible to identify each user's power allocation and combine their results to produce the ideal solutions using this technique. The network throughput is improved by allocating optimal transmission power. Let x(i,p) be the maximum throughput of the ith SU with power p,Y(i,p) be the previous SU's throughput with power p, accordingly the optimized power of the ith SU is defined as O(i,p). By using this optimization, power consumed is decreased by considering the power of previous (i−1) users to find how much power is needed to allocated to the ith SU in an optimal way.

The challenge of optimization can be stated as follows:

$$P1 : \max \eta_{EE}$$

$$P2 : \max N$$

$$\alpha_{SUi}, P_{SUi} \qquad (10)$$

$$P3 : maxN \sum_{i=1}^{N} R_{SUi}$$

$$\alpha_{SUi}, P_{SUi}$$

Subjected to

$$C1 : P_{SUi} \leq Pmax$$

$$C2 : \gamma_{SUi} \geq \gamma_{Sui}^{th}$$

$$C3 : P_{PUi} \leq Pmax$$

$$C4 : \gamma_{PU} \geq \gamma_{PU}^{th} \qquad (11)$$

$$C5 : \sum_{i=1}^{N} P_{SUi} h_{SUi,PU} \leq I_P U^{th}$$

$$C6 : Pm \leq Pmax$$

$$C7 : Pm \geq 0$$

P_{SUi} is the signal power vector of the i-th SU that can access the system; N is total number of SU; α_{SUi} is the power allocation of secondary user SU_i; C1, C3 depicts the power constraint, C2,C4 the SU's QoS, and C5 the SU's interference temperature constraint. The goal of P3 is to increase the secondary network's throughput under power constraints. The maximized power limits are indicated by C6, C7 (Fig. 2).

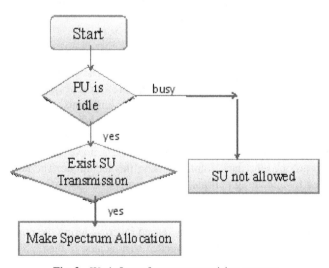

Fig. 2. Work flow of resource provision process

Let us look at the work flow diagram of the resource provision process, From this we can able to understand that, how the resources or spectrum is distributed to multiple users instead of allocating it to single user request, depending on their channel condition, and the location of the subordinate users which do not have any authority to access the spectrum without meeting the interference constraints of the (licensed primary users) in the small cell with coverage area of 50 m and the licensed users are located at the macro cell with coverage area of 500 m as already shown in the system model Fig. 1.

From workflow spectrum sensor initially senses the channel's busy or idle state. If the channel being occupied by any licensed primary users means, eventually the secondary unlicensed users are not allowed to access the spectral environment; it has to wait until it gets the resource from licensed users. If the sensor senses the channel as inactive means; that is primary licensed user is unoccupied, it permits the secondary user transmission and makes the spectrum owed to the unlicensed secondary users (Table 1).

Algorithm for Dynamic Search Power Allocation in CR-NOMA

```
1. Initialize the networkparameters:i,N,P_MBS P_SBS, α_SUi,h_SUi,PU;
2. The "power allocation term" α_SUi and Number of SU is
   obtained by constrained optimization technique;
3. max R_SUi  is obtained from the QoS constraint;
4. max η_EE is obtained from the power constraint;
5. i=i+1;
6. Repeat steps 2 to 5 until N;
7. For each SU_i  request "request count= SU_i  request ++"
      Search for resource
      If the resource available
      Allocate to SU_i  request
8. Allocating power to SU_i until ( 0<p_m≤ P_max)
9. Else put the request in queue
10. Repeat until P*_SUi
11. Output: α_SUi and the "optimized transmission power"
   P*_SUi
```

Table 1. Simulation parameters and values

Simulation parameters	Values
Multiplexing mode	NOMA
Network region	500 m × 50 m
Transmitter power	40 (dBm)10 w
Total Bandwidth	5 MHz
Maximum no. of users	40
Channel	AWGN
Noise power density	−174 dBm/Hz

5 Simulation Scenario

The proposed methodology is analyzed using MATLAB simulation tool. For the simulations, "(HCRN) based on NOMA" accessing scheme is used, with K small cells having multiple secondary users placed randomly throughout the macro cell coverage areas with primary licensed users. The coverage radius of a macro cell and a small cell are 500 m and 50 m respectively with total base station transmit power of 40 (dBm) 10 w. And the total bandwidth used here is 5 MHz bandwidth, with maximum of 40 multiple secondary users in the network.

The basic "Additive White Gaussian Noise channel model (AWGN) " is used with noise power spectral density of −174 dBm/Hz.

The performance metrics sum-rate, spectral and energy-efficiency are considered for the proposed technique. The proposed Dynamic Search Power Allocation (DSPA) approach is analyzed with the "Fixed Power Allocation (FIPA) and Fractional Transmit Power Allocation (FTPA)" methods. In the existing approach, preset amount of broadcast power is allocated to all the users which have good and poor channel condition, and fractional power using the binary decisions of zero with fixed power and one with greater power to the multiple users. To mitigate this drawback we go for DSPA approach.

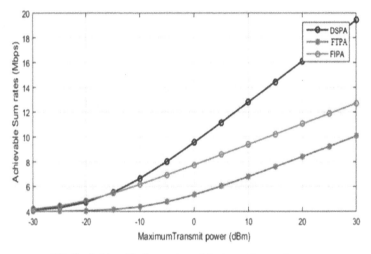

Fig. 3. Achievable Sum rate vs Maximum transmit power

Figure 3 relates the system performance as achievable sum rate vs transmitted power. For all power allocation methods, the system's feasible sum rate grows as transmit power increases. Our proposed Dynamic Search Power Allocation (DSPA) approach, obtains a greater overall sum rate than both FIPA and FTPA algorithms by selecting the best set of power levels based on the system's performance gain considering each user's channel state, resulting in optimal solutions.

Figure 4 shows that, NOMA enhanced multiple user HCRN spectrum efficiency increases as the transmitted power increase. From the figure, the Dynamic search power allocation provides a better spectral efficiency compared to the existing methods.

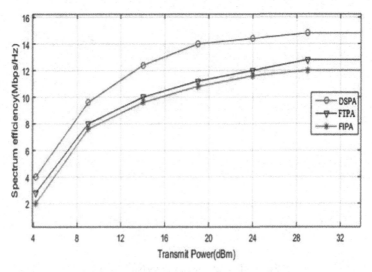

Fig. 4. Spectrum efficiency vs Transmit Power.

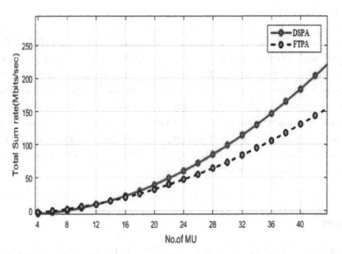

Fig. 5. Total Sum rate vs No. of MU.

Figure 5 depicts the proposed method's and FTPA method's total sum rate. The system is designed to service up to 40 users per cell at 30 dBm transmission power. As the multiple users (MU) served by the system grows, so does the total sum rate.

Figure 6 represents the Energy- efficiency of the DSPA and existing FTPA method. The total EE increases with the increase in number of multiple users. The proposed DSPA outperforms the previous technique because it considers user fairness and maximizes spectrum usage, allowing DSPA to achieve good EE (e.g., allows multiple SUs to share one sub channel).

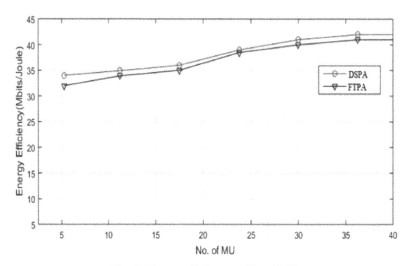

Fig. 6. Energy efficiency vs No. of MU.

6   Conclusion

This paper presented an "efficient resource allocation approach for (MU-HCRN) based on (NOMA)" with assured quality of services (QoS) under perfect spectrum sensing. Under transmission power and QoS constraints, performance indicators like spectrum efficiency, energy efficiency, and sum rate were examined. The proposed Dynamic Search Power Allocation algorithm, when compared to traditional power allocation methods, achieves improved energy efficiency, Sum rate, Spectrum efficiency and higher transmission rates for multi-user (MU."Efficient power allocation methods with high spectral efficiency can be extended in the future by including co-operative relaying systems and security issues related with multiple user access will be analyzed with evolutionary algorithms".

References

1. Shi, H., Prasad, R.V., Onur, E., Niemegeers, I.G.M.M.: Fairness in wireless networks: issues, measures and challenges. IEEE Commun. Surv. Tut. **16**(1), 5–24 (2014). https://doi.org/10.1109/SURV.2013.050113.00015
2. Alabbasi, A., Rezki, Z., Shihada, B.: Energy efficient resource allocation for cognitive radios: a generalized sensing analysis. IEEE Trans. Wirel. Commun. **14**(5), 2455–2469 (2015). https://doi.org/10.1109/TWC.2014.2387161
3. Mili, M.R., Musavian, L., Hamdi, K.A., Marvasti, F.: How to increase energy efficiency in cognitive radio networks. IEEE Trans. Commun. **64**(5), 1829–1843 (2016)
4. Feng, L., Kuang, Y., Fu, X., Dai, Z.: Energy-efficient network cooperation joint resource configuration in multi-RAT heterogeneous cognitive radio networks. Electron. Lett. **52**(16),1414–1416 (2016)
5. Awoyemi, B.S., Maharaj, B.T., Alfa, A.S.: Resource allocation in heterogeneous cooperative cognitive radio networks. Int. J. Commun. Syst. **30**(11), e3247 (2017). https://doi.org/10.1109/ACCESS.2019.2914185

6. Xu; Y., Hu, Y., Chen, Q., Zhang, S.: Optimal power allocation fo rmultiuser OFDM-based cognitive heterogeneous networks. Commun. Theor. Syst. **14**(9), 1–4 (2017). https://doi.org/10.1109/CC.2017.8068764

7. Sun, X., Wang, S.: Energy-efficient power allocation for cognitive radio networks with minimal rate requirements. Int. J. Commun. Syst. **30**(2), e2953 (2017). https://doi.org/10.1002/dac.2953

8. Sindhu, P., Deepak, K.S., Abdul Hameed, K.M.: A novel low complexity power allocation algorithm for downlink NOMA networks. IEEE Recent Adv. Intell. Comput. Syst. (2018).https://doi.org/10.1109/RAICS.2018.8635048

9. Zhang, H., et al.: Energy-Efficient Resource Allocation in NOMA Heterogeneous Networks IEEE Wireless Communications (2018). https://doi.org/10.1109/MWC.2018.1700074

10. Xu, W., Qiu, R., Jiang, X.-Q.: Resource allocation in heterogeneous cognitive radio network with non-orthogonal multiple access. IEEE Access (2019).https://doi.org/10.1109/ACCESS.2019.2914185

11. Mahendru, G., Shukla, A., Banerjee, P.: A novel mathematical model for energy detection based spectrum sensing. Cogn. Radio Netw. Wirel. Personal Commun. (2019). https://doi.org/10.1007/s11277-019-06783-3

12. Alghasmari, W.F., Nassef, L.: Power allocation evaluation for downlink non-orthogonal multiple access (NOMA). Int. J. Adv. Comput. Sci. App. **11**, 4 (2020). https://doi.org/10.14569/IJACSA.2020.0110417

13. Tian, J., He, X., Sun, Y., Dong, H., Li, X.: Energy efficiency optimization-based resource allocation for underlay RF-CRN with residual energy and QoS guarantee. EURASIP J. Wirel. Commun. Netw. (2020). https://doi.org/10.1186/s13638-020-01824-z

14. Shyleshchandra Gudihatti, K.N., Roopa, M.S., Tanuja, R., Manjulaa, S.H., Venugopal, K.R.: Energy aware resource allocation and complexity reduction approach for cognitive radio networks using game theory. Phys. Commun. (2020). https://doi.org/10.1016/j.phycom.2020.101152

15. Kakkavas, G., Tsitseklis, K., Karyotis, V., Papavassiliou, S.: A software defined radio cross-layer resource allocation approach for cognitive radio networks: from theory to practice. IEEE Trans. Cogn. Commun. Netw. (2020).https://doi.org/10.1109/TCCN.2019.2963869

16. Xu, Y., Hu, R.Q., Li, G.: Robust energy-efficient maximization for cognitive NOMA networks under channel uncertainties. IEEE Internet of Things J. (2020). https://doi.org/10.1109/JIOT.2020.2989464

17. Eappen, G., Shankar, T.: Hybrid PSO-GSA for energy efficient spectrum sensing in cognitive radio network. Phys. Commun. (2020). https://doi.org/10.1016/j.phycom.2020.101091

18. Khasawneh, M., Azab, A., Agarwal, A.: Towards securing routing based on nodes behavior during spectrum sensing in cognitive radio networks. IEEE Access (2020).https://doi.org/10.1109/ACCESS.2020.3024662

19. kockaya, K., Develi, I.: Spectrum sensing in cognitive radio networks: threshold optimization and analysis. EURASIP J. Wirel. Commun. Netw. **2020**(1), 1–19 (2020). https://doi.org/10.1186/s13638-020-01870-7

20. Kumar, A., Pandit, S., Singh, G.: Threshold selection analysis of spectrum sensing for cognitive radio network with censoring based imperfect reporting channels. Wirel. Netw. **27**(2), 961–980 (2020). https://doi.org/10.1007/s11276-020-02488-9

CV Based Person Detection System for Smart Transportation

Shreedhar Bhatt$^{(\boxtimes)}$, Neev Shah, and Samir Patel

Pandit Deendayal Energy University, Gandhinagar, India
Shreedharmb22@gmail.com, samir.patel@sot.pdpu.ac.in

Abstract. This paper describes an implementation method for a person counter system which detects people using a fixed single camera. Here the system counts the number of people sitting in a transportation bus and displays the count at the next station so that the crowd can be reduced significantly. This computer vision based crowd detection system updates the real-time seat availability in the public buses. Also maintaining the live tracking can cost a lot of money. Our solution provides the answers of these queries. Using computer vision based automated techniques we are receiving optimum output.

Keywords: Person detection · Database · ImageAI · Vision-based system · Smart transportation · openCV

1 Introduction

1.1 Need of the Hour

In today's world public transportation is very crucial in terms of time management, pollution management and traffic management. It has been seen that the number of people using public transport is decreasing day by day. Nowadays, people are preferring personal vehicles for commuting to their workplaces. In India there are several cities which are having public transport in the form of buses instead of metro trains. In such cases managing the whole network and providing buses on the basis of public requirement is a difficult task. Many people prefer personal vehicles or taxis/autos just because they don't get seats often. There is no system which shows how many seats are available in the upcoming bus. Our model provides solutions to these problems.

1.2 Literature Survey

There are some work where researchers have suggested the real time people tracking, the number of people is maintained through its video processing [2]. In this case there are a lot of drawbacks like internet disconnection, high cloud storage & higher cost of the system. There have been some other instrumental solutions like RFID tags & Wi-Fi [3] tags but these solutions don't work in the complex transport networks where there are multiple routes & multiple buses from the same station. In public transport you

© Springer Nature Switzerland AG 2022
N. Chaubey et al. (Eds.): COMS2 2022, CCIS 1604, pp. 286–295, 2022.
https://doi.org/10.1007/978-3-031-10551-7_21

cannot control the user to pick a particular bus. It can be labelled as a part of the fleet management system. With some increased functionalities like safety management, fuel management, mechanical damage can call it a fleet management system [1]. Researchers have also worked on computer vision, to count algorithms to track the flow of boarding and alighting passengers in bus stop areas [4]. Some have suggested [5] a single camera vertically mounted on the door that keeps track of the number of people entered and exited from the province and then calculates the amount of people, they have also developed a GUI based application which helps in security purposes, combining our logic with this system can give a higher range of accuracy. A system was tested at Kaunas city transport and it's analysis and results are stated [6] where the methodology is divided into four main algorithms that are simulation, intensity detection, zone and correlation based movements. They have tested and compared the results but did not develop any application which helps users. In paper [8] there has been a system proposed which counts the number of passengers waiting for bus transit using three machine learning techniques. Gaussian Mixture Model, Running Gaussian Average, and Adaptive Gaussian Mixture Model, they try to predict and identify the number of passengers but this system does not help in solving the bigger picture that is to ease the process of transportation with comfort. [7] suggests to use optical flow for image acquisition, color processing and image histogram analysis which helps in counting passengers they extended the algorithm that connected the bus departure and arrival based on fuzzy logic, the only drawback to this system is the whole algorithm is time consuming that means it cannot be used in real life scenario.

1.3 Impact on People's Life

As our system drives towards smart transportation, benefits can be availed by end users, first and foremost is the ease and efficiency to people who commute using public provisions. It not only helps the users but also the authority as management and monitoring can be observed properly. Major insists/data can be outflows from this system which might help the government build a better platform. With API support we can provide data to transportation's application, which can be useful to people while opting for public transportation. Computer vision provides a great value addition to the transportation system. Our model helps administrators to decide very crucially in terms of managing the vehicle flow. They can even plan dynamic pricing according to the demand of the system for business enhancement.

2 Method

2.1 Computer Vision Model

Computer Vision is one of the important fields of Artificial Intelligence. The science of software systems and computers which can understand images and scenes. Computer Vision is additionally made up of varied aspects like recognising an image, image super-resolution, detecting an object, generation of an image and more. Object detection is perhaps the erudite aspect of computer vision because the amount of use cases are practical.

ImageAI has always been a reliable python library constructed for an entitle developers to creates software and system applications which free standingly contain computer vision and deep learning abilities while just writing some line of code. ImageAI makes use of comparatively small codes. It also includes a python execution of nearly all of the state-of-the-art deep learning algorithms. This python library uses numerous APIs that work without internet connection – including detection of object, detection of video and various APIs to track object that can be called offline. This advanced library uses a pre-trained model which can be effortlessly modified. ImageAI library's Object Detection class includes functions that can carry out detection of an object in set of images or a single image, utilizing pre-trained models. With ImageAI, one is able to detect and identify more than 85 different sorts of common and simply available objects. Here we will be using this library to detect people (Fig. 1).

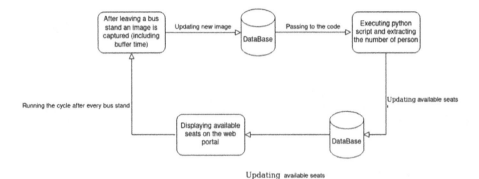

Fig. 1. System architecture

Python dependencies which this project needs are as follows (Table 1):

Table 1. Dependencies

pip install tensorflow==2.4.0
pip install keras==2.4.3 pillow==7.0.0 matplotlib==3.3.2 scipy==1.4.1
pip install h5py==2.10.0 opencv-python keras-resnet==0.2.0 numpy==1.19.3
pip install imageai

Model: A RetinaNet based pretrained model used here is known as resnet50_coco_best_v2.1.0.h5 which is highly compatible with imageai library.

```
ALGORITHM:
detect = ObjectDetection()
detect.setModelTypeAsRetinaNet()
detect.setModelPath(
os.path.join(execution_path,"resnet50_coco_best_v2.1.0.h5"))
detect.loadModel()
detection=detect.detectObjectsFromImage(input_image=os.path.join(
execution_path , "input_image.jpg"), out-
put_image_path=os.path.join(execution_path , "output_image.jpg"))
```

Here firstly we define our object detection class, secondly we set the model type to RetinaNet, after that setting the model path to the path of our RetinaNet model, loading the model into the object detection class, finally calling the detection function and parsing the input image path and the output image path.

After we obtain the classification of the object present in the image firstly we inilitize counter to 0, i.e. count $= 0$.

Following with checking whether the detected object is a person or not. If yes then increment the counter by 1.

```
for eachObject in detections:
    if eachObject["name"] == "person":
        increment count
```

Subsequently checking the seat availability i.e. subtracting the threshold value of seats by the number of persons detected (count) and finally updating the database's available seat column.

2.2   Database Configuration

One has to integrate our model with their security cameras in such a way that whenever a bus passes through the bus station, the system should process the picture of the bus in the model's database which eventually will update the number of available seats in the bus. Every transportation system will have different policies in terms of seat arrangements, route management. All things can be taken care of through this system.

We have written SQL queries to configure the database. It selects the upcoming bus from the database. When the bus passes from station A, it will be updated in the database. At the same time, the picture from the bus also reaches the database & after processing the number of available seats are updated. The database also stores information like drivers, routes, buses, stations and users.

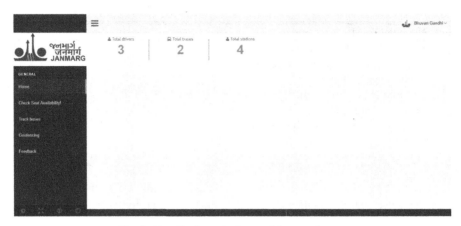

Fig. 2. Details about the buses, drivers and route

We have used the Update function to change the number of available seats. Our model is configured through the DbConn function, which passes the query to the database.

Query 1

qry = "UPDATE bus_seats SET bus_available_seat = '" + str(available_seats) + "' WHERE bus_code = (SELECT bus_code FROM bus_list WHERE bus_number = 'A2')"

We have used a select query in the backend. Which will give the data like bus route, bus number, characteristic and number of available seats as shown in Fig. 2. We have used PHP to configure the database into a website (Fig. 3).

Query 2

$result = $myDb->selectQry("SELECT route_list.route_number, bus_list.bus_number, bus_list.acOrNot, bus_list.expressOrNot, bus_seats.bus_available_seat FROM route_list, bus_list, route_bus_list, bus_seats WHERE bus_list.bus_code = bus_seats.bus_code and bus_list.bus_code = route_bus_list.bus_code GROUP BY bus_list.bus_number");

---

3 Result

See Figs. 4, 5, 6 and 7.

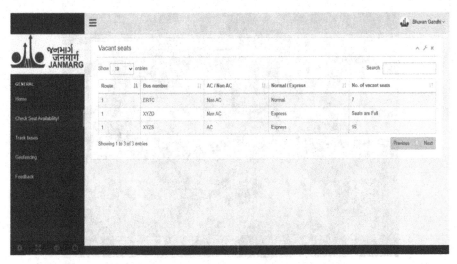

Fig. 3. Number of people updating on the website

Fig. 4. Performance Analysis I

Our model also works in this COID era. As modern problem requires modern solution, our model works with the people who have worn the mask. Our model doesn't fully depend upon face recognition. The model has a balanced approach at looking at the various body parts of the people. In the post-covid-era, public transportation is one of the biggest issues in the world. Some highly populated countries have to call off their biggest commutative public transport due to excessive usage of it can lead to the

Fig. 5. Performance Analysis II

Fig. 6. Performance Analysis III

COVID outbreak in the country. In this case our system would be beneficial, authorities can manage and limit the number of people through our system. COVID outbreak has increased the use of private transportation in recent times and looking at the point of view of the environment, running back to public transport would be ideal. With the use of our model we can track the social distancing norms and other safety measures with little bit modifications (Figs. 8 and 9).

Fig. 7. Performance Analysis IV

Fig. 8. Performance Analysis V

We have been getting accurate numbers in terms of seat availability. It is mostly in the range of 95–97%. The update of the seat is taking no time. The website illustrates the upcoming bus at a particular station & its available seats in the bus.

Fig. 9. Performance Analysis VI

4   Conclusion and Future Work

In this paper, we addressed an optimal solution for hassle-free public transportation with the help of person detection, we are able to check the number of seats available in a bus and display the number so that the crowd can be divided significantly. In the future, our goal would be to increase the accuracy rate of our proposed logic by expanding the number of cameras and fixing it to different angles so the person detection rate can be escalated significantly. We can also insert infrared sensors at the entry of every bus so that it can count the number of entries and exits of people. After that, comparing the output of infrared sensors to our output by this way the precision level of the system can be improved.

References

1. Singh, P., Suryawanshi, M., Tak, D., Sant, J.: Smart fleet management system using IoT, computer vision, cloud computing and machine learning technologies. https://easychair.org/publications/preprint/XrnF
2. Zhao, X., Delleandrea, E., Chen, L.: A People Counting System based on Face Detection and Tracking in a Video. https://hal.archives-ouvertes.fr/hal-01437717
3. Raghavachari, C., Aparna, V., Chithira, S., Balasubramanian, V.: A Comparative Study of Vision based Human Detection Techniques in People Counting Applications. https://www.sciencedirect.com/science/article/pii/S1877050915021754/pdf?md5=5f4f725c219d14dcf2a1b76fa9e683a1&pid=1-s2.0-S1877050915021754-main.pdf

4. Billones, R.K.C., et al.: Vision-Based Passenger Activity Analysis System in Public Transport and Bus Stop Areas. https://ieeexplore.ieee.org/document/8666357

5. Kim, J.-W., Choi, K.-S., Choi, B.-D., Ko, S.-J.: Real-time Vision-based People Counting System for the Security Door. http://mesh.brown.edu/en193s05-2004/pdfs/kimetal-itc2002.pdf

6. Lengvenis, P., Simutis, R., Vaitkus, V., Maskeliunas, R.: Application of Computer Vision Systems for Passenger Counting in Public Transport. https://eejournal.ktu.lt/index.php/elt/art icle/view/1232

7. Passenger demand forecast using optical flow passenger counting system for bus dispatch scheduling. https://ieeexplore.ieee.org/document/7848347

8. Lumentuta, J.S., Gunawanb, F.E., Diana: Evaluation of Recursive Background Subtraction Algorithms for Real-Time Passenger Counting at Bus Rapid Transit System. https://research.binus.ac.id/publication/739C2E30-4521-4E77-BA51-84C3545BFBE2/evaluation-of-recurs ive-background-subtraction-algorithms-for-real-time-passenger-counting-at-bus-rapid-tra nsit-system/

9. Kniess, J., Rutke, J.C., Castaneda, W.A.C.: An IoT Transport Architecture for Passenger Counting: A Real Implementation. https://dl.ifip.org/db/conf/im/im2021short/211069.pdf

10. Yahiaoui, T., Khoudour, L., Meurie, C.: Real-time passenger counting in buses using dense stereovision. https://www.researchgate.net/publication/238982016_Real-time_p assenger_counting_in_buses_using_dense_stereovision

11. Sun, F., Pan, Y., White, J., Dubey, A.: Real-time and Predictive Analytics for Smart Public Transportation Decision Support System. https://www.researchgate.net/publication/301676 425_Real-Time_and_Predictive_Analytics_for_Smart_Public_Transportation_Decision_ Support_System

12. Amina, I.J., Taylor, A.J.: Automated people–counting by using low–resolution infrared and visual cameras. MIT Press (2007). https://repository.lboro.ac.uk/articles/journal_cont ribution/Automated_people-counting_by_using_low-resolution_infrared_and_visual_cam eras/9561314

13. Petkevičius, M., Vegys, A., Proscevičius, T., Lipnickas, A.: Inspection system based on com-puter vision. Elektronika ir Elektrotechnika (Electronics and Electrical Engineering), no. 10, pp. 81–84 (2011). https://eejournal.ktu.lt/index.php/elt/article/view/889

14. Roqueiro, D., Petrushin, V.: Counting people using video cameras. MIT Press (2007). https://www.semanticscholar.org/paper/Counting-people-using-video-cameras-Roq ueiro-Petrushin/fe904d95d13b8b26d70bb078678e79f4d1084ab8

A Performance of Low-Cost NVIDIA Jetson Nano Embedded System in the Real-Time Siamese Single Object Tracking: A Comparison Study

Abbas Aqeel Kareem[1], Dalal Abdulmohsin Hammood[1]([⊠]), Ahmed A. Alchalaby[2], and Ruaa Ali Khamees[3]

[1] Electrical Engineering Technical College, Department of Computer Technical Engineering, Middle Technical University (MTU), Al Doura, 10022 Baghdad, Iraq
Dalal.hammood@mtu.edu.iq
[2] Computer Techniques Engineering Department, Dijlah University College, Baghdad, Iraq
ahmed.alchalaby@duc.edu.iq
[3] Institute of Technology, ICT Department, Middle Technical University, Baghdad, Iraq
dr.ruaakhamees@mtu.edu.iq

Abstract. The tracking of objects is a complex mission computer vision and machine learning (ML). There are several types of objects tracking like tracking one object or more than one. The tracking of one object is applied in video frames as the tracking of more than one object is applied to tracking for multiple objects in the video. Single object tracking is usually implemented using the method of correlation filter-based or of Siamese Network-based. Siamese Network, the state of art method, has an active search area, nowadays, due to its good achievements in accordance with localization real-time and accuracy application. Especially within a new surveillance system that is built on UAV to get unbounded tracking. GPU-based embedded systems give superior performance in comparison with CPU-based systems in the implementation of ML in the terms of speed. In this paper low-cost NVIDIA Jetson nano embedded system performance was evaluated for real-time Siamese single object tracking. 14 Siamese single object tracking algorithms were tested using NVIDIA Jetson nano board. The result shows that the bord gives the best performance with the Lighttrack algorithm with 8.3 frames per second speed. Such performance can be used in real-time tracking applications.

Keywords: Siamese neural network · Object tracking · ML · Embedded system · Jetson nano

1 Introduction

Nowadays, computer vision has been improved quickly improvement, the reason for that is its wide range of applications like surveillance systems, robots, drones, and many others. Computer vision has several tasks like single-object tracking, multi-object tracking, video object detection and image object detection, video object detection [1]. tracking

© Springer Nature Switzerland AG 2022
N. Chaubey et al. (Eds.): COMS2 2022, CCIS 1604, pp. 296–310, 2022.
https://doi.org/10.1007/978-3-031-10551-7_22

is a big problem in computer vision. Some high-level application like video surveillance requires tracking some objects specified in the first frame to corresponding objects in the next frame [2]. In this work Single Object Tracking (SOT) will be used as a computer vision task. This task is still a complicated problem the reason for that is the variation in target appearance due to the change in the size, light changing, deformation, rotation, occlusion, fast motion, low resolution, and background clutter [3]. SOT is a fundamental technique in computer vision for several applications like UAV tracking, video surveillance, etc. The main task of SOT is to choose the target object from the background and another object in the next frame. To accomplish this task of computer vision, several types of algorithms were proposed. These algorithms are based on two methods, the first one is the generative method and the latter is a discriminative method [4]. The solution by the generative method can be the extraction of the object's feature map specified initially in frame number one and locate the region that is mostly matching in the search region. The discriminative method relies on the classifier that can classify the selected object from the background and other objects [5]. This work focuses on Siamese Neural Network (SNN) most of these trackers are based on the discriminative method. This Siamese-based tracker has high active research area in object tracking due to its balanced between accuracy and speed. The tracking of single objects can be considered as a computer vision's primary function for several applications like UAV, surveilling, due to huge improvements in neural networks especially Convolution Neural Network (CNN) which improves the accuracy of detecting even small objects by extracting the features map of the object which is used then for tracking the object in the next frame. Luca et al. 2016 introduced the first Siamese object tracking which is based on the powerful backbone and uses a correlation filter for increasing accuracy [6]. Bo et al. 2018 presented a tracker based on the region proposal subnetwork in the same year Zheng et al. proposed a tracker with distracter aware modules which develops the model's discriminating [7, 8]. In 2019 Bo Li et al. improved the Siamese trackers which rely on region proposal subnetwork using more deep CNN as a backbone [9]. Changhong et al. 2020 introduced a tracker with an anchor suggestion subnetwork for producing an anchor for all points in the feature map which decreases the negative sample in the classification [10]. This algorithm contains millions of parameters to accomplish this task, so it's required more processing capability and memory capacity. This gives a limitation in using embedded systems with AI applications. For this reason, Bin et al. in 2021 introduced a tracker by using neural architecture search technique to reduce this huge number of parameters and FLOPS requirements [11]. And with the improvement of AI chipset can find solutions for these problems. For example, NVIDIA Xavier is one of the most AI chipsets. Which can compute the SSD300/MobileNetV1 (SSD/MobileNet) object detection CNN model which contains 6.91M parameter [12, 13] at a speed of 665 Frames per Second (FPS) [14]. There are other problems, one of them is the cost of the chip (exceed 1000$ for NVIDIA Xavier). So, it needs to find a good tradeoff between the cost and capabilities of the development board. Here, NVIDIA jetson nano development kit can be utilized for evaluating the speed of Siamese SOT algorithms. Siamese SOT algorithms consist of two CNN branches, one for search region and another for target. The output of two branches is joined by a similarity computing function to produce a similarity map [15].

The study in [16] evaluates only the CNN backbones on Jetson nano and other accelerators for comparison purposes. This work compares the results of Siamese single object tracking algorithms which use some of these CNN backbones like Alexnet and resnet50.

The contributions of this work are the following:

- Evaluation of NVIDIA jetson nano board performance on 14 different Siamese SOT algorithms in terms of speed to reach real-time.
- Comparison of the evaluated results on standard benchmarks and the speed of these algorithms.

2   Siamese Network

Siamese neural network consists of two or more sisters' neural networks, as shown in Fig. 1. Each of them receiving input the output from each subnetwork is used to compute the similarity between the elements. This is done by using the distance similarity function which is a return value close to zero if the inputs are similar. Then all results will be used to create the confusing matrix [17].

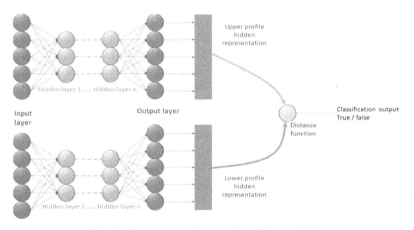

Fig. 1.   Siamese neural network architecture [17].

SNN has been used in different applications type like speech and audio signal processing [18–20], biological applications [21, 22], Pharmacology and Chemistry [23], Graphics and Geometry [24], Analyzing images which can be considered as the highest field for using Siamese neural network [25, 26], and have many other applications but in our task, Siamese neural network is widely used in object tracking in recent years. Siamese neural networks are non-linear models which contain capabilities to produce embeddings that mainly aim to increase accuracy and take full advantage for real-time applications [15]. Siamese trackers which are matching-based strategy the peruse from it is to find the similarity between the patch and the target object for robust tracking the target [2]. SNN performs that similarity check through two stages; firstly, feature extracting by deep neural network share same weights. Secondly, finding the similarity between these feature maps [27]. Siamese based method proposes many techniques for providing a robust discriminative target object such as distractor aware [8], target aware features [28], Combining deep features from multi-layer [29] or combining confidence map [30], removing silent background object by considering the angle of the target [31], etc., One problem with the conventional tracker is adaptive changing with the appearance of target and relying on offline training data can lead to unseen the target. To solve that Siamese tracker proposes an online update strategy to reduce the risk of overfitting [32], deactivating the background [8], performing tracking tasks as one-shot local task detection [7], increasing the weights of important feature channels [30], and other techniques.

3 Siamese SOT Algorithms

This section describes state of art Siamese SOT algorithms used in the evaluation:

SiamFC [6] equipped a fully-convolutional Siamese tracking algorithm trained using the ILSVRC15 object tracking dataset. The tracking algorithm work at a speed near realtime and, regardless of its extreme simplicity, reaches the most modern performing in more than one benchmark. The internal structure of SiamFC algorithm appears in Fig. 2.

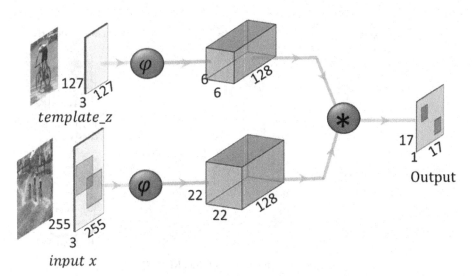

Fig. 2. The architecture of SiamFC [6].

SiamFC++ [33] presented a set of realistic target state estimate methods for object tracking with high performance. These criteria guided the development of a Fully Convolutional Siamese tracker++ (SiamFC++). SiamFC++ includes a classification and target state calculation branch (G1), a classification degree without ambiguity (G2), and tracking. Figure 3 shows the structure of SiamFC++

SiamRPN [7] proposes the region proposal network (RPN), which was trained offline end to end along with large picture pairings. It is made up of two subnetworks, as shown

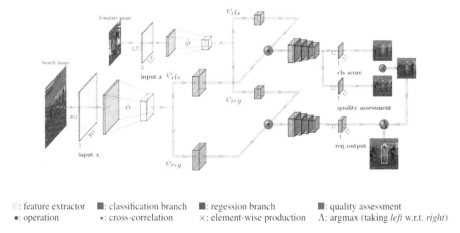

: feature extractor   ■: classification branch   ■: regession branch   ■: quality assessment
●: operation   ⋆: cross-correlation   ×: element-wise production   Λ: argmax (taking *left* w.r.t. *right*)

Fig. 3. Architecture of SiamFC++ [33].

in Fig. 4. A subnetwork for extracting the features and a subnetwork for proposing the regions that consist of the regression as well as classification branches.

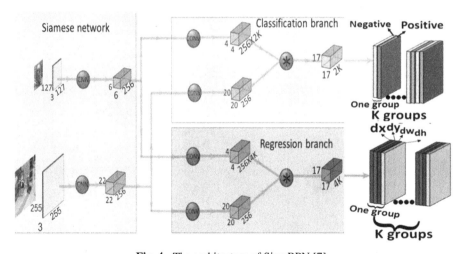

Fig. 4. The architecture of SiamRPN [7].

SiamRPN++ [9], is an updated version of SiamRPN. It broke the lack of rigorous translation invariance constraint by a sampling strategy. Also, effectively train a Resnet Siamese tracker with a considerable performance increase. As well as, it suggested a novel model design for layer- and depth-wise aggregations, which not only increases accuracy but also decreases the model size. Figure 5 shows the algorithm's block diagram.

DaSiamRPN [8] implemented an effective sampling technique during the off-line training phase to regulate the distribution of the training data. Also, it directed the model's attention to the semantic distractors. It is also introduced a plain successful

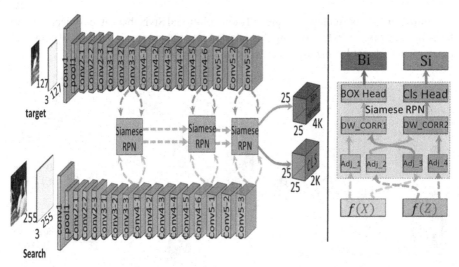

Fig. 5. Architecture of SiamRPN++ [9].

local-to-global searched area technique to expand the suggested method for continuous tracking.

SiamMask [34] used a single straightforward technique to accomplish both tracking the object and object segmentation in real-time. SiamMask enhances their offline training procedure. Once trained, SiamMask ran networked and produced objected and class-agnostic segmenting and localizing tasks at a rate of 55 FPS over NVIDIA RTX 2080 GPU. SiamMask's architecture appears in Fig. 6.

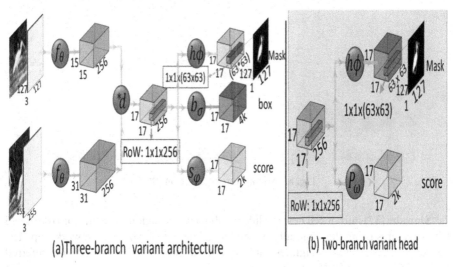

Fig. 6. The architecture of SiamMask [34].

SiamCar [35] presented a unique fully convolutional SNN that solves object tracking tasks in a per-pixel way by dividing this mission into two minor issues: classifying pixel category and object localization regression as shown in Fig. 7.

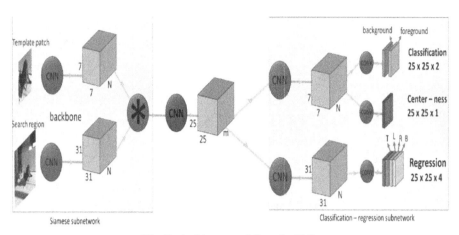

Fig. 7. Architecture of SiamCar [35].

Siamban [36] is a system that took advantage of the completely convolutional network's expressive capabilities. Siamban approaches the issue of visual tracking like a an issue of parallel classifying and regression. The architecture of Siamban is shown in Fig. 8.

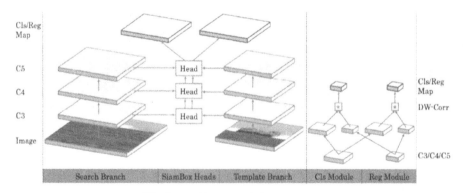

Fig. 8. Architecture of Siamban [36].

Siamdw [37] introduced new modules to alleviate the padding effect. It also designed new structures using these modules with planned open field size and network step. The introduced structures are weightless and warrant real-time following speed when referred to SiamFC and SiamRPN.

SiamAPN [10] is a unique Siamese network-based mechanism of two stages in pursuit of UAV tracking, as shown in Fig. 9. Stage number one generates anchor proposals of high quality and stage number two improves them. Furthermore, the framework outperforms anchor-free approaches is enhanced at stage-2 refinement.

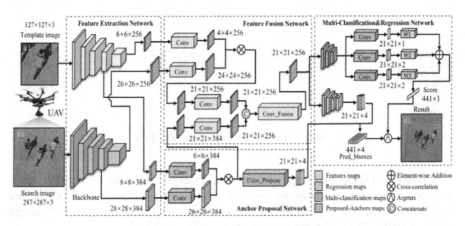

Fig. 9. The architecture of SiamAPN [10].

SiamAPN++ [3] performed a particular AAN (Attentional Aggregation Network) comprised of cross-ANN and self-AAN. AAN eventually enhances the exemplification capability of characteristics by attention mechanism through spatial and channel dimensions, as shown in Fig. 10. Furthermore, a dual-featured anchor proposal network was developed to improve the robustness of tracking objects of varied sizes.

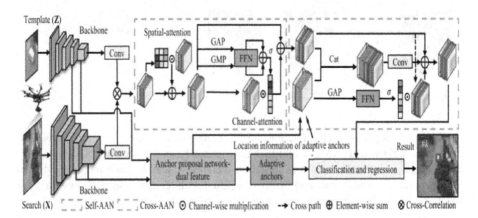

Fig. 10. Architecture of SiamAPN++ [3].

SiamGat [38] suggested the use of a full bipartite graph to design part-to-part correspondence between the goal and the search template. Then it used the graph attention strategy to transfer selected object data from the template feature to the search feature, As shown in Fig. 11.

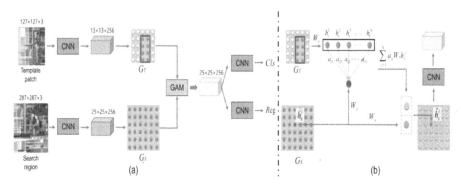

Fig. 11. The architecture of SiamGat [38].

UpdateNet [32] toke the original template, the accumulated template, and the current frame's template. For estimating the following frame's optimal template. The Updatenet was small enough to fit inside current Siamese trackers. UpdateNet improves the findings of DaSiamRPN. The architecture of UpdateNet is in Fig. 12.

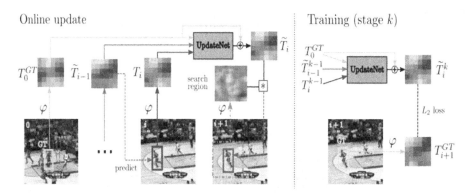

Fig. 12. The Architecture of UpdateNet [32].

LightTrack [11] was a lightweight and efficient objected tracker that employs Neural Architecture Searched (NAS). Lighttrack is proposed based on one-shot NAS used only for object tracking problems. It is based on weightless search space including depthwise separable convolutions and inverted residual architecture, which allows tracking by efficient structure. Figure 13 illustrates the architecture of this algorithm.

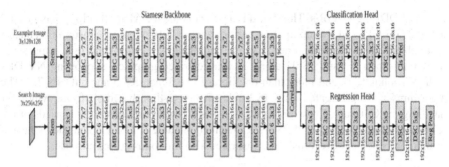

Fig. 13. Architecture of LightTrack [11].

4   Evaluation

We have got three well known typical benchmarks used to evaluate object tracking algorithms: **vot_2018**, **vot_2016**, **got_10k**, and **UAV123**.

4.1   VOT Benchmark

VOT is a standard benchmark to evaluate the object tracking algorithms that are suitable to deploy in the real application for object tracking. The main evaluation measure is Expected Area Overlap (AEO) and accuracy (A), and robustness (R). We use vot_2016 [39] and vot_2018 [40] for comparison purposes.

4.2   GOT-10K Benchmark

The two main parameters to evaluate tracker in this benchmark is AO which is average overlap and the R which is the success rate when the overlap exceeds the predefined threshold (i.e., 0.5 or 0.75). GOT-10K [41] Is the largest data set containing about 1000 videos in the subset of training, and 180 in the test as well as validate subsets.

4.3   UAV123 Benchmark

UAV123 [42] is a new benchmark for the aerial video that has got one hundred twenty-three video sequences shot from an aerial perspective that is low in attitude. This benchmark evaluates the tracker in precision and accuracy score.

5   Results and Discussion

The deep learning base tracker shows low performance on CPU-based embedded systems (Arduino, Raspberry Pi, etc.) While giving higher performance when running on GPU-based boards. The development kit of NVIDIA Jetson nano was utilized to test the speed of the after-mentioned algorithms in terms of FPS. The embedded system NVIDIA Jetson nano is coming with Quad-core ARM A57 @ 1.43 CPU and memory is 4 GB

64-bit LPDDR4 25.6 GB/s. This board is a good choice for AI applications, jetson nano has 472 GFLOPS of FP16 computing performance at 5-10W power consumption makes it suitable for the Unmanned aerial vehicle application. Jetson nano uses jetpack 4.6 SDK built upon Ubuntu 18.04 along with accelerated graphics, supporting NVIDIA CUDA Toolkit 10.0, and more than one library like TensorRT 5 and cuDNN 7.3. The algorithms are implemented using PyTorch 1.7.0 AI python-based platform, cython for handling the C library, Cuda toolkit 10.0 for GPU cores parallelism. The speeds of the tested algorithms in terms of FPS were presented in Table 1. The adapted backbone and evaluation benchmark records were illustrated also for comparisons purpose.

Table 1. Comparisons of tracking algorithms of four standard benchmarks with speed

Tracker	FPS	Adapted backbone	Bemchmark									
			VOT_2018			GOT-10K			UAV123		Vot_2016		
			A	R	EAO	AO	R0.5	R0.75	ACU	PRC	A	R	EAO
SiamFC	2	Alexnet	0.503	0.585	0.188	34.8	35.3	9.8	—	—	0.53	0.46	0.235
SiamFC++	4.5	Alexnet	0.556	0.183	0.400	49.3	57.7	32.3	—	—	—	—	—
SiamRPN++	5.5	Alexnet	0.6	0.234	0.414	51.8	61.8	32.5	0.549	0.739	0.642	0.196	—
SiamRPN	6.6	Alexnet	0.586	0.276	0.383						0.56	0.26	0.344
SiamMask	2.2	Resnet50	0.609	0.276	0.380	—					0.639	0.214	0.433
Updatenet	1.8	Alexnet	0.518	0.454	0.244	—			—	—	0.610	0.206	0.481
Siamban	0.7	Resnet50	0.597	0.178	0.452	—			—	—	—		—
DaSiamRPN	5.8	Alexnet	0.586	0.276	0.383			—	0.491	0.96	0.61	0.22	0.411
SaimCar	6.25	Alexnet	—	—	—	56.9	67.0	41.5	—	—	—	—	—
Siamdw_FC	2.8	CIR_Restnet	—	—	—				—	—	0.54	0.38	0.30
SiamAPN	2.8	Alexnet	—	—	—				0.566	0.752	—	—	—
SiamAPN++	4.7	Alexnet	—	—	—				0.58	0.764	—	—	—
SiamGat	1.5	Googlenet	—	—	—	62.7	74.3	48.8	0.592	0.779			—
Lighttrack	8.3	Supernet	—	—	—	62.3	72.6		—	—	—	—	—

NVIDIA Jetson nano with 128 GPU cores gives the ability to handle real-time tracking when used with the LightTrack. LightTrack algorithm gives the best performing with reference to accuracy 62.3% and speed 8.3 FPS. Which achieves real-time object tracking. Because this algorithm introduces lightweight models with NAS. Which is effective can decrease the FLOPs and parameters required for the model. For example, SiamMask uses 15.5G FLOPs and have 16.6M parameter for accomplishing a very modern performing while LightTrack uses 0.53G FLOPs and have a 1.97M parameter for accomplishing a very modern performing. The board also shows acceptable performance with the other two algorithms SiamRPN 6.6 FPS, 56% accuracy, and SiamCar 6.25 FPS, 56.9%. Figure 14 summarizes the algorithm speed on the jetson nano embedded system.

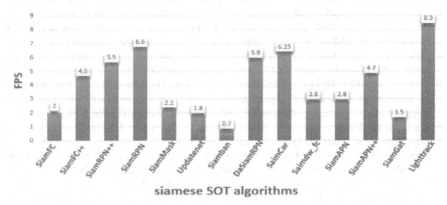

Fig. 14. Single object tracking algorithms speed.

6 Conclusion

Recently, object tracking has attracted applications, especially in a surveillance systems. The new surveillance system is built based on UAV to get the benefits of UAV unbounded tracking. Weights and power consumption give the limitations of using high-performance object tracking embedded systems with UAVs. Jetson nano is a low-cost lightweight embedded system from NVIDIA that performs the deep learning process based on GPU. This work investigates the performance of modern Siamese tracking for one object on jetson nano board. LightTrack, SiamRPN, SiamCar algorithms give the most superior performing respecting speed (8.3, 6.6, 6.25 FPS) respectively. Obtained Lighttrack algorithm speed can be considered in the applications of real-time tracking systems based on UAVs.

References

1. Zhu, P., et al.: Vision meets drones: past, present and future. IEEE Access **9**, 110149–110172 (2020). https://doi.org/10.1109/ACCESS.2021.3101988
2. Ondrasovic, M., Tarabek, P.: Siamese visual object tracking: a survey. IEEE Access **9**, 110149–110172 (2021). https://doi.org/10.1109/ACCESS.2021.3101988
3. Cao, Z., et al.: SiamAPN++: Siamese Attentional Aggregation Network for Real-Time UAV Tracking (2021)

4. You, S., Zhu, H., Li, M., Li, Y.: A review of visual trackers and analysis of its application to mobile robot. arXiv preprint arXiv:1910.09761 (2019)
5. Fu, C., et al.: Correlation filters for unmanned aerial vehicle-based aerial tracking: a review and experimental evaluation. IEEE Geosci. Remote Sens. Mag. **10**, 1–28 (2021). https://doi.org/10.1109/MGRS.2021.3072992
6. Bertinetto, L., Valmadre, J., Henriques, J.F., Vedaldi, A., Torr, P.H.S.: Fully-convolutional siamese networks for object tracking. In: Hua, G., Jégou, H. (eds.) ECCV 2016. LNCS, vol. 9914, pp. 850–865. Springer, Cham (2016). https://doi.org/10.1007/978-3-319-48881-3_56
7. Li, B., et al.: High performance visual tracking with siamese region proposal network. In: Proceedings of the IEEE Computer Society Conference on Computer Vision and Pattern Recognition, pp. 8971–8980 (2018). https://doi.org/10.1109/CVPR.2018.00935
8. Zhu, Z., et al.: Distractor-aware Siamese Networks for Visual Object Tracking. arXiv:1808.06048v1 [cs.CV]. ECCV 2018, pp. 1–17 (2018)
9. Li, B., et al.: SIAMRPN++: evolution of siamese visual tracking with very deep networks. In: Proceedings of the IEEE Computer Society Conference on Computer Vision and Pattern Recognition, 2019-June, pp. 4277–4286 (2019). https://doi.org/10.1109/CVPR.2019.00441
10. Fu, C., et al.: Siamese Anchor Proposal Network for High-Speed Aerial Tracking (2020). https://doi.org/10.1109/icra48506.2021.9560756
11. Yan, B., et al.: LightTrack: Finding Lightweight Neural Networks for Object Tracking via One-Shot Architecture Search (2021). https://doi.org/10.1109/cvpr46437.2021.01493
12. Liu, W., et al.: SSD: single shot MultiBox detector. In: Leibe, B., Matas, J., Sebe, N., Welling, M. (eds.) ECCV 2016. LNCS, vol. 9905, pp. 21–37. Springer, Cham (2016). https://doi.org/10.1007/978-3-319-46448-0_2
13. Reddi, V.J., et al.: MLPerf inference benchmark. In: Proceedings - International Symposium on Computer Architecture, 2020-May, pp. 446–459 (2020). https://doi.org/10.1109/ISCA45697.2020.00045
14. Jo, J., Jeong, S., Kang, P.: Benchmarking GPU-accelerated edge devices. In: IEEE International Conference on Big Data and Smart Computing (BigComp), pp. 117–120 (2020). https://doi.org/10.1109/BigComp48618.2020.00-89
15. Marvasti-Zadeh, S.M., et al.: Deep learning for visual tracking: a comprehensive survey. IEEE Trans. Intell. Transp. Syst. (2021). https://doi.org/10.1109/TITS.2020.3046478
16. Jo, J., Jeong, S., Kang, P.: Benchmarking GPU-accelerated edge devices. In: Proceedings - 2020 IEEE International Conference on Big Data and Smart Computing, BigComp 2020, pp. 117–120 (2020). https://doi.org/10.1109/BigComp48618.2020.00-89
17. Bock, C., Moor, M., Jutzeler, C.R., Borgwardt, K.: Machine learning for biomedical time series classification: from shapelets to deep learning. In: Cartwright, H. (ed.) Artificial Neural Networks. MMB, vol. 2190, pp. 33–71. Springer, New York (2021). https://doi.org/10.1007/978-1-0716-0826-5_2
18. Thiollière, R., et al.: A hybrid dynamic time warping-deep neural network architecture for unsupervised acoustic modelling. In: Proceedings of the Annual Conference of the International Speech Communication Association, INTERSPEECH, 2015-January(2), pp. 3179–3183 (2015). https://doi.org/10.21437/interspeech.2015-640
19. Barnard, E., et al.: The NCHLT speech corpus of the South African languages. In: Spoken Language Technologies for Under-Resourced Languages, (May), pp. 194–200 (2014)
20. Siddhant, A., Jyothi, P., Ganapathy, S.: Leveraging native language speech for accent identification using deep Siamese networks. In: 2017 IEEE Automatic Speech Recognition and Understanding Workshop, ASRU 2017 - Proceedings, 2018-January, pp. 621–628 (2018). https://doi.org/10.1109/ASRU.2017.8268994
21. Jindal, S., et al.: Siamese networks for chromosome classification. In: Proceedings - 2017 IEEE International Conference on Computer Vision Workshops, ICCVW 2017, 2018-January, pp. 72–81 (2017). https://doi.org/10.1109/ICCVW.2017.17

22. Zheng, W., et al.: SENSE: Siamese neural network for sequence embedding and alignment-free comparison. Bioinformatics **35**(11), 1820–1828 (2019). https://doi.org/10.1093/bioinf ormatics/bty887

23. Jeon, M., et al.: ReSimNet: drug response similarity prediction using Siamese neural networks. Bioinformatics **35**(24), 5249–5256 (2019). https://doi.org/10.1093/bioinformatics/btz411

24. Sun, Z., et al.: Embedded spectral descriptors: learning the point-wise correspondence metric via Siamese neural networks. J. Comput. Des. Eng. **7**(1), 18–29 (2020). https://doi.org/10. 1093/jcde/qwaa003

25. Kassis, M., Nassour, J., El-Sana, J.: Writing Style Invariant Deep Learning Model for Historical Manuscripts Alignment (2018)

26. Cheng, G., et al.: Remote sensing image scene classification meets deep learning: challenges, methods, benchmarks, and opportunities. IEEE J. Sel. Top. Appl. Earth Obs. Remote Sens. **13**, 3735–3756 (2020). https://doi.org/10.1109/JSTARS.2020.3005403

27. Roy, S., et al.: Siamese networks: the tale of two manifolds. In: Proceedings of the IEEE International Conference on Computer Vision, 2019-October, pp. 3046–3055 (2019). https:// doi.org/10.1109/ICCV.2019.00314

28. Li, X., et al.: Target-aware deep tracking. In: Proceedings of the IEEE Computer Society Conference on Computer Vision and Pattern Recognition, 2019-June, pp. 1369–1378 (2019). https://doi.org/10.1109/CVPR.2019.00146

29. Cen, M., Jung, C.: Fully convolutional siamese fusion networks for object tracking. In: 25th IEEE International Conference on Image Processing (ICIP), pp. 3718–3722 (2018)

30. Yang, L., et al.: Region-based fully convolutional siamese networks for robust real-time visual tracking. In: 2017 IEEE International Conference on Image Processing (ICIP), pp. 1–5 (2017)

31. He, A., Luo, C., Tian, X., Zeng, W.: Towards a better match in Siamese network based visual object tracker. In: Leal-Taixé, L., Roth, S. (eds.) ECCV 2018. LNCS, vol. 11129, pp. 132–147. Springer, Cham (2019). https://doi.org/10.1007/978-3-030-11009-3_7

32. Zhang, L., et al.: Learning the model update for siamese trackers. In: Proceedings of the IEEE International Conference on Computer Vision, 2019-October, pp. 4009–4018 (2019). https:// doi.org/10.1109/ICCV.2019.00411

33. Xu, Y., et al.: SiamFC++: towards robust and accurate visual tracking with target estimation guidelines. In: AAAI 2020 - 34th AAAI Conference on Artificial Intelligence, pp. 12549–12556 (2020). https://doi.org/10.1609/aaai.v34i07.6944

34. Wang, Q., et al.: Fast online object tracking and segmentation: a unifying approach. In: Proceedings of the IEEE Computer Society Conference on Computer Vision and Pattern Recognition, 2019-June, pp. 1328–1338 (2019). https://doi.org/10.1109/CVPR.2019.00142

35. Guo, D., Wang, J., et al.: SiamCAR: siamese fully convolutional classification and regression for visual tracking. In: Proceedings of the IEEE Computer Society Conference on Computer Vision and Pattern Recognition, pp. 6268–6276 (2020). https://doi.org/10.1109/CVPR42600. 2020.00630

36. Chen, Z., et al.: Siamese box adaptive network for visual tracking. In: Proceedings of the IEEE Computer Society Conference on Computer Vision and Pattern Recognition, pp. 6667–6676 (2020). https://doi.org/10.1109/CVPR42600.2020.00670

37. Zhang, Z., Peng, H.: Deeper and wider siamese networks for real-time visual tracking. In: Proceedings of the IEEE Computer Society Conference on Computer Vision and Pattern Recognition, 2019-June, pp. 4586–4595 (2019). https://doi.org/10.1109/CVPR.2019.00472

38. Guo, D., et al.: Graph Attention Tracking (2020). http://arxiv.org/abs/2011.11204

39. Mishra, D., Matas, J.: The Visual Object Tracking VOT2017 Challenge Results The Visual Object Tracking VOT2017 challenge results. ICVC, vol. 1, no. November 2017, pp. 777–823 (2019). https://openaccess.thecvf.com/content_ICCVW_2019/papers/VOT/Kristan_The_ Seventh_Visual_Object_Tracking_VOT2019_Challenge_Results_ICCVW_2019_paper.pdf

40. Kristan, M., et al.: VOT2018 results. Chinese Acad. Sci. **26**(1), 1–15 (2018). http://vision.fe. uni-lj.si/cvbase06/
41. Huang, L., Zhao, X., Huang, K.: Got-10k: a large high-diversity benchmark for generic object tracking in the wild. IEEE Trans. Pattern Anal. Mach. Intell. **43**(5), 1562–1577 (2021). https:// doi.org/10.1109/TPAMI.2019.2957464
42. Zhu, X., Badr, Y.: Benchmarking deep trackers on aerial videos Abu. Sensors **18**(12) (2018). https://doi.org/10.3390/sxx010005

Author Index